The Dawning of Christianity in Poland and across Central and Eastern Europe

POLISH STUDIES
TRANSDISCIPLINARY PERSPECTIVES

Edited by Krzysztof Zajas / Jarosław Fazan

VOLUME 26

Igor Kąkolewski / Christian Lübke /
Przemysław Urbańczyk (eds.)

The Dawning of Christianity in Poland and across Central and Eastern Europe

History and the Politics of Memory

Bibliographic Information published by the Deutsche Nationalbibliothek
The Deutsche Nationalbibliothek lists this publication in the Deutsche Nationalbibliografie; detailed bibliographic data is available in the internet at http://dnb.d-nb.de.

Library of Congress Cataloging-in-Publication Data
A CIP catalog record for this book has been applied for at the Library of Congress.

This publication was funded by the Centre for Historical Research of the Polish Academy of Sciences and Leibniz Institute for the History and Culture of Eastern Europe.

Cover illustration: Courtesy of Benjamin Ben Chaim

ISSN 2191-3293
ISBN 978-3-631-78725-0 (Print)
E-ISBN 978-3-631-79091-5 (E-PDF)
E-ISBN 978-3-631-79092-2 (EPUB)
E-ISBN 978-3-631-79093-9 (MOBI)
DOI 10.3726/b15997

© Peter Lang GmbH
Internationaler Verlag der Wissenschaften
Berlin 2020
All rights reserved.

Peter Lang – Berlin · Bern · Bruxelles · New York · Oxford · Warszawa · Wien

All parts of this publication are protected by copyright. Any utilisation outside the strict limits of the copyright law, without the permission of the publisher, is forbidden and liable to prosecution. This applies in particular to reproductions, translations, microfilming, and storage and processing in electronic retrieval systems.

This publication has been peer reviewed.

www.peterlang.com

Contents

Introduction 7

Part I: New perspectives

Oleksiy Tolochko
Christians and pagans in Kiev during the 10th c. 11

Martin Wihoda
The beginnings of Christianity in Bohemia 33

Christian Lübke
Between reception and aversion. The earliest traces of Christianity
among the Polabian Slavs 43

Matthias Hardt
Magdeburg and the beginnings of the Diocese of Poznań 57

Przemysław Urbańczyk
Archaeology on the beginnings of Christianity in Poland 65

Eduard Mühle
Mieszko I's baptism and the *Poloni* as reflected in historiographic
sources from the 10th to the 14th c. 77

Marian Rębkowski
The beginnings of Christianity in Pomerania 91

Teresa Rodzińska-Chorąży
Early-Piast architecture in the context of early-medieval European
architecture 111

Andrzej Buko
The archaeological discoveries at Bodzia near Włocławek (Kuyavia
region) and their significance for Poland's early-medieval history 141

Part II: Modern Myths

Igor Kąkolewski
The roads by which Christianization proceeded in the history of Poland and in the Poles' culture of memory – new research perspectives and modern myths 159

Philip Earl Steele
Homo religiosus: the phenomenon of Poland's Mieszko I 185

Mikołaj Banaszkiewicz
Searching for the meaning of the Russian way. The ideological setting of the 900th anniversary celebrations of the Baptism of Rus' (1888) 219

Bartłomiej Noszczak
History as a tool in the state's struggle against the Catholic Church during the celebrations of the One-Thousand Years of the Polish State (1956–1966/1967) 241

Vasyl' M. Tkachenko
The inseparable heritage of early medieval Rus'. On the celebration of the 1,150th anniversary of the origin of Russian statehood 279

List of affiliations of the authors 305

List of figures 307

Editors' remarks 309

Introduction

The present volume arose from two inspirations. Firstly, it is a result of the international conference "The early processes of Christianization in Central and Eastern Europe: the broad historical canvas and aspects of Mieszko I's baptism in 966". That conference was held by the Center for Historical Research of the Polish Academy of Sciences in Berlin (CBH PAN) on June 10 and 11, 2016, in co-operation with the Institute of Archaeology and Ethnology PAN and the Leibniz-Institut für Geschichte und Kultur des östlichen Europa (GWZO) in Leipzig. In the first part of this volume, we showcase the conference's fruits – namely, the papers by archeologists, historians, and art historians who present the latest results of research into the origins of Polish statehood and the process of Christianization in the realm of the early Piast dynasty against the background of contemporary Central and Eastern Europe. This part represents a summary of the input of Polish, German, Czech, and Ukrainian historiographies in the genesis and unique nature of the roads whereby Christianization proceeded in Polish lands in the early Middle Ages in the context of the parallel processes underway in neighboring lands from the 10th c.

The second part was provided by the years-long research tradition at CBH PAN in Berlin into cultures of memory and the politics. Besides the critical analysis of the paradigms present in Polish historiography in regard to the beginnings of Christianization in the early Piast monarchy, this part of the volume includes papers that analyze the politics of memory as applied to the beginnings of Christianity and statehood in Poland and the Kievan Rus'. Chosen as examples of this are: the state celebrations in Russia in 1888 of the 1,000th anniversary of Vladimir the Great's baptism*; communist Poland's 1966 rival celebrations of "1,000 Years of Polish Statehood" vs. the "Millennium of Poland's Baptism"; and the celebrations in the Russian Federation in 2012 of the 1,050th anniversary of the Rus'. These examples reveal the uniqueness and the evolution

---

* The form *Vladimir* in relation to the Grand Prince of Kiev, and the ruler of Kievan Rus' from 980 to 1015 is used only here and below in the text: "Searching for the meaning of the Russian way. The ideological setting of the 900th anniversary celebrations of the Baptism of Rus' (1888)" by Mikołaj Banaszkiewicz, as it is the transcription of the most common linguistic form used in Russian language. In the remaining texts in this volume the form *Volodimer* is used as it appears in the *Primary Chronicle* or *Tale of Bygone Years* (see: editor's remarks).

of various politics of memory in regard to the founding myths of statehood in today's Poland, Russia, and Ukraine in modern times, i.e., from the late 19th c. to the early 21st c.

Igor Kąkolewski, Christian Lübke, Przemysław Urbańczyk

Part I: New perspectives

Oleksiy Tolochko

Christians and pagans in Kiev during the 10th c.

Abstract: The author discusses two themes: the supposed growth of Christianity in pre-conversion Kiev and the parallel developments within the traditional "pagan" beliefs. He argues that descriptions of pagan idols and the image of the pre-conversion Eastern Slavs as idolaters in the earliest historical sources lie at the core of the contemporary understanding of pagan "religion". As in any other aspect of early Rus' history, the principal text here is the *Primary Chronicle* that emerged in the early 12th c. However, the idea of paganism that arises in this text was mostly shaped by literary sources (Byzantine chronicles) and the models of the pagans and their idols known from the Old Testament. Also the archeological discoveries, generally viewed as more reliable that are discussed in the chapter were interpreted within what is termed "text-driven archeology". No wonder that the number of pagan shrines, as well as their locations, are in perfect agreement with the *Primary Chronicle*'s account.

Keywords: Kievan Rus', Grand Prince Volodimer, Varangians, Baptism of Rus', paganism

"State of the Union"

In no other field of medieval history have sources exercised such a tyrannical grip over what scholars tend to think or believe as in the study of Kievan Rus'. The discipline was cursed with what otherwise might have been a blessing: possession of an unparalleled, rich in details, and brilliantly entertaining account of "ancient days" found in the *Primary Chronicle*. Ever since the dawn of history as an academic branch of knowledge in the 18th c., the *Primary Chronicle* was recognized as a surpassingly important source, factual and reliable both in its particulars and in its general presentation of past reality. Being essentially the only source offering a systematic and coherent narrative, the *Primary Chronicle* suggested itself as a convenient template for history-telling – and indeed, it has been incorporated in every major synthesis to the point of rendering them but a translation of the medieval story into academic language. True, other sources were gradually added into the discussion, but they were absorbed into the already existing interpretative scheme supplied by the *Primary Chronicle*. The ongoing effect is obvious, if not always recognized: everything we think we know about the early Kievan state (as well as things we think we do not know) is framed by merely a few medieval narrative sources and their ideas about the past.

The above applies of course to both themes of my discussion: the supposed growth of Christianity in pre-conversion Kiev and the parallel developments within the traditional "pagan" beliefs. Without going into much detail, the standard narrative runs as follows.[1] Eastern Europe was introduced to Christianity shortly after the first Rus' attack on Constantinople in 860.[2] However, what exactly happened, who the Rus' requesting baptism were – and even whether the event actually took place at all – is not quite clear.[3] The results of this first attempt to institute a new religion are assessed as ephemeral at best, nonetheless it is believed that from that time on Christianity never ceased to exist in Eastern Europe, and that it persisted, against all odds and the total lack of evidence, into the 10th c. Since the early 900s, the close and regular (if not always happy) relationships established by the Kievan Rus' with Byzantium, their annual travels to Constantinople and prolonged stays there, should have encouraged at least some among the Varangian Rus' elite to explore the new set of ideas and beliefs associated with the splendor, wealth, and prestige of the Empire. Indeed, by the 940s a sizable Christian community organized around the "Cathedral Church" of Saint Elijah is discernible in Kiev. Not yet including any members of the ruling clan, these Christians nevertheless formed an influential faction within the Kievan society, judging from the fact that their approval in the form of a Christian oath was needed in order to endorse the treaty with Byzantium. The next decade saw Christianity penetrating the core institution of the Rus': the princely clan itself. In the 950s, the regent of Kievan Rus' (940–960), Princess Olga († 969), travelled to Constantinople where she was baptized with at least some members of her (mostly female) entourage.[4] After that but one final step

---

1 A good guide to the traditional research agenda is: H. Birnbaum, "Christianity before Christianization. Christians and Christian Activity in Pre-988 Rus' Christianity and the Eastern Slavs: Slavic Cultures in the Middle Ages", *California Slavic Studies* 16, 1993, p. 42–62.
2 The event is described by several Byzantine authors, most extensively by Constantine Porphyrogenitus in his biography of Basil I, see: S. A. Ivanov, *"Pearls Before Swine": Missionary Work in Byzantium*, Paris 2015, p. 101–102.
3 Cf. Ihor Ševčenko's insightful remarks that Constantine's account, full of missionary "topoi" and culminating in a miracle, is precious as much for the historical information it provides, as for its "historical misinformation", see: I. Ševčenko, "Religious Missions seen from Byzantium", *Harvard Ukrainian Studies* 12, 1989, p. 24.
4 Everything associated with Olga's journey to Constantinople – the number of visits, their dates and even whether she was indeed baptized there – has been a matter of a lively debate generating an amount of literature no single footnote can do justice to. Among the more recent additions see: C. Zuckerman, *Le voyage d'Olga et la*

remained to be taken: for an actual ruler to set an example to his followers and the whole realm by accepting baptism. In 988, Prince Volodimer the Great (980–1015) travelled to the Byzantine city of Kherson where he received baptism and was rewarded with marriage to the Byzantine Princess Anna Porphyrogenita, sister of the sitting emperors. Christianity had arrived in Eastern Europe for good and Rus' had entered the family of Christian nations.

Oddly, this picture of Christianity ever enlarging its territory and constantly gaining new ground, thus paving the way to final conversion – indeed, making it bound to happen and even inevitable – coexists in the literature with the story of the concurrent development of paganism and how it evolved into a complex set of beliefs and practices tailored to the ever increasing demands of the maturing state organization and culminating in the creation of the "pagan pantheon" by Volodimer shortly before he made his choice in favor of the Christian faith. The two developments run parallel, as if mirror reflections of one another. Whether or not such a scenario is plausible or if we should rather expect the new religion to expand at the expense of the old, is beyond the point, for the two stories are lifted almost verbatim from the pages of the *Primary Chronicle*. They reflect how a medieval cleric understood his realm's path to conversion and thus have a very limited value for the reconstruction of past reality.

It would seem that the only conceptual innovation in recent years has been the notion of "Varangian Christianity" suggested by John Lind.[5] At the core of this concept lies the vision of Eastern Europe as part of the large periphery of Christendom stretching from Anglo-Saxon Britain to the Byzantine Empire and its principal "movers and shakers" – namely, the Scandinavians (called the Varangians in Byzantium and in Rus'), apparently the only international player in Eastern Europe, as their enterprises alone made them transcend the local experience of other communities in Eastern Europe. Being exposed to Christianity in the extreme points of this space and also being either indifferent to or unaware

---

première ambassade espagnole à Constantinople en 946, (ser.: Travaux et Mémoires, 13), Paris 2000, p. 647–672, M. Featherstone, "Olga's Visit to Constantinople in De ceremoniis", *Revue des études byzantines* 61, Lyon 2003, p. 241–251; A. Poppe, "Once Again Concerning the Baptism of Olga, Archontissa of Rus'", [in:] *Christian Russia in the Making*, ed. A. Poppe (ser.: Variorum Collected Studies Series, 867), Adlershot, Burlington VT 2007, with addendum on intervening literature; F. Butler, "Olga's Conversion and the Construction of Chronicle Narrative", *The Russian Review* 67, 2008, p. 230–242.

5 J. Lind, "The Christianization of North and Eastern Europe c. 950–1050 — A Plea for a Comparative Study", *Ennen ja Nyt* 4, 2004, p. 1–18, [electronic resource] available at: http://www.ennenjanyt.net/4-04/lind.html.

of dogmatic and institutional differences between the Latin and Greek Churches, or else simply being opportunistic, the Scandinavians must have created a phenomenon which John Lind termed "Varangian Christianity", i.e., a practice of Christianity on the grassroots level and in the absence of fixed ecclesiastical structures. While potentially departing from the standard narrative, this concept has the same fundamental flaw: it is inspired by the same chronicle tradition.

Idol-worshipers and heretics

Since the 19th c., the majority vote among historians and archeologists favors the idea that the early reports on the pre-conversion Eastern Slavs, including those on their religious beliefs, however deficient in scope and detail, do contain some bits of authentic information and may serve as a reliable base for the reconstructions of their traditional system of beliefs. This attitude was certainly dominant throughout the 20th c. and, with the number of works growing and their volume increasing, it is firmly established as the principal approach to the topic. It is becoming increasingly obvious, however, that the immensely complex and sophisticated edifice of "Eastern Slavic paganism" embodied in these writings belongs to what was aptly termed "an armchair mythology" (*kabinetnaia mifologia*) – i.e., an artificial construction quite removed from the past reality.

It would therefore be useful to return to the sources and reexamine them in the absence of the interpretative burden imposed by tradition. For my discussion, I have carved out only one aspect from within this vast field: the descriptions of pagan idols and the image of the pre-conversion Slavs as idolaters. I would argue that for the authors of our earliest reports on pagan practices among the Eastern Slavs, these two issues feature most prominently and lie at the core of their understanding of pagan "religion".

A few words about the evidence might be handy at the onset of the discussion. As in any other aspect of early Rus' history, our principal text here is, expectedly, the *Primary Chronicle*. It emerged in the early 12th c. and bears all the marks of its time. It was conceived and written within a monastery setting by a pious Christian cleric whose exposure to genuine pagan practices was limited or nonexistent. At best, his idea of paganism might have been shaped by some vestiges of traditional beliefs still practiced in rural and remote areas by the common folk. I will have the opportunity to revisit this suggestion in due course. What his sources might have been for the paganism of the ancient past remains a complete mystery. We know, however, that when needing to explain the nature of the pagan deities or the origin of some pagan practice (as in the entries for 912 or 1114), the chronicler would resort to literary sources, normally the Byzantine chronicles of John Malala or George Hamartolos. His "paganism" was thus of a learned nature, read from books rather than experienced in practice. Chances are, therefore, that the rest of his knowledge on the past religious life came from a similar source.

The most persistent theme in the chronicler's portrayal of pagans and their heathen ways is their idols. Idols and idol-worship are so conspicuous an attribute of the pagans that, within the framework of the chronicle, to be a pagan or to live the life of a pagan means primarily to worship idols and sacrifice before idols.

The Primary Chronicle is not alone in this respect. It may have built upon established models. Somewhat earlier the Metropolitan Ilarion develops the same topic and with much vigor in his *Sermon on Law and Grace*.[6] The author is a notable figure: he was a preacher at the court church of the Holy Apostles and in 1051, he was appointed to the Metropolitan See of Kiev. *The Sermon on Law and Grace* is, most probably, an Easter Sermon, delivered sometime in the late 1040s in the Tithe Church built by Volodimer shortly after his conversion, or in Saint Sophia Cathedral in Kiev, but definitely before the entire royal family of the baptizer's son Yaroslav the Wise (1019–1054). This is the earliest known attempt to explain to the ruling dynasty their pagan past and their Christian present, along with the difference between the two, and how the two can be reconciled.

Ilarion is quite single-minded on the subject: of all the terms reserved in Slavonic for heathens and heathen ways he employs only those semantically tied to the noun idol. He calls the pagans of old exclusively "idol-worshipers" and "idolaters" (*idolosluzhiteli*). Indeed, he knows no other aspect of pagan beliefs and practices but the worshiping of idols. To be a pagan means to venerate idols (*moliti idoly, polklaniatisia idolom*); to share heathen beliefs is to remain in the "darkness of idol-worship" or "delusion of idol-worship". The contrast with Christians lies in pagans having "multiple deities of idolatry" (*mnogobozhestvo idolskoe*). Ilarion is so graphic here that he describes conversion as the process of demolishing the heathen temples with their idols (*kapishcha idolskie*) and erecting Christian churches in their stead. He is emphatic, but scant in details. Pagan gods are but demons controlled by Satan that demand human sacrifices. Slavic paganism in the *Sermon on Law and Grace* is devoid of any historical or "ethnographical" dimension. It is faceless and impersonal, and Ilarion's audience would learn nothing about their ancestors' wicked ways of praising their gods. Ilarion's rigid approach is unsurprising and even expected considering his

---

6   For an English translation see: S. Franklin, *Sermons and Rhetoric of Kievan Rus'* (ser.: Harvard Library of Early Ukrainian Literature, 5), Cambridge MA 1991, p. 3–30.

principal topic: the contrast between the idol-worshipers of the Old Testament and the Christians of the Gospel. Thus, Ilarion's image of paganism is deeply Christianized; it is the paganism of Scripture.

Ilarion might have set the standard or may have followed an established discourse; we have no way of knowing, for his sermon is an isolated phenomenon without proper context in the 11th c. Yet some seventy years later, the same descriptive model of pagans as primarily or even exclusively idol-worshipers proved rather productive for historical narrative.

The theme of idols and of the veneration of idols feature in several episodes of the *Chronicle*, for instance in the famous scene of Prince Igor's (†945) making an oath before the idol of Perun in 945, yet most prominently in those parts that deal with Prince Volodimer, his pagan delusions, his choice of a new faith, and his eventual conversion. The most famous of those is, of course, the story of what is termed in the literature "the pagan reform of Volodimer" and "Volodimer's pantheon." According to the *Chronicle*'s account, upon occupying the principal town of Kiev, Volodimer ordered several, in fact, six, idols to be erected "on the hill outside his palace":

> And [Volodimer] set up idols on the hill outside the castle with the hall: one of Perun, made of wood with a head of silver and a mouth of gold, and others of Khors, Dazhbog, Stribog, Simargl, and Mokosh. The people sacrificed to them, calling them gods, and brought their sons and their daughters to sacrifice to these devils. They desecrated the earth with their offerings, and the land of Rus and this hill were defiled with blood.[7]

In the *Chronicle*'s passage we immediately recognize the motifs known already from Ilarion's treatise: the multitude of pagan deities who are, in fact, mere demons; idols representing these false "gods"; and human sacrifices as the principal way of offerings.

However, this account is much celebrated in the literature on Eastern Slavic paganism for here we have not only the names of all six idols, but also the description of the physical appearance of the most prominent of them all, Perun. There exists a long tradition of exegesis on this passage, mostly in a "realistic" vein.[8] Scholars would speculate about the exact place in Kiev where this "pantheon"

---

7   *The Russian Primary Chronicle*, ed., trans. S. H. Cross, Cambridge MA 1930, p. 180. Volodimer also sent his uncle Dobrynia to Novgorod, which apparently had hitherto lacked a proper temple, to set up an idol there so that people could offer sacrifices.

8   One of most recent samples in this genre is M. Vasilev, *Iazychestvo vostochnych Slavian nakanune kreshcheniia Rusi: Religiozno-mifologicheskoie vzaimodeistviie s iranskim mirom. Iazycheskaia reforma kniazia Vladimira*, Moscow 1997.

might have been constructed; about the reasons that compelled Volodimer to undertake his "pagan reform"; about its role in the program of state-building; about its relationship to future conversion, etc. The general conclusion is that with his "pagan reform" (manifested in the construction of idols) Volodimer aimed to unify the diverse pagan beliefs of his realm in order to fuse them into a single "state paganism". Also, it is believed that this "reform" betrays Volodimer's attempts at "fishing" for a new religion, which eventually would bring him to Christianity.

For us, two issues are of key importance here: could there indeed have been a pagan pantheon and is the description of the idols authentic? Some scholars, among them Viljo J. Mansikka and Henryk Łowmiański, would argue convincingly that the pagan pantheon could not be supported by authentic data.[9] There simply is no evidence for the suggestion that the Slavic pagan gods were ranked or arranged in hierarchical order and formed a closed community with clearly divided responsibilities. This is the idea of a Christian cleric who tried to arrange pagan deities in accordance with his own idea of how the heavenly forces should operate.

Yet if there was no "pantheon", how are we to explain the multitude of idols? Why was it not enough to have a single idol of Perun? We have to bear in mind that Ilarion insists that idolaters always venerate many idols (*mnogobozhestvo idolskoe*), which is their most obvious distinction from Christians who believe in one god. The multitude of idols produces a diversity of "laws" and "customs" among the pagans, and this is contrasted by the single law of the Christians. The whole story of Volodimer erecting a multitude of idols near his palace is simply an extended gloss to this common notion.

---

[9] V. J. Mansikka, *Religiia vostochnykh Slavian*, Moscow 2005, p. 76–78; (Russian translation of a work first published in 1922); H. Łowmiański, *Religia Słowian i jej upadek (w. VI – XII)*, Warszawa 1979, p. 113–115. Both scholars insisted that the selection of the idols in the "pantheon" is an artificial product of the chronicler's activity. They differed, however, as to how he came up with the names. While Mansikka suggested that the chronicler picked up at random whatever the name he could find, Łowmiański argued that the list was the result of a deliberate inquiry. On a possible Old Testament model for the account, see: S. Albrecht, "Vladimir der Heilige und Nebukadnezar – Bemerkungen zu einem typologischen Verständnis des slawischen Pantheons", [in:] *Die frühen Slawen – von der Expansion zu gentes und nationes. Beiträge der Sektion zur slawischen Frühgeschichte des 8. Deutschen Archäologiekongresses in Berlin*, ed. F. Biermann, T. Kersting, A. Klammt, vol. 1, Langenweissbach 2016, p. 275–285.

Before converting to Christianity, in the *Chronicle*'s story, Volodimer had explored the extremes of pagan idolatry, which, within the chronicler's narrative strategy, makes the conversion of this utmost idolater clearly miraculous. The description of idols erected in Kiev is followed by the grim story of how this act incited people to willingly sacrifice their sons and daughters to the idols. This fragment is a close paraphrase of Psalm 105:

> And they served their idols: which were a snare unto them. Yea, they sacrificed their sons and their daughters unto devils, And shed innocent blood, even the blood of their sons and of their daughters, whom they sacrificed unto the idols of Canaan: and the land was polluted with blood. Thus were they defiled with their own works.[10]

The chronicle passage (and its Old Testament prototype) has its echo later in the *Chronicle* – namely, in a very marked fragment usually called "The Philosopher's Admonition" to Volodimer, where a Greek missionary instructs the pagan prince in the Christian version of history:

> They undertook to build idols, some of wood, some of brass, others of marble, and still others of gold and silver. They not only worshiped them, but even brought their sons and daughters and killed them before these images, so that all the earth was defiled.[11]

The philosopher's lecture made a first dent in Volodimer's stubbornness, but it did not convinced him entirely. Yet while listening to the missionary, the prince could not have missed a strange and disturbing semblance of the Old Testament idols to the ones he himself had erected.

Indeed, the idol of Perun is described as "made of wood with a head of silver and a mouth of gold". This description is attested to in the following entry by the observation made by a Varangian Christian whose son was chosen for a sacrifice: "These (i.e., the idols) are not gods, but only idols of wood. Today it is, and tomorrow it will rot away. These gods do not eat, or drink, or speak; they are fashioned by hand out of wood."[12] It would appear that the "wooden" nature of idols is their most consistently stressed attribute, and, we may gather, their most important one.

These descriptions have been recognized as "hidden citations" from Scripture.[13] Their main task is to demonstrate the man-made nature of pagan

---

10 L. Müller, *Die Taufe Russlands. Die Frühgeschichte des russischen Christentums bis zum Jahre 988*, München 1987, p. 93.
11 *The Russian Primary*..., p. 188.
12 *The Russian Primary*..., p. 182.
13 I. Danilevsky, *Povest vremennykh let. Germenevticheskie osnovy izucheniia letopisnych tekstov*, Moscow 2004, p. 104.

gods. The theme of idolatry is so conspicuous in the Old Testament that it is quite difficult to pick any single example that served for our descriptions. The words of the Christian Varangian echo Deuteronomy 4, 28: "And there you will serve gods of wood and stone, the work of human hands, that neither see, nor hear, nor eat, nor smell". They also echo Psalm 115, 4–6: "Their idols are silver and gold, the work of human hands. They have mouths, but do not speak; eyes, but do not see. They have ears, but do not hear; noses, but do not smell." Here we find not only the principal material for the manufacture of idols – i.e., wood – but also silver and gold, which are emblematic of the Perun idol.

These examples, whose number might be increased[14], suggest that both the general characteristic of idols and the individual description of Perun are but a collective portrait of the Old Testament idols. The "paganism" of old for the later clerics could only have been grasped as a form of the "idolatry" known from Old Testament precedents.

The end of the Rus' idols was dramatic – but, it would seem, it was performed according to a scenario drawn from a written source. Upon baptism, Volodimer,

> directed that the idols should be overthrown, and that some should be cut to pieces and others burned with fire. He thus ordered that Perun should be bound to a horse's tail and dragged along Borichev to the river. He appointed twelve men to beat the idol with sticks, not because he thought the wood was sensitive, but to affront the demon who had deceived man in this guise [...] After they had thus dragged the idol along, they cast it into the Dnieper.[15]

Several literary prototypes have been suggested for this scene: similar episodes from the chronicle of George Hamartolos are known, and even closer parallels are found in the *Vita of the First Kherson Martyrs*.[16]

In setting up the "pagan pantheon" on the hill outside the princes' hall, the author of the *Primary Chronicle* failed to comment upon the individual functions of the deities. This he left to modern scholars who, indeed, have come up with ingenious conjectures about their origins and responsibilities. In the entire

---

14 The theme of idolatry is readily invoked by the prophets who develop the idea of their man-made nature (Isa 37: 19; Jer 10: 3–5; Hab 2: 18–1; Dan 5: 23). A very close parallel to the chronicle passage is found in Ps 135: 15–17. The idols' lack of awareness is important to the *New Testament* as well, and we found the theme in Acts 17: 19 and in Rev 9: 20.

15 *The Russian Primary...*, p. 204.

16 T. Vilkul, *Litopys i khronohraf. Studii z tekstolohii domonholskoho kyivskoho litopysannia*, Kiev 2015, p. 133; M. Andreicheva, "Siuzhet izgnaniia Peruna v statie 6496 g. Povesti vremennykh let", *Drevnyaya Rus. Voprosy medievistiki* 65, Moscow 2016, p. 95–110.

Chronicle, only one god's duty is vaguely referred to: "Volos, the god of livestock". This laconic remark the chronicler borrowed verbatim from the original document that was at his disposal: the charter of Prince Svyatoslav's (c. 963–972) treaty with Byzantium of 971. Ironically, this Volos was not included in the pantheon.

The chronicler dealt with the issue of the gods' personalities toward the end of his work, in the entry for 1114.[17] Here he discusses two pagan deities – Svarog and Dazhbog, the latter, importantly for us, being listed among the idols of the "pantheon". We are told that Svarog was an Egyptian king also known as Hephaestus ("Theost"). He is responsible for teaching humankind how to produce iron weapons and also for establishing monogamy, for which, the chronicler remarks elliptically, he received his other name, Svarog. Svarog was succeeded on the Egyptian throne by his son Helios (translated as *Solntse tsesar*, sun-king), also known as Dazhbog. "He was a strong man," yet his only noted achievement was enforcing his father's law of monogamy.

It has long been recognized that the whole passage is an almost word for word quotation from the Slavonic translation of John Malalas' chronicle.[18] A (Bulgarian?) translator of the Byzantine chronicle glossed the Greek names of Egyptian kings with the names of pagan deities. The chronicler apparently had nothing to add of his own.

One arrives at the conclusion (almost inevitable in light of the previous observations) that those in the 11th and the early 12th c. who had a chance to reflect on pagan religion knew virtually nothing about the actual beliefs or practices of their ancestors. They modeled their pagans and their idols after the fashion of the Old Testament. Paganism, obviously, had not been "nationalized", so all the pagans were alike. There was no notion of specifically "Slavic" or "Germanic" or "Finnish" paganisms. Since the "sacred history" as described in the Old Testament was assimilated as part of one's own "national" past, it was only natural for someone writing about the old times to suppose that all the idolaters were the same. Thus, their only point of reference (which they tried to impose on readers) was not some "historical memory", but that of Scripture.

---

17 *Polnoie sobranie russkikh letopisei*, vol. 2: *Ipatievskaia letopis*, Saint Petersburg 1908, p. 278–279.

18 V. J. Mansikka, *Religiia vostochnykh Slavian...*, p. 90–94. See also the most exhaustive treatment of the passage, as well as its place within the structure of the *Primary Chronicle*: T. Vilkul, *Litopys i khronohraf...*, p. 142–147.

So what about the actual paganism still supposedly practiced on the margins of Christian Rus'? Could it serve as a useful source for constructing the image of the past pagans?

We have two rather detailed reports on contemporary pagans for the 1070s, one, importantly, was passed on to the chronicler by an eyewitness.[19] 1071 was apparently a bad year: the failure of crops caused famine and popular unrest. For this year, the *Chronicle* reports that several pagan priests (called *volkhvy*) appeared in Kiev, Novgorod, and the Rostov region inciting people and stirring up mutinies. Of these instances, the most interesting for our purposes is the story told by Ian', son of Vyshata, a member of a prominent Kiev family and one of the principal chronicler's informants. That year Ian' happened to be sent by Prince Svyatoslav to the Rostov region to collect taxes. While there, he learned that two pagan priests (*volkhvy*) had appeared in the region inciting people and accusing the members of the local elite of causing the failure of crops and famine. The *volkhvy* were proceeding through the land killing those better off and seizing their possessions. Ian' confronted the *volkhvy* and the band of their followers, managed to capture them, and before meting out punishment, entered into a theological dispute with them. The exchange proved fascinating and the *volkhvy* were forced to reveal the basics of their beliefs. This is a puzzling text for it turns out that deep in the woods of the upper Volga the pagan priests (most probably, of Finno-Ugric extraction) articulated something suspiciously similar to the Bogomil heresy prominent in the Balkans. This has forced some scholars to speculate whether the Bogomils were active in Rus'.[20] But the solution here is simple. Whatever the *volkhvy* had said to Ian', it was of no consequence: he was either unable to understand them or unwilling to take them seriously. Many years after the incident, Ian' Vyshatych and his interlocutor the chronicler were able to envision the pagans as Christian heretics.

In terms of the *Chronicle*'s narrative, this and other episodes of encounters with pagan priests are intended to serve as a useful lesson for the Christians. The most important ability of the *volkhvy* was believed to be their ability to predict the future. Ian' had demonstrated that to be false: not only were they unable to learn of someone else's future, they could not foresee their own end. Prince Gleb Svyatoslavich (c. 1068–1078) in Novgorod in similar circumstances staged the same demonstration.[21] And this was again shown in Kiev, where two pagan

---

19 For the text see: *The Russian Primary...* p. 240–243.
20 N. Kazachkova, "Kym vyprosa za bogomilska eres v Drevna Rusia prez XI vek", *Istoricheski pregled* 13, 1957, p. 45–77; D. Angelov, "Bogomilstvo v istoriata na slavianskite narodi", *Slavianska filologia* 5, 1963, p. 173–178.
21 *The Russian Primary...*, p. 243–244.

priests were dispatched with no consequences for true believers. The *volkhvy* could boast of their great future, while in fact, they were easily killed and no pagan gods came to their rescue. This simple lesson on the impotence of pagans and their priests is an instantly recognizable theme for anyone reading the *Chronicle*. It is the subject of probably the most famous of all the stories of "preconversion times": the death of Prince Oleg (879–912) who was believed to be a soothsayer himself, but was unable to foresee his own end.[22]

The conclusion is rather trivial: it would appear that aside from several minor bits of authentic information, there is no "authentic" paganism in the *Chronicle*. This paganism is deeply Christianized: the ancient pagans are being imagined as idolaters from the Old Testament, while the current pagans are imagined as Christian heretics of a sort, and both images are used instrumentally in order to reaffirm the Christian identity of the reader.

Folkways as the heathen ways

By the turn of the 12th c., the realm of Rus' was considered, both by outsiders as well as its natives, a firmly Christianized country. Very few, and then only on the fringes of the society and in extreme circumstances, would dare to profess their non-Christian beliefs. All the same, Christian propagandists would maintain that the purity of faith had not been fully achieved and some vestiges of the old religion were still there, still to be eradicated from people's habits and attitudes.

Under the year of 1068, on the occasion of the crushing defeat suffered by the Christian Rus' princes from the heathen Cumans, the chronicler inserted an admonition on the causes of God's wrath. It has been established that he used as his template a medieval Slavic text known as *The Sermon on the Drought and the Punishments Inflicted by God*.[23] However, the chronicler took a liberty in adding to the list of transgressions some items not found in his original – namely, what he believed to be traces of pagan mores:

> Do we not live like pagans as long as we attach superstitious significance to meetings? For he turns back who meets a monk, a boar, or a swine. Is that not pagan? [...] Other people attach special significance to sneezing, which is healthy for the head. By these

---

22 *The Russian Primary...*, p. 155.
23 I. I. Sreznevsky, "Istochnik pouchenia, vnesennogo v Povest vremennykh let i pripisannogo Feodosiiu Pecherskomu", [in:] *Svedenia i zametki o maloizvestknykh i neizvestnykh pamiatnikakh*, part 3, Saint Petersburg 1867, p. 34–43; I. Miltenov, "Slovo za zasukhata i za bozhie nakazania: Tekstologichesko i izvorovedsko izsledvanie", *Izvestia na Institut za balgarski iezik* 30, 2017, p. 214–261.

and other similar customs the devil deceives us [...] For we behold the playgrounds worn bare by the footsteps of a great multitude, who jostle each other while they make a spectacle of a thing invented by the devil. The churches still stand; but when the hour of prayer is come, few worshipers are found in the church.[24]

The daily life of a Christian folk, predictably, was a far cry from the monastic ideal for a model Christian, and beyond the relative safely of the cloister walls a pious monk would have numerous occasions to be appalled or disgusted – just as Saint Theodosius, the Abbot of the Caves monastery, obviously was upon witnessing profane entertainment with music and dancing right in the princely palace. The Saint's *Vita* conceded that that was "a custom in the royal presence", yet Prince Svyatoslav was chastised nevertheless. Unlike the common people, however, "the faithful prince" had not been accused of heathen inclinations and had not abandoned his habits: rather, a silent agreement was reached that he would abstain from impious amusements during the abbot's visits.

"Pagan ways" are thus folkways, customs, and habits that are traditional. The source of this lingering "paganism" is not any evil intent, but rather human ignorance and "simplicity" to be cured by persistent enlightenment.

Yet, if pagan ways stem from tradition, which by definition is something stretching back in time, pagans of old can be imagined as a simple folk living in the past and practicing more of the same.

The chronicler had a chance to comment on the mores of pre-conversion Slavic tribes in the opening pages of his work. Most pagan tribes – the Derevlians, the Radimichis, the Vyatichians, the Severians – are described as living a life of uncivilized, almost beast-like existence. They, too, "gather together for games, for dancing, and for all other devilish amusements".[25] They eat all sorts of "unclean" food (in which we register an echo of dietary accusations from contemporaneous anti-Latin polemics), know neither Christian marriage, nor Christian burial. Instead,

> whenever a death occurred, a feast was held over the corpse, and then a great pyre was constructed, on which the deceased was laid and burned. After the bones were collected, they were placed in a small urn and set upon a post by the roadside, as the Vyatichians do even to this day.[26]

The practice of cremation is obviously a non-Christian custom and this description seems authentic enough. Yet the final remark – "as the Vyatichians do even

---

24 *The Russian Primary...*, p. 237.
25 *The Russian Primary...*, p. 142.
26 *The Russian Primary...*, p. 142.

to this day" – betrays that the chronicler used the "ethnography" of his time for historical lesson. The chronicler draws on his ethnography again, noting that "even in our own day" the nomadic Cumans practice exactly the same heathen customs as the Slavs once had. Rural backwardness was equated with the historical backwardness of paganism.

Varangian Christians

Two themes are of paramount importance for the author of the *Primary Chronicle*: the origin of the Varangian dynasty that came to rule over the Slavs and the way its pagan realm came to be converted to Christianity.

Metropolitan Ilarion had solved the latter issue by treating conversion as an obvious miracle. Prince Volodimer had presided over the land of the pagans; he was a pagan himself and had no means of learning about the true faith: he had not heard the words of wisdom, he had not read from the books, he had not witnessed miracles performed by the holy men, he had seen no apostle visiting his land. There were no Christians around Volodimer, and so his decision to convert came about as a result of a sudden divine inspiration, a truly miraculous event.

There are echoes of these ideas in the *Primary Chronicle*, too. However, its author's task was quite different from that of Ilarion's: the chronicler had to tell stories and preferably in as many details as could be found. He opted for a "long" story of Christianity slowly infiltrating Rus' and gradually winning over more and more adepts.

In the chronicler's vision, Rus' was predestined to become Christian from the beginning. Long before the Varangian dynasty came along and even before the town of Kiev was built, the land had been visited by the apostle Andrew who prophesied its great Christian future. The land was blessed.[27]

For the Christian cleric writing in the early 12th c., Byzantium served as the ultimate source of piety and true faith. The chronicler, therefore, used any opportunity of Rus' coming into contact with Constantinople to introduce heathens to at least some aspects of Christian ways.

We are told that in 911, when the Rus' envoys came to Constantinople to conclude a treaty, the Emperor Leo VI the Wise (886–912), upon successful negotiations, ordered his courtiers

> to show them the beauties of the churches, the golden palace, and the riches contained therein. The thus showed the Russes much gold and many palls and jewels, together

---

27 *The Russian Primary...*, p. 139.

with the relics of our Lord's Passion: the crown, the nails, and the purple robe, as well as the bones of the Saints. They also instructed the Russes in their faith, and expounded to them the true belief.[28]

This bizarre story of pagans appreciating the relics of the Passion and "the bones of the Saints" while being instructed "in true belief" is a pure invention of the chronicler[29] modeled after an episode found in the chronicle of George Hamartolos and featuring Emperor Leo and Muslim envoys.[30] But for the participants of the tour, the experience did not go without consequences. The seeds were sown, and when the time came to sign a new treaty with Byzantium in 944, we discover a whole Christian community of the Varangians dwelling in Kiev. They were asked to endorse the charter as a separate group: "The Christian Russes took oath in the Church of St. Elias [...] This was, in fact, a cathedral church, since many of the Varangians were Christians".[31]

"The cathedral church" together with its name, as well as "the Christian Russes" were lifted by the chronicler from the charter of the treaty to create a colorful scene in Kiev. In fact, it all happened in Constantinople on the premises of the Grand Palace, and "the Christian Russes" noted in the text of the treaty were, most probably, those serving in the Byzantine army.[32] The chronicler located his imaginary "Varangian church" as standing "by the Stream" (the name of a rivulet into which the idol of Perun will later be cast), which indicates that he placed his Christian community within the Lower Town of Podil, a mercantile district by the river.

In the next generation we find Christian Varangians residing in a very prominent spot: in the aristocratic Upper Town, next to the princely hall, on the site where in due course the first masonry Tithe Church would be erected by Volodimer upon his baptism. The chronicle vignette, sometimes called the "Life of the Varangian Martyrs" (and indeed later reworked into one), is placed within the first years in the "pagan" period of the baptizer's reign. We read that there was a certain Varangian in Kiev who "came from the Greeks" and "adhered

---

28 *The Russian Primary...*, p. 154.
29 J. Wortley, C. Zuckerman, "The Relics of Our Lord's Passion in the Russian Primary Chronicle", *Vizantiyskiy vremennik* 63, 2004, p. 67–75.
30 O. P. Tolochko, "Letopisnoie obramlenie rusko-vizantiiskogo dogovora 911 goda", [in:] *Dubitando. Studies in History and Culture in Honor of Donald Ostrowski*, ed. B. J. Boek, R. E. Martin, D. Rowland, Bloomington 2012, p. 61–66.
31 *The Russian Primary...*, p. 164.
32 See: O. P. Tolochko "Church of St. Elijah, 'Baptized Ruses,' and the Date of the Second Ruso-Byzantine Treaty", *Byzantinoslavica* 71, 2013, p. 111–128.

to the Christian faith".[33] It so happened that the pagans lead by the Prince were looking for the next victim for their sacrifices. The lot fell on the Varangian's son, also a Christian. In the end, both father and son were killed – but not before the Varangian Christian took the opportunity to preach before the mob of pagans on the nature of their idols (wooden and senseless products of human hands, as we know already). The Varangian's speech is modeled after the similar episode in the *Vita of the First Kherson Martyrs*.[34]

In the end, contacts with Byzantium proved crucial. First a Greek missionary came to Kiev and taught Volodimer the basics of the faith, and then Volodimer sent his emissaries to Constantinople to examine "the Greek faith." The emissaries went straight to the Emperor and stated their purpose. The Emperor ordered the Patriarch to set up a service and took the heathen "Russes" to the cathedral church where together they enjoyed a liturgy:

> The Emperor accompanied the Russes to the church, and placed them in a wide space, calling their attention to the beauty of the edifice, the chanting, and the offices of the archpriest and the ministry of the deacons, while he explained to them the worship of his God.[35]

This final episode is a companion to the very first one of 911 and indeed was borrowed from the same Byzantine source. The second tour of Hagia Sophia staged by an emperor for the benefit of the heathen envoys proved decisive: they were deeply impressed by the Christian service and upon their return strongly advocated baptism for Volodimer. Attentive readers of historical records, they also cited the example of his grandmother Olga who accepted baptism while in Constantinople.

It would appear that within the generally fictitious chronicle story of Christianity's steady advancement through the 10th c., the case of Princess Olga is the only authentic – i.e., supported by evidence – episode. The chronicler probably learned of her visit to Constantinople from some Byzantine source, and he got the dating almost right (955 instead of 957). Beyond that, he knew of no actual details and entertained his readers instead with a romantic story of the Emperor suddenly falling in love with Olga and fancying to marry her. Olga's

---

33 *The Russian Primary…*, p. 182.
34 See: O. P. Tolochko "Varangian Christianity in Kiev in the Tenth Century", [in:] *Early Christianity in Scandinavia and Rus': Contacts And Influences*, ed. I. H. Garipzanov, O. P. Tolochko, Kiev 2011, p. 58–69.
35 *The Russian Primary…*, p. 198.

request for baptism, with the Emperor acting as the godfather, was a trick that helped the poor widow to escape the ordeal.

Certain uncertainties

As I have argued elsewhere[36], there are only three fragments in the *Primary Chronicle* of unquestionably authentic substance that are fit for historical reconstruction. These are the three Byzantine charters with texts of the treaties concluded with Rus' in 911, 944, and 971. They are believed to have been discovered at the turn of the 12th c., translated into Slavonic and copied *in extenso* into the chronicle.[37] They are set roughly thirty years apart, and thus provide us with snapshots of Rus' society in three consecutive generations of their ruling elite.

All three treaties consistently treat the Rus' as pagans and their land as remaining outside of Christendom. The treaty of 911 generally makes a clear distinction between the "Christians" (synonymous to the "Greeks") and "the Rus'".[38] The contrast is less pronounced in the other two charters, which mostly resort to ethnic names, yet several provisions in the 944 treaty discriminating between "the Christians" and "the Rus'" make it abundantly clear that no radical change in the confessional composition of Rus' society occurred in thirty years and "the Rus'" in the usage of the imperial chancellery was still synonymous with the heathens. The treaties, moreover, affirm this attitude by the formulas of oaths, which, at the demand of the Byzantines, the Rus' performed according to their custom and in the name of their traditional gods.

The formula of the oath in the treaty of 911 does not invoke any deity. The Rus' party stated that they confirm the provisions of the agreement "under a firm oath sworn upon our weapons according to our religion and our law", a rite performed (as again stated towards the end of the treaty) "according to our own faith and the custom of our nation."[39]

The ritual requested in 944 was of the same nature, also involving weapons, but was prescribed with more precision. The Rus' were expected to "lay down their shields, their naked swords, their armlets, and their other weapons, and swear to all that is inscribed upon this parchment."[40] The sanction for breaking

---

36 See: A. Tolochko, *Ocherki nachalnoi Rusi*, Kiev and Saint Petersburg 2015.
37 See: J. Malingoudis, *Die russisch-byzantinischen Verträge des 10. Jh. aus diplomatishcher Sicht*, Thessaloniki 1994.
38 On the notion of a "Christian" in the treaties, see: A. Alberti, "Ot Boga i ot Peruna. I trattati tra la Rus' e Bisanzio", *Studi Slavistici* 4, 2007, p. 9–11.
39 *The Russian Primary...*, p. 151, 154.
40 *The Russian Primary...*, p. 163.

the oath was the wrath of the god Perun, who would turn the weapons against the perpetrators: "May he receive help neither from God nor from Perun; may they not be protected by their own shields, but may they rather be slain by their own swords, laid down by their own arrows or by any of their own weapons, and may they be in bondage forever"; he who violates the terms of the accord "shall merit death by his own weapons, and be accursed of God and of Perun because he violated his oath."[41]

Unfortunately for us, the manner in which Prince Svyatoslav and his men performed their oath in 971 has not been put in writing (it is simply noted that they did so), but the formula of oath with the sanction was recorded:

> But if we fail in the observance of any of the aforesaid stipulations, either I, or my companions, or my subjects, may we be accursed of the God in whom we believe, namely, of Perun and Volos, the god of flocks, and may we become golden as gold, and be slain with our own weapons.[42]

And this is about the scope of our knowledge on the "pagan religion" as practiced in Kiev during the 10th c.: two names of the deities and several descriptions of a single ritual associated with the sphere of the sacrum. No idols, no pantheon, no sacrifices, and certainly no rich mythology.[43]

To this frustratingly meagre selection, three descriptions, all by outsiders, of the sacrificial practices of the Rus' should be added. Writing on Svyatoslav's Balkan campaign of the 970s, Leo the Deacon reports that the Rus', while cremating their dead warriors after the battle, made human sacrifices: they killed captives, men and women, "according to the custom of their ancestors" and also drowned infants and roosters in the Danube.[44]

---

41 *The Russian Primary…*, p. 160, 163. On the possible interpretation of the formula, see: A. Fetisov, "Ritualnoe soderzhanie kliatvy oruzhiem v russko-vizantiiskikh dogovoraeh 10 veka", [in:] *Stanovlenie slavianskogo mira i Vizantia v epokhu rannego srednevekovia*, Moscow 2001, p. 113–119; O. Gubarev, "O kliatvakh Rusov i Slavian", *Stratum plus* 5, 2013, p. 239–245.

42 *The Russian Primary…*, p. 176. On the enigmatic formula of men turning into gold and its possible meaning, see most recently: A. Romenky, "Kliatva na zolote v dogovore Sviatoslava s Ioannom Tsymiskhiem", *Ruthenica* 13, 2016, p. 142–149, with exhaustive treatment of the previous literature.

43 Cf. the somber remarks about the evidence on Eastern Slavic paganism in A. Nazarenko, "O iazychestve slavian", [in:] *Drevniaia Rus i Slaviane. Istoriko-filologicheskie issledovania*, ed. A. Nazarenko, Moscow 2009, p. 298–300.

44 *The History of Leo the Deacon. Byzantine Military Expansion in the Tenth Century*, intr., trans., A. M. Talbot, D. F. Sullivan, Washington 2005, p. 193. The editors note

We also have a report from the 920s by the Arab traveler Ybn Fadlan on his encounter with the Rus' on the Middle Volga River. He, too, observed the Rus' sacrifices, but of a less sanguinary nature: they offered to their gods "bread, meat, onions, milk, and alcohol." The deity was represented in the form of a tall piece of wood set up in the ground that had a human face and was surrounded by smaller figurines.[45] This description of idols: anthropomorphic, "made of wood" and arranged in a sort of "pantheon", seems to support the possibility of an analogous "pantheon" in Kiev. However, the connection of the Volga Rus' to their Varangian fellows in the Middle Dnieper, as well as to the polity centered in Kiev, is quite problematic. Chances are, we are dealing with two different cultural communities.

In the 940s, Emperor Constantine VII Porphyrogenitus (913–959) described the sacrifices of the Rus' performed on the road to Constantinople as follows:

> They reach the island called St. Gregory, on which island they perform their sacrifices because a gigantic oak-tree stands there; and they sacrifice live cocks. Arrows, too, they peg in round about, and others bread and meat, or something of whatever each may have, as is their custom. They also throw lots regarding the cocks, whether to slaughter them.[46]

All three contemporaneous reports have some recurrent themes, and yet they describe rites so diverse in appearance, selection, and sequence of elements and perhaps overall meaning that it is difficult to piece together an underlying system of beliefs. If anything, these accounts would suggest that there was no unified "pagan religion" common to Eastern Europe during the 10th c. Traditional beliefs were manifested as a varying assemblage of practices and rituals whose performative aspect as well as significance were determined by ever changing context.

Compared to the narrative sources, archeological evidence is generally viewed as more reliable and, by virtue of being material remains of past life, more authentic. It has no agenda and thus is honest. Yet archeology is notoriously ambiguous about what in material culture should be interpreted as vestiges of past religious life and how to make artifacts speak.

---

the influence of Herodotus on Leo the Deacon's treatment of "Scythian" sacrifices by the Rus'.
45 J. E. Montgomery, "Ibn Faḍlān and the Rūsiyyah", *Journal of Arabic and Islamic Studies* 3, 2000, p. 24–25.
46 C. Porphyrogenitus, *De administrando imperio*, Greek text ed. G. Moravczik, English trans. R. J. H. Jenkins. New, rev. edition, Washington DC 1967, p. 61.

Two sites in medieval Kiev have been identified as remnants of pagan shrines. In 1908, Vikenty Khvoika, an amateur archeologist active in Kiev, discovered in the midst of the ancient hill-fort a structure that consisted of various-sized sandstone slabs mixed with clay. The structure had an ellipsoid shape with four-cornered projections emerging from the four sides and oriented to the points of the compass. The unusual structure was interpreted as a pagan shrine or an altar – indeed, the one where, according to the *Chronicle*, the idol of Perun must have stood.[47] In 1975, another enigmatic structure, or rather its foundation, was discovered just outside the ancient hill-fort. It had the shape of a rectangle with six rounded symmetrical projections protruding from its three sides. The unusual configuration of the foundations together with its clear north-south orientation, as well as the presence of early material, suggested its possible use for religious purposes. There were also indications that the structure had been deliberately destroyed at some point. It was interpreted as the new temple built by Prince Volodimer to house his "pantheon" of six idols.[48]

In 1951–1952, in the locality called Peryn' near Novgorod another site interpreted as a pagan shrine was excavated. It was of circular shape, 21 m in diameter, and surrounded by a ditch with eight widened sections supposedly housing ritual bonfires. No constructions of any kind were discovered, but it was assumed that the idol of Perun (as intimated by the place name) stood in the middle. It had been cut and destroyed when the site came to be demolished in antiquity.[49]

All three discoveries were made, or rather interpreted, within what is termed "text-driven archeology".[50] No wonder the number of pagan shrines, as well as their locations, are in perfect agreement with the *Chronicle* account.

---

47 P. P. Tolochko "Religious Sites in Kiev During the Reign of Volodimer Sviatoslavich", *Harvard Ukrainian Studies* 11, 1987, p. 317–318.
48 P. P. Tolochko "Religious Sites in Kiev ...," p. 319–320.
49 V. Sedov, "Drevnerusskoe iazycheskoe sviatilishche v Peryni", *Kratkie soobshchenia Instituta istorii materialnoi kultury* 50, 1953, p. 92–103; B. Rybakov, *Iazychestvo Drevnei Rusi*, Moscow 1987, p. 255–256.
50 For a critical reexamination of the archeological evidence, see: L. Klein, "O drevnerusskikh iazycheskikh kapishchakh", [in:] *Tserkovnaia arkheologiia. I: Rasprostranenie khristianstva v Vostochnoi Evrope*, Saint Petersburg, Pskov 1995, p. 71–80; V. Konetskii, "Nekotoryie aspekty istochnikovedeniia i interpretatsii kompleksa pamiatnikov v Peryni pod Novgorodom", [in:] *Tserkovnaia arkheologiia. I: Rasprostranenie khristianstva v Vostochnoi Evrope*, Saint Petersburg, Pskov 1995, p. 80–85.

Up until recently, the most solid proof for the conviction that idols once were numerous in Eastern Europe and were a normal element of pagan temples was the most famous of them and the only one in existence: the "Idol of Zbruch", a stone slab with anthropomorphic images carved on its four facets, discovered in the river Zbruch in 1848. The Idol of Zbruch's authenticity received a boost when in the 1980s archeological excavations on the nearby hill discovered a pagan shrine with an altar and even pinpointed the exact spot where the idol's pedestal had once been.[51]

However, lately a strong case was made that the "Idol of Zbruch" is in fact a nineteenth-century forgery.[52] That, in turn, would render the "sacral hill-fort" with the pagan temple on Bokhit hill, along with similar discoveries rashly made, but artifacts of modern scholarship rather than of past reality.

Studying Christianization based on archeological evidence has a long history. Generally, it is believed that successes in spreading Christianity among the pre-conversion Eastern European population can be measured by the shift toward inhumation graves with east-west orientation and by dissemination of specific objects associated with Christianity, most often cross-shaped pendants.[53] By their nature, cross-shaped pendants are the most visible and obvious way to manifest one's belonging to Christian faith. However, as has been recently demonstrated, virtually all finds of cross-shaped pendants come from female graves.[54] The clear gender specific distribution of these Christian symbols is puzzling and suggests that during the 10th c., crosses, usually of precious metal, were viewed as ornaments and valued for being exotic accessories and not for the religious meaning they projected. If even the obvious Christian symbols as markers of an individual's faith are problematic, then the rest of the evidence is even more controversial. But then, why would scholars expect to discover signs of Christianization in a region yet to be converted in the first place? Is it not because the archeological hunt for traces of Christianity is being driven by the

---

51 I. Rusanova, B. Tymoshchuk, *Iazycheskie sviatilishcha drevnikh Slavian*, Moscow 2007, p. 63–113.
52 A. Komar, N. Khamaiko, "Zbruchskii idol: pamiatnik epokhi Romantizma?" *Ruthenica* 10, 2011, p.166–217; A. Komar, N. Chamajko, *Idol ze Zbrucza: zabytek z epoki romantyzmu?* (ser.: Suplement do Materiałów i Sprawozdań Rzeszowskiego Ośrodka Archeologicznego, 34), Rzeszów 2013.
53 F. Androshchuk, "Symbols of Faith or Symbols of Status? Christian Objects in Tenth-Century Rus'", [in:] *Early Christianity in Scandinavia and Rus': Contacts and Influences*, ed. I. H. Garipzanov, O. P. Tolochko, Kiev 2011, p.70–71.
54 F. Androshchuk, "Symbols of Faith or Symbols of Status..." p. 78–79.

narrative of "Christianization before Conversion" developed outside their discipline and imposed on them by historians?[55]

This narrative is based on the image of Christianization as a grassroots movement, a bottom-up development spreading horizontally within the community and eventually effecting the upper strata of the society (something analogous to the phenomenon of Early Christianity). Yet as we have seen, in all of the 10th c., in only three instances can the baptism of someone from Eastern Europe be documented: members of the warrior elite accepting Christianity in Constantinople in order to advance in the Byzantine army; Princess Olga's baptism together with her escort while in Constantinople; and finally Prince Volodimer's conversion of 988. All three episodes testify to the upper class, aristocratic even, nature of a Christianization driven by specifically elite concerns for power, prestige, and acceptance.

---

55 It is in historians' interpretations that "the archeological data seems to tally with the literary evidence quite well", see: J. Shepard, "The Coming of Christianity to Rus: Authorized and Unauthorized Versions", [in:] *Conversion to Christianity from Late Antiquity to the Modern Age. Considering the Process in Europe, Asian, and the Americas*, ed. C. B. Kendall et al., Minneapolis MN 2009, p. 193–197.

Martin Wihoda

The beginnings of Christianity in Bohemia[1]

Abstract: In the year 806 Bohemian Slavs swore allegiance to Pepin, son of Charlemagne. The regular trips made by the Bohemians to the Bavarian lands on the Danube helped establish a closer relationship with Frankish counts, and once it turned out that the adoption of Christianity might be beneficial for mutual relations, fourteen Bohemian dukes, together with their retinues, accepted baptism in 845. They probably did not represent the entire tribe (*gens*), and regarded the faith as a symbol of status and a key to the world of Carolingian monarchs. This was the reason why on the fringe of the assembly ground, and in the immediate vicinity of a pagan burial ground and place of sacrifice (Žiži Hill), a temple with a tomb/sarcophagus could be built. After his victory over Strojmir, Duke Bořivoj († c. 889) had the temple rebuilt into the Virgin Mary's church, thus demonstrating to the Bohemians that their community was entering a new epoch – that of Christianity.

Keywords: Christianization, Bohemia, Přemyslid dynasty, Duke Bořivoj, Great Moravia, paganism

It does not call for much effort to answer the question when, or how, the Bohemians adopted Christianity. Suffice it to refer to the legend which tends to be dated (more or less concordantly) to around the end of the 10th c., and whose authorship is ascribed (more or less unanimously) to Christianus (Kristián, also known as Strachkvas, † 996), son of Bohemian Duke Boleslaus I the Cruel (Boleslav I Ukrutný, 935–972).[2] As we can read in the second chapter of the legend, the Bohemian Slavs (*Sclavi Boemi*) worshipped their idols and until they were overwhelmed by the bubonic plague, they lived without laws, without a duke or any other ruler, and without a capital city (*sine lege, sine ullo principe vel rectore, vel urbe*). Therefore, they requested a soothsayer for prophecy and

---

1 This study has been prepared as part of a project within the Centre of excellence GACR 14-36521G (*Centrum pro transdisciplinární výzkum kulturních fenoménů ve středoevropských dějinách: obraz, komunikace, jednání*/Centre for trans-disciplinary research of cultural phenomena in Central European history: image, communication, action), with support from the Faculty of Philosophy, Masaryk University.
2 D. Třeštík, "Přemyslovec Kristián", *Archeologické rozhledy* 51, 1999, p. 602–612.

subsequently had a castle built in Prague, and elected Přemysl the Ploughman their ruler.³

As the legend further tells us, the Bohemians nonetheless went on cultivating their pagan rites until Bořivoj (c. 870–c. 889) came to power. This man had once travelled to Moravia, where he was amicably received by the local Duke Svatopluk I (870–894), and by Bishop Methodius. From the latter he could hear the teachings on the primacy of the Christian faith and the assurance that once he accepted baptism, he would become a lord of his lords (*dominus dominorum tuorum efficieris*); that he should subjugate all his enemies, and that his offspring would flood all over like a great river. Bořivoj returned home accompanied by a priest named Kaich, to whom he bestowed Saint Clement's church in Levý Hradec. The populace was so incensed at hearing the news that Bořivoj had to seek refuge with the Moravians. Strojmir was then elected as his replacement; however, the latter, having spent a number of years with the Germans (*qui aput Theutonicos profugus exulabat*), had forgotten his native language (*diuturna tamen exulatio eum proprii privaverat labii eloquio*), and thus voices were raised amongst the Bohemians demanding that Bořivoj join the people again.⁴

The general reconciliation was to be restored at the assembly ground (*in campo*) in front of Prague Castle; however, Strojmir's followers decided to kill off all their opponents. As their design came to light, and Bořivoj's supporters subsequently achieved victory over them, the "new old" Duke Bořivoj was elevated to the throne. As Bořivoj swore to God that with his dignity and position regained (*ad propria cum honore reducerret*) he would build a church at Prague Castle to worship Virgin Mary, he eventually became the first founder of "sacred places" or sanctuaries (*primus fundator locorum sanctorum*) and a promoter of the Christian faith (*religionis institutor*).⁵

Shortly before the year 1000, Christianus' message was quite clear and pointed. It was the faith that ensured to Bořivoj's successors primacy in Bohemia and control over Moravia. And, if we take the chronicler at his word, the Bohemians joined the community of Christian peoples owing to Methodius; this might have happened shortly before his death during the Easter of 885.⁶ Yet the attentive reader will notice that this natural course of occurrences has two inaccuracies

---

3   *Legenda Christiani* (*Vita et passio sancti Wenceslai et sancte Ludmile ave euis*), ed. J. Ludvíkovský, Praha 1978, chap. 2, p. 16, 18.
4   *Legenda Christiani…*, chap. 2, p. 18, 20, 22.
5   Ibidem, p. 24.
6   D. Třeštík, *Počátky Přemyslovců. Vstup Čechů do dějin (530–935)*, Praha 1997, p. 312–347.

to it. First, whereas Christianus makes Prague the main event stage, he sends Bořivoj's personal chaplain to Levý Hradec.[7] Second, once the Bohemians rejected Bořivoj and Christianity, they established Strojmir as his replacement; but Strojmir, we are told, had spent quite a part of his life among Germans[8], where he supposedly would not have admitted his worshipping the lesser gods of his heathen ancestors.

The story told by Christianus was also accepted without much objection by the chronicler Cosmas of Prague, who decided, as early as the beginning of the 12th c., that Prague – rather than Levý Hradec – was where Adalbert (Vojtěch), Prague's second Bishop, was elected in 982.[9] In the time of Duke Sobeslaus I (Soběslav I, 1125–40), Levý Hradec was clearly associated with the local origins of Christianity (*ubi christianitas incepta est*).[10] However, one should consider how reliable the story is. True, it does have a lasting place in the history of Bohemian dukes, but Christianus told it not until the late 10th c., with the apparent intention of warning the Bohemians against disrespect toward the Christian faith.[11]

To make his message powerful, Christianus placed a moralistic interpolation before the baptism of Bohemians, reminding that the Moravians had accepted the Christian faith in the time of Saint Augustine and invited to their country an ethnic Greek, Cyril, who developed a new script, translated the Old and the New Testament from Greek and Latin, and resolved that masses and matins would be celebrated in the language of the common folk.[12] After some time, Cyril was called to Rome where the Pope accused him of breaching Canon Law. With his humble and wise attitude, Cyril managed to persuade those assembled that the traditional rituals were useless with uneducated and defiant Slavs. With consent from the papal Curia, Cyril decided to enter a monastic order in Rome, and had his brother Methodius continue his work. With the support offered by the ruler of Moravia, he was appointed archbishop and had seven suffragans assigned to assist him. But his luck did not last long: once Svatopluk came to power, he left it for his people to choose whether they were willing to serve Christ – or the

---

7   *Legenda Christiani...*, chap. 2, p. 20.
8   Ibidem, p. 22.
9   *Cosmae Pragensis Chronica Boemorum I/25*, ed. B. Bretholz, W. Weinberger (ser.: Monumenta Germaniae Historica, Scriptores rerum Germanicarum. Nova series, 2), Berlin 1923, p. 47.
10 *Codex diplomaticus et epistolaris regni Bohemiae I. (805–1197)*, ed. G. Friedrich, Prague 1904–1907, p. 129–131, no. 124.
11 D. Třeštík, *Počátky Přemyslovců...*, p. 117–137.
12 *Legenda Christiani...*, chap. 1, p. 12.

devil. This elicited condemnation that affected his country and its people, and brought down on Moravia the disasters from which the land is suffering "still till this day" (*usque in hodiernum diem*)[13], the interpolation obviously referring to the author's time.[14]

The tragic collapse of Svatopluk's domain in the early years of the 10th c. could incline the Bohemians to think.[15] The question remains, though: how to consider the Christianization of this people? The legend unambiguously associates the baptism with Bořivoj, whilst the *Annals of Fulda* noted that as many as fourteen dukes of the Bohemians (*XIIII ex ducibus Boemanorum*) appeared before King Louis II the German (c. 843-876) already in 845 to declare that they and their people (*cum hominibus suis*) desire to accept the Christian faith (*christianam religionem desiderantes suscepit*). This is why the East Frankish King ordered (*iussit*) that they be christened on the Octave of the Epiphany – that is, January 13, 845.[16]

This is but one modest gloss on the margin of the other events the chronicler from Fulda seems to have considered particularly important. We can only guess where the Bohemian dukes travelled to be baptized: was it, perhaps, Regensburg, or some other place not far from Bohemia's frontier, where the royal court stopped on their way? Were they really christened by Drogo, Archbishop of Metz?[17] Whom did they represent and what were their intentions? Hence the dilemmas among historians, who have yet to agree whether the occurrence was of primary significance, or was it, perhaps, some rather insignificant attempt at gaining the King's esteem and establishing a closer relationship with eastern Frankish counts? It is also not at all surprising that the nationalist-inclined debate with a state-building tint has led to a not-quite-credible conclusion that the baptism was meant to prevent a war against the Franks, whilst King Louis

---

13 *Legenda Christiani…*, chap. 1, p. 14, 16.
14 D. Kalhous, *Anatomy of a Duchy. The Political and Ecclesiastical Structures of Early Přemyslid Bohemia*, Leiden and Boston 2012, p. 193–208.
15 M. Wihoda, "Cyrilometodějská tradice v paměti přemyslovského věku", [in:] *Cyrilometodějská misie a Evropa. 1150 let od příchodu soluňských bratří na Velkou Moravu*, ed. P. Kouřil, Brno 2014, p. 298–302.
16 *Annales Fuldenses sive Annales regni Francorum orientalis*, ed. F. Kurze (ser.: Monumenta Germaniae Historica. Scriptores rerum Germanicarum in usum scholarum separatim editi, 7), Hannover 1891, p. 35.
17 P. Charvát, "Dona ferentes: Ratisbonne 845, la christianisation de la Bohême et l´archeologie", [in:] *Famille, violence et christiansation au Moyen Âge. Mélanges offerts à Michel Rouche*, ed. M. Aurell, T. Deswarte, Paris 2005, p. 219–227.

the German apparently consented to a covenant whereby the Bohemians would acknowledge their subordination to the Empire in exchange for some other beneficial terms or conditions. Yet when King Louis sent his troops to face the Christian Moravians, the Bohemians purportedly came to the conclusion that the baptism had done them no good; they consequently renounced their faith, and in spite of the numerous wars they had to subsequently wage, did not quit their inimical attitude.[18]

Admittedly, the baptism of 845 left no visible trace in the memory of ducal Bohemia – nonetheless, the question need be posed: can the act of baptism as such be deprecated? If we place it among the events occurring at the time along the eastern border of the Carolingian empire, it becomes apparent that the Bohemian Slavs were noticed by Charlemagne (768–814) as the warfare against the Avars started unfolding in 791.[19] The location of the Vltava River valley, which Charlemagne found interesting from the strategic viewpoint, inclined the King of the Franks to dispatch his army to Bohemia in 805, with his son Charles as the commander.[20] The first attack struck the north of Bohemia, where a Duke named Lech was killed (*ducem eorum nominem Lechonem occidit*)[21] and the vicinity of a fortress *Cannburg* was ravaged.[22] In the summer of 806, the Bavarians invaded Bohemia again, supported by Alleman and Burgundian troops[23]; it was the sight of their desolated lands that, reportedly, inclined the Bohemians to agree to negotiate.[24]

---

18 D. Třeštík, "Křest českých knížat roku 845 a christianizace Slovanů", *Český časopis historický* 92, 1994, p. 423–457.
19 W. Pohl, *Die Awaren. Ein Steppenvolk in Mitteleuropa 567–822 n. Chr.*, München 2002, p. 312–317.
20 *Einhardi Vita Karoli Magni*, ed. Holder-Egger (ser.: Monumenta Germaniae Historica. Scriptores rerum Germanicarum in usum scholarum separatim editi, 25), Hannover 1911, p. 16–17.
21 *Annales regni Francorum inde ab a. 741 usque ad a. 829, qui dicuntur Annales Laurissenses maiores et Einhardi*, ed. F. Kurze (ser.: Monumenta Germaniae Historica. Scriptores rerum Germanicarum in usum scholarum separatim editi, 6), Hannover 1895, p. 120.
22 *Ex Chronico Moissiacensi*, ed. G. H. Pertz (ser.: Monumenta Germaniae Monumenta Germaniae Historica. Scriptores, 2), Hannover 1829, p. 258; *Annales Mettenses priores*, ed. B. von Simson (ser.: Monumenta Germaniae Historica. Scriptores rerum Germanicarum in usum scholarum separatim editi, 10), Hannover 1905, p. 93–94.
23 *Annales regni Francorum...*, p. 122.
24 D. Třeštík, *Vznik Velké Moravy. Moravané. Čechové a střední Evropa v letech 791–871*, Praha 2001, p. 244–245.

As we learn from the *History of the Longobards*, it was not Charles but Pepin who commanded the Frankish troops at *Beowinidis*.[25] The substitution clearly stemmed from Charlemagne's last will of February 6, 806, whereby Pepin was apportioned the Longobard part of Italy, with Bavaria, Allemania, and Rhetia (*Raetia*), up to the Danube River, along with the obligation to secure the Frankish border against enemies.[26] In the summer, he led another expedition against the Bohemians, whom he forced to pay a tribute, as Cosmas recorded in his chronicle from the early 12th c.[27] The money thus collected was transferred to nearby Bavaria – probably to Regensburg, which thus became a symbol of the Carolingian empire for the Bohemians. The situation was repeated in 817, with the Central Danubian territory afforded to Louis the German.[28] In 876, the peacemakers again resolved – in line with the *Ordinatio Imperii* – to bequeath Bavaria, Pannonia, Carinthia, and the Slavic lands of the Bohemians and Moravians (*regna Sclavorum, Behemensium et Marahensium*) to Louis's son, Carloman of Bavaria, (876–879).[29]

The special nature of the Bavarian-Bohemian relationship came to light in 890. King Arnulf (887–899), made peace with the Moravian Duke Svatopluk and sealed their agreement with an unusual gift: he conceded (*concessit*) power to his ally over the Duchy of Bohemia, so that its people might have a ruler of their own blood, and remain loyal to the Franks (*ducatus Behemensium, qui hactenus principem suae cognationis ac gentis super se habuerant Francorumque regibus fidelitatem promissam inviolato foedere conserverant*).[30] Five years afterwards, the Bohemians incited an insurrection and, represented to this end by the Dukes Spytihněv I (c. 895–915) and Vitislav took sides with the people of Bavaria.[31] Arnulf did not object, and conferred the case to Count Luitpold, who assumed

---

25 *Historia Langobardorum codicis Gothani*, ed. G. Waitz (ser.: Monumenta Germaniae Historica. Scriptores rerum Langobardicarum et Italicarum saec. VI-IX), Hannover 1878, p. 11.
26 *Divisio regnorum*, ed. A. Boretius (ser.: Monumenta Germaniae Historica. Capitularia regum Francorum, 1), Hannover 1883, p. 126–130, no. 45, art. 2.
27 *Cosmae Pragensis Chronica Boemorum II/8...*, p. 93–94.
28 *Ordinatio imperii (2)*, ed. A. Boretius (ser.: Monumenta Germaniae Historica. Capitularia regum Francorum, 1), Hannover 1883, p. 270–273, no. 136; ibidem, p. 271.
29 *Reginonis abbatis Prumensis Chronicon cum continuatione Treverensi*, ed. F. Kurze (ser.: Monumenta Germaniae Historica. Scriptores rerum Germanicarum in usum scholarum separatim editi, 50), Hannover 1890, p. 112.
30 *Reginonis abbatis Prumensis Chronicon...*, p. 134.
31 *Annales Fuldenses...*, p. 126.

the title of Duke of the Bohemians (*dux Boemanorum*).³² The honorable title was evidently meant to announce to the outside world that Luitpold was made the representative of this people to the East Frankish Carolingian court.

The fact that the Bohemians began paying tribute was meticulously noted down by the Carolingian chroniclers of the Reich.³³ Although the disputes between the neighbors could occasionally lead to war³⁴, there is no evidence the Bohemians endeavored to free themselves from the non-coercive dependence on the Carolingians – except for the Fulda chronicler's sigh at the Bohemians pretending to be loyal (*Boemani more solito fidem mentientes*).³⁵ The memorable year 806 affected the course of events in more than one way. The obligation imposed by Pepin called for unity and therefore collaboration between the noble families was a must. How many of those families were there, was remarked on not only in the 845 baptism record³⁶, but also in a contemporary description of the lands situated north of the Danube. The latter source tells us that a tribe named *Betheimare* consists of fifteen communities (*civitates*)³⁷, which was probably meant to mean housing estates or strongholds where the local dukes resided, and whose rule was succession-based.³⁸ Louis the German subdued some of those hubs in 856 and 857³⁹, finding the struggle for the fortress of Vistrach particularly grueling, for the Duke Slavitah offered him resistance for a number of years – until he was expelled and had to seek refuge with Duke Rastislav (Rostislav, 846–870) in Moravia.⁴⁰ The strife and skirmishes over this land extended until 869⁴¹, and although the Bohemians (*Behemi*) requested peace⁴², a battle involving five dukes occurred in 872, somewhere not far from

---

32 *Zwentibaldi et Ludovici infantis Diplomata*, ed. T. Schieffer (ser.: Monumenta Germaniae Historica. Diplomata regum Germaniae ex stirpe Karolinorum, 4), Hannover 1960, p. 125–127, no. 20; ibidem, p. 126.
33 E. Mikušek, "Ideové pojetí vztahu českého státu k říši německé v dílech dějepisců 10. a 11. století", *Sborník historický* 26, 1979, p. 5–52; ibidem, p. 39–40.
34 *Annales Fuldenses*..., p. 36.
35 Ibidem, p. 38–39.
36 D. Třeštík, *Počátky Přemyslovců*... p. 69–73.
37 *Descriptio civitatum et regionum ad septentrionalem plagam Danubii*, [in:] *Magnae Moraviae fontes historici III*, ed. D. Bartoňková, R. Večerka, Brno 2011, p. 249.
38 D. Třeštík, "České kmeny. Historie a skutečnost jedné koncepce", *Studia Mediaevalia Pragensia* 1/1988, p. 129–143.
39 *Annales Fuldenses*..., p. 47.
40 J. Sláma, "Civitas Wiztrachi ducis", *Historická geografie* 11, 1973, p. 3–30.
41 *Annales Fuldenses*..., p. 67.
42 Ibidem, p. 70.

the Vltava.[43] At long last Spytihněv and Vitislav submitted in 895 a complaint on behalf of the Bohemians against the Moravian patronage and requested that an alliance with the Bavarian nation be resumed.[44]

The Fulda Chronicler offers us a mention of internal Bohemian relations: namely, in 857 Louis the German got even with Slavitah who was considered a tyrant (*qui tyrannidem tunc in ea exercebat*). It may be supposed that this was meant to suggest that the latter exercised power not in keeping with his native tradition. Should this supposition be correct, the interests of the tribe (*gens*) must have been represented by a body of dukes who, if need be, could have sought assistance from the East Frankish Carolingians, who enjoyed the regularly renewed right, additionally confirmed by the tribute, to uphold internal peace.[45]

As is now apparent, the baptism of 845 did not affect the constellation of power that had prevailed since 806. The fact that the christening took place on the Octave of the Epiphany, rather than on Pentecost or during Easter is not surprising, since the other feasts – Epiphany among them – were tolerated, to an extent, by the synods in Carolingian times. Thus, if we ascribe the date of 845 with its deserved significance, the question arises: why does Christianus' legend confine itself to praising Duke Bořivoj?

The key to the answer probably rests in the differing content of the two events. In other words, neither of the two events necessarily stands in contradiction with the other. In 845, the Dukes could only ask for baptism for themselves and their retinues – in order, perhaps, to unperturbedly negotiate with the Frankish counts. Once they returned home, Christ was merely made a figure in the pantheon of the indigenous deities. Bořivoj, in turn, superimposed Christian values on others, and thus incurred the anger of his people. Therefore, Christianus could see in him a martyr who had to suffer exile at Svatopluk's court due to his devout faith. Nevertheless, it cannot be precluded that some of the dukes accepted christening with great conviction.

It has to be borne in mind that the year 872 saw five dukes rise against the Franks; one of them was named Hermann[46], and this uncommon, possibly baptismal name might suggest that he had already become a Christian. Alongside Hermann, Vitislav took part in the warfare. Together with Bořivoj's son Spytihněv, Vitislav represented the Bohemians in 895, which might indicate that

---

43 Ibidem, p. 76.
44 Ibidem, p. 126.
45 M. Wihoda, *První česká království*, Praha 2015, p. 94–100.
46 *Annales Fuldenses*…, p. 76.

he also opted for the Christian faith. Let us complement these considerations with the history behind the Church of the Virgin Mary at Prague Castle, whose remains were discovered by Ivan Borkovský (as part of an excavations project).[47] Although this longitudinal-shaped structure, rebuilt several times, whose apse is 815 cm long (at its maximum length), in nowise resembles the basilica mentioned by Christianus and the earliest phase of its construction is not precisely datable[48], authors tend to accept that it had been Bořivoj's church from the end of the 9th c. A detailed analysis of the find has proved, however, that the space within that small church was predominantly occupied with a carefully built sarcophagus and the church should thus be regarded as a funeral chapel (if not a mausoleum)[49], which was later rebuilt, the earlier tomb (if it did really exist) having been replaced with a stone burial chamber in which the corpse of a man or a woman was eventually deposited.[50]

The jewelry found in the sarcophagus/tomb indicate that the funerals were carried out in the early 10th c., which attests that the structure in question was rebuilt in the time of Spytihněv I at the latest. But if the church was founded by Bořivoj in 885, the question arises: why did it need being so thoroughly reconstructed after only twenty years? And how can the known and available historic records be combined into one reasonable story?

Let us ponder for a while the Bohemians' duty to pay tribute, which Cosmas described (in the early 12th c.) as defined by Pepin, Charlemagne's son, as a title payable in silver and cattle. This is confirmed by the Carolingian annals, which tell us that in 805 and 806 Charlemagne had the Bohemians obey him, and that a Duke named Lech was killed in a skirmish. Astonishingly, no one has been intrigued by the fact that whilst the levy's burden had been laid upon the politically compact tribe of Bohemians (*gens Bohemanorum*), authority remained distributed among the dukes. Furthermore, the 991 charter for Saint Laurence's Cathedral in Magdeburg mentions that the levy was to be paid in gold, silver, cattle, as well as other objects, large and small[51], which meant that the families

---

47 I. Borkovský, *Pražský hrad v době přemyslovských knížat*, Praha 1969, p. 90–102.
48 A. Merhautová-Livorová,"Nejstarší dosud známý kostel na Pražském hradě", *Folia Historica Bohemica* 6, 1983, p. 81–89.
49 J. Maříková-Kubková, I. Herychová,"Revize první stavební fáze kostela Panny Marie na Pražském hradě/Hradčanech. Návrat po šedesáti pěti letech", *Staletá Praha* 31, 2015, p. 62–74.
50 I. Borkovský, "Kostel Panny Marie na Pražském hradě", *Památky archeologické* 44, 1953, p. 129–200; ibidem, p. 147–153.
51 *Ottonis III. Diplomata*, ed. T. Sickel (ser.: Monumenta Germaniae Historica. Diplomata regum et imperatorum Germaniae, 2/2), Hannover 1888, no. 71, p. 478–479.

had to convene in order to have the tribute distributed by item, then collect the items, and ultimately to dispatch them to where agreed upon.[52]

If our chain of assumptions is correct, the deliberations could have been held on a regular basis on the hill by Prague Castle, at the site where an assembly field was organized, surrounded with a ditch, next to the hill Žiži where the sacrifices were offered and funerals carried out.[53] Around 845, a mausoleum might have been set up there, and then redeveloped by Bořivoj, in 885, into a church.

In generalized terms, we can trace the Christianization of Bohemian Slavs back to the year 806, when they swore allegiance to Pepin, son of Charlemagne, and undertook to pay an annual tribute as a gesture of good will. To fulfil this obligation cooperation was required, the terms of which had been determined in detail at the assemblies that, most evidently, took place on the hill by the Vltava riverside, where later on Prague Castle was erected. The regular trips made by the Bohemians to the Bavarian lands on the Danube helped establish a closer relationship with Frankish counts, and once it turned out that the adoption of Christianity might be beneficial for mutual relations, fourteen dukes, together with their retinues, accepted baptism in 845.

As it seems, they did not represent the entire tribe (*gens*), and regarded the faith as a useful instrument, perhaps as a symbol of status and a key to the world of Carolingian rulers. This was the reason why on the fringe of the assembly ground, and in the immediate vicinity of a pagan burial ground and place of sacrifice (Žiži Hill), a temple with a tomb/sarcophagus could be built. After his victory over Strojmir, Bořivoj had the temple rebuilt into the Virgin Mary's church, thus demonstrating to the Bohemians that their community was entering a new epoch – that of Christianity.[54] And this, perhaps, is how the legend told by Christianus/Strachkvas ought to be retrospectively understood.

Translated by Tristan Korecki

---

52 M. Wihoda, "Sněmy Čechů", [in:] *Šlechta v proměnách věků*, ed. T. Knoz, J. Dvořák, Brno 2011, p. 17–37.
53 I. Borkovský, "Poloha kopce 'Žiži' na Pražském hradě", *Časopis Společnosti přátel starožitností* 52, 1954, p. 15–21.
54 Z. Smetánka, *Hledání zmizelého věku. Sondy do středověkých Čech*, Praha 1987, p. 9–31.

Christian Lübke

Between reception and aversion. The earliest traces of Christianity among the Polabian Slavs

Abstract: In recent decades Polish and German perspectives have changed in regard to the previous notions presented in nation-centered historiographies on the history of the Polabian Slavs and their role in early German-Slavic relations. Thanks to new archeological finds and the mounting scientification of historical research, today Christianization in the Middle Ages is not understood as a one-way, inevitable process – and pre-Christian Slavic beliefs are no longer dismissed as irrational or backward. The chapter presents the penetration of Christianity into the Slavic Polabian regions as a slow process that gathered pace in the 10th c. when Henry I and Otto I exerted military pressure and at the same time made overtures to the Slavic princes of the Polabian Slav population who fluctuated between reception and aversion toward the Christian religion. Otto was focused on his plans to found the Archbishopric of Magdeburg, but he underestimated the adherence of the Polabian Slavs to their gods. Unlike in Mieszko's realm, neither the Emperor's power nor the autochthonous princely power over the Polabian Slavs was yet strong enough to leverage Christianity permanently in the 10th c.

Keywords: Polabian Slavs, Christianization, Lutizians, Slav Uprising 983, paganism

An overview of contemporary research on the historical circumstances surrounding the baptism of Mieszko I (c. 960–992) and, in particular, investigations into the Polabian Slavs, suggests that we are dealing with events, along with the sources describing them, that have been familiar for a long time already.[1] No new written sources have emerged in the last years or even decades, while recent archaeological studies on the Elbe marches – i.e., the regions located roughly

---

1 In the 1980s, as part of a German Research Foundation (DFG) project, the author collected and edited *Regesten zur Geschichte der Slaven an Elbe und Oder*, which constitute a comprehensive documentation of events that occurred between the Elbe/Saale and Oder in the 10th and early 11th c., while also taking into account the earlier history of the area's neighboring regions and a broad spectrum of historic sources and of specialized literature in history, archaeology and onomastics. See: C. Lübke, *Regesten zur Geschichte der Slaven an Elbe und Oder (vom Jahr 900 an)*, vol. 1–5, Berlin 1984–1988. A digital edition can be found now at [electronic resource] https://bibdorm. bsb-muenchen.de/q/bv/BV045370824.

between the Oder and Elbe/Saale Rivers east to west, and between the Baltic Sea and Ore Mountains north to south – have likewise yielded few significant findings relating to the influence of Christianity there.[2]

Within German historiography a new approach became evident in the first post-WWII decades, when the role of the Slavs who inhabited these territories in the early Middle Ages (and which only later could be labelled "German" in respect to social and, ultimately, national norms) was also taken into account. Broadly speaking, earlier studies had shown little interest in the Slavs, other than to designate them as a mass that hindered the progress of civilization and Germanization.[3] As for Polish research, what long dominated was the view tabled in 1903 by Kazimierz Wachowski in his study on Western Slavdom (*Słowiańszczyzna Zachodnia*) that the Polabian Slavs, in particular the Luticians, formed a protective wall against the German *Drang nach Osten*, or "eastward push", thus enabling the formation of the medieval Polish state in the shadow of this wall.[4] In recent decades, these two contrary perspectives on the historical circumstances, both being products of nation-centered historiography, have gradually been overcome as a more scientific approach has emerged that avoids privileging the position of the nation and state. Nonetheless, investigations into the Polabian Slavs have not become a prominent theme in German historiography on the medieval period, with regional and local history dominating the field. Archaeology, however, is becoming increasingly significant in this respect. Thanks to research in this discipline, interest in the Slavic past of the Polabian regions has grown notably. Important contributions are also emerging from Slavic onomastics, although

---

2   See: *Die Slawen in Deutschland. Geschichte und Kultur der slawischen Stämme westlich von Oder und Neiße vom 6. bis 12.-Jahrhundert. Ein Handbuch*, ed. J. Herrmann, Berlin 1985.

3   J. Hackmann, C. Lübke, "Die mittelalterliche Ostsiedlung in der deutschen Geschichtswissenschaft", [in:] *Historiographical Approaches to Medieval Colonization of East Central Europe: A comparative analysis against the background of other European inter-ethnic colonization processes in the middle ages*, ed. J. M. Piskorski, New York 2002, p. 179–217; C. Lübke, "Germany's Growth to the East: from the *Polabian Marches to Germania Slavica*", [in:] *The making of medieval history*, ed. G. A. Loud, M. Staub, York 2017, p. 167–184.

4   K. Wachowski, *Słowiańszczyzna zachodnia*, Warszawa 1902 (2nd ed. Poznań 1950, 3rd ed. Poznań 2000).

this field has become less effective following the most productive period of the Leipzig school of onomastics in the 1970s and 1980s.[5]

The same pattern applies in respect to Christianization: it is the sites of German Church institutions and secular rule, as well as anniversaries related to them, which have provided the inspiration for large-scale exhibitions, including one at the Magdeburg Museum of Cultural History. Such exhibitions have noted the Polabian regions, but do so, naturally enough, as entities that would come to form elements of the Church structures of the East Frankish, and increasingly Germanized Empire. Particular focus has been placed on the Archbishopric of Magdeburg and its subordinate dioceses, although the Hamburg-Bremen Archbishopric has also featured.[6] Large swathes of these dioceses, founded before 968, were lost to their Christian institutions as a result of the Great Polabian Slav Uprising in 983. The large-scale Christianization of these areas began not until the second half of the 11th c., thus significantly outside the context of the baptism of Mieszko I. The uprising of 983 was initiated by an association of Polabian tribes whose members were collectively known as Luticians. Indeed, it was in the context of this uprising that their name first appeared in written sources, which fact gives meaning to the second term in the title of this paper, "Reception and Aversion". More precisely, it is owing to the 983 uprising against Christianity that we first learn anything of the reaction of the Polabian Slavs to the challenges that confronted them following the arrival of Christians, who demanded the absolute domination of their God, their Church, and their secular representatives.[7]

The events connected to this basic constellation of circumstances, as well as their interpretations, are broadly familiar to specialists working in this field. Particularly noteworthy are the studies by Wolfgang H. Fritze and Jerzy Strzelczyk, while I myself have also made several contributions to research on

---

5 See the series: *Deutsch-slawische Forschungen zur Namenkunde und Siedlungsgeschichte*, vol. 1–41, Leipzig 1956–2007, published mainly under the editorship of E. Eichler and H. Walther.

6 D. Claude, *Geschichte des Erzbistums Magdeburg bis in das 12. Jahrhundert*, vol. 1–2, Köln 1972, 1975; J. Petersohn, *Der südliche Ostseeraum im kirchlich-politischen Kräftespiel des Reiches, Polens und Dänemarks vom 10. bis 13. Jahrhundert: Mission, Kirchenorganisation, Kultpolitik*, Köln 1979.

7 W. H. Fritze, "Der slawische Aufstand von 983 – eine Schicksalswende in der Geschichte Mitteleuropas", [in:] *Festschrift der Landesgeschichtlichen Vereinigung für die Mark Brandenburg zu ihrem hundertjährigen Bestehen, 1884–1984*, ed. E. Henning, W. Vogel, Berlin 1984, p. 9–55; J. Strzelczyk, "Tysiąclecie powstania Słowian połabskich, 983–1983. Naukowe rezultaty jubileuszu", *Studia Historica Slavo-Germanica* 14, 1985, p. 241–260.

the subject.[8] It is particularly important to draw attention to the fundamental difference between pagan religion (heathenism) and universal religion, something that Hans-Dietrich Karl developed in his study of the Polabian Slavs.[9] This difference is fundamental to the issue of the reception of Christianity. To put it briefly, heathen or "gentile" communities (of the *gentes*) each have their own divine figures that they consider responsible for the welfare and fate of the *gens*, with their authority limited to the territory of the *gens*. It was obvious to the pagans that other *gentes* would have their own divine figures and thus that the Germans e.g. would pray to their *deus teutonicus*. According to Christian teaching, however, this was a universal deity, one that was omnipotent and exercised power over all *gentes*. Indeed, one of the Christian commandments was: "Thou shalt have no other gods before me!". This laid the foundations for the central conflict between the gentiles and the universalists that came to the fore in the Lutician Uprising of 983.

Speaking of the Luticians, it is worthwhile going into greater detail on the current state of research, in particular by highlighting the single monograph that, at the time of writing, has been published on this exceptional case in European history – namely, Wolfgang Brüske's 1955 work on the Lutician Alliance, which was reissued in 1974 with a new foreword.[10] Brüske argued that the "fate of the Polabian and Baltic Slavs" was determined primarily by their attitude towards the issue of Christianization. Brüske herein presented two lines of development

---

8   J. Strzelczyk, "Missionsstrategie und Missionspraxis der westlichen Kirche im frühen Mittelalter", [in:] *Rome, Constantinople and Newly converted Europe. Archeological and Historical Evidence*, ed. M. Salamon et al., vol. 1, Kraków 2010, p. 33–42; C. Lübke, "Das Christentum als Herausforderung gentilreligiöser Gesellschaften im östlichen Europa", [in:] *Dynamika przemian społecznych i religijnych średniowieczu (III Kongres Mediewistów Polskich, Łódź, 22–24 wrzesnia 2008 roku)*, ed. T. Grabarczyk, T. Nowak, Warszawa 2011, p. 155–168; idem, "Ein Fall von 'challenge and response'?: Die autochthonen Bewohner des südlichen Ostseeraums gegenüber Macht und Pracht des Christentums", [in:] *Glaube, Macht und Pracht. Geistliche Gemeinschaften des Ostseeraums im Zeitalter der Backsteingotik*, ed. O. Auge et al., Rahden 2009, p. 39–48.
9   H. D. Kahl, *Slawen und Deutsche in der brandenburgischen Geschichte des zwölften Jahrhunderts*, vol. 1–2, Köln 1964, p. 77–78. The use of the term "Gentilreligion" (and "Universalreligion") has been proven by the same author: idem, "Heidnisches Wendentum und christliche Stammesfürsten. Ein Blick in die Auseinandersetzung zwischen Gentil- und Universalreligion im abendländischen Hochmittelalter", *Archiv für Kulturgeschichte* 44, 1962, p. 72–119.
10 W. Brüske, *Untersuchungen zur Geschichte des Lutizenbundes. Deutsch-wendische Beziehungen des 10.-12. Jahrhunderts*, Köln 1983.

that emerged following the epoch of Charlemagne (768–814), whereby "the Sorbs maintained their folklore, while the northern branches of the Wends disappeared almost without a trace."[11] Brüske used the term "Wends" as a synonym for the Polabian and Baltic Slavs. He argued that the year 983 was the decisive moment that caused the two paths to split, thus shaping the future historical existence of the two Slavic groups. "The Sorbs", he wrote,

> like the Czechs remained loyal to the German Empire and did not participate in the 983 Wend Uprising. Even if it was unintentional, this proved to be a very wise, far-sighted policy. [...] The fate of the north-western Slavic group turned out differently. It cast off German rule and thus Christianity towards the end of the 10th c. Initially, the group had seemingly restored its freedom. In the long run, however, its position proved untenable. Wedged between the increasingly powerful and ambitious German Empire on the one side and a Poland that had been Christian since the age of Otto I and was pushing powerfully westwards on the other, the Wend group was destined to be destroyed sooner or later. Had it accepted Christianity and adopted German culture, it would have had the chance to rescue its folklore for posterity, since voluntarily adopting Christianity would have taken the wind out of the sails of the Empire's aggressive policies. When the territory between the Elbe and Oder was ultimately secured by the Empire [...] in the third quarter of the 12th c., the cultural differences between West and East Polabia had grown so large in the course of almost two hundred years since 983 that the Wends were very quickly absorbed.[12]

It is not possible at this juncture to go into greater detail on the developments occurring after 983, thus it will have to suffice to indicate the "aversion" towards Christianity that was associated with the heathenism that had helped shape the surprisingly stable Lutician power structures that remained in place until the mid-11th c.[13] But how had this aversion evolved since the age of Charlemagne? Which early traces of Christianity are to be found despite the fundamental conflict between the gentile and universal believers? In order to produce any answers to these questions, it is necessary to first look to the south, to the Bavarian-Carantanian realms and the activities of the Bavarian Church whose reorganization resulted in the founding of the Archbishopric of Salzburg in 798. We can trace its history thanks to a "white paper" – namely, the *Conversio Bagoariorum et Carantanorum*, which documented the successes of the missionary work

---

11 This quotation and all following quotations from non-English sources were translated into English by the translator of the chapter.
12 W. Brüske, *Untersuchungen...*, p. 1–2.
13 See: C. Lübke, *Regesten...*, p. 742–743.

originating in Salzburg in the 9th c.[14] It reveals the close relationship between missionary work and politics that was early on evident among the Carantanians, with the Franks offering support to their favored political allies or supporting regional rulers outside their own jurisdiction. This was how the Bavaria-educated Cacatius/Karastus (†c. 752) became the ruler of Carantania in 749/750 *per iussonem Francorum*. One of his successors, Waltunc (772–784), came to power in a very similar manner, thanks to the support of the Bavarian Duke Tassilo III (748–after 794). According to sources left by Cacatius/Karastus, we are able to establish that he was brought to Bavaria in 740 as a hostage together with his cousin Cheitmar, before being baptized and raised as a Christian. Both of them later returned to Carantania as Christian rulers.[15]

The strategy here is essentially very simple to outline: the Franks evidently believed that they would be able to impose Christianity from above in an area that was being controlled from outside, albeit not yet incorporated into their own jurisdiction, by means of a converted, baptized prince who was politically dependent on them. An almost identical method was used much later in relation to the Havelland Polabian Slavs, the Hevellians, and in their stronghold of Brandenburg. It was also applied in a slightly different form in relation to the Moravian rulers, while the baptism of fourteen Bohemian princes – who, according to the *Annals of Fulda*, appeared in 845 before the King Louis II the German (c. 806 – 876) of East Francia "with their men" (*cum hominibus suis*) in Regensburg and demanded to be accepted into Christianity – can be seen in a similar light, at least in respect to the strategic intentions.[16]

The fact that similar methods were not applied against the Polabian and Baltic Slavs further north, except a few exceptions, is thus surprising. Opportunities to apply such measures did present themselves, as when Charlemagne personally undertook a successful campaign against the Veleti (*Wilzi*) in 789. As Charles' chronicler Einhard recorded, the King of Franks (and later Emperor) reached as

---

14 *Conversio Bagoaroirum et Carantanorum: das Weißbuch der Salzburger Kirche über die erfolgreiche Mission in Karantanien und Pannonien*, ed. H. Wolfram, Ljubljana 2012.
15 A. Angenendt, *Kaiserherrschaft und Königstaufe. Kaiser, Könige und Päpste als geistliche Patrone in der abendländischen Missionsgeschichte*, Berlin, New York 1984, p. 230; M. Hardt, "Salzburg und Hamburg. Christianisierung am südöstlichen und nördlichen Rand des Frankenreiches", [in:] *400–1000. Vom antiken Erbe bis zu den Anfängen der Romanik*, ed. C. Lübke, M. Hardt (ser.: Handbuch der Geschichte der Kunst in Ostmitteleuropa, 1), Berlin 2017, p. 176-178.
16 A. Angenendt, *Kaiserherrschaft...*, p. 237.

far as the fort of prince Dragovit with his forces, ensuring not only that the Duke subjugated himself and released hostages, but that other Slav leaders followed Dragovit's lead.[17] Nevertheless, Charles evidently did not use this success for missionary purposes, meaning that in the following decades emissaries from the Polabian Slavs were present at imperial courts, thus demonstrating the Emperor's power. However, they were present as gentiles, meaning that the Christian Church considered them heathens. The fact that such imperial parliamentary gatherings were used for ceremonial baptisms is indicated by the experience of the Saxon Widukind who was christened at Christmas in 785, with Charlemagne as his godfather; in 796 the ruler (*Tudun*) of the Pannonian Avars was baptized in Aachen, while in 826 the Danish King Harald Klak (812–814 and 819–827) accepted Christianity in Ingelheim, being baptized at the behest of Emperor Louis the Pious (813–840).[18] Despite numerous testimonies confirming the presence of Obotrite and Veletian Dukes and other representatives of the Polabian Slav elites in the imperial diets into the 920s, there is only one case that mentions the use of baptisms. It relates to the Obotrite prince Sclaomir (810–821), whom Charlemagne declared a prince at a gathering in Verden in 810. The Frankish imperial annals recorded that Sclaomir was awarded the title *regia potestas* in 817. Later, however, he disregarded the Emperor's decisions in relation to the division of his powers. Sclaomir was thus captured by Frankish-Saxon forces and brought to Aachen in 819. Nevertheless, two years later he was considered to be so trustworthy that Emperor Louis again pronounced him ruler of the Obotrites. However, Sclaomir died on the journey back to his homeland, having asked to be re-baptized shortly before his death.[19] During his time in Aachen he was thus successfully familiarized with Christianity and baptized there, although any missionary use of his sudden death was not possible. This was however the only case during the period, as has been stressed, where diplomatic-strategic means were applied – i.e., when a high-level representative of a pagan Polabian Slav community converted to Christianity far from his own country and was then sent back home as a potential future ruler and promoter of Christianity there.

In principle, it is possible to jump forward about a century from here, since during this time Christianity and missionary work did not play a role in the

---

17 *Annales regni Francorum inde a. 741 usque ad 829, qui dicuntur Annales Laurissenses maiores et Einhardi*, ed. F. Kurze, (ser.: Monumenta Germaniae Historica. Scriptores rerum Germanicarum in usum scholarum, 6), Hannover 1895, p. 85, 87 (*Annales qui dicuntur Einhardi*, 789).

18 M. Hardt, "Salzburg und Hamburg...", p. 184.

19 *Annales regni Francorum...*, p. 147, 149, 157.

lives of Polabian Slavs. However, I would like to briefly mention one case that highlights Charlemagne's fundamental interest in the conversion of the Slavs – namely, the foundation of fourteen Slav churches that were placed under the control of Bernwelf, the Bishop of Würzburg, in 793/794. They were to be established in the *terra Sclavorum* of the Main and Rednitz Wends in Upper Franconia.[20] Peaceful coexistence and neighborly relations between the Slavs and Frankish inhabitants and landowners can be assumed to have existed in this region, as evidenced by the mixed German-Slavic names of the settlements. This case may be considered an element in the process of Slavs becoming familiar with the Christian religion beyond the limited areas of the Main and Rednitz Wends. Christians and heathens lived along the East Frankish border of the Empire without adhering to any strictly demarcated frontier. Instead, they inhabited a broad swathe either side of the Elbe and Saale Rivers, where, according to the *Fulda Annals*, in the mid-9th c. the Margrave Thakulf (*dux Sorabici limitis*) was renowned for his knowledge of Slavic language and customs.[21]

This situation did not change until the rule of Henry I the Fowler (919–936) when he developed a form of Saxon *Ostpolitik*[22] that was based on ensuring defenses against Hungarian incursions as well as on securing the strategic aim of hindering a strong coalition and competition in areas east of his strongholds in Thüringen, particularly in the Merseburg region. This policy developed during the nine-year cessation in hostilities with the Hungarians that was secured in 924. After making the necessary preparations, the King undertook a series of targeted military campaigns between the winter of 928 and the summer of 934 to secure dominion over the Slavic marches of Thuringia and Saxony. These campaigns were directed against a succession of potential enemies in order to preclude a possible coalition between the Polabian Slavs, Bohemians, and Hungarians. Each followed a similar pattern, shaped by the defensive tactics of the Slavic groups: occupying and conquering the central forts of each tribe, imprisoning or even killing the rural populations that had fled there, removing distinguished hostages, and enforcing annual tributes for the future.[23]

---

20 M. Hardt, "Salzburg und Hamburg...", p. 183, 184.
21 *Annales Fuldenses sive annales regni Francorum orientalis*, ed. F. Kurze (ser.: Monumenta Germaniae Historica. Scriptores rerum Germanicarum in usum scholarum, 7), Hannover 1891, ad a. 849, p. 366.
22 L. Dralle, "Zu Vorgeschichte und Hintergründen der Ostpolitik Heinrichs I.", [in:] *Europa slavica – Europa orientalis. Festschrift für Herbert Ludat zum 70. Geburtstag*, ed. K.-D. Grothusen, K. Zernack, Berlin 1980, p. 99–126.
23 *Widukindi monachi Corbeiensis rerum gestarum Saxonicarum libri tres*, ed. P. Hirsch et al. (ser.: Monumenta Germaniae Historica. Scriptores Rerum Germanicarum in usum

It is striking that the inhabitants of Brandenburg were not subject to the same drastic measures that other forts had faced. The fact that the family of the Hevellian rulers who resided in the Brandenburg fort had almost certainly converted to Christianity was a factor in this. It even seems that Henry, as with Bohemian Duke Wenceslas I (921–935), had ascribed particular functions (albeit ones still under Saxon control) to the Slavic ruler of Brandenburg, since he was personally unharmed.[24] Quite exceptionally, a significant amount of attention was devoted to the Brandenburg dynasty of Slavonian rulers, with some research even suggesting that a legitimate marriage between the Ottonians and Havellians was considered for a while. The heir to the throne, Otto, entered into such close relations with a prince's daughter from the Brandenburg fort that an illegitimate son named Wilhelm was conceived, one who later took on the important post of Archbishop of Mainz.[25] Another scion of the Brandenburg family, Tugumir († after 940), was formally taken hostage by the Saxons and then most probably raised as a Christian in a Saxon monastery. He is said to have later proved himself as a decisive figure in the battle for this important fort when it had temporally been lost by the Ottonians. Released from captivity, Tugumir was made the rightful heir to the fort and took control of it in 940 and then left it, together with the entire tribute under his rule "up to the Oder", to the ruling King, Otto I (936–973).[26]

Only a brief reference can be made here to Bohemia, although it too is an important region in this context, as Heinrich I also forced Prague's Duke Wenceslas into paying tribute, having conquered Brandenburg in 929. A material manifestation of this phase of Saxon dominion over Bohemia is the Cathedral of St. Vitus in Prague's Hradčany district, which was dedicated to the Saxon saint.[27] Otherwise only in the very north among the Obotrites did Henry's efforts produce any elements related to Christianity, with his campaign of the summer of 931 resulting in the baptism of one of the tribe's princes. In the south, on the other hand, the heathen elites were eliminated to such an extent that they no

---

scholarum separatim editi, 60), Hannover 1935, I/35–36; *Thietmari Merseburgensis episcopi Chronicon*, ed. R. Holtzmann (ser.: Monumenta Germaniae Historica Scriptores rerum Germanicarum Nova Seria, 9), Berlin 1935, I/16. C. Lübke, *Regesten...*, no. 25, 27, 28, 29, 31, 33, 36, 37, 42, 43.

24 *Widukindi... libri tres*, I/35, p. 49–50; C. Lübke, *Regesten...*, no. 25.
25 *Widukindi... libri tres*, II/73, p. 150; C. Lübke, *Regesten...*, no. 32.
26 *Widukindi... libri tres*, II/20, p. 85; C. Lübke, *Regesten...*, no. 66.
27 *Widukindi... libri tres*, I/35, p. 50–51; C. Lübke, *Regesten...*, no. 29; J. K. Hoensch, *Geschichte Böhmens. Von der slavischen Landnahme bis ins 20. Jahrhundert*, München 1992, p. 45.

longer formed an independent political power and thus played no role in potential deliberations on the introduction of Christianity. However, the foundation of the fort of Meissen by the Saxons should be considered a measure that was influenced by the need for surveillance and for securing the surrounding territory. Over the next hundred years, Meissen proved to be the most strategically important site in the entire southern reaches of the Polabian Slav region, and as such was made into the seat of the new diocese that was established in 968.[28]

The foundation of this diocese formed part of the efforts of Henry's son Otto to incorporate the territories of the Polabian Slavs that were already under military control into his empire's church structures. Upon his election as King in 936 at a ceremony in Aachen that saw him placed on Charlemagne's throne, Otto might already have had plans in place to continue his father's military activities in the east as newly-elected King, and this would have aligned him with Charlemagne's imperial ambitions. He ultimately achieved this aim in 962 when he was crowned Emperor by the Pope in Rome. Along the way, he had had to overcome significant opposition, including resistance in the Slavic regions. Otto demonstrated his intention to be active in the east from the outset through his selection of personnel to serve in the Polabian marches, through measures strengthening the Ottonian positions in east Saxony, and through gifts that initially affected the regions east of the Elbe.[29] Otto provided generously for the new women's convent of the Ottonian House in Quedlinburg, awarding it estates in Thuringia and the Harz, to which numerous Slavic families (*familiae Sclavorum*) from the Saale region belonged, although it is not possible to establish their religion. In any case, archaeological findings have made clear that even decades later entire groups of Slavs had maintained their particular lifestyle in Thuringia, including their pagan religious beliefs.[30] There had certainly been no missionary offensive under Otto's rule.

The plan was for Quedlinburg to become an increasingly regular host of court and imperial diets. Of even greater significance was the establishment of, and investment in the Abbey of St. Maurice in Magdeburg in 937, which laid the foundations for the Archbishopric of Magdeburg (founded 968). Slavic families were also ascribed to the Abbey of St Maurice, although its income came largely from the Slavic lands of the *Moraciani*, *Liezizi*, and *Heveldun* east of the Elbe and from the right to collect timber, slaughter pigs, and graze animals there. This was

---

28 C. Lübke, *Regesten….*, no. 142, 145, 151, 152.
29 C. Lübke, *Regesten…..*, no. 46, 47, 58.
30 C. Lübke, "Slaven und Deutsche um das Jahr 1000", *Mediaevalia Historica Bohemica* 3, 1993, p. 59–90.

therefore the first time that the King had also made a Church institution responsible for Slavic lands east of the old imperial border. With the almost simultaneous transfer of virtually all of the customs duties collected in Magdeburg to the Abbey of St. Maurice, he thereby made clear the intended consequences of his measures for trade policy.[31]

There was a general expansion at this time of the range of people and institutions that showed an interest in the Slavic lands. Like the Abbey of St Maurice in Magdeburg, noble families from east Saxony and Thuringia were awarded land in the form of numerous donations affecting the regions between the Saale and Mulde Rivers. An undoubtedly new aspect of the expansion of the instruments of power came in 948, in the form of the founding of two dioceses that (until 968) were subordinate to the Archbishopric of Mainz – namely, Brandenburg and Havelberg. The territories, estates, and income ascribed to them show that the dioceses mainly encompassed the mid-Polabian lands that had belonged to the Hevellian principality.[32] However, the lands in the north, where the Archbishopric of Hamburg-Bremen exercised mission rights, and in the south, where Bohemian influence still prevailed, remained outside the control of the new church organizations. Little is known about the subsequent fate of Tugumir, the Slavic ruler of Brandenburg who was so significant in shaping these developments. It is possible that he died at the Saxon Abbey of Möllenbeck, since his name is recorded in its book of deaths. The fact that King Otto I termed the fort of Magdeburg "our possession" (*predium nostrum*) in the founding document of the diocese, awarding half of it to the bishop, has led to the conclusion that the Hevellian prince was no longer alive at this point. There are, though, several pieces of evidence which must be taken seriously, ones that suggest that his Christian family survived and achieved notable significance again towards the end of the 10th c.[33]

In any case, the initial round of founding dioceses in these regions led to a phase of intensified imperial rule that was to eliminate any surviving traces of Slavic autonomy. The Slavic commanders of strongholds were replaced by Saxon

---

31 C. Lübke, *Regesten...*, no. 51–54, 62.
32 *Conradi I Heinrici I et Ottonis I diplomata*, ed. T. Sickel (ser.: Monumenta Germaniae Historica. Die Urkunden der deutschen Könige und Kaiser, 2), vol. 1, Hannover 1878–1884, no. 76 (Havelberg), no. 105 (Brandenburg);
33 E.g. Pribislav, who married margrave Dietrich's daughter Mathilde in Brandenburg before 983, was a member of Tugumir's family, most probably; see: *Thietmari Merseburgensis....*, IV/64. The topic is discussed at C. Lübke, *Regesten...*, no. 216.

representatives and garrisons, with the intention of securing tributes for the King and tithes for the bishops in Brandenburg and Havelberg. These were, after all, the basis for their economic survival, with Otto having signed Slavic lands over to the dioceses. The pressure created by these measures caused new Polabian Slavic uprisings, particularly in the north, starting with the Ukrani in 954, a group that had been made to pay tithes to the Diocese of Brandenburg since 948.[34]

King Otto's I Saxon troops were at this time preparing for military battles with the Hungarians, against whom he finally achieved victory at the Battle of Lechfeld in 955. Contemporaries presented the events there as the decisive battle in the Christians' fight against the heathens, with Otto's victorious forces proclaiming him "father of the fatherland and emperor" (*pater patriae imperatorque*), as the chronicler Widukind von Corvey reported, before adding:

> He thus ordered the dedication and praise of almighty God in the individual churches, spreading the word to his honourable mother through messengers before returning jubilant and gloriously to Saxony where he was received by his people with the greatest of joy. For two hundred years, no king had been able to celebrate such a victory.[35]

Beyond the significance of this triumph for his reputation, Otto also wanted to use the huge forces that he had gathered at this point for a second purpose – namely, to put down the resistance that had flared up among the Polabian Slavs. While he was still busy preparing for the coming military campaign, Slavic emissaries representing numerous tribes came to him in a final effort to move the King to recognize their cultural identity and autonomy. They explained that as allies (*socii*) they were fully prepared to continue to pay tributes as before, so long as they enjoyed royal approbation of their *dominatio regionis*, which entailed the recognition of their communities' internal autonomy, including their religious beliefs – otherwise they would enter into battle "for their freedom".[36] For Otto, accepting this request would have meant nothing less than ending what he himself had initiated with the investment of the margraves and bishops in the Slavs' areas of settlement. This option was therefore out of the question for King Otto, particularly after the victory over the pagan Hungarians and having vowed to expand Church structures in Slavic lands by establishing a Diocese in Merseburg. The subsequent military campaign in the autumn of 955 ended with Otto's victory at the Battle on the Raxa, whereupon he then exacted bloody punishment with the execution of an estimated 700 captured Slavs.[37] There were nevertheless

---

34 *Widukindi... libri tres*, III/42, p. 122; C. Lübke, *Regesten...*, no. 91.
35 *Widukindi... libri tres*, III/49, p. 128.
36 *Widukindi... libri tres*, III/53, p. 132; C. Lübke, *Regesten...*, no. 100.
37 *Widukindi... libri tres*, III/55, p. 135; C. Lübke, *Regesten...*, no. 102.

further battles and it was only a final military campaign in 960 that seemed to have ensured a temporary peace, since the sources give no indication of any further military encounters between 960 and 965, when Otto bequeathed the Magdeburg Abbey of St Maurice with the tithes from a silver tax that was demanded from the subjugated Slavic tribes (*a subditis nobis Sclauorum nationibus*) – namely, the Ukrani, Rečani, Redarians, Tollensians, and Circipanians.[38]

The peace in the Slavic lands might also have been a consequence of Otto having shifted certain accents of his policies. Indeed, in 961 he set off for Italy, seeking to secure the imperial Roman crown. His coronation took place on February 2, 962, with later papal documents showing that it was Otto's previous successes in battle against the heathens that provided the core arguments in favor of trusting the King of Saxony with the greatest worldly honor that the Roman Church could bestow.[39]

Otto had already established contact with the Roman Curia thanks to the extension of his oath, given before the Battle of Lechfeld, to include the promise of establishing a Diocese in Merseburg. What he had in mind then was a complete restructuring of ecclesiastical organization in the east of his empire, with Magdeburg becoming central to his plans. Otto wanted to establish an archbishopric there, to create a large metropolis for the entirety of Slavic lands, and Pope John XII approved the transformation of the Abbey of Saint Maurice into an archbishopric in February 962. In this respect, he issued a papal bull that offers insight into the broad scope of Ottonian plans for the east. Fundamental to them, according to this document, were Otto's victories over the Hungarians and other heathen peoples (*barbarae gentes*) and the aim of leading the Slavs into Christianity.[40] The Pope awarded the Emperor the right to transfer the taxes from the converted peoples to each of the newly-established dioceses in the Polabian Slavic lands, with the bishops to be appointed by the Archbishop of Mainz, who at the time was Otto's son, the abovementioned Wilhelm, born of the Emperor's illegitimate relationship with a Slav woman. She was, most probably, a sister of Tugumir, prince of Brandenburg. As comparison with documents that were created a few years later in different conditions shows, during the early phase of planning the new Archbishopric in Magdeburg there was no indication of a limit being placed on its eastern domain. However, with the foundation of the Archbishopric of Magdeburg delayed by the resistance of German

---

38 C. Lübke, *Regesten...*, no. 132.
39 C. Lübke, *Regesten...*, no. 121.
40 *Urkundenbuch des Erzstifts Magdeburg*, ed. F. Israel, W. Möllenberg, Magdeburg 1937, no. 28; C. Lübke, *Regesten...*, no. 121.

bishops that lasted until 968, eastward limitations were, in fact, created in 966 by the baptism of the first Polish historic ruler Mieszko I and the existence of a missionary bishop in his dominion. The Archbishopric of Magdeburg thus encompassed only the existing Dioceses of Brandenburg and Havelberg, as well as the new Bishoprics of Merseberg, Zeitz, and Meissen. A short while afterwards, the Diocese of Oldenburg was incorporated into the Archbishopric of Hamburg-Bremen, thus completing the Christianization of the Polabian Slavs, at least in terms of ecclesiastical structures. However, in contrast to the experience of neighboring Slavs in Bohemia and Poland, who developed a regional church, the Polabian structures were incorporated into the Ottonian imperial church.[41]

The Polabian Slavs' aversion to these developments had already been evidenced by the numerous battles waged since the age of Henry I. This aversion was obscured only superficially by the foundation of the Archbishopric of Magdeburg, as it continued to smolder in the central and northern areas of the Polabian marches before ultimately leading to the outbreak of rebellion in the form of the great Lutician-led Uprising of 983. However, reception occurred only sporadically, with only a few members of the Polabian Slavic elites accepting collaboration with the imperial powers and voluntarily adopting Christianity. This, nonetheless, encouraged the empire to accept the Slavs into the Christian community. The continued existence of this intention to convert them after the Uprising of 983 was evident in the presence of the Slavic land (*Sclavinia*) in the group of four provinces paying tribute in the famous image in the Gospels of Otto III, produced at Reichenau Abbey.[42]

Translated by Tristan Korecki

---

41 C. Lübke, *Regesten...*, no. 142, 146, 148, 149, 150–154.
42 It is about the *Gospels of Otto III* today preserved in Bayerische Staatsbibliothek München, Clm 4453, fol. 23v–24r. Sclavinia in one row with Germania, Gallia and Roma, is paying homage to the emperor like the other provinces in the shape of a virgin.

Matthias Hardt

Magdeburg and the beginnings of the Diocese of Poznań

Abstract: The author discusses the links between the Archdiocese of Magdeburg founded in 968 and the first diocese on the Polish territories created in the wake of Mieszko's baptism. Since Poznań was not mentioned in Pope John XIII's Ravenna deed from 967, it is wholly improbable that it was founded at an earlier date, around the time of Mieszko's baptism. Bishop Jordan may have first acted as a missionary bishop without a permanent seat, as initially could have his successor Unger, as well. There is also no evidence that could suggest any supremacy of the Archdiocese Magdeburg over Poznań. The author agrees with Johannes Fried's conclusion that regardless of the later claims from Magdeburg, the Diocese of Poznań was never legally incorporated into the German ecclesiastical province.

Keywords: Diocese of Poznań, Archdiocese of Magdeburg, Metropolinate of Gniezno, Congress of Gniezno, Ottonian Empire

On April 20, 967, Pope John XIII decreed that Magdeburg on the Elbe was to be elevated to metropolitan status at the Easter Synod of Ravenna; this was where Roman Emperor Otto I the Great (936/962–973) gathered the bodies of Saint Maurice and numerous martyrs, establishing an *ecclesia mirae magnitudinis*.[1]

---

1 G. Althoff, "Die Gründung des Erzbistums Magdeburg", [in]: *Otto der Große, Magdeburg und Europa*, vol. 1: *Essays*, Mainz 2001, p. 344–352; W. Huschner, *Transalpine Kommunikation im Mittelalter. Diplomatische, kulturelle und politische Wechselwirkungen zwischen Italien und dem nordalpinen Reich (9.-11. Jahrhundert)*, vol. 2 (ser.: Schriften der Monumenta Germaniae Historica, 52/II), Hannover 2003, p. 624–658. For the status of excavations on the cathedral hill in Magdeburg cf. most recently: R. Kuhn, "Die Grablege der Editha und die Bedeutung Magdeburgs in ottonischer Zeit", [in:] *Dome – Gräber – Grabungen. Winchester und Magdeburg. Zwei Kulturlandschaften des 10. Jahrhunderts im Vergleich,*, Regensburg 2016, p. 27–47; for information on the patrocinia of Magdeburg's churches in the early period, see: M. Hardt, "Mauritius, Innocentius, Petrus, Christus Salvator, Paulus und andere. Von Laurentius kaum eine Spur. Zu den ottonenzeitlichen Kirchenbauten auf dem Magdeburger Domplatz", [in:] *Aedificatio Terrae. Beiträge zur Umwelt- und Siedlungsarchäologie Mitteleuropas. Festschrift für Eike Gringmuth-Dallmer zum 65. Geburtstag*, Rahden/Westfalen 2007, p. 177–183.

In so doing, the Pope made great strides towards completing the King and Emperor's preparations, which for more than two decades had been marred by resistance from William, the Archbishop of Mainz, and Bernhard, the Bishop of Halberstadt. The new metropolinate should not rank behind the older archsees; its suffragans were the Bishoprics of Brandenburg and Havelberg founded in 948, which hitherto had belonged to the Metropolinate of Mainz. The Archbishop of Magdeburg should have the *potestas per congrua loca, ubi per illorum predicationem christianitas creverit, episcopos ordinare, nominative nunc et presentaliter Merseburg, Cici et Misni* [...].[2]

In the elevation of the Saint Maurice Monastery to an archdiocese (which, though not implemented, had been announced by John XII in 962), only Merseburg was mentioned as a suffragan. However, since Magdeburg was located in the vicinity of the *gentes*, it should be possible to found further suffragans amongst the subjugated in adjacent areas: *quia vicinus id locorum gentibus est, in archiepiscopalem transferatur sedem, que per subditos suffraganeos totum die gregem regere et gubernare valeat* [...]. Moreover, it was stated that all future *gentes* subjugated by Emperor Otto and his successors were to be subjugated to Magdeburg and its dioceses:

> Et quia tot gentes sub uno pastore regi minime possunt, volumus et per nostre auctoritatis privilegium censemus, ut censum et decimationem omnium gentium, quas predictus piissimus inperator baptizavit vel per eum suumque filium equivocum regem successoresque eorum deo annuente baptizande sunt, ipsi sucessoresque eorum potestatem habeant distribuendi, subdendi Magdaburgensi, Merseburgensi vel cuicunque velint future unicuique sedi.[3]

Though notions of future expansion into areas occupied by the *gentes* were similarly unspecified in 967, they had a considerably less enthusiastic form than five years earlier. In addition, John XIII insisted that the mission was more a duty of the Pope and the bishops than of the Emperor.[4]

Based on the deed from 967, the actual founding of the archdiocese was finally effected in the autumn of 968. The importance of the Emperor for the archdiocese and its mission was again highlighted in the memorandum created for it. According to that document, establishing new archdioceses nevertheless

---

2 *Urkundenbuch der Stadt Magdeburg*, vol. 1: *Bis 1403*, ed. G. Hertel, Halle 1892, no. 52, p. 74; W. Huschner, *Transalpine Kommunikation II...*, p. 626–627.

3 *Urkundenbuch der Stadt Magdeburg I...*, no. 28, p. 42; W. Huschner, *Transalpine Kommunikation II...*, p. 626.

4 D. Claude, *Geschichte des Erzbistums Magdeburg bis in das 12. Jahrhundert*, part 1, Köln, Wien 1972, p. 90.

remained the duty of the archbishops, a position that remained in place in the deed issued by John XIII in naming Adalbert as the first Archbishop of Magdeburg. However, the deed contained no provisions for expansion east of Magdeburg: it was only in a further charter issued by the Pope in October 968 that granted this permission, *ut ab eius rectoribus episcopi, qui ultra Albiam et Salam constituti et constituendi sunt, post futuris temporibus consecrentur et ipsi eiusdem tue scilicet ecclesie archiepiscopos, sicut pro tempore fuerint, consecrent*.[5]

However, Otto I the Great made no secret of his intentions. The new archdiocese of *vir venerabilis* Adalbert, *Rugis olim predicatorum destinatum et missum*, should *totius ultra Albiam et Salam Sclauorum gentis modo ad deum converse vel convertende fieri*.[6]

This detailed account of what was written in the earliest sources regarding the Archdiocese of Magdeburg's expansion eastward was necessary so that we may now address the question of whether the Archdiocese of Magdeburg may also have initially held jurisdiction over the Piast dominion. This view, which may not be clearly ascribed to the early texts, has the approval of the chronicler Thietmar, the Bishop of Merseburg. Though written shortly before 1018, his description of the Archdiocese of Magdeburg's founding appears to contain more information alluding to this. Thietmar writes that Adalbert was

> accepted by the clergy and the population with great fervor and appointed Boso as the first Bishop of Merseburg, Burchard as the first Superior of Meissen and Hugo as the first Bishop of Zeitz during the festive period; then there was also Dudo, who had earlier been appointed the Bishop of Havelberg. Each of them was assigned to their particular diocese, and all vowed obedience to him and his successors. In addition to these clergymen (*additus*), Thietmar was anointed before them as the first Bishop of Brandenburg – and Jordan as the first *episcopus Posnaniensis*.[7]

When Emperor Otto III (983/996–1002) met Prince Boleslaus the Brave (Bolesław Chrobry, 992–1025) at the Congress of Gniezno in the year 1000, he was reverently received *ab episcopo eiusdem Ungero* and led into the church. Unger[8] was Jordan's successor. However, when the Archdiocese of Gniezno was

---

5   *Urkundenbuch der Stadt Magdeburg I...*, no. 64..., p. 93.
6   *Diplomatum regum et imperatorum Germaniae. Conradi I., Heinrici I. et Ottonis I. diplomata*, vol. 1, ed. T. Sickel (ser.: Monumenta Germaniae Historica. Die Urkunden der deutschen Könige und Kaiser, 2), Hannover 1879-1884, reprinted: Berlin 1956, no. 366, p. 502-503; *Urkundenbuch der Stadt Magdeburg I...*, no. 67, p. 97.
7   *Thietmari Merseburgensis episcopi Chronicon*, ed. R. Holtzmann (ser.: Monumenta Germaniae Historica Scriptores rerum Germanicarum Nova Seria, 9), Berlin 1935, reprinted: München 1996, p. 64.
8   M. Hardt, "Unger", [in:] *Neue Deutsche Biographie*, vol. 26, Berlin 2016, p. 629–630; J. Strzelczyk, "Unger", [in:] *Lexikon des Mittelalters*, vol. 8, München 1997, p. 1234–1235.;

founded a short time later[9] (*ut spero legitime*, as Thietmar revealed), the Bishop of Merseburg's account states that Unger was left out in the cold, since he refused to grant his consent (*sine consensu tamen prefati presulis, cuius diocesi omnis haec regio subiecta est* […] *Vungero Posnaniensi except*), Reinbern of Kołobrzeg, Poppo of Kraków, and John of Wrocław appointed Adalbert of Prague's Bohemia-born brother Radim Gaudentius as the Archbishop of Gniezno.[10]

It was of course natural to link the inconsistency of Unger's subsequent exclusion with his affiliation to the Archdiocese of Magdeburg. Many academics from earlier German research – including Rudolf Köpke, Ernst Dümmler[11], Albert Hauck[12], and Gerhard Sappok[13] – took this approach, since the clergy in Magdeburg had left a trail of clues via falsifying documents early on. Before these can be examined, we must come back to Thietmar, as his accounts may be able to shed light on the beginnings of the Diocese of Poznań. He highlighted the close relationship Bishop Jordan had maintained with Boleslaus the Brave's parents: Mieszko I (c. 960–992)[14] and Doubravka[15], his Christian wife from Bohemia.

> Their first bishop Jordan made great efforts for them, as the zealous man invited them to work on the Vineyard of the Lord in word and deed. The two spouses, the man and noble woman, were rightly delighted by this and everyone subject to them was pleased with their marriage in Christ.[16]

The majority of Polish researchers concluded from this account that Jordan came to the Piasts as part of Doubravka's entourage. She was of Bohemian origin, a

---

J. Leśny, J. Tazbirowa, "Unger", [in:] *Słownik starożytności słowiańskich*, vol. 6, Wrocław, Warszawa, Gdańsk 1977, p. 264.

9 E-D. Hehl, "Die Gründung des Erzbistums Gnesen unter kirchenrechtlichen Aspekten", [in:] *Europas Mitte um 1000. Beiträge zur Geschichte, Kunst und Archäologie*, vol. 1, Darmstadt 2000, p. 498–501.

10 *Thietmari Merseburgensis…*, 45, p. 182–184.

11 R. Köpke, E. Dümmler, *Jahrbücher des deutschen Reiches unter Otto I*, Leipzig 1876, reprinted in Darmstadt 1962, p. 452.

12 A. Hauck, *Kirchengeschichte Deutschlands*, part 3, unchanged 3rd and 4th edition Leipzig 1920, p. 200–202.

13 G. Sappok, *Die Anfänge des Bistums Posen und die Reihe seiner Bischöfe von 968–1498 (Deutschland und der Osten 6)*, Leipzig 1937, p. 74–78.

14 P. Urbańczyk, *Mieszko Pierwszy tajemniczy*, Toruń 2012.

15 J. Strzelczyk, "Polen, Tschechen und Deutsche in ihren Wechselwirkungen um das Jahr 1000", [in:] *Polen und Deutschland vor 1000 Jahren. Die Berliner Tagung über den "Akt von Gnesen"* (ser.: Europa im Mittelalter, 5), Berlin 2002, p. 43–59, here p. 47–49.

16 *Thietmari Merseburgensis…*, 56, p. 194–196.

daughter of the Přemyslid, Prince Boleslaus I the Cruel (935–972), which is why various academics (including Gerard Labuda) surmised that Jordan came from the Diocese of Regensburg to Poznań via Prague.[17] However, the question of who could have appointed him as bishop remains unanswered. Dietrich Claude believed the appointment could only have been possible with Otto I the Great's consent, but found it unlikely that Jordan would have been appointed by the Pope.[18]

Jordan's successor was Unger (*Vungerus, Vnger*) from Saxony, who, in fact, might have come from the middle Danube region and probably assumed office around 982/984. His personality and actions have also been interpreted differently in German and Polish research. If he is the same person as the *Vvunnigerus episcopus*[19] recorded in 991, he was also the Abbot of Memleben Abbey on the Unstrut River at this time and owed his promotion to Emperor Otto II (973–983) and his wife Theophanu. He is sometimes credited[20] as having taken part in preparing Mieszko's bestowal of the *civitas Schinesghe* to Saint Peter in Rome in 991[21], as recorded in the *Dagome iudex regesta*. The bronze door of Gniezno Cathedral depicts a bishop attending the repatriation of Bishop Adalbert of Prague's body from Prussia and witnessing the first interment of the saint.[22] In light of the historical detail conveyed by the cast-bronze depictions, the bishop depicted can only be Unger rather than Radim Gaudentius, whose inclusion would have had to be an act of prescience.

---

17 G. Labuda, "Der 'Akt von Gnesen' vom Jahre 1000. Bericht über die Forschungsvorhaben und – ergebnisse", *Quaestiones Medii Aevi Novae* 5, 2000, p. 145–188. For older Polish research, see also: M. Banaszak, "Das Problem der kirchlichen Abhängigkeit Poznańs von Magdeburg in der polnischen Geschichtsschreibung", [in:] *Beiträge zur Geschichte des Erzbistums Magdeburg*, Leipzig 1968, p. 214–228, here p. 219–220.
18 D. Claude, *Geschichte des Erzbistums Magdeburg I...*, p. 110–111.
19 *Diplomatum regum et imperatorum Germaniae. Ottonis III* (ser.: Monumenta Germaniae Historica, Die Urkunden der deutschen Könige und Kaiser, 2/2), 2nd unchanged edition, Berlin 1957, no. 75, p. 482–483.
20 J. Fried, *Otto III. und Boleslaw Chrobry. Das Widmungsbild des Aachener Evangeliars, der "Akt von Gnesen" und das frühe polnische und ungarische Königtum*, Stuttgart 1989, p. 144.
21 Ch. Warnke, "Ursachen und Voraussetzungen der Schenkung Polens an den Heiligen Petrus", [in:] *Europa slavica – Europa orientalis. Festschrift für Herbert Ludat zum 70. Geburtsta*, ed. K.-D. Grothausen, K. Zernack, Berlin 1980, p. 127–177.
22 A. Bujak, A. S. Labuda, *Porta regia. Drzwi Gnieźnieńskie*, Gniezno 1998, Scena XVII; J. Strzelczyk, "Polen im 10. Jahrhundert", [in:] *Europas Mitte um 1000. Beiträge zur Geschichte, Kunst und Archäologie*, vol. 1, Darmstadt 2000, p. 446–457, here p. 455; J. Fried, *Otto III. und Boleslaw Chrobry...*, p. 106.

After the Congress of Gniezno in 1000, in which Unger – termed the "the unruly bishop" by Ernst-Dieter Hehl[23] – was involved in a conflicting manner, he arranged as *episcopus terrae* for the burial of the *quinque fratres*, i.e., the five Camaldolese monks killed in 1003.[24] During a trip to Rome, which probably took place in 1006 and was intended for preparing the monks' canonization, and which may have served Unger's own interest in declaring the successor to the deceased Radim Gaudentius, the *Vita quinque fratrum* states that he was captured on the order of King Henry II (1002–1024) and taken to a monastery in Magdeburg.[25] The name of any successor in Poznań is unknown. Unger died on June 9, 1012, i.e., thirty years after his *ordinatio*. When announcing his death, Thietmar of Merseburg referred to him as the *Posnaniensis cenobii pastor*, and as the *consacerdos et suffraganeus* of Archbishop Tagino of Magdeburg, who died on the same day.[26] Unger's date of death was recorded in the necrologies of Merseburg and Saint Michael's in Lüneburg. Dietrich Claude regards the latter instance as an indication that Unger had good relations with Rikdag, the Abbot of Lüneburg, who had occasionally served as the Abbot of the Berge Monastery in Magdeburg.[27] The late-medieval chronicler Jan Długosz claimed that Unger was buried in Brandenburg at the Havel. Herbert Ludat did not want to rule out the possibility that Unger had been staying there for negotiations with Polish envoys at the time of his death.[28] The question is often raised as to whether during his captivity the Bishop had agreed to subordinate the Diocese of Poznań to the Archdiocese of Magdeburg[29], which was often assumed as being the case already from its founding in 968.

Dietrich Claude wrote in 1972 that Thietmar of Merseburg believed that Poznań belonged to Magdeburg's union of metropolinates. However, he also indicated that the chronicler's knowledge of the events of 968 was incomplete.

---

23 E. D. Hehl, "Der widerspenstige Bischof. Bischöfliche Zustimmung und bischöflicher Protest in der ottonischen Reichskirche", [in:] *Herrschaftsrepräsentation im ottonischen Sachsen*, Sigmaringen 1998, p. 295–344, here especially p. 313–315.

24 *Vita Quinque fratrum eremitarum*, ed. J. Karwasinska (ser.: Monumenta Poloniae Historica. Nova Series, 4/3), Warszawa 1973, p. 27–84, here p. 67; J. Fried, *Otto III. und Boleslaw Chrobry...*, p. 108.

25 *Vita quinque fratrum eremitarum...*, p. 72.

26 *Thietmari Merseburgensis ...*, 65, p. 356.

27 D. Claude, *Geschichte des Erzbistums Magdeburg bis in das 12. Jahrhundert*, part 2, Köln, Wien 1975, p. 297.

28 H. Ludat, *An Elbe und Oder um das Jahr 1000. Skizzen zur Politik des Ottonenreiches und der slavischen Mächte in Mitteleuropa*, Köln, Wien 1971, p. 63–64.

29 M. Banaszak, "Das Problem der kirchlichen Abhängigkeit...", p. 216.

Even so, there was "no reason to reject his message about Poznań being subordinate to Magdeburg, even during Jordan's lifetime".[30] So when was the Diocese of Poznań founded? Supported by more recent annals, older research literature maintained that the founding took place in 968.[31] Since Poznań is not mentioned in Pope John XIII's Ravenna deed from 967, it is wholly improbable that it was founded at an earlier date, around the time of Mieszko's baptism. As the Poznań School of Polish Medieval Studies similarly argues[32], Bishop Jordan may have first acted as a "missionary bishop without a permanent seat"[33], as could have Unger initially. In this instance though, both would have been directly answerable to the Pope, thus failing to explain why Unger remained outside of the new Metropolinate of Gniezno in 1000.[34]

Dietrich Claude suggested that Poznań had *de facto* recognition closely resembling "consuetudinary law", since "it is probable that Jordan and Unger appealed to the Archbishop of Magdeburg [...] to procure books, vestments, and perhaps also to enlist priests". Claude added that canonical sanctioning from Rome was not forthcoming.[35] However, Johannes Fried argued in 1989 that Unger had "full independent rights from Magdeburg" and acted against their curtailment.[36] Fried also stated that Unger was Boleslaus the Brave's original candidate for the Polish Archdiocese; perhaps with the Prince's consent, Unger now blocked the legal capacity of the incumbent in Gniezno. In so doing, however, he prevented the probable planned elevation of Boleslaus to king with a religious ceremony. He must be considered a "decisive opponent of all Magdeburg's claims to Poznań".[37] However, Johannes Fried postulated that four dioceses already existed in 1000, namely those at Kołobrzeg, Wrocław, and Kraków in addition to Unger's.[38]

If there was any evidence that could at most suggest the validity and recognition of a claim from Magdeburg to a Diocese in Poznań, it has become apparent that there are no documents in Magdeburg that could support such claim. In particular, Paul Kehr demonstrated this in a paper *The Archdiocese of*

---

30 D. Claude, *Geschichte des Erzbistums Magdeburg bis in das 12. Jahrhundert*, part 1..., p. 108.
31 M. Banaszak, "Das Problem der kirchlichen Abhängigkeit...", p. 220–221.
32 Ibidem, p. 221–222.
33 D. Claude, *Geschichte des Erzbistums...*, p. 110.
34 Ibidem, p. 111.
35 Ibidem, p. 112.
36 J. Fried, *Otto III. und Bolesław Chrobry...*, p. 103.
37 Ibidem, p. 106.
38 Ibidem, p. 105.

Magdeburg and the First Organization of a Christian Church in Poland, which he presented at the Prussian Academy of Sciences in 1920.[39] There was an attempt in Magdeburg to remedy this by drafting a papal deed, which, according to Helmut Beumann's studies at the Curia in Rome, was nevertheless not accepted.[40] It is claimed in the manuscript that Otto I the Great took the initiative to found archdioceses *ultra fluvios Albiam et Salam et Odoram*; the list has Poznań behind Zeitz, Merseburg, Brandenburg, and Havelberg. In order for these locations to have a common metropolinate, Otto ultimately ordered the Archdiocese of Magdeburg to be established, while the suffragans were appointed by Adalbert. Magdeburg was expressly guaranteed the right for this: *ut idem archiepiscopus cum suis successoribus et cum loco sibi conmisso munduburdio sancti Petri suique vicarii perpetuo subiectus potestatem haberet supradictarum civitatum episcopos ordinare.*[41] Helmut Beumann and Walter Schlesinger take the stance that the manuscript ascribed to Archbishop Giselher may well have made its way as far as the Apostolic Chancery; however, it was not executed on the evidence of the glaring inaccuracies. Magdeburg's attempt to gain supremacy over Poznań by means of a papal deed also failed.

With all of this evidence now discussed, Johannes Fried is left with the final word: "No matter which claims were brought from Magdeburg's side, the Diocese of Poznań was never legally incorporated into the German ecclesiastical province".[42]

Translated by Tristan Korecki

---

39 P. Kehr, *Das Erzbistum Magdeburg und die erste Organisation der christlichen Kirche in Polen*, Berlin 1920, p. 33, 37–40, 45–46.

40 H. Beumann, W. Schlesinger, "Urkundenstudien zur deutschen Ostpolitik unter Otto III", *Archiv für Diplomatik* 1, 1955, p. 132–256.

41 *Urkundenbuch der Stadt Magdeburg I…*, no. 130.

42 J. Fried, *Otto III. und Boleslaw Chrobry…* p. 146.

Przemysław Urbańczyk

Archaeology on the beginnings of Christianity in Poland

Abstract: During the reign of Boleslaus I the Brave we witness an acceleration of the country's Christianization. That ruler invested in church architecture, expanded the personnel conducting evangelization, and compelled his subjects to observe the basic requirements of Christianity. The period when his father Mieszko I ruled, however, prompts many difficult questions. This is because neither written nor material sources provide information enabling us to discern a change of religion in any of the lands Mieszko ruled – except for Poznań itself. There is no archaeologically observable change in the eschatology that should be visible in a new burial rite – that is, we see no shift from cremation to inhumation. And after all, there are controversies concerning the very baptism of Mieszko I. Indeed, if the available historical, onomastic, and archaeological knowledge permit us to suggest a hypothesis that his ancestors hailed from Great Moravia, then Mieszko I was born into a Christian family – and thus the baptism of 966 would signify rather only the admission of his realm to Latin Europe.

Keywords: archeology, Mieszko I, Boleslaus I the Brave, Christianization, Great Moravia

Despite his marked malevolence toward Boleslaus the Brave (Bolesław Chrobry, 992–1025), Thietmar, the Bishop of Merseburg, did consider the Polish ruler's state to be a truly Christian one. He even emphasized the orthodoxy of Boleslaus himself, who did not refrain from applying cruel methods to impose on his subjects in line with the moral expectations of the Church.[1] Indeed, Thietmar noted that Boleslaus went so far as to consult the guidelines of Canon Law.[2] Thietmar moreover appreciated the determination of the Christian defenders of Niemcza, who in the year 1017 desperately resisted the attacks of the pagan Luticians (*Lutici*) allied at that point with Emperor Henry II (1002/1014–1024).[3]

The point is, it was during the rule of Boleslaus the Brave that Poland experienced a distinct acceleration of the Christianization process. During the first decade of his rule he promoted the idea of *imitatio imperii* to the rank of state strategy, part of which included support for the Church. Thus, he made

---

1 Thietmar, *Kronika Thietmara*, ed. M. Z. Jedlicki, Poznań 1953, Book VIII, p. 2.
2 Ibidem, Book VI, p. 92.
3 Ibidem, Book VII, p. 60.

investments in ecclesial architecture (in Giecz, Gniezno, Kałdus, Kraków, Łekno, Ostrów Lednicki, Poznań, Przemyśl, and, probably, Wrocław), expanded the evangelization staff, and compelled observance of the basic requirements of Christianity. This was part of the important changes that Boleslaus introduced to the method of ruling the country and to the geopolitical strategy he pursued.

Boleslaus the Brave's active propagation of Christianity is confirmed by archaeological evidence, which is not limited to ecclesiastic stone architecture, with its impressive scale and size, but also includes: the coinage, which strongly emphasized Christian symbolism; the funeral rite progressively changing from cremation to inhumation; and artefacts related to the new religion, such as personal crosses, fragments of ornamented reliquaries, and book bindings.

This situation cannot be automatically extrapolated to the earlier time when his father, Mieszko I ruled (c. 960–992), for a series of difficult questions arises regarding the chronology, course, extension, and effects of the Christianization efforts of that period. Neither the available written sources nor material evidence provide us with information that help us unambiguously portray the religious change taking place in the territory then subjected to Piast rule. There is even controversy surrounding the baptism of Mieszko, the date of which is hard to precisely determine, and the location of which remains completely unknown.

The traditional vision coincided with Gallus Anonymus' conviction in his *Chronicle*, whereby owing to Mieszko I, "the Polish nation was saved from death in paganism".[45] Accordingly, the baptism of our first historic ruler was to initiate a radical ideological breakthrough, followed by an expeditious Christianization of the whole country. In time, this vision assumed the dimensions of a national emblem, with the baptism of Mieszko being considered the cornerstone of an eternal Poland understood as a demographic, geographical, and political unity of Christians. In this way, an individual act of conversion became "the Baptism of Poland" – as was emphasized in the watchwords of all the anniversary celebrations held in April 2016. This "1,050th anniversary of the Baptism of Poland" was even commemorated by a special-edition contemporary banknote featuring an appropriate motto.

Yet, archaeological evidence offers no convincing arguments that would testify to Mieszko's pursuit of extensive Christianization. Apart from the central

---

4   Gall Anonim, *Kronika polska*, ed. R. Grodecki, Wrocław et al. 1996, Book I, p. 6.
5   This quotation and all following quotations from non-English sources were translated into English by the translator of the chapter.

stronghold in Poznań, no investments in ecclesiastic infrastructure have been discovered – one possible exception being the (rather carelessly made) rotunda found beneath the Gniezno cathedral church. Hence, our present knowledge conjures a vision of an ostensibly Christian country that for a quarter-century had virtually nowhere to celebrate the liturgy. This denies what we are told by the fourteenth-century annal, *Rocznik Traski*, which says that Mieszko founded and furbished a number of monasteries and churches.[6]

Similarly, there are no archeologically observable effects of the conversion in the eschatological sphere, which should have manifested itself in the transition of the funeral rite – namely, from cremation into burial of whole dead bodies in line with the Christian principle. There are no reliably dated inhumation graves identified even in the very heart of Mieszko's state. These doubts surrounding the progress of Christianization are reinforced by no finds of objects related to the liturgy or individual devotion that could be dated to the time of Mieszko's reign. This telling lack of relevant material evidence leads to the conclusion that Mieszko attained no archeologically observable successes in the evangelization of his subjects.

We do not know if this was owing to Mieszko's weak personal involvement in the promotion of the new faith, or if it resulted from difficulties he encountered in overcoming the conservative attitude of his people, who either actively opposed a radical religious change, or showed passive but efficient resistance. We know such "ideological" conflicts from other countries that entered Christian Europe during the Early Middle Ages, for Mieszko I was not the only one who had to seek compromise between what the Church expected and his subjects' attachment to traditional customs and habits. Bishop Adalbert (Czech: Vojtěch; Polish: Wojciech) painfully experienced such developments in his native Bohemia, a country that had formally been Christianized for several dozen years. His missionary zeal in enforcing the requirements of the Church provoked an acute political conflict with the Bohemian Duke Boleslaus II the Pious (972–999) and the Bohemian aristocracy, one which resulted in the Bishop having twice fled his Prague Diocese – specifically, in 988 and 994.[7]

---

6   *Rocznik Traski*, ed. A. Bielowski, (ser.: Monumenta Poloniae Historica, 2), Lwów 1872, Book 2.

7   *Świętego Wojciecha żywot pierwszy*, trans. K. Abgarowicz, [in:] *Piśmiennictwo czasów Bolesława Chrobrego*, ed. J. Karwasińska, Warszawa 1966, p. 23–86, here p. 13 and 19; Brunon z Kwerfurtu, *Świętego Wojciecha żywot drugi*, trans. K. Abgarowicz, [in:] *Piśmiennictwo czasów Bolesława Chrobrego*, ed. J. Karwasińska, Warszawa 1966, p. 87–154, here p. 11–12 and 16.

Perhaps the reason for the infinitesimal progress of Christianization in the earliest Piast state related to the lack of external missionary assistance? After all, the "fraternal" Bohemian Church was too weak to support its neighbor with appropriately prepared missionaries, whilst the German Church had no political interest in supporting the diocese it could not control institutionally. Or, what if Mieszko I forcefully converted his subjects, but they – without being evangelized on a regular basis – quickly reverted to the faith of their ancestors? This is the sort of trouble Polish Duke Boleslaus III the Wrymouth (Bolesław III Krzywousty, 1107–1138) dealt later with respect to the Pomeranians who, once conquered militarily, would frequently "seek salvage in baptism, but once having recovered their strength again, recanted the Christian faith".[8] Whatever the case, archaeology today undermines the once-cherished dogma of the rapid conversion of the Piasts' subjects to Christianity after 966. The earlier vision of the swift conversion of the inhabitants of the whole country was not recorded by abundant historic sources. On the contrary, it made use of the scarcity of records written down in the crucial period of transition.

The disappointment of archaeologists over the lack of evidence of Mieszko's efficiency, or perhaps of his missionary determination, is rooted in our inclination to use sharp definitions of what was Christian and what was non-Christian. Contrasting the two "worlds", ones perceived as unambiguously separated, in order to attain typological and chronological clarity, implies a tendency to view paganism as a form of opposition to Christianity, defined in turn as a monolithic entity. Such an assumption implied a simple periodization that followed the vision of early-medieval ecclesiastic chroniclers who purposefully "dichotomized" the past into two separable epochs, the former having been concluded by the divine plan of reordering the previously reigning moral and religious chaos.

This has allowed creating a heuristically convenient opposition and to avoid problems related to analyzing the complex situation of the coexistence of two worldviews, something which probably lasted for a long time. It is easier to describe a religious transition with the use of a (pre)assumed "revolutionary" model than to wrestle with a long-lasting dialectical confrontation that was probably composed of periods of accelerated and decelerated evangelization, if not periodic decline (as, for instance, in the fourth decade of the 11th c. when the Christian Kingdom of Poland collapsed). Moreover, it is easier to assume religious homogeneity in as large a territory as possible, since the arduous task of taking local specificities into account is thus eliminated. Use of such generalized

---

8   Gall Anonim, *Kronika...*, Book I, Introduction.

contrasts is much more comfortable than the effort required to trace the historically diversified processes of transformation.

The recent State and Church celebrations of the 1,050th anniversary of Mieszko's baptism reinforced its simplified image, rendering it even more precise by indicating the date of his formal conversion to Christianity as April 14, 966 (which was Easter Sunday that year). Nonetheless, our knowledge on what actually happened is far from explicit. Doubts are prompted not only by archaeological evidence, but also by scattered pieces of historic information.

The Saxon Bishop Thietmar of Merseburg was the first to have written about Mieszko I's conversion. In his *Chronicle*, composed between 1012 and 1018, he openly admits that the date of the event is uncertain: 966, or maybe 968? Thietmar mentions "hard labors" performed by Bishop Jordan who arrived in Mieszko's dominion, to support the Christianization, and "indefatigable in his efforts, he [eventually] induced them, by word and deed, to cultivate the Lord's vineyard".[9] Driven by missionary enthusiasm, the Saxon chronicler optimistically declared that "all their subjects entered into matrimony with Christ" then.[10] Still later rewriters of the medieval annals, compiled on the Polish territories, differed in their chronological opinion: most of them pointed to the year 966, but some say the event took place in 967 – or even in 960. The lack of sources from the time of Mieszko's baptism and the chronological discord between the accounts written down at later dates commends critical caution when attempting unambiguous chronological adjudications.

The issue has become further complicated with the discovery at the former river island of Ostrów Tumski (in Poznań) of a *palatium* (stone palace-and-church complex) which was most probably built before 966.[11] This inclines one to ask the serious question about the religious situation at this early-Piast political center prior to the commonly accepted date of Mieszko I's baptism. While the answer is not easy, the very consideration of this question, inspired by archaeological discoveries, has an important heuristic value as it undermines the prevailing conviction that "it was the celebration of baptism that marked for

---

9 Thietmar, *Kronika...*, Book IV, p. 56.
10 Ibidem, Book IV, p. 56.
11 H. Kóčka-Krenz, *Na wyspie Ostrów, przy której dziś jest Poznań*, Poznań 2012; eadem, "Poznań w czasach panowania pierwszych Piastów", [in:] *Ziemia, człowiek, sztuka. Interdyscyplinarne studia nad ziemią. Archeologia – historia – kultura – sztuka*, ed. U. Mazurczak, Lublin 2015, p. 71–98.

Fig. 1: A visualization of the Poznań residential-ecclesial complex from Mieszko I's time (after H. Kóčka-Krenz, Ziemia, człowiek, sztuka. Interdyscyplinarne studia nad ziemią, [in:] *Archeologia – historia – kultura – sztuka*, ed. U. Mazurczak, Lublin 2015, pp. 71–98). The visualition made by Andrzej Gołembnik according to Hanna Kóčka-Krenz.

the Polish ruler the first event that enabled his contact with the symbolic sphere of Western culture".[12]

If the current archaeological findings remain unchanged, then the functioning in Poznań of an early enclave of Christians – strong in their association with the dynasty ruling the small state in Greater Poland (Wielkopolska) region – *before* the "canonical" date of 966 ought to be considered in all earnestness. The construction of a church/chapel forming an integral wing of the ducal palace[13] leaves no doubt with regards to the political status of the founder of this project, whose Christian connotation is clear [**Fig. 1**]. The temple's small size (approximately 10 sq. m) does not change the fact that it was a material demonstration of the presence of Christ's followers in Poznań.

I will skip here the detailed argument I have presented elsewhere.[14] It is sufficient to recall that the available historical, onomastic, and archaeological

---

12 L. Wetesko, *Piastowie i ich państwo w łacińskiej Europie. Studia z dziejów kultury politycznej X i XII wieku*, Poznań 2013.
13 H. Kóčka-Krenz, *Poznań in the 10th Century*, Poznań 2011.
14 P. Urbańczyk, *Mieszko Pierwszy tajemniczy*, Toruń 2012, p. 129–166.

information enables us to hypothesize a Great Moravian background of Mieszko I's ancestors: it was not without good reason that the Polish ruler named his second son Svatopluk thus referring to the dynastic name of the Moravian Moimirids. The Moravian ruling house was a fundamentally Christian family, although their Church followed the Cyrillo-Methodian variety of liturgy and evangelization, which was deemed by the Latin Church in the late 9th c. as virtually a heresy.

If Mieszko's predecessors indeed descended from the Moravian Christian family, then, after emigrating to central Greater Poland, they had to face the effects of their detachment from the ecclesial network. Mieszko would thus have been part of at least the second generation of Christians who remained isolated for a longer time from permanent contact with the institutional Church. The basic spiritual ministry could have been provided by visiting priests, ones who used the books and paraphernalia they had brought with them. However, there is no source that tells us about such visits prior to the official date of Mieszko's christening.

Even a single priest permanently present in Poznań, at the center of a small pre-Mieszko state, would not have solved the problems related to the lack of (albeit intermittent) contact with a bishop. Only a bishop, be it a visiting one, could ensure that the doctrinal requirements of performing the liturgy within a minutely defined sacral space were fulfilled. The ordainment of priests, consecration of altars, blessing of the holy oils, administration of the sacrament of Confirmation were the tasks of a bishop – as was the sacral assignment of a burial space and commencement of the construction of a church. The canonical requirements of the Latin Church with respect to the site of celebrating the Eucharistic liturgy have always been unambiguous: a church has to be a temple formally consecrated by a bishop and have a permanent pastoral staff. Absent a priest, a temple becomes a chapel or shrine. The lack of a consecrated altar would degrade the object to an oratory – a space designed for prayerful contemplation, but certainly not for the liturgy of transubstantiation. And of course, the basic obligation of a Christian is to take part in such liturgy, at least from time to time, and to receive the subsequent sacraments.

The problem of there being no consecrated ecclesial altar present could have been solved in Poznań by the use of portable altars which were a popular way of coping with the unavailability of a network of permanent churches in early-medieval Europe.[15] Nonetheless, the long-lasting relative isolation from the centers of institutionalized Christianity could have caused a degeneration of the

---

15 M. Budde, *Altare portatile. Kompendium der Tragaltare des Mittelalters 600–1600*, vol. 1-3, Münster 1998.

religion professed in the Greater Poland region. The fact that somebody had had a church built in Poznań before 966 certainly attests that he considered himself a Christian – which would not be tantamount to him being regarded from outside as a "true" Christian.

Archaeology cannot help resolve these doubts; what it can do is indicate the directions of the architectural inspiration for the small temple built in Poznań. Its closest formal analogies – Molzbichl in Carinthia, Uznach in Saint Gallen Canton, Switzerland, and Eldagsen near Hildesheim in Saxony – are dated between the 8th and 10th c.[16] A sort of parallel is also offered by a not much larger church that was built in Prague, probably by Doubravka's great-uncle, *Spytihněv* I, (c. 895–915). The Poznań and Prague churches were both erected at the central hubs of monarchal authority, and both were dedicated to Our Lady; moreover, the rulers are believed to have been buried in each of these temples.[17] With respect to the Poznań church, such a parallel is not surprising at all, given the context of the suggested arrival of Mieszko's ancestors from beyond the southern mountains in the early years of the 10th c.

Apart from the significant example of the Poznań temple, the only material evidence of an early (possibly, episodic) presence of some Christian people in the basins of the Odra and the Vistula Rivers are the so-called "tablets" made of fired clay found in Podebłocie in southern Mazovia (Mazowsze) [**Fig. 2**]. These exceptional artefacts are dated to the 9th c. and seem to have been engraved with acronyms of sacred names (*nomina sacra*) in the Greek alphabet (*IXCI* and *IXCH* = *I[HCOYC] X[PICTO]C H[NIKA]*) before the clay was fired.[18]

***

Surprisingly, with respect to the ca. three decades following the symbolic date of 966, no material traces whatsoever of Christianity's expansion are presently ascribable. It may thus be guessed that during of Mieszko I's rule, Christianization only encompassed the center of political power, i.e., the monarch's closest milieu. There is no historical source or archaeological testimony that would be indicative of any efficient missionary effort elsewhere than Poznań. But it also might have been that Mieszko "was not strongly concerned about Christianity" and,

---

16 H. Kóčka-Krenz "Poznań w czasach panowania..."
17 Z. Pianowski, "Który Bolesław? – Problem początku architektury monumentalnej w Małopolsce", [in:] *Początki architektury monumentalnej w Polsce*, ed. T. Janiak, D. Stryniak, Gniezno 2004, p. 269; P. Urbańczyk, *Mieszko Pierwszy...*, p. 416–418.
18 A. Łukaszewicz, "Dwadzieścia lat później. O tabliczkach z Podebłocia", [in:] *Przez granice czasu*, ed. A. Buko, W. Duczko, Pułtusk 2008.

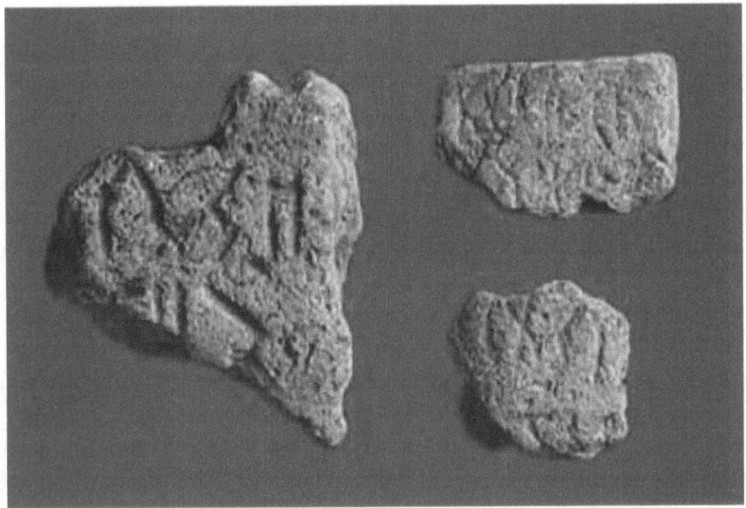

Fig. 2: The 'tablets' from Podebłocie (after E. Marczak, *Wczesnośredniowieczna osada przygrodowa w Podebłociu (stanowisko 3) na tle zespołu osadniczego*, Warszawa 2014 [doctoral thesis submitted at the Faculty of History, University of Warsaw; typescript]).

driven by political pragmatism, imposed upon his subjected community "only as much as those people could bear".[19]

The difficulties encountered by the Christianizers in eradicating traditional religious beliefs are illustrated by the situation in neighboring Bohemia, where several dozen years after the local dynasty's official conversion, the first Bishop of Prague, Dietmar (Dětmar; 973–982), baptized the pagan people[20] (*populum gentilem baptizans*). Yet in 1003 Bohemian Duke Boleslaus III the Red (999–1003) observed that the Bohemians were still attached to "pagan practices".[21] It can be suspected that the neophytes won over at the time but "for the most part they did not understand the sacramental *character indelebilis* of baptism".[22]

---

19 S. Zakrzewski, *Mieszko I jako budowniczy państwa polskiego*, Warszawa 1921.
20 Kosmas, *Kosmasa kronika Czechów*, ed. M. Wojciechowska, Wodzisław Śląski 2012, Book I, p. 24.
21 Thietmar, *Kronika...*, Book V, p. 29.
22 S. Albrecht, "Der Mauerbau von Stará Boleslav", *Medieval and Early Modern Studies for Central and Eastern Europe* 2, 2010, p. 25.

Hence, "Both the missionaries and Church authorities were fully aware of the ignorance of their new flock in Christian matters and of that flock's inability to comprehend Christian teaching in its complexity as well as its particulars."[23]

This slowed change in eschatological convictions, was expressed in the continued funeral rite of cremation. True, no universal guideline is conceivable that could help archaeologists establish which specific elements, appearing at which specified time, may be deemed an unambiguous indication of accepted Christian eschatology. For the method of burying deceased Christians took precise form in the early Middle Ages via practices that gradually took shape in various areas. The simplified interpretation of the change in the funeral rite, based on the conviction that there should be no real problem in differentiating between pagan (cremation) versus Christian (skeletal) funerals in Poland – as the two modes are separated by an evident borderline – is nevertheless unsustainable. This convenient vision is undermined, for instance, by the earlier bi-ritualism of many pre-Christian communities (as in Scandinavia or Rus'), where some dead bodies were cremated and others were buried in their entirety, for reasons and/or in circumstances we are unaware of today.

Similarly, a truly Christian early-medieval funeral remains indefinable. There were no clearly determined rules in place which would define sepulchral orthodoxy. Thus, the homogeneous eschatological doctrine was not followed by homogeneous rituals related to death, which fact initially allowed some freedom when it came to choosing the funeral practice. In any case, "… no document produced by any of the ecumenical councils of antiquity and the Middle Ages contains any detailed instructions whatsoever with respect to the funeral rite recommended by the Church".[24] Apart from the Carolingian codices of the early 9th c., nor are indications to this end provided elsewhere by the Church authorities.

Neither did early-medieval legislation define the exact form of the grave (in terms of presence/absence of a specified structure, or otherwise). No method of "wrapping up" the corpse was recommended (such as, e.g., coffin and/or shroud); the position of the dead body inside the grave was not rigorously determined (as, for instance, in a supine position, or the hands positioned in a specified way).

---

23 E. Melnikova, "How Christian were Viking Christians?", [in:] *Early Christianity on the way from the Varangians to the Greeks*, ed. I. Garipzanov, O. Tolochko, Kiev 2011, p. 97.

24 M. Rębkowski, "Kilka uwag w sprawie genezy orientacji pochówków szkieletowych we wczesnym średniowieczu", [in:] *Świat Słowian wczesnego średniowiecza*, ed. M. Dworaczyk, A. B. Kowalska, S. Moździoch, M. Rębkowski, Szczecin 2006, p. 516; M. Rębkowski, *Chrystianizacja Pomorza Zachodniego. Studium archeologiczne*, Szczecin 2007, p. 90.

Fig. 3: A visualization of the first cathedral church in Poznań (after A. Bukowska and Z. Cozac).

There were no constraints in respect to putting some objects into the grave – apart from food, which would suggest a belief in an instantaneous journey to the netherworld. Nor is any codification dated before the 13th c. concerning the obligatory burial of Christian dead with their heads pointing west known to us.[25] None of this facilitates tracking the progress Christianity was making in the initial period of its onerous struggle with earlier traditions.

***

The strategy adopted by Mieszko I might have changed in the last period of his rule, as may be testified by the commencement of the construction of a monumental cathedral church at Ostrów Tumski in Poznań [**Fig. 3**]. The situation of the Piast Church in the ninth decade of the 10th c.[26] provokes the suspicion that this was an effort whose overtone and resonance was mainly political. The initiation of this ambitious investment project might have been an attempt to reinforce the arguments in favor of "releasing" Abbot-Bishop Unger from Saxony, who after his investiture in 982–983 apparently delayed his arrival in Poland.

---

25 M. Rębkowski, "Kilka uwag w sprawie genezy...", p. 517.
26 P. Urbańczyk, *Mieszko Pierwszy...*, p. 248–253.

Mieszko eventually decided to have a cathedral church erected, one equal in rank to the Emperor's foundation in Memleben.[27] The construction of a monumental cathedral without a bishop exercising his office on-site was a political manifestation of the determination of the Christian ruler and a form of symbolic pressure on the imperial court, the German Church, and the Pope. Bearing in mind that Carolingian Canon Law already banned the commencement of constructing any church without consent from the bishop, it has to be assumed that either Bishop Jordan had granted such consent before his death in 980–982, and that the progress of the work was hindered due to various circumstances – or perhaps that his successor did in fact briefly stay in Poland, and allowed the project to get underway.

Whatever the case, in light of our current knowledge, Mieszko I's "possible" conversion (which certainly extended to his inner circle) was most probably a primarily outward element of geopolitical strategy; the initiative might also have stemmed from Mieszko's personal conviction[28], which however remained limited to his private devotional practices. As to the other inhabitants of Mieszko's state, no historical sources or archaeological testimonies exist that would be indicative of any extensive missionary campaign he might have launched. After all, being a strongly formalized one-book and single-institution religion, one of standardized buildings and specific paraphernalia, Christianity needed strong organizational and financial support from the political authorities, it received only during the reign of Boleslav I the Brave, i.e. after 992.

Translated by Tristan Korecki

---

27 A. Bukowska, "Forma i geneza pierwszej katedry w Poznaniu", [in:] *Architektura romańska w Polsce. Nowe odkrycia i interpretacje*, ed. T. Janiak, Gniezno 2009; A. Bukowska, *Najstarsza katedra w Poznaniu. Problem formy i jej genezy w kontekście architektury około roku 1000*, Kraków 2013.

28 Ph. E. Steele, *Nawrócenie i chrzest Mieszka I* (2nd edition), Kraków 2016, p. 9–98.

Eduard Mühle

Mieszko I's baptism and the *Poloni* as reflected in historiographic sources from the 10th to the 14th c.

Abstract: In analyzing the fragments of the early written sources from the late 10th and early 11th c., along with later Polish chronicles describing the baptism of Mieszko, the author concludes that this event did not attract much attention of the literate Polish elite between the 10th and 14th c. Admittedly Gallus's chronicle from the beginning of the 12th c. offers a complete presentation of the caesura of Christianization, but the author assigns no lesser merit to Mieszko's son Boleslaus the Brave for the "increment of the true religion". In the *Chronica Polonorum* written at the turn of the 13th c. by Vincentius Kadłubek, the occurrence of conversion further loses in importance within the framework of the narrative. The meager records related to the Piast period compiled after Kadłubek's chronicle do not provide more information.

Keywords: Mieszko I's baptism, early-Piast monarchy, medieval historiography, Gallus Anonymus, Vincentius Kadłubek

From a historical perspective, the baptism of Mieszko I (960–992) is a fundamental caesura in Poland's early-medieval history.[1] However, even in medieval Poland the event aroused astonishingly little attention. It appears as if that act,

---

1 Given the abundance of publications on the topic, let us refer to just a handful of those recently issued: J. Shepard, "Conversions and Regimes Compared: The Rus' and the Poles, ca. 1000", [in:] *East Central and Eastern Europe in the Early Middle Ages*, ed. F. Curta, A. Arbor, Koninklijke 2005, p. 254–282; P. Urbańczyk, S. Rosik, "Poland", [in:] *Christianization and State Formation in North Europe*, ed. N. Berend, S. Bagge, Cambridge 2005, p. 263–318; R. Michałowski, "Piast Monarchy in the 10th and 11th Centuries", *Acta Poloniae Historica* 101, 2010, p. 5–35; D. A. Sikorski, *Kościół w Polsce za Mieszka I i Bolesława Chrobrego. Rozważania nad granicami poznania historycznego*, Poznań 2011; idem, *Początki Kościoła w Polsce. Wybrane problemy*, Poznań 2012; S. Rosik, *Die Anfänge des Christentums in Polen*, in *Credo. Christianisierung Europas im Mittelalter*, vol. 1: *Essays*, ed. Ch. Stiegermann, Petersberg 2013, p. 380–388; F. Biermann, "Überzeugung und Zwang bei der Christianisierung Polens unter den ersten Piasten", [in:] *Schwertmission. Gewalt und Christianisierung im Mittelalter*, ed. H. Kamp, M. Kroker, Paderborn 2013, p. 67–91; T. Jurek, "O czasie i okolicznościach chrztu Mieszka", *Roczniki Historyczne* 81, 2015, p. 35–56; G. Pac, "Chrystianizacja i prawo we wcześniejszym średniowieczu", *Kwartalnik Historyczny* 122, 2015, p. 817–23;

willingly used in historical memory contexts by modern descendants as an opportunity for historical-and-political celebrations, did not capture the attention of Polish society in the Middle Ages – the literate Polish elite, at the very least – or move those people in some special way. When reviewing the available records, one cannot avoid the impression that between the 10th and the 14th c. not much fuss was made about the act of baptism, or the Christianization, of the domains of the Piasts and their subjects.[2]

Even some of the authors living between 960 and 1010 failed to mention the occurrence, though some did – albeit superficially. In any case, we can find no report of a "baptism"/Christianization of the *Poloni* whether in Widukind of Corvey, in the *Vitae of Saint Adalbert*, or even not clearly in the writings of Bruno of Querfurt. Taking interest in the Christianization of the Danish people, Widukind did not utter a word about the christening of Mieszko and his *Licicaviki* people, though we can find mentions about those in his *Deeds of the Saxons*.[3] Whether the *rex Misaca*, attacked by Margrave Gero – similarly as King Harald (c. 958 – c. 986) and his Danes – continuously paid homage to his pagan idols (*idolis ritu gentili servientes*), Widukind does not tell us; we cannot learn from him whether that ruler actually became a Christian himself, not much later as a friend of the Emperor (*amicus imperatoris*). All the same, the Saxon chronicler was aware of certain important details – one of them being Mieszko's marriage to a daughter of Bohemia's Duke Boleslaus I (935–972). Why did Widukind make no use of his knowledge to mention Bohemian Mieszko's wife Doubravka's conjectured, or factual, role in her husband's baptism, or to show how the *Licicaviki* converted to the new faith – like he had done in respect to the Danes?

The earliest surviving *Vita of Saint Adalbert*, compiled a mere thirty years later in either Liège or in Rome (*Vita prior*), assumed as an obvious point that the

---

A. Buko, "1050-lecie chrześcijaństwa na ziemiach polskich. Państwo Mieszka I i problem wczesnej chrystianizacji Polski w perspektywie badań archeologicznych", *Nauka* 2, 2016, p. 7–38; D. A. Sikorski, "Chrzest Polski i początki Kościoła w Polsce (do pierwszej połowy XI wieku)", [in:] *Chrzest – św. Wojciech – Polska. Dziedzictwo średniowiecznego Gniezna, Katalog wystawy*, ed. T. Janiak, Gniezno 2016, p. 25–38; P. Urbańczyk, *Co się stało w 966 roku?*, Poznań 2016.

2 Originally a lecture, this chapter is complemented by certain remarks and comments and is effectively a *miscellanea*.

3 *Widukindi monachi Corbeiensis rerum gestarum Saxonicarum libri tres*, ed. P. Hirsch et al. (ser.: Monumenta Germaniae Historica. Scriptores Rerum Germanicarum in usum scholarum separatim editi, 60), Hannover 1935, III, p. 65.

Piast *regnum* was not persevering with the "error of infidelity" (*infidelitatis errore preuenta*). For the author of the *Vita* of the missionary, former Bishop of Prague, and friend of Emperor Otto III (983/996–1002), the Polish Duke Boleslaus I the Brave (992–1025) and his subjects had long been among those residents of the country of Slavs (*Sclauoniae*) who "have the good faith and do good deeds"[4] (*bene credunt et ... bona opera agunt*). It is Boleslaus, after all, who offered the future martyr shelter at his court after Adalbert's *family was slaughtered* in Libice by the Bohemian Duke Boleslaus II the Pious (c. 930- 999) of the Přemyslid dynasty. As the *Vita* emphasizes, the Polish ruler buoyed him up with great promises and friendly assistance (*magnis promissis et amicis opibus eum solatur*).[5] Also Bruno of Querfurt, author of the second Vita (*Vita altera*) from about 1004, considered it needless to mention exactly how the Piast benefactor and protector of Saint Adalbert, and/or his country and subjects, had come to the "good faith", although the course of the narrative offered an adequate opportunity: i.e., contrary to the earlier version of the *Vita prior*, it makes a clear reference to Mieszko's conflict with Margrave Hodo, in the context of the complaint about the Christian life (*christiana religio*) in the empire of the Ottons. Mieszko's son, *princeps Bolezlaus*, is for Bruno a *christianissimus dominus* and there is no need to revert to the history of his baptism.[6] Such is the case also with the *Vita of Five Martyr Brethren* penned by Bruno, where Boleslaus is mentioned as a blameless Christian. With the five brethren arriving in the land of the *Poloni*, the *Vita* praises the Duke, explaining his Slavonic name as "Praiseworthy" (*nomen Bolizalao [...] quod interpretatum maior glorie sonat*), and lauds him for having originally sent Saint Adalbert on a mission to be carried out among the Prussians. After Adalbert's martyr's death, Boleslaus found a place of last repose for him in his dominion

---

4 This quotation and all following quotations from non-English sources were translated into English by the translator of the chapter.

5 S. *Adalberti Pragensis episcopi et martyris vita prior [antiquior]*, ed. J. Karwasińska (ser.: Monumenta Poloniae Historica. Nova Series, 4/1), Warszawa 1962, p. 3–47, here, p. 3 and 38; J. Hoffmann, *Vita Adalberti. Früheste Textüberlieferungen der Lebensgeschichte Adalberts von Prag*, Essen 2005, p. 126 and 153; for an English translation of the *Vita*, see: *Vitae Sanctorum Aetatis Conversionis Europae Centralis (saec. X–XI)/Saints of the Christianization Age of Central Europe (Tenth–Eleventh Centuries)*, ed. G. Klaniczay, Budapest 2013, p. 97–181; quotes from p. 97 and 165.

6 S. *Adalberti pragensis episcopi et martyris vita altera [posterior] auctore Brunone Querfurtensi*, ed. J. Karwasińska (ser.: Monumenta Poloniae Historica. Nova Series, 4/1), Warszawa 1969, p. 32 (full edition: *De terra Polanorum quam Bolizauus proximus christiano domino procurat*), and p. 63 (abridged edition: *De terra Polonorum quam Bolzet princeps christianissimus dominus procurat*).

(*qui cum solus ex omnibus nostri eui raram auem martyrem Adalbertum, et in predicatonem mittere, occisumque in suo regno collocare meruisset*). This *Vita* stresses, moreover, that not only did Boleslaus bid a wholehearted welcome to the brethren, but also ordained that an appropriate hermitage be built and furnished with everything necessary (*consuetudinem gratissimo animo et magno desiderio seruos Dei suscepit exhibensque illis omnem humanitatem, in quieta heremo qualem huic uite congruum locum ipsi inuenerunt, diuite uoluntate edificauit et uitę necessaria sine labore ministrauit*).[7] The Christianity of the *Poloni* and of their ruler seemed so obvious to Bruno that it never occurred to him that the "baptism" of Mieszko might be referred to, although it had taken place just a few dozen years earlier. Since Bruno's time, at the latest, the occurrence was taken note of in Polish annals (those from that time are not surviving) in a manifestly brief and lapidary fashion, typical of annalistic style, with no room for a more detailed story.[8]

Nearly ten years after Bruno, the Saxon chronicler Thietmar of Merseburg made the first-ever unambiguous and extensive reference to the Polish ruler's baptism. Thietmar did this as he made corrections to his chronicle, compiled in 1012–1018. The section describing Otto III's time originally mentioned Mieszko as a loyal ally to the Emperor. In the amended version, the chronicler added

---

7   *Vita quinque fratrum eremitarum seu vita vel passio Benedicti et Iohannis sociorumque suorum*, ed. J. Karwasińska (ser.: Monumenta Poloniae Historica. Nova Series, 4/3) Warszawa 1973, p. 6–84; here, p. 41–42. Also, cf. B. Kürbis, "Purpureae passionis aureus finis. Brun von Querfurt und die Fünf Märtyrerbrüder", [in :] *Europas Mitte um 1000*, vol. 1: *Beiträge zur Geschichte, Kunst und Archäologie*, ed. A. Wieczorek and H. M. Hinz Stuttgart 2000, p. 519–526 ; S. Trawkowski, "Die Eremiten in Polen am Anfang des 11. Jahrhunderts", [in:] *Svatý Vojtěch, Čechové a Europa*, ed. D. Třeśtik, J. Žemlička, Praha 1998, p. 167–179.

8   The origins/evolution and transmission/heritage of Polish annals has been subject to (not infrequently controversial) scientific debate; of the more recent considerations, cf. W. Drelicharz, *Idea zjednoczenia królestwa w średniowiecznym dziejopisarstwie polskim*, Kraków 2012, p. 22–47; and T. Jurek, "O czasie …", p. 35–38. The earliest preserved annals date to the early 12th c. (*Rocznik [świętokrzystki] dawny*) and the latter half of the 13th c. (*Rocznik kapituły krakowskiej*). The former dates the: *Dubrouka venit ad Miskonem* and: *Mysko dux baptizatur* events: *ad annum* 965 and 966, resp.; the latter refer the *Dubrouka ad Meskonem venit* and *Mesco dux Polonie baptizatur* to the same dates; cf. *Annales Cracoviensis priores cum kalendario/Najdawniejsze roczniki krakowskie i kalendarz*, ed. Z. Kozłowska-Budkowa (ser.: Monumenta Poloniae Historica. Nova Series, 5), Warszawa 1978, p. 4–5, 43.

more details regarding the Polish Duke, his rule, and his conversion. I reckon that these aspects came to the author's mind by way of association or, more plausibly perhaps, chance. Thietmar initially makes a reference to Widukind's account of Mieszko's Bohemian spouse and explains how the Duke introduced into his house a "noble spouse from Bohemia [...] whose life verily corresponded with what she essentially was. Her name, in Slavonic, was, namely, Dobrawa [i.e. Doubravka], which in the German language is interpretable as The-Good-One" (*a Boemia regione nobilem sibi uxorem [...] duxerat sororem. Quae, sicut sonuit in nomine, apparuit veraciter in re. Dobrawa enim Slavonice dicebatur, quod Teutonico sermone Bona interpretatur*).[9] Here, Thietmar once again demonstrates his command of Slavonic languages; it might be that he mentions the Přemyslid princess Doubravka for this very reason.[10] Referring to her "good-natured" personality, he prompts himself to explain the "very essence" of her, and so confronts the figure of a faithful Christian (*Christo fidelis*) against her husband who is "still entangled in various errors of heathendom" (is it not a really easy thing to do?). Doubravka, therefore, strove to render Mieszko "allied for her faith" (*hunc sibi sociaret in fide*) – which does not mean that he had not been christened yet or had been a complete unbeliever. Eventually, Doubravka's attempt to purposefully provoke her husband by breaking the observance of lent and "conciliate his zeal" (*placare contendit*) could only have been successful had he actually been a Christian already, knowledgeable of the rules of fasting. Thietmar's remark makes sense only if Mieszko attempted to prevent such a "trespass" (*delictum*). A misdemeanor once committed calls, from the standpoint of the chronicler and his readers, for explanation and apologies. Being a clergyman, Thietmar has it at the ready: as is known, the end justifies the means, so the story goes on – and has as-yet nothing to do with a history of the baptism. Thus, we learn that the "handsome fruit" yielded by Doubravka's "pious endeavours" (*fructum eligantem piae voluntatis*) has justified her trespass. "She thus worked on the conversion of her spouse" (*laboravit enim pro conversione coniugis sui*), whilst the "persistent

---

9 *Thietmari Merseburgensis episcopi chronicon*, ed. R. Holtzmann (ser.: Monumenta Germaniae Historica Scriptores rerum Germanicarum Nova Seria, 9), Berlin 1935, IV, p. 55–56; *Ottonian Germany. The Chronicon of Thietmar of Merseburg*, trans. D. A. Warner, Manchester, New York 2001.
10 Cf. D. Fraesdorff, *Der barbarische Norden. Vorstellungen und Fremdheitskategorien bei Rimbert, Thietmar von Merseburg, Adam von Bremen und Helmold von Bosau*, Berlin 2005, p. 139–142; H. W. Goetz, "Die Slawen in der Wahrnehmung Thietmars von Merseburg zu Beginn des 11. Jahrhunderts", *Lětopis* 62, 2015, p. 103–118; esp., p. 108–111.

incitation of his beloved spouse" (*dum crebro dilectae uxoris oratu*) eventually caused him to actually get rid of his "innate venom of Christianity" (*innatae infidelitatis toxicum evomuit*), "wiping-away the stain of the original sin by means of the holy baptism" (*in sacro baptismate nevam originalem detersit*). The story of the Piast's baptism described by Thietmar is, to my mind, a rather casual insert. The mention of Mieszko's and his people's conversion is, apparently, not a thoroughly conceived aspect of a well-thought-out story, or a significant event that is worth reminding. It seems, instead, to be a product of a narrative strategy where one content is associatively derived from the other. As part of this strategy, the chronicler combines his specific knowledge of the details (for instance, he knows that the name of the Bishop who arrived in Mieszko's dominion after his baptism was Jordan) with general abstracts, partly embellished with biblical phrases, which create for the world a *topos* of the conversion of the *Polani*.[11]

The first reference to this image ever made in Poland dates to a hundred years later and is to be found in the *Cronicae et gesta ducum sive principum Polonorum*, compiled in 1113–1116 by Gallus Anonymus. This chronicle presents the image in its modified form, complemented by new elements that most evidently come from other sources.[12] This earliest Polish chronicle attaches no extreme importance to the act of baptism and the associated occurrences. Although, as a letter of dedication in Book I states, the *Chronicle* was meant to deal "also with the deeds of bishops of the time of yore" (*veterum eciam gesta antistitum*)[13], its clergyman author quite expectedly praises "great Divine deeds" and devotes much attention, *inter alia*, to the Piast rulers' endeavors to win the pagan Pomeranians

---

11 Cf. also the various interpretations of history: J. Banaszkiewicz, "Dąbrówka christianissima i Mieszko poganin (Thietmar, IV, 55–56; Gall, I, 5–6)", [in:] *Nihil superfluum esse. Prace z dziejów średniowiecza ofiarowane Profesor Jadwidze Krzyżaniakowej*, ed. J. Strzelczyk, J. Dobosz, Poznań 2000, p. 85–93; P. Wiszewski, "Die Frau, der Fürst, die Taufe und die Quellen der Familientradition der Piasten (Thietmar, IV, 55–56) – Problementwurf", *Biuletyn Polskiej Misji Historycznej* 4, 2007, p. 163–168; S. Rosik, "Chrzest Mieszka I i Polaków, ale czy Polski? Postrzeganie konwersji władcy i społeczeństwa w świetle najdawniejszych przekazów (Thietmar z Merseburga, Gall Anonim)", *Kwartalnik Historyczny* 122, 2015, p. 833–840.

12 *Galli anonymi cronicae et gesta ducum sive principum Polonorum/Anonima tzw. Galla kronika czyli dzieje książąt i władców polskich*, ed. K. Maleczyński (ser.: Monumenta Poloniae Historica. Nova Series, 2), Kraków 1952; for an English translation of the chronicle, see: *Gesta principum Polonorum. The Deeds of the Princes of the Poles*, (ser.: Central European Medieval Text, 3), trans. and annotated P. W. Knoll, F. Schaer, Budapest 2003.

13 Ibidem, p. 2, resp. 5 (Eng. trans.).

for the Christian faith. However, the related accounts and references ought not to be read above all as stories about the history and development of the Piast Church or about the Christianization of the *Polani*. They basically seem to have been appended in the context of the work's main intention, which was to apotheosize the works and deeds of dukes, the secular rulers of the *regnum Poloniae*.[14] For instance, Gallus's account of Boleslaus the Brave's meeting with Otto III in the year 1000 undeniably puts the spotlight on the political elevation of the Duke of Poland to the rank of "the Emperor's brother and co-operator" (*fratrem et cooperatorem imperii*); the establishment of an archbishopric on this occasion is mentioned, as it were, in passing.[15] In the description of the unrest in the 1030s, the chronicler is moved by the political rebellion much more than by the populace's departure from the Christian faith. The main lesson Gallus had learned from "the destruction of Poland" (*de Polonie destructione*) was not the necessity to stay loyal to the Church, but rather the appeal to the *Polani* to preserve faithfulness to "their natural lords", i.e., the secular dukes (*dominis naturalibus fidem [...] servant*).[16]

As a duke in power, Mieszko is initially presented as a secular ruler who "oftentimes assailed the [neighboring] peoples all around" (*nationes per circuitum bello sepius attemptare*).[17] Afterwards, there follows a concise mention of his conversion – as if it were some abstract act. In fact, it was not a single act but a process extending over time. Mieszko long remained "involved in such errors of heathendom that, according to his custom, he abused VII [seven] wives" (*in tanto gentilitatis errore involvebatur, quod sua consuetudine VII uxoribus abutebatur*). He abandoned this "wicked custom" (*pravam consuetudinem*) only when he "requested into matrimony one exquisite Christian woman from Bohemia, her name being Dubrovka" (*christianissimam de Bohemia Dubroucam nomine in matrimonium requisivit*). She then demanded of Mieszko that he "accept the sacraments of the Christian faith" (*fidei christiane sacramenta suscepturum*) before she ever arrives, with her court, in Poland. However, once there, "she would refrain from federating with him maritally until he,

---

14 In respect of the recent studies on Gallus, cf. E. Mühle, "*Cronicae et gesta ducum sive principium Polonorum. Neue Forschungen zum so genannten Gallus Anonymus*", *Deutsches Archiv zur Erforschung des Mittelalters* 65, 2009, p. 459–496; idem, "*Exul apud vos et peregrinus. Najnowsze badania nad tzw. Gallem Anonimem*", *Studia Źródłoznawcze* 50, 2012, p. 89–98.
15 *Galli anonymi cronicae* ..., p. 20; *Gesta principum Polonorum* ..., p. 37.
16 Ibidem, p. 43, resp. 81 (Eng. trans.).
17 Ibidem, p. 15, resp. 29 (Eng. trans.).

gradually and diligently contemplating the Christian custom and the ecclesial ordinances, abnegated the errors of heathendom and co-united with the bosom of Church, the Mother" (*necdum tamen thoro sese maritiali federavit, donec ille paulatim consuetudinem christianitatis et religionem ecclesiastici ordinis diligenter contemplans, errorem gentilium abnegavit, seque gremio matris ecclesie counivit*). This expressly refers to the associative and "adventitious" history by Thietmar, which Gallus condenses into a more compact narrative. The figures of both, the Piast Duke and his Bohemian consort act in a more distinct manner, focused on the purpose they pursue. The narrative leads to the statement that no-one other than Mieszko has deserved the fame and glory for the grace of baptism, although his believing wife was the driving force behind it. Gallus puts this as follows: "in his time and through him did the heavenly light visit the Kingdom of the *Poloni*" (*suo tempore et per eum oriens ex alto regnum Poloni visitatvit*).[18] The highlighted role of the Duke in the conversion process is fully correspondent with the general assumption behind the work, which was to praise the deeds and acts of the Piast rulers and the dignity of *Polonia*. In addition, Gallus makes use of one more narrative motif – the legend of Mieszko's childhood blindness and regained sight on his seventh birthday.[19] The author was possibly inspired by a similar Rus' legend of the time, the *Tale of Bygone Years*, being a story of Volodimer's (Volodimer the Great, 980–1015) blindness. In Gallus, this known motif is transformed in a way so as to reveal to the reader, through the applied narrative technique, not only the secular/political, but also the spiritual/religious significance of the caesura marked by Mieszko's reign. What the blindness and regained sight are supposed to signify is: "Poland was blind before then, as it were, [...] yet thenceforth is to be illuminated by Mesco [Mieszko] and exalted above the adjacent nations" (*Poloniam sic antea fuisse quasi cecam [...], sed de cetero per Mesconem illuminandam et exaltandam super naciones contiguas*). Moreover, "Verily, Poland was blind prior thereto, knowing not the worship of the true God nor the doctrine of the faith, but by the [wondrously] illuminated Mesco has it become illuminated as well, for with him faithful, the Polish people was exempt from death in infidelity" (*Polonia ceca prius erat, que nec culturam*

---

18 Ibidem, p. 16, resp. 31 (Eng. trans.).
19 Cf. also J. Banaszkiewicz, "Dąbrówka *christianissima* ..."; P. Wiszewski, "Struktur, Fabel und Geschichte. Die Erzählung über das Wiedergewinnen des Augenlichtes von Mieszko I (*Galli Anonymi Cronica ducum Poloniae*, I, 4)", *Biuletyn Polskiej Misji Historycznej* 5, 2009, p. 215–237; S. Rosik, "Chrzest Mieszka ..."

veri Dei nec doctrinam fidei cognoscebat, sed per Meschonem illuminatum est et ipsa illuminata, quia eo credente Polonica gens de morte infidelitatis est exempta).[20]

Gallus's *Cronicae et gesta* offers a complete presentation of the caesura of Christianization, making a comprehensive use of it in its narrative; still, this author assigns no lesser (and perhaps even bigger) merit to Mieszko's son Boleslaus the Brave for the "increment of the true religion" (*ad vere religionis incrementum*); hence, the act of conversion is ultimately not highlighted in some particular way, given the entire context of the *gesta ducum et principum*.[21] This might have been the case simply because the chapter following the description of Mieszko's baptism states, on the occasion of the arrival of Saint Adalbert, that "the faith has already somewhat spread in Poland, and the sacred Church grown" (*iam in Polonia fidem pullulasse et sacnctam ecclesiam excrevisse*).[22]

In the *Chronica Polonorum*, written eighty or perhaps ninety years later (at the turn of the 13th c.) by Master (Magister) Vincentius (Wincenty Kadłubek), the occurrence of conversion further loses in importance within the framework of the narrative.[23] Vincentius was a clergyman too; the 1180s–1190s saw him lecture at the Cathedral School in Kraków, and then served as provost with the Collegiate Church of Sandomierz (attested as such as from 1206). In 1208–1218, he was Bishop of Kraków. He spent his last five years at the monastery in Jędrzejów. All the same, the chronicle he penned is *not* a history of the Church with special emphasis on the processes of conversion and Christianization. Vincentius deliberately made the *Chronica* a historical dissertation on a secular history of Poland, meant to present the reader, in the spirit of the period's *gesta*, a selection of memorable and imitable deeds of the ancestors, thereby legitimizing the actions of his contemporary rulers and reinforcing community awareness among the political elite. Yet Vincentius does not appear merely as a historian using his personal views to support an agenda of "historical politics". He would often pair his narration on historical events with another – i.e. moralizing – purpose. This author shapes his subject matter as a moralist and educator, striving

---

20 *Galli anonymi cronicae* …, p. 14; *Gesta principum Polonorum* …, p. 27, 29.
21 *Galli anonymi cronicae* …, p. 30; *Gesta principum Polonorum* …, p. 55.
22 *Galli anonymi cronicae* …, p. 17; *Gesta principum Polonorum* …, p. 35.
23 *Magistri Vincentii dicti Kadłubek Chronica Polonorum*, ed. M. M. Plezia (ser.: Monumenta Poloniae Historica. Nova Series, 11), Kraków 1994. For a review of recent studies Master Vincentius/Wincenty Kadłubek, see: my Introduction to *Die Chronik der Polen des Magisters Vincentius/Magistri Vincentii Chronica Polonorum*, ed. E. Mühle (ser.: Ausgewählte Quellen zur Geschichte des Mittelalters, Freiherr-vom-Stein-Gedächtnisausgabe, 48), Darmstadt 2014, p. 13–86.

to fill the public life and customs of his country with ethical values, legal norms, and Christian ideals. He did this to confront his Duke with the criteria of ideal power and authority, whilst exhorting his compatriots to love their homeland and care for the commonweal, or public good. The ruler and the political elite were expected to accept the law and virtues as the uppermost values without which, in his view, no value-based community, the *patria* and the *res publica* – or, the *regnum Poloniae* – could possibly blossom.[24] It is in this spirit that Master Vincentius wanted to bring up and educate the readers: not in line with a narrowly conceived ecclesial/religious education, but in a broadly-comprehended humanistic fashion, inspired by the heritage of Antiquity.

Seen from this perspective, Vincentius imbues the history of religious conversion with a peculiar antique-rhetorical tint. Apart from presenting it in a weird dialogical from, he has embroidered its language and style, applying a hardly bearable mannerism, described as *ornatus difficilis*. He immerses himself deep down into the early history of Poland, which could apparently be traced back as far as Antiquity; an account of this early history filled the entire Book I of his *Chronicle*. It is only at the beginning of the second that Vincentius makes a reference to the legend of the Piasts, known from Gallus Anonymus. Vincentius, to be specific, does not approach Christianization as a historical caesura that ultimately ensures salvation, but foremost refers it to the historical connections and contacts between Poles and ancient Greeks and Romans. This translates into a further relativizing of the momentousness and significance of the historical caesura of Christianization and conversion, as they are seen (whilst also relativized) in Gallus.

It is significant that – in the utterance of Matthew, his dialogue partner – Vincentius deprives the story of little Mieszko's seven-year-long blindness of its symbolic meaning, which is present in Gallus's account. The miracle of the boy regaining his sight is not primarily comprehended in terms of a religious illumination of Poland, but as an epitome of the repentance of the young Duke. This is reflected in his sending away of his "seven harlots" and "coupled himself by matrimony with a [woman] from Bohemia, named Dambrovca" (*de Bohemia quandam Dambroucam nomine matrimonio copulat*).[25] Up to this moment, the story is no different from Thietmar's account: the latter also assumed that it was only at the marriage stage that Mieszko could have actually been won

---

24 Cf. E. Mühle, "'Przezornie bowiem powinni władcy władać', czyli jak funkcjonowała monarchia piastowska w XII-XIII wieku", *Roczniki Historyczne* 79, 2013, p. 41–55.
25 *Magistri Vincentii ... Chronica ...*, p. 37; the following three quotations are cited after ibidem.

for the faith. Master Vincentius describes this as follows: "The felicitous consortium with her causes the ices of infidelity to thaw, and the wild-vine of our heathens turns into a noble young grapevine spring" (*Cuius felici consortio glacies infidelitatis dissoluitur et nostrorum labrusca gentilium in uere uitis palmitem transmigrat*). Vincentius (though he may well not have known the Merseburg Bishop's chronicle) complements the Gallus account – which somewhat differed from Thietmar's – by adding:

> For she [i.e., Doubravka], sincerely attached to the Catholic faith, would not be willing to be married ere the entire Kingdom of Poland, together with the King himself, have received the mark of the Catholic profession. She has namely learned [this being the author's own comment: Vincentius willingly presented himself as an extremely learned man] that the diversity of cult was one of the impediments to matrimony. Thus, the first King [*sic!*] of Poland, Mesco, received the grace of baptism. (*Huic enim catholice fidei amantissime non prius nubere collibuit, quam uniuersum Polonie regnum cum ipos rege Christiane professionis suscepit caracterem. Didicerat namque dispar cultus unum erat impeditiuorum matrimonii. Primus itaque rex Mesco gratiam baptismi suscepit*).

In line with the specific division of roles designed by Vincentius for the partners in the dialogue within the narrative frame, the history told by Matthew had to be commented on by his interlocutor, John. And it is this narrative scheme that implies the latter's summary of Mieszko's merits from the standpoint of religious history; John emphasizes that:

> He was the primary and the worthiest of all the kings; it was him through whom the radiant light of a new star inundated this homeland of ours; through him, that a font of grace so great flowed down onto the bottom of our quagmire. (*Omnium omnino hic primus regum ac serenissimus, per quem huic patrie noui iubar sideris est infusum; per quem tante fons gratie ad nostri usque luti alueos manauit*).

This is another reference to Mieszko's blindness; again, like in Gallus, we are reassured, in metaphorical terms, that the time before the baptism was one of "ignorance of all of us, of our error" (*nostre insipiente, nostri erroris uniuersitatem*), "the darkness of our obstinacy" (*nostre obstinationis*); now, however, "the light of grace" (*gratie lux*) is rising.[26]

The accounts by Gallus and Vincentius, fairly extensive as they are, were further abridged in the 13th and early 14th c. Written in the 1250s by Wincenty of Kielcza, a Dominican friar, the *Vitae of Saint Stanislaus* (both the *Vita minor* and the *Vita maior* were compiled after 1253 – after the canonization of the Kraków Bishop murdered in 1079) contain no story of the christening of Mieszko, merely

---

26 Ibidem, p. 37–38.

mentioning the ruler as Poland's "first Christian".[27] The *Chronicle of Dzierżwa*, probably written in 1306–1320 by a Kraków Franciscan friar, largely expands on Vincentius' *Chronicle* and offers very brief, summarized descriptions of the events. One short sentence directly refers to Vincentius ("From Siemomysł, begotten is the famous Mieszko the Blind, who was being brought up in his blindness of seven years")[28] and then the reader is referred, for more detailed information, to the *Annales Polonorum*. As we can read there, "he [Mieszko] was explained how every night he had copulated with seven concubines, and how afterwards he led Dambrowka home as a wife [...] and how through her the King [sic!] and the people was converted to the faith" (*quomodo illuminatus sit, quomodo septem pelicibus omni nocte abutebatur et quomodo ultimo duxit Dambrowkam [...] et qualiter per ipsam rex et populus conversus est ad fidem*).[29] The occurrence is also presented, again very concisely, in the earlier part of the *Chronica Poloniae Maioris* (*Chronicle of Greater Poland* [i.e., Wielkopolska]), dated late 13th c. This source mentions Mieszko's blindness without no comment or attempt at interpreting it; there is a reference to the marriage with Doubravka, which allegedly took place in 931 (Mieszko's consort being erroneously referred to as a sister of Wenceslaus I), and ascertains, briefly and concisely: "Advised to this end by his spouse, [Mieszko] in the following year accepted the sacred baptism, with the entire people of Lechiti, i.e., the Polish people, out of inspiration by Divine grace" (*Anno sequenti cum tota gente Lechitarum seu Polonica uxore suadente et divina gracia inspirante sacrum baptisma suscepit*).[30] The dating, 932, is a novelty – a version that followed from some other incorrect annalistic records. A dating of the event is also found in the *Polish-Silesian Chronicle* (*Chronicon Polono-Silesiacum*) compiled by a Cistercian monk from Lubiąż in the 1280s probably, on commission of Silesian Henry IV the Righteous (Henryk IV Probus, 1266–1290) from the Polish Piast dynasty. It moreover offers an

---

27 *Vita sancti Stanislai episcopi Cracoviensis (Vita minor)*, ed. W. Kętrzyński (ser.: Monumenta Poloniae Historica, 4), Lwów 1884, reprinted: Warszawa 1961, p. 253–285; here, p. 269: *de Polonia dux primus baptizatus*; *Vita sancti Stanislai Cracoviensis episcopi (Vita maior). Auctore fratre Vincentio de ordine fratrum praedicatorum*, ed. W. Kętrzyński, [in:] ibidem, p. 362–438; here, p. 364: *primus fuit Christianus*.

28 *Chronica Dzirsvae/Kronika Dzierzwy*, ed. K. Pawłowski (ser.: Monumenta Poloniae Historica. Nova Series, 15), Kraków 2013, p. 22: *De Zemomisl autem famosus ille Mesko cecus gignitur, cecus septennio educatur*; cf. *Magistri Vincentii ... Chronica ...*, p. 37.

29 *Chronica Dzirsvae...*, p. 22.

30 *Chronica Poloniae Maioris/Kronika Wielkopolska*, ed. B. Kürbis (ser.: Monumenta Poloniae Historica. Nova Series, 8), Warszawa 1970, p. 16.

extremely concise account of the events otherwise known from the annals by Master Vincentius and Gallus Anonymus. What the Silesian chronicle says is, "The first Duke and King of the Poles, *Mesico* [*sic!*], received the grace of baptism in the year of our Lord 966" (*Primus itaque Polonorum princeps et rex Mesico baptismi graciam suscepit anno Domini 966*).[31]

Hence, the question becomes: do these late attempts at dating, or the lack of any dating – as in Gallus and Vincentius – merely ensue from the fact that both of the earliest annalists included no dating at all in their chronicles, as a matter of principle, whereas the *Chronica Poloniae Maioris* basically attached dates to its records from the year 913 onwards? Otherwise, the actual reason might have been that the earliest accounts of Mieszko's marriage with Doubravka and of his baptism, as mentioned or described in the annals, were not part of a wider knowledge or awareness in medieval Poland. The scarce records related to the Piast period compiled after Vincentius' time do not provide more information compared to the earlier sources and known annalistic records. There, the focus on Mieszko's baptism is even smaller and is ascribed lesser importance than in Gallus and Vincentius. What may be concluded is that the historical caesura of the Christianization and the baptism of Mieszko, having occurred in 965, 966 or 967, every so often strongly highlighted by modern historiographers and history-oriented politics, did not quite enjoy a worthy place in Piast memory between the 12th and the 14th c. Nor did Mieszko's contemporaries attach a comparable significance to the event. They satisfied themselves with the view that the Piasts and their subjects had always been Christians and their conversion did not require detailed description or historical-and-political justification. Or perhaps they felt ashamed that their ancestors had not become Christian much earlier. This would possibly explain their refraining from excessive notoriety around a conversion to Christianity that was delayed compared to many other European peoples.

Nonetheless, the late-medieval chroniclers took a different stance. The *Chronica principum Poloniae*, dated to the 1380s, offers a rather early instance of detailed compilation of Gallus Anonymus' and Master Vincentius' accounts, referring the occurrence in question to the year 966.[32] In the 15th c., Jan Długosz

---

31 *Kronika Polska*, ed. L. Ćwikliński (ser.: Monumenta Poloniae Historica, 3), Lwów 1878, reprinted: Warszawa 1961, p. 604–656; here, p. 616.

32 *Kronika książąt polskich*, ed. Z. Węclewski (ser.: Monumenta Poloniae Historica, 3), Lwów 1878, reprinted: Warszawa 1961, p. 428–578; here, p. 437–438.

became the precursor of this new historiographic tradition: he provides us with an altogether detailed description of Mieszko's baptism, which he dates to 965: the preparations for the event, its course and effects, giving free rein to his literary muse in describing the surrounding details.[33]

Translated by Tristan Korecki

---

[33] *Ioannis Dlugossii Annales seu Cronicae incliti regni Poloniae. Liber primus, liber secundus*, ed. J. Dąbrowski, Warszawa 1964, p. 175–178.

Marian Rębkowski

The beginnings of Christianity in Pomerania

Abstract: This chapter discusses the earliest traces of Christianity's spread into Pomerania (Pomorze) during the two centuries before a lasting Church organization was finally built in the 12th c. As evidenced through archaeological finds, already in the late 10th /early 11th c. do we observe an erosion of the traditional sepulchral behaviors and the appearance of new grave and burial-site forms among the Slavic Pomeranians. This phenomenon might be associable with the stronger penetration of Christianity into this region, i.a., during the short-lived conquest of Pomerania by the Piasts at the end of the 10th c. Moreover, the rhythm of economic development in the early-urban residential merchant settlements in this Baltic region, ones which functioned in the pre-state (tribal) period, implied a regular arrival of merchants, including Christian ones. In contrast to the early-Piast monarchy, the penetration of Christianity into Pomerania before the 12th c. was not supported by powerful structures of centralized power.

Keywords: archeology, Pomeranian Slavs, paganism, Christianization, early medieval merchant settlements

With respect to the expansion of *Christianitas* in Europe, one may observe that Pomerania (Pomorze) was included at a very late date. The region was part of the "pagan enclave" that stretched along the southern coast of the Baltic Sea well into the 12th c. From today's standpoint, it is only the period of 1124–1140 - marked by the missions of Bishop Otto of Bamberg (1124/1125, 1128) and the resulting establishment of the Pomeranian Bishopric with its seat in Wolin (1140) - that can be recognized as a breakthrough moment in the reception of Christianity. The creation of an episcopal see marked the beginning of a durable (as time was to show) ecclesial administration related to the Duchy of Pomerania.[1] Things developed differently in the eastern part of the region, situated along today's Gulf of Gdańsk (Pomorze Gdańskie), which established stable bonds with Poland earlier on: thus it will not be covered in depth here.

The twelfth-century dating of the baptism of Pomerania clearly does not mean that the first people who professed Christianity turned up in that part

---

1 See: J. Petersohn, *Der südliche Ostseeraum im kirchlich-politischen Kräftespiel des Reichs, Polens und Dänemarks vom 10. bis 13. Jahrhundert. Mission – Kirchenorganisation – Kultpolitik*, Köln 1979, p. 211–484.

of Baltic lands only in the 12th c. There are several arguments to support this remark: firstly, Pomerania was conquered by the Piasts in the late 10th c.; a Polish Bishopric was subsequently set up in Kołobrzeg in 1000, however, it proved ephemeral. Secondly, there are other premises, including archaeological sources, indicative of Christianity's penetration of Pomerania long before the first half of the 12th c. Hence, the appearance of the new religion locally should be shifted, roughly, one and a half centuries earlier. This chapter seeks to trace the earliest years of Christianity's spread into Pomerania – a period that was crowned by the commencement of building of a lasting Church organization in the first half of the 12th c.

To consider this problem relying only on written sources, one would have to assume that Christianity began penetrating into Pomerania in the late 10th and early 11th c. There are several premises in favor of this conclusion: the foremost being that the region was conquered in the last decades of the 10th c. by the first two Christian rulers of Poland, Mieszko I (c. 960–992) and his son Boleslaus I the Brave (Bolesław Chrobry, 992–1025).[2] In the aftermath, a Polish Bishopric was established at the Congress of Gniezno in the year 1000, with its seat in Kołobrzeg, which was most probably meant to encompass the entire land of Pomerania. However, the project did not survive long.[3] That Christians turned up in the milieu of pagan Pomeranian Slavs is also attested by somewhat later information from Adam of Bremen, who in Book II of his *Gesta Hammaburgensis ecclesiae pontificum* mentions a locality named *Iumne* (i.e. Wolin). Apart from the Slavs, the city was said to be populated by Greeks, barbarians, and Saxons – so long as they refrained from flaunting their Christianity.[4] Included in this body of written sources is also the one contained in the *First Vita of Saint Adalbert*,

---

2 *Historia Pomorza*, vol. 1: *Do roku 1466*, part 1–2, ed. G. Labuda, Poznań 1972, p. 307–309; J. Strzelczyk, *Mieszko Pierwszy*, Poznań 1992, p. 81–83; G. Labuda, *Mieszko I*, Wrocław 2002, p. 72; B. Śliwiński, *Początki Gdańska. Dzieje ziem nad zachodnim brzegiem Zatoki Gdańskiej w I połowie X wieku*, Gdańsk 2009, p. 23–31.

3 Thietmar, *Kronika Thietmara*, ed. M. Z. Jedlicki, Poznań 1953, Book IV, chap. 45; G. Labuda, "Aspekty polityczne i kościelne tzw. 'zjazdu gnieźnieńskiego' w roku 1000", [in:] *Ziemie polskie w X wieku i ich znaczenie w kształtowaniu się nowej mapy Europy*, ed. H. Samsonowicz, Kraków 2000, p. 17–34; J. Petersohn "Der Akt von Gnesen im Jahre 1000 und die Errichtung des Bistums Salz-Kolberg. Zur historischen Substanz eines Jubiläums", *Baltische Studien* NF 87, 2001, p. 24–35.

4 *Adami Bremensis Gesta Hammaburgensis ecclesiae pontificum*, ed. B. Schmeidler (ser.: Scriptores rerum Germanicarum in usum scholarum ex MGH separatum editi), Hannover 1917, II, p. 19: *Est sane maxima omnium quas Europa claudit civitatum, quam incolunt Sclavi cum aliis gentibus, Graecis et barbaris. Nam et advenae Saxones*

where the visit of the future martyr (murdered by Prussians in 997) to an *urbs Gyddanyzc* is mentioned, this description generally being connected to Gdańsk.⁵ Taking these facts as the point of departure, let us first try and answer whether the appearance of Christianity in Pomerania can indeed be dated to the late 10th c. Also, let us ask when the new religion could have become influential, or outright adopted by the local inhabitants. Given the very limited information contained in the written sources, we are compelled to consider the issue primarily on the basis of archaeological sources, whose three categories come into play: cemeteries (enabling us to trace how funeral customs evolved), discoveries of religious symbols and objects associated with the celebration of the cult, and sites of cult activity – i.e. churches. Before passing to the heart of the matter at hand, we should provide some brief comments on the interpretations derived from analysis of the changes observed in the funeral customs and on researchers' attempts at associating some of them with the spread of Christianity. One has to remark that no uniform Christian funeral rite, lasting from Antiquity into the Middle Ages, existed. In the fully Christianized medieval European countries, the major features of the rite – approached by contemporaries as the *mos christianorum*, a custom or usage typical of Christians⁶ – included inhumation and situating the corpses on their backs, orientated along an East-West axis (with the heads pointing west). The internment sites were located beside churches, and thereby, at the centers of settlements.⁷ I myself am convinced, though, that in

---

    param cohabitandi legem acceperunt, si tamen christianitatis titulum ibi morantes non publicaverint. Omnes enim adhuc paganicis ritibus oberrant.

5 S. *Adalberti Pragensis episcopi et martyris vita prior*, ed. J. Karwasińska (ser.: Monumenta Poloniae Historica. Series Nova, 4/1), Warszawa 1962, p. 27; see: G. Labuda, *Święty Wojciech*, Wrocław 2000, p. 184–190; more recently B. Śliwiński, *Początki Gdańska*, p. 11–14.

6 *Ebonis Vita S. Ottonis episcopi Babenbergensis*, ed. J. Wikarjak, K. Liman (ser.: Monumenta Poloniae Historica. Series Nova, 7/2), Warszawa 1969, II, 12: *sicut mos est omnium christianorum*.

7 The features characteristic of medieval Christian funeral rite have been dealt with by abundant literature. Exemplary studies include: M. Müller-Wille, *Death and burial in medieval Europe*, Lund 1993, p. 10; H. Zoll-Adamikowa, "Formy konwersji Słowiańszczyzny wczesnośredniowiecznej a problem przedpiastowskiej chrystianizacji Małopolski", [in:] *Chrystianizacja Polski południowej*, Kraków 1995, p. 133–134; F. S. Paxton, *Christianizing Death. The creation of a Ritual Process in Early Medieval Europe*, Ithaca 1996; J. Kieffer-Olsen, "Christianity and Christian Burial. The religious background and the transition from paganism to Christianity from the perspective of a churchyard archaeologist", [in:] *Burial & Society. The Chronological and Social Analysis of Archaeological Burial Data*, ed. C. Kjel Jensen, K. Høilund Nielsen, Aarhus

the initial years of Christianization, practice must have diverged from religious custom in this respect.

* * *

There is a peculiarity to the culture and economy of the Slavic communities inhabiting Pomerania in the early Middle Ages, one identifiable in a number of aspects, as when compared to e.g. Greater Poland (Wielkopolska). The local specificity manifested itself in the early urbanization processes that dated back to the tribal period (9th c. at the latest). This resulted from Pomerania having become part of the "Baltic Sea-region economic zone", which was formed by the activity of Scandinavian people.[8] A number of the crafts-and-trade settlements emerging at the time in the lands spreading along the Baltic coast were multiethnic, and thus there was a religious diversity among their dwellers. This phenomenon is well illustrated by the diversity of the funeral rites; inhumation appeared among them, as is clearly inferred from the graveyards situated beside the crafts-and-trade settlements, both those found in Scandinavia (Birka, Hedeby, and elsewhere) and in the Slav-populated areas (Gross Strömkendorf

---

1997, p. 185-189; H. Valk, "About the transitional period in the burial customs in the region of the Baltic Sea", [in:] *Culture Clash or Compromise? The Europeanisation of the Baltic Sea Area 1100-1400 AD*, (ser.: Acta Visbyensia, 11), ed. N. Blomkvist, Visby 1998, p. 237-239; A. Schülke, "'Die Christianisierung' als Forschungsproblem der südwestdeutschen Gräberarchäologie", *Zeitschrift für Archäologie des Mittelalters* 27-28, 1999-2000, p. 115; D. Quast, "Christianisierung im archäologischen Befund. Ein Vergleich unterschiedlicher Regionen Mitte-, Nord- und Osteuropas", [in:] *Zwischen den Zeiten. Archäologische Beiträge zur Geschichte des Mittelalters in Mittelauropa*, ed. J. Pfrommer, R. Schreg, Rahden 2001, p. 234; M. Rębkowski, *Die Christianisierung Pommerns. Eine archäologische Studie*, Bonn 2011, p. 63-68.

8 L. Leciejewicz, *Początki nadmorskich miast na Pomorzu Zachodnim*, Wrocław 1962; idem, "Early towns of the Baltic Slavs and their Scandinavian parallels", [in:] *Archaeology and History of the Middle Ages*, Forli 1996, p. 47-53; W. Łosiński, "W sprawie genezy osiedli wczesnomiejskich u Słowian nadbałtyckich", *Slavia Antiqua* 35, 1994, p. 101-128; idem, "Zur Genese der frühstädtische Zentren bei den Ostseeslawen", [in:] *Burg – Burgstadt – Stadt. Zur Genese mittelalterlicher nichtagrarischen Zentren in Ostmitteleuropa*, ed. H. Brachmann, Berlin 1995, p. 68-91; M. Bogucki, "Viking Age ports of trade in Poland", *Estonian Journal of Archaeology* 8, 2004, p. 100-127; H. Jöns, "Ports and emporia of the southern coast from Hedeby to Usedom and Wolin", [in:] *Wulstan's Voyage. The Baltic Sea Region in the Early Viking Age as Seen from Shipboard, Maritime Culture of the North*, vol. 2, ed. A. Englert, A. Trakadas, Roskilde, p. 160-181; S. Kleingärtner, *Die frühe Phase der Urbanisierung an der südlichen Ostseeküste im ersten nachchristlichen Jahrtausend* (ser.: Studien zur Siedlungsgeschichte und Archäologie der Ostseegebiete, 13), Neumünster 2014.

being one example).⁹ It is in this context that we should identify the oldest known early-medieval skeleton graves from Pomerania, ones discovered between the cremation burial mounds in Świelubie near Kołobrzeg and dated to the latter half of the 9th c. The entire local settlement context indicates that in all likelihood a crafts-and-trade settlement functioned somewhere in the vicinity; the buried dead ought probably to be identified with Scandinavians.¹⁰ The single burial in Kępsko near Bobolice is of a similar date.¹¹

Whether or not the fact that a few inhumations at each of the two cemeteries dated to the second half of the 9th c. may be approached as testimony to eschatological beliefs remains unsolved. However, it need be noted that the 9th c. is also the identified date for the fragments of Tating jugs discovered in Wolin and in the nearby (though, in fact, located just outside Pomerania) Menzlin on the Peene, the latter being another crafts-and-trade settlement from the period concerned. Jugs of the Tating type, embellished with the repeating motif of an isosceles cross made of tinfoil, were manufactured in the area between the north of France and the Rhine and distributed almost exclusively in northern and north-western Europe.¹² Taking into account the decorative art and ornamentation styles, the scarce number of finds, and the context in which the earliest specimens were

---

9   E.g., A. S. Gräslund, *Birka IV. The Burial Customs*, Stockholm 1980; U. Arends, S. Eisenschmidt, *Die Gräber von Haithabu*, vol. 1-2, Neumünster 2010; M. Gerds, *Das Gräberfeld des frühmittelalterlichen Seehandelsplatzes von Groß Strömkendorf, Lkr. Nordostmecklenburg* (ser.: Frühmittelalterliche Archäologie zwischen Ostsee und Mittelmeer, 6), Wiesbaden 2015.
10 W. Łosiński, *Początki wczesnośredniowiecznego osadnictwa grodowego w dorzeczu dolnej Parsęty (VII-X/XI w.)*, Wrocław 1972, p. 263, 270; idem, "Wczesnośredniowieczny zespół osadniczy w Bardach i Świelubiu pod Kołobrzegiem", *Koszalińskie Zeszyty Muzealne* 3, 1973, p. 102-119; H. Zoll-Adamikowa, *Wczesnośredniowieczne cmentarzyska ciałopalne Słowian na terenie Polski*, part 1: *Źródła*, Wrocław 1975, p. 229-232.
11 J. Olczak, K. Siuchniński, *Źródła archeologiczne do studiów nad wczesnośredniowiecznym osadnictwem grodowym na terenie województwa koszalińskiego*, vol. 2, Poznań 1968, p. 75, no. 40; H. J. Eggers, *Funde der wendisch-wikingischen Zeit in Pommern*, Kiel 1978, p. 178.
12 H. Stilke, "Tatinger Ware", [in:] *Handbuch zur mittelalterlichen Keramik in Nordeuropa*, vol. 1, ed. H. Lüdtke, K. Schietzel, Neumünster 2001, p. 257-270; U. Müller, "Tatinger Ware im Gebiet des Mare Balticum", [in:] *Aus der Frühgeschichte des südwestlichen Ostseegebietes*, ed. G. Mangelsdorf (ser.: Greifswalder Mitteilungen, 5), Frankfurt am Main 2002, p. 9-24; U. Schoknecht, *Menzlin. Ein frühgeschichtlicher Handelsplatz an der Peene*, Berlin 1977, p. 111-112, 136, Taf. 50; B. Stanisławski, *Garncarstwo wczesnośredniowiecznego Wolina, a rekonstrukcja procesów kulturowych*, Wolin 2004, typescript, p. 97.

discovered (close to, or not far from, the supposed manufacture sites), it may be guessed that the original purpose of such jugs or pitchers could have related to the Christian liturgy (Eucharist or baptism). In any case, it is hard to clearly define whether the finds from the Baltic-area crafts-and-trade settlements actually attest to a reduction of their original function into the secular sphere, or if they had perhaps ensued from Christianity penetrating into local clusters of the population. The fact that finds of this sort have also been identified for richly furnished graves, both skeletal and cremation ones, would rather point to a reduced function of pitchers in the Norman elitist milieu, though these objects might still have been used in religious rites or ceremonials.[13]

All these scarce, almost singular discoveries hitherto identifiable as dating to the 9th c. attest to nothing more than the fact that Christians could have turned up at the period's trading centers in the Baltic area. It does however seem all but certain that this implied no impact on the native Slavic people inhabiting the Pomeranian coast of the Baltic. No essential change in the funeral rite or ceremonies, nor any premises in favor of such evolution, can be reported for that period whatsoever.

An evident turn in this respect stands out in the last years of the 10th c., or in the late 10th/early 11th c., when an erosion of the traditional sepulchral behaviors among the Slavic Pomeranians is clearly observable, as evidenced through archaeological finds. This erosion is visible owing to the appearance of new grave and burial-site forms which diversified the funeral rite. This diversity proved to be regional for the entire 11th c. In the context of the issues here considered, the appearance in that period of a group of flat-surfaced skeletal burial sites in the lower Oder River area seems to be a phenomenon of particular importance. Apart from inhumation, these graveyards have a lot more in common. All these necropolises (including Wolin-Mühlenberg (Młynówka); Lubin; Usedom (Uznam)/"Am Hain"; Cedynia, site 2a; Stargard; Drense) were situated next to considerable settlement centers of the stronghold type (*gród* in Polish); the Wolin emporium was at the time an important crafts-and-trade center with an early urban character.[14] It is quite probable that the earlier phase

---

13 J. Staecker, "Legends and Mysteries. Reflections on the Evidence for the Early Mission in Scandinavia", [in:] *Visions of the Past. Trends and Traditions in Swedish Medieval Archaeology*, ed. H. Andersson, P. Carelli, L. Ersgård, Stockholm 1997, p. 430–431; idem, "Die Christianisierung des westlichen Ostseeraumes – die archäologische Perspektive", [in:] *Culture Clash or Compromise?*, p. 212–214.

14 J. Wojtasik, *Wczesnośredniowieczne cmentarzysko na wzgórzu 'Młynówka' w Wolinie*, Szczecin 1968; idem, "Cmentarzysko wczesnośredniowieczne na wzgórzu 'Młynówka' w Wolinie (badania z 1969 r.)", *Materiały Zachodniopomorskie* 16, 1970, p. 289–323;

of the cemetery site in Dębczyno near Białogard, the necropolis of Santok and Stolpe upon Oder were of a similar character. A trace of such similarity is discernible also for the burial found not far from the stronghold of Kołobrzeg. The latter four sites date most probably to the 11th c.[15]

Some of the aforementioned skeletal graveyards, where the method of handling the dead bodies was completely different from what was common practice among the Baltic Slavs – i.e. cremation – are akin to the traditional burial grounds in terms of situation: they were set up close to, if not within sites where cremated corpses were buried. Another extremely characteristic feature of these necropolises is their quite irregular and diverse orientation of the graves vis-à-vis the cardinal points, which suggests there was no governing rule in this respect. The dead bodies were usually placed in the graves on their backs, their hands stretched out along their bodies. Objects potentially identifiable as actual grave goods, scarce as they are, have rather rarely been found along with the skeletons. Traces of coffins or other wooden grave constructions are also rare with the burial sites.[16]

W. Łosiński, J. Wojtasik, "Cmentarzysko wczesnośredniowieczne na wzgórzu 'Młynówka' w Wolinie" (review of the publication), *Sprawozdania Archeologiczne* 22, 1970, p. 501–504; W. Filipowiak, "Badania archeologiczno-konserwatorskie w Lubinie, pow. Wolin", *Materiały Zachodniopomorskie* 5, 1959, p. 319–320; F. Biermann, *Bootsgrab – Brandgrab – Kammergrab. Die slawischen Gräberfelder von Usedom im Kontext der früh- und hochmittelalterlichen Bestattungssitten in Mecklenburg und Pommern* (ser.: Archäologie und Geschichte im Ostseeraum, 7), Rahden 2009, p. 20–39, 54–97; A. Porzeziński, *Wczesnośredniowieczne cmentarzysko szkieletowe na stanowisku 2a w Cedyni, województwo zachodniopomorskie*, Szczecin 2006; V. Schmidt, *Drense. Eine Hauptburg der Ukrane* (ser.: Beiträge zur Ur- und Frühgeschichte der Bezirke Rostock, Schwerin und Neubrandenburg, 22), Berlin 1989, p. 18–22; M. Majewski, "Ecclesia sub ecclesia – czyli o świątyni odkrytej pod kościołem augustiańskim w Stargardzie", [in:] *Kościoły w dobie chrystianizacji*, ed. M. Rębkowski (ser.: Wolińskie Spotkania Mediewistyczne, 3), Szczecin 2016, p. 247–249.

15 A. Sikorski, T. Szczurek, "Monety z wczesnośredniowiecznego cmentarzyska szkieletowego w Dębczynie na Pomorzu", [in:] *Moneta i kontakty mennicze w rejonie Morza Bałtyckiego XIII-XVIII w.*, ed. A. Musiałowski, Toruń 2002, p. 7–32; H. Kóčka-Krenz, A. Sikorski, "Grób 'księżniczki' z Dębczyna koło Białogardu w woj. koszalińskim (stan. 53)", [in:] *Kraje słowiańskie w wiekach średnich. Profanum i sacrum*, ed. H. Kóčka-Krenz, W. Łosiński, Poznań 1998, p. 525–535; J. Brzeżycki, "Cmentarzysko i grodziska średniowieczne na stanowisku 2 Santoku", [in:] *Santockie zamki*, ed. D. Rymar, Z. Czarnuch (ser. Biblioteczka Nadwarciańskiego Rocznika Historyczno-Archiwalnego, 3), Gorzów Wielkopolski 1997, p. 7–41; *Kołobrzeg. Wczesne miasto nad Bałtykiem*, ed. L. Leciejewicz, M. Rębkowski, Warszawa 2007, p. 161, 163.

16 M. Rębkowski, *Die Christianisierung Pommerns...*, p. 79–81, 106.

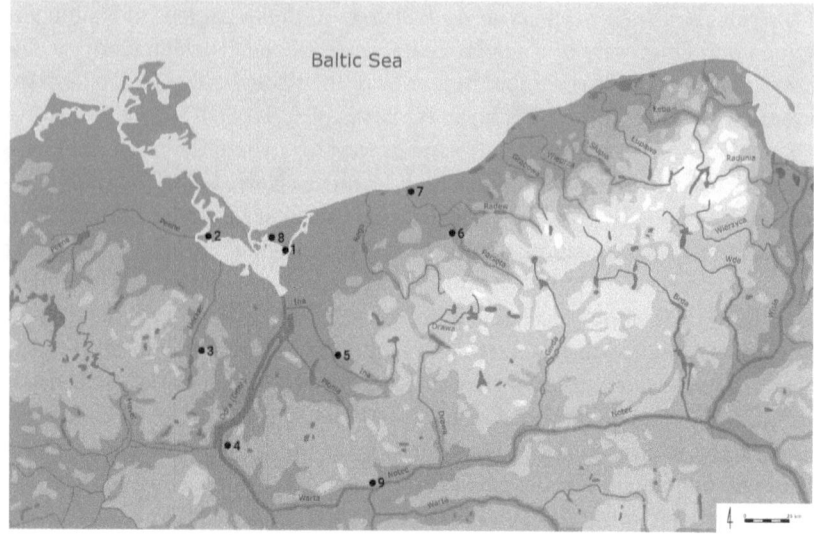

Fig. 1: The spread of flat skeletal burial grounds in the 11th c.
1 – Wolin-Młynówka, 2 – Usedom-Am Hain; 3 – Drense; 4 – Cedynia 2a; 5 – Stargard; 6 – Dębczyno; 7 – Kołobrzeg; 8 – Lubin; 9 – Santok

In terms of the problems central to this paper, these necropolises raise above all the following question: is their appearance in the lower Oder River and Kołobrzeg area in the late 10th and early 11th c. at all associable with the influence (albeit indirect) of Christianity? We may begin our answer with the skepticism related, for instance, to the frequently voiced opinions that inhumation contributed to social prestige in certain parts of the *Barbaricum*[17], and thus did not necessarily reflect Christian eschatological content. Such a skeptical approach is buttressed by the peculiarly diverse orientations of burials in these necropolises, which is seemingly contrary to the Christian custom of the period. Yet these are probably not the decisive arguments: after all, comparative studies have offered evidence that in a number of territories that were Christianized in the early medieval period, skeletal burial grounds with diversely oriented burials

---

17 L. Leciejewicz, "Die sozialen und politischen Voraussetzungen des Glaubenwechsels in Pommern", [in:] *Rom und Byzanz im Norden. Mission und Glaubenwechsel im Ostseeraum während des 8.-14. Jahrhunderts*, vol. 2, ed. M. Müller-Wille, Mainz 1997, p. 45.

tended to appear in the initial period, when the influence of Church institutions was still negligible; necropolises arranged into rows developed at a later stage. This had been the case with the Franks but, later on, probably also in Silesia (Śląsk), in Sweden, and (in a still later period) in the Lutician territories. This leads one to conjecture that inhumation as such was of much higher importance in the early days of Christian influence than the orientation of graves.

Let us leave the issue aside for a while and note that the earliest finds in Pomerania of objects being individual symbols of Christian cult, such as crosses and other pendants, are dated at the same point in time as the appearance and use of the above-described skeletal burial grounds. In regard to some of these cult symbols, which were hidden amidst silver treasures together with coins, one ought to suppose that their value and importance were perceived – at least at the moment of hiding – primarily in terms of ore and jewelry, rather than mostly as religious symbols. This is true for the silver Hiddensee-type cross found in the Gralewo hoard (hidden after 996)[18], for the cross found in the Noskowo/Bzowo hoard made of silver sheet metal and empty inside (11th c.)[19], as well as for two silver crosses of the Blumenhagen hoard (in fact, outside Pomeranian territory) that were made in a similar manner (late 11th c.).[20]

There is indeed a series of finds of this sort that have been discovered in settlement contexts. The immediately outstanding aspect is that all these objects, apart from one, have been found within Wolin – the exception being a bronze cast crucifix found in Żółte near Drawsko-Pomorskie, in a lake, at the place where a harbor adjacent to the local stronghold had been situated.[21] The cross features a sculptural relief of Christ Crucified, attired in a short tunica; the discoverers have discerned Greek letters on its rear side. The object is dated to the 11th c. at the latest. In the stratifications related to an erosion-stricken Wolin wharfage, a fragment of another silver cross has recently been found, one whose date of make

---

18 J. Żak, '*Importy*' *skandynawskie na ziemiach zachodniosłowiańskich od IX do XI wieku (część katalogowa)*, Poznań 1963, p. 145–146.

19 T. Kiersnowska, R. Kiersnowski, *Wczesnośredniowieczne skarby srebrne z Pomorza. Materiały*, Warszawa 1959, p. 76.

20 W. Karbe, "Der wendische Silberschatz von Blumenhagen", *Prähistorische Zeitschrift* 16, 1925, p. 76–80, Taf. VVI; A. Hollnagel, *Die vor- und frühgeschichtlichen Denkmäler und Funde des Kreises Neustrelitz*, Schwerin 1958, p. 31, Taf. 55–56; J. Żak, "Importy...", p. 30–31, Fig. 21; R. Kiersnowski, *Wczesnośredniowieczne skarby srebrne z Połabia. Materiały*, Wrocław 1964, p. 28.

21 *The Island in Żółte on Lake Zarańskie. Early Medieval Gateway into West Pomerania*, ed. W. Chudziak, R. Kaźmierczak, Toruń 2014, p. 269.

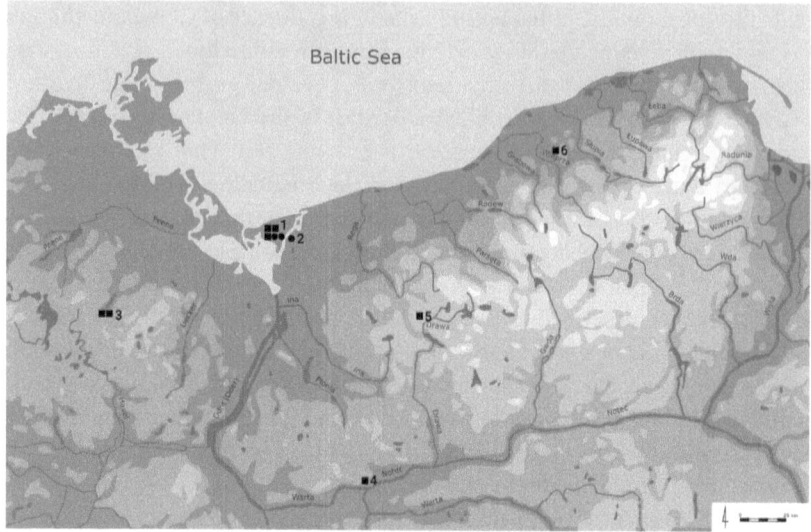

Fig. 2: The spread of the discoveries of Christian religious symbols, end of the 10th and the 11th c.

1 – Wolin; 2 – Drabino-Piaski; 3 – Blumenhagen; 4 – Gralewo; 5 – Żółte; 6 – Noskowo/Bzowo

has been determined as the end of the 10th c.[22] A bone pendant discovered in Wolin's Old Town area, featuring a cross motif whose plaited form is characteristic for Scandinavian decorative art, has a similar chronology (dated late 10th/ early 11th c.).[23]

Identical dating has been determined for two other historical objects found in Wolin whose Scandinavian provenance has been proved. Two circular Terslev style brooches feature characteristic motifs of an equal-armed cross in the form of a ribbon plait.[24] An eagerly accepted hypothesis has it that such pins, worn by members of the Scandinavian social elite, functioned as Christian symbols

---

22 A. Janowski, *W wolińskim porcie...*, p. 31.
23 W. Filipowiak, *Wolin-Jomsborg. Ein Vikingetids – Handelsby i Polen*, Roskilde 1991, p. 27; B. Stanisławski, "Sztuka wikińska z Wolina", *Średniowiecze polskie i powszechne*, vol. 4, ed. I. Panic, J. Sperka, Katowice 2007, p. 32, 43, 46, Fig. 20.
24 W. Filipowiak, "Some aspects of the development of Wolin in the 8th–11th centuries in the light of the results of new research", [in:] *Polish Lands at the Turn of the First and the Second Millennia*, ed. P. Urbańczyk, Warszawa 2004, p. 65, Fig. 19.

in this milieu.²⁵ Let us add that a fragment of a similar ornament was probably also found in a hoard hidden in the late 10th c. in Dramino-Piaski, not far from Wolin.²⁶

To complete this survey, let us stress the importance of another Wolin find, discovered in the 1930s but "rediscovered" only recently based on field documentation of the research then made (which has been kept over the years at the Arbeitsgemeinschaft für Heimatkunde Oldenburg/Ostholstein).²⁷ It is, namely, a small metal cross (possibly, an application) that has probably been lost and is known to us today only from a drawing. The context in which it was discovered – namely, the aforementioned Wolin-Mühlenberg (Młynówka) burial ground – is of special significance, enabling us to date the object at, most probably, the 11th c.

As a brief summary of the data tabled so far, we find that at the turn of the millennium (or even earlier, in the late 10th c.) the thitherto traditional Pomeranian funeral customs eroded. This was marked, among other things, by the emergence of a peculiar form of skeleton graveyards concentrated in the lower Oder River area and, apparently to a lesser extent, in the Kołobrzeg/Białogard area. Consequently, over the entire 11th c. and partly in the subsequent century, a multivector trend is observable in the funeral rite, along with its regionalization.²⁸ The same period saw the appearance, in various contexts, of symbols of Christian cult whose accumulation is discernible in Wolin and the nearby area. Let us moreover add that another two fragments of Tating jars discovered in Wolin and Usedom are dated to the 10th c., as well.²⁹

There are possibly two, not mutually exclusive, options that may help explain the origins of these phenomena. One explanation is related to the subordination

---

25 S. Kleingärtner, "Der Terslev-Schmuck – Zeugnis christlicher Missionierung?", *Archäologie in Schleswig* 9, 2001, p. 105–114.

26 T. Kiersnowska, R. Kiersnowski, *Wczesnośredniowieczne skarby...*, p. 80–1, Taf. XIV.2.

27 W. Filipowiak, M. Gierke, K. Kokora, M. Kowalska, "Zaginiona dokumentacja z przedwojennych badań archeologicznych w Wolinie", [in:] *Kościoły w dobie chrystianizacji...*, p. 25.

28 M. Rębkowski, "Christian mission, state formation and the changes in burial customs", *Archaeologia Polona* 48, 2010 (2015), p. 259–260.

29 I. Gabriel, "Hof- und Sakralkultur sowie Gebrauchs- und Handelsgut im Spiegel der Kleinfunde von Starigard/Oldenburg", [in:] *Oldenburg – Wolin – Staraja Ladoga – Novgorod – Kiev. Handel und Handelsverbindungen im südlichen und östlichen Ostseeraum während des frühen Mittelalters*, ed. M. Müller-Wille, (ser.: Berichte der Römisch-Germanischen Kommission, 69), Mainz am Rhein 1988, p. 135, ftn. 107; B. Stanisławski, *Garncarstwo...*, p. 97.

of Pomerania to the Piasts' state in the late 10th c., while the other focuses on the influence of the Scandinavian milieu that presumably were particularly active at the time in the Oder estuary.

The Piasts' expansion toward Pomerania had extended along the Oder since the seventh decade of the 10th c.; Mieszko I subdued the entirety of Pomerania shortly thereafter.[30] From that moment, the land remained dependent on the Piast rulers for several dozen years, at least until the 1st decade of the 11th c. The Piasts had recently adopted Christianity and set about Christianizing their country; hence, the newly conquered lands must also have been subjected to attempted Christianization, the most outstanding manifestation of this trend being the establishment in the year 1000 of the Bishopric of Kołobrzeg. It was then that in the stronghold rebuilt by the Piasts, the first Christian temple in the territory of our present focus arose.[31] Although no physical remains of the episcopal church have ever been found, there do exist archaeological premises that are indicative of at least the fact that construction of such a church had been commenced. Unfortunately, not much more than can be read in Thietmar of Merseburg on the destructions of pagan temples is known to us today about the possible Christianization efforts of Bishop Reinbern.[32] Similarly, we still lack reliable archaeological traces of the short-lived functioning of the local episcopal see – one possible reason being the altogether limited reach of the excavations carried out to date.[33]

Among the skeletal burial grounds dating to the period in question and known to us today, the necropolises of Santok and Cedynia site 2a – the localities situated along the northward expansion of the Piasts – as well as in Kołobrzeg itself and, possibly, in Stargard and Dębczyno, might possibly relate to the said expansion. An analogous interpretation of the finds from Wolin and Usedom would, in turn, be rather unjustified. After the conquest of Pomerania, Wolin presumably continued to enjoy independence or perhaps freed itself earlier than the other Pomeranian lands from Piast rule. Hence, the reasons behind Christian

---

30 See: the reference literature in footnote 2.
31 For more on Reinbern's cathedral, see: L. Leciejewicz, "Czy biskup Reinbern budował katedrę w Kołobrzegu?", *Archaeologia Historica Polona* 15/1, 2005, p. 59–67; M. Rębkowski, *Die Christianisierung Pommerns...*, p. 19–20.
32 S. Rosik, "Reinbern – Salsae Cholbergiensis aecclesiae episcopus", [in:] *Salsa Cholbergiensis. Kołobrzeg w średniowieczu*, ed. L. Leciejewicz, M. Rębkowski, Kołobrzeg 2000, p. 87–90.
33 For results of the excavations done to date, see: *Kołobrzeg. Wczesne miasto...*

symbols appearing and the inhumations practiced in that particular area should be traced elsewhere.

The latter half of the 10th and the beginning of the 11th c. were marked by the contacts of Wolin – then a large trading emporium at the height of its importance in the Baltic trade – with Scandinavia, primarily Denmark. These contacts are quite traceable in various archaeological sources, and this includes representatives of the Danish elite, Christianized as they were by then, sojourning in the town on the Dziwna Strait. The collection of the finds from Wolin and the mouth of the Oder, dated to the turn of the millennium, includes ornaments that were Christian religious symbols produced in a Scandinavian environment, of which at least some are characteristic for the Danish aristocracy.[34] If Adam of Bremen is to be trusted, the Saxons were the other alien group of baptized people dwelling in the multiethnic emporium of Wolin in the 11th c.[35] In this context, the hypothesis can be proposed that in the late 10th and in the 11th c. a group of Christians dwelled in the still predominantly pagan Wolin, which was mainly composed of aliens: Saxons, Scandinavians and, presumably, Ruthenian merchants ("Greeks"). As I have elsewhere endeavored to prove, it was the tradition of a Christian commune once existing in Wolin that was the main reason behind the setting of the Pomeranian Bishopric there, in 1140, a time when the town's splendor was already a matter of the past.[36] Taking into account the political situation in the second quarter of the 12th c., one should rather expect to have seen the bishopric established in Kamień, where the main ducal seat was situated. An analogy with Denmark is apparent: according to researchers, Hedeby and Ribe were chosen as the seats of bishoprics founded in 948 just because communities of Christians had dwelled there already in the 9th c.[37]

Given the current state of archaeological research, any attempt at a reliable and well-informed evaluation of the influence of the Bishopric of Kołobrzeg and of the alien Christians inhabiting the Oder estuary on the local Slavs would

---

34 For archaeological traces of presence of Scandinavians in Wolin, see: W. Duczko, "Obecność skandynawska na Pomorzu i słowiańska w Skandynawii we wczesnym średniowieczu", [in:] *Salsa Cholbergiensis...*, p. 25–30; B. Stanisławski, *Sztuka wikińska...*, p. 28–50; idem, "Norse culture in Wolin-Jómsborg", [in:] *Scandinavian Culture in Medieval Poland*, ed. S. Moździoch, B. Stanisławski, P. Wiszewski, Wrocław 2013, p. 193–246.

35 Cf. footnote 4.

36 M. Rębkowski, *Die Christianisierung Pommerns...*, p. 146.

37 M. Müller-Wille, "Ansgar und die Archäologie. Der Norden und das christliche Europa in Karolingischer Zeit", *Germania* 82/2, 2004, p. 451.

be a difficult and rather unproductive task. Let us nonetheless note that some historiographers conjecture that even after the collapse of the Piast domination over Pomerania, a part of the local elite may have remained Christian. One example is the (still mysterious) Pomeranian Duke *Zemuzil* who, according to the *Annales Altahenses*, was received in 1046 at the Merseburg court of Emperor Henry III (1028/46-1056), on a par with the Bohemian Duke Bretislav I (1055) and the Polish ruler Casimir the Restorer (Kazimierz Odnowiciel, 1034-1056) from the Piast dynasty.[38] Some historians argue that this would not have been possible if *Zemuzil* had not been a Christian. Whether such reasoning is legitimate is not for us to resolve here. For whatever the case, it is a fact that several dozen years later, Bishop Otto, during his missions in Pomerania, encountered some members of the urban elites of Wolin, Usedom, and Szczecin who had become Christian long before he arrived there. Pomeranian Duke Wartislav himself was reportedly a Christian too – and so was his spouse, described as a *matrona nobilissima et christianissima* who managed to preserve her faith in spite of dwelling amongst heathens.[39]

As I mentioned in the introductory section, the missions of 1124-1128 and the ensuing construction of a lasting ecclesial infrastructure – the first sites of the cult and, shortly afterwards, the episcopal see in Wolin – came as a groundbreaking moment for the Christianization of Pomerania. Compared to the situation in Poland, this series of occurrences was of a corresponding importance to the baptism of Mieszko in 966 and the formation of a Bishopric in Poznań a couple years later. Otto of Bamberg's mission journeys are at the root of the actual Christianization of the Pomeranians, a process that was to unfold over at least a hundred years. Leaving aside the trajectory and the clearly traceable regionalization of that process, which was initially concentrated in administrative and economic centers of the Duchy of Pomerania, I shall instead focus briefly on the question whether the available archaeological sources reflect the consequences of the events that took place in the second quarter of the 12th c.

---

38 *Annales Altaheuses maiores*, ed. W. Giesebrecht, E. Oefele (ser.: Scriptores Scriptores Rerum Germanicorum in usum scholarum ex Monumentis Germaniae Historicis recusi), Hannover 1891, p. 41. See: E. Rymar, *Rodowód książąt pomorskich*, Szczecin 2005, p. 77-82.

39 *Ebonis Vita*, II 8, 9, III 6; *Herbordi Dialogus de Vita S. Ottonis episcopi Bebenbergensis*, ed. J. Wikarjak, K. Liman (ser.: Monumenta Poloniae Historica. Series Nova, 7/3), Warszawa 1974), II, 21, III, 3); *S. Ottonis episcopi Babenbergensis Vita Prieflingensis*, ed. J. Wikarjak, K. Liman (ser.: Monumenta Poloniae Historica. Series Nova, 7/1), Warszawa 1966), II, 3 i 9.

Beginning with the aforesaid period, we can observe a decline of all the forms of necropolises we know of, particularly those using cremation as part of the funeral rite. It was then that the mound grave form eventually faded out in Pomerania. In lieu of it, we observe ever after a rapid increase in the number of skeletal burial grounds; two categories of the latter are discernible, apart from individual graves of dynasty members and top-ranked clerics buried inside Christian temples. It is rather apparent that all these forms of the period's necropolises were accepted by the Church during the 12th c.[40]

The first category is that of cemeteries adjacent to churches: still quite scarce at the time, they were mostly situated at the edges of settlements located near strongholds. As based upon the fragmentarily recognized burial sites of this sort (Gützkow, Wolgast, Usedom, Lubin)[41], one finds that the dead were buried there in rows orientated in line with the orientation of the churches – i.e. along the W–E axis, their heads pointing west. A tendency of turning these burial sites into multilayered cemeteries became clear already in the course of the 12th c., which must have been due to the limited burial space inside the settlements.

The other type of necropolis was that of cemeteries situated outside the settlements, and thus with no spatial relationship with the churches. A majority of them can be described as countryside cemeteries: very rarely do they appear in close vicinity to stronghold centers (as in Cedynia, e.g. site 2a): usually they are situated at a far distance from them. The row arrangement of burials, stemming from the orientation of graves along the W–E axis with the heads pointing west, is an important characteristic feature of these burial grounds; burials orientated otherwise amount to a small fraction. The burial site in Penkun is a good

---

40 M. Rębkowski, *Christian Mission…*, p. 258–259.
41 The territories situated west of the lower Oder, where the first three of the enumerated localities are located, fell under control of Pomeranian rulers in the 1120s; see: J. Spors, *Studia nad wczesnośredniowiecznymi dziejami Pomorza Zachodniego. XII – pierwsza połowa XIII w.*, Słupsk 1988, p. 73–75, 201–202. For more on the burial sites, see: H. Schäfer, T. Hoche, "Die Ausgrabungen auf dem Marktplatz und in der Pommerschen Straße 53 in Gützkow, LKr. Ostvorpommern", *Bodendenkmalpflege in Mecklenburg. Jahrbuch* 48, 2000 (2001) p. 351–358, Abb. 4; A. Poggensee, "Die slawische Vorbesiedlung der Altstadt von Wolgast, LKr. Ostvorpommern", *Bodendenkmalpflege in Mecklenburg. Jahrbuch* 50, 2002, p. 48–49; F. Biermann, *Bootsgrab*, p. 40–53; M. Rębkowski, "The Cultural Character and Chronology of the Cemetery on the Castle Hill in Lubin", [in:] *Lubin. Early Medieval Stronghold at the Mouth of the Oder River*, ed. M. Rębkowski, Szczecin 2018, p. 201–212.

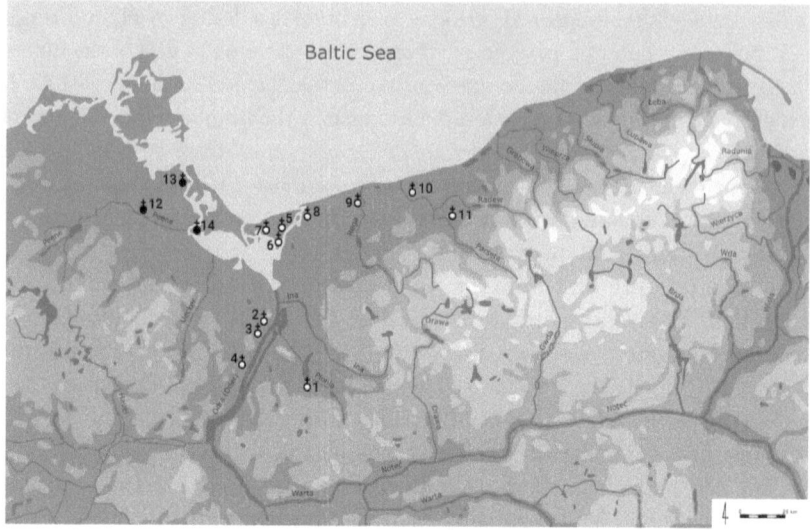

Fig. 3: Distribution of the churches founded by Bishop Otto of Bamberg in 1124–1125 (white) and 1128 (black), according to the *Vitae of Saint Otto*.

1 – Pyrzyce; 2–3 – Szczecin; 4 – Gridiz; 5–6 – Wolin; 7 – Lubin; 8 – Kamień; 9 – Clodona; 10 – Kołobrzeg; 11 – Białogard; 12 – Gützkow; 13 – Wolgast; 14 – Usedom

example: the regularly arranged rows of burials are dated, thanks to a whole series of coins, to the last two decades of the 12th c.[42]

Beside the main argument, let us add that for some of the cases an outright chronological relation occurring between Otto of Bamberg's missions and the change in the funeral rite can be proved. This is well illustrated by the instance of Usedom, where a sequence of burial sites existed: the aforementioned Am Hain necropolis was in use during the whole 11th c.; in the early 12th c. it was replaced, as it were, by a multilayered cemetery arranged into rows (remains of the site have been found in Priesterstrasse area).[43] Analysis of the dates of the issuance of the coins discovered on both the former and the subsequent graveyard proves that the burial site was moved at the end of the third decade or in

---

42 A. Pollex, "Das spätslawische Gräberfeld von Penkun, Fundplatz 28, Lkr. Uecker-Randow", *Bodendenkmalpflege in Mecklenburg. Jahrbuch* 53, 2005 (2006), p. 183–239.
43 F. Biermann, *Bootsgrab...*, p. 40–53.

the fourth decade of the 12th c.[44] Analogous processes are observable with Wolin or Lubin.

The graves of the dead buried at graveyards adjacent to churches appear to contain Christian cult symbols, such as metal (as in Gützkow) or amber crosses (Lubin). The raw material used to make cross-shaped pendants in Pomerania in the course of the 12th c. is symptomatic: the finds discovered in the settlement strata of Szczecin, Wolin, or Usedom indicate that such artefacts were made almost exclusively of the local amber.[45]

Church graveyards obviously emerged as a consequence of the construction of the first durable sites of Christian cult. As we are told by the *Vitae* of Bishop Otto, at least fourteen churches were erected in twelve localities at the initiative of this particular missionary; one of these churches became, in 1140, the seat of the Pomeranian Bishopric in Wolin. These remained Pomerania's only sites of Christian cult for the following three decades. Their scarce number and specific location must have contributed to a limited access to the centers of the new religion. Except for the currently mysterious locality of *Clodona*, churches were situated in the political centers of the realm of Wartislav I († 1135) Duke of Pomerania, which assumed its shape at the time. The centers were formed of settlement complexes composed of the stronghold and its surrounding settlements. Not long afterwards, most of them became centers of administrative authority of the Pomeranian Duchy. The regularity observable with the distribution of the network of those earliest churches was certainly related to the pragmatics of the missions, which were targeted at the largest clusters of the population. But most probably there was also an ideological rationale behind it: the churches became elements of the infrastructure of early-state power. As to the shapes and forms of these earliest temples in Pomerania, until quite recently we had only to rely on the *Vitae* of Bishop Otto. These accounts tell us about the constructional simplicity of the wooden structures, some of which were made with "tree branches" and thatched, the others having been constructed exquisitely.[46] The

---

44 M. Rębkowski, "Św. Otton a archeologia. O potrzebie i perspektywach badań", [in:] *Populi terrae marisque. Prace poświęcone pamięci Profesora Lecha Leciejewicza*, ed. M. Rębkowski, S. Rosik, Wrocław 2011, p. 110–111.

45 M. Rębkowski, *Die Christianisierung Pommerns*..., p. 131–132.

46 *Ebonis Vita*, II 5, 15, 18, III 1, 7, 9; *Herbordi Dialogus*, II 17, 22, 37, 38, III 14; *Vita Prieflingensis*, II 13, 14, 16, 17, 19, 20; III 4. See, for instance: R. Kiersnowski, "Budownictwo zachodnio-pomorskie wieku XII w świetle źródeł pisanych", *Wiadomości Archeologiczne* 19, 1953, p. 129–131; 297–299; 619–624; M. Rębkowski, *Die Christianisierung Pommerns*..., p. 20–31; S. Rosik, "*Ecclesias de ramis arborum, ut novella tunc plantatio exigebat, construxit*. Pierwsze pomorskie kościoły w świadectwie

excavations carried out in recent years at the strongholds in Lubin and Szczecin led to the discovery of two objects that may be associated with the churches existing there around the middle of the 12th c. These were buildings founded upon clay-and-stone benches in which poles forming the base of construction of the walls were embedded; the walls, at least in Lubin, were made of wattle and clay, and whitewashed on the inside. These single-nave structures (whose width was around 7 to 9 m) were orientated along the E–W axis, with a presbytery or apse added at the eastern end.[47]

* * *

To summarize these observations, let us make some brief remarks that basically refer to a comparison of the emergence and initial reception of Christianity in Pomerania and in the adjacent territory of Poland. In both cases, a lasting ecclesial structure, whose impact on the Christianization of the society became critical later on, was formed at the stage of the development of statehood. The emergence of such a structure resulted from the decisions made by the early-state power center: this is true both for Mieszko's baptism as well as for Wartislav's consent for the missionary activity of the Bamberg Bishop. Certainly there were more than 150 years between the two events. Moreover, in the case of Pomerania, the political factor of the expansion led by the Polish ruler – Boleslaus III the Wrymouth (Bolesław Krzywousty, 1107–1138) – did exert a direct influence. The processes taking place in both countries in the first decades after those developments seemingly took a similar course all the same. The early period marked the development, in both countries, of ecclesial hubs situated at the main centers of state power. The scarcity, or even lack of churches outside these centers, must have led to a phenomenon that can be today described as the "regionalization" of Christianization. As a result, similarities observable in the transformations of the funeral rite appeared. During the first 100–150 years after the "baptism", a sort of dualism was practiced with respect to funeral sites: apart from churchyards established, let us remark, in settlement centers also, single-layer row graveyards situated outside settlements were in use, and thus must have been accepted by the Church. The funeral rite was made uniform in this

---

o misyjnych dokonaniach św. Ottona z Bambergu (XII wiek)", [in:] *Kościoły w dobie chrystianizacji...*, p. 203–214.

47 M. Dworaczyk, "Kościół świętego Wojciecha w Szczecinie", [in:] *Kościoły w dobie chrystianizacji...*, p. 215–224; M. Rębkowski, *Ecclesia sancti Nicolai...*, p. 225–238; M. Rębkowski, P. Romanowicz, "The Church of St. Nicholas", [in:] *Lubin. Early Medieval Stronghold...*, p. 183–190.

respect at a much later date, as the ecclesial infrastructure expanded and more churches appeared and parochial structure developed. This basically took place in the 12th c. in Poland. In Pomerania, the process commenced not until the last decades of that century; a network of parishes took shape not until the second quarter of the 13th c., with the colonization of these lands. As a result, cemeteries other than ones adjacent to churches began disappearing.[48]

When comparing Poland with Pomerania, I discern certain differences above all with respect to the earliest penetration of Christianity. For Greater Poland (Wielkopolska), we have so far obtained no data whatsover which would be indicative of any such penetration prior to the baptism of Mieszko. The unique rhythm of economic development of the Baltic territories and the appearance of early-urban residential settlements which functioned in the pre-state (tribal) period must have implied the regular arrival of merchants, including Christian ones, long before Wartislav I came to power. This phenomenon of Christianity penetrating into Pomerania long before Otto's missions was, paradoxically, associated with the rather late crystallization of the structures of centralized power. This facilitated active interest on the part of Christianized neighbors, which manifested itself in the short-lived conquest of Pomerania by the Piasts at the end of the 10th c. and the setting up of the ephemeral Diocese of Kołobrzeg. In all probability, these developments and influences did however contribute to an erosion of the sepulchral customs traditional among the Pomeranians long before Bishop Otto of Bamberg set out on his first mission to them.

Translated by Tristan Korecki

---

48 M. Rębkowski, *Die Christianisierung...*, p. 147–150.

Teresa Rodzińska-Chorąży

Early-Piast architecture in the context of early-medieval European architecture

Abstract: The author uses the term "early-Piast architecture" for works created between the third quarter of the 10th c., after Mieszko's adoption of Christianity, until the late 11th c., when the role of magnates in the shaping of Poland's architectural landscape grew markedly. The form of the first Piast rulers' residential complexes around the year 1000 distinguished itself in Central Europe with its concise concept and single-axial layout, and with the diverse shapes of its palace chapels. These complexes testify that the first Piasts established close contacts with highly educated architects from the Empire and took advantage of their services. Also, the forms of the first cathedrals on Polish territories, partly rebuilt or replaced by new edifices in the 2nd half of the 11th c., testify to a deepening assimilation of the western models from the Empire's territory, whereas the impact of early Bohemian architecture on early-Piast structures seems to be much less important.

Keywords: early medieval architecture, Christianization, early-Piast dynasty, early medieval cathedrals, early medieval residential complexes

For Polish art, the reception of baptism by Mieszko I (c. 960–992) is an event of surpassing significance, regardless of its date as indicated in written sources or the place where it occurred.[1] For the ruler himself, one of the obvious effects of baptism was the necessity to ensure adequate conditions for evangelization, as well as a new garb for the exercising of power, for its character had changed in line with Christian doctrine. Mieszko's christening initiated not only the long and toilsome process of converting the populace inhabiting the territory under his rule, as it also involved relevant and measurable material consequences. Foundations were part of the Christian ruler's array of obligations, which included the erection of churches and establishment of monasteries where the relics of saints and liturgical celebrations would ensure fortune and prosperity to the ruler as

---

1　D. A. Sikorski, *Kościół w Polsce za Mieszka I i Bolesława Chrobrego*, Poznań 2011, p. 91–129; K. Ożóg, 966. *Chrzest Polski*, Kraków 2015, p. 102–110; P. Urbańczyk, *Co się stało w 966 roku?*, Poznań 2016, p. 95–113; T. Jurek, "O czasie i okolicznościach chrztu Mieszka", *Roczniki Historyczne* 81, 2015, p. 35–56; *Chrzest Mieszka I i chrystianizacja państwa Piastów*, ed. J. Dobosz, M. Matla, J. Strzelczyk, Poznań 2017.

well as his subjects.² Since there had been no local tradition in building stone constructions, the works commissioned by Piast rulers and their spouses could only have been accomplished by architects and building workshops imported from outside Piast lands.

Thus, together with the Christian religion, masters of the art of designing and erecting monumental stone edifices arrived from distant shores to the lands on the Warta, the Oder, and the Vistula Rivers. Their works have been preserved to our day as remains that are unveiled during archaeological-architectural explorations, with none of them remaining extant in their original form. This does not facilitate their interpretation, something compounded by the fact that no written sources are available. Indeed, no known records reveal the names of the builders or where they came from. The only signature of those artists is, in fact, the form of the residences and churches they built – as far as they prove re-constructible based on the surviving relics. However, analysis of their form may indicate inspirations and relationships with foreign artistic milieu. European architecture between the 9th and the 11th c. embraces a wide scope within which one can try and identify the architectural solutions applied in the country of the first Christian Piasts.

Among the many dilemmas involved with research into early architecture in Poland, the terminology used in the literature is of primary importance.³ It is not at all easy to unambiguously classify the styles in the context of the above-described condition of surviving historical substance. I therefore refer the term "early-Piast architecture" to works created in the period that began in the third quarter of the 10th c. with Mieszko's adoption of Christianity. What we describe today as artistic sponsorship or patronage was for over a century the exclusive domain of the main power center concentrated around the ruler. A broadening of the circle of founders, a process attested by written sources, is observable with the activities of the palatine Sieciech of the Starż-Toporczyk family in the late 11th c. And so it seems quite correct to mark the end of the period in art described as "early-Piast" within the last two decades of that century. "Early-Piast architecture" would not therefore be a style-denoting category; rather, it extends to works created at the initiative not only of the first two historical rulers of Poland: Mieszko

---

2   R. Michałowski, *Princeps fundator. Studium z dziejów kultury politycznej w Polsce X-XIII wieku*, Warszawa 1993; idem, "Podstawy religijne monarchii we wczesnym średniowieczu zachodnioeuropejskim. Próba typologii", *Kwartalnik Historyczny* 105, 1998, p. 3–34; L. Wetesko, *Historyczne konteksty monarszych fundacji artystycznych w Wielkopolsce do początku XIII wieku*, Poznań 2009, passim.

3   T. Rodzińska-Chorąży, *Zespoły rezydencjonalne i kościoły centralne na ziemiach Polskich do połowy XII wieku*, Kraków 2009, p. 264–289.

I and his son Boleslaus I the Brave (Bolesław Chrobry, 992–1025), but also of their successors: Mieszko II Lambert (1025–1034), Casimir I the Restorer (Kazimierz I Odnowiciel, 1034–1058), Boleslaus II the Bold/Generous (Bolesław Śmiały/ Szczodry, 1058–1079), and Ladislaus I Herman (Władysław I Herman, 1079– 1102). The material remains of the baptism of Mieszko I and his contemporary elite have been among the most frequently discussed issues related to the origins of the state. Research carried out in the 1950s and 1960s resulted in discoveries of what were deemed baptismal fonts in Wiślica and Poznań; the publications of Zofia Wartołowska and Krystyna Józefowiczówna inspired a long-lasting discussion on the actual purpose of those objects.[4] That dispute, with its telltale socio-political context in the background, was pursued in association with the interdiscipline of the archaeology of architecture then emerging in Poland and elaborating its research methods. Two different interpretations of both the aforementioned "fonts" have been reappearing in the literature to this day. However, a definite majority of researchers acknowledge that the "baptismal fonts" known from Poznań do not testify to a baptism: their function was associated, instead, with the construction process.[5] Several dozen similar objects discovered in various places across Europe and considered everywhere else to be remains of basins for mixing mortar have not convinced the "font theory adherents" that in Poznań what we encounter is a grand architectural investment project, rather than something attesting to the liturgy of christening. The structure found in Wiślica, in turn, is distinct, for it is neither a baptismal basin nor a mortar bowl, nor even a natural geological formation.[6]

Nonetheless, the few adherents of the "baptismal font" interpretation maintain the hypothesis once proposed by Zofia Kurnatowska, whereby the largest of the Poznań fonts was originally kept inside a small baptistery building, which itself

---

4 Z. Wartołowska, *Dzieje Wiślicy*, typescript, Archive of the Institute of Archaeology, University of Warsaw; K. Józefowiczówna, "Uwagi w spornej sprawie 'baptysteriów' w Polsce X i XI wieku", *Slavia Antiqua* 14, 1967, p. 31–129.

5 T. Rodzińska-Chorąży, "Koliste struktury w Poznaniu i Wiślicy – misy chrzcielne czy urządzenia do mieszania zaprawy?", [in:] *Wiślica. Nowe badania i interpretacje*, ed. A. Grzybkowski, (ser.: Biblioteka Muzealnictwa i Ochrony Zabytków, series B, 86/98), Warszawa 1997, p. 61–81; P. Urbańczyk, "Czy istnieją archeologiczne ślady masowych chrztów ludności wczesnopolskiej?", *Kwartalnik Historyczny* 102, 1995, p. 3–18; idem, "Jeszcze o funkcji wczesnośredniowiecznych 'mis' wapiennych", *Kwartalnik Historyczny* 103, 1996, p. 65–68.

6 J. Kalaga, W. Gliński, "Wiślicka 'misa chrzcielna' w świetle nowych badań archeologicznych", [in:] *Dzieje Podkarpacia*, vol. 5, ed. J. Gancarski, Krosno 2001, p. 161–170.

was part of a purported mission outpost.[7] However, the Poznań baptistery, square in plan, as hypothetically reconstructed by that scholar, is a thoroughly imaginary structure that was conceived based on a misinterpretation of the earliest cathedral's walls. To create the structure, negatives of some enigmatic older structures were used, along with the foundations of the inter-nave walls and the transept of the earliest basilica erected on the islet of Ostrów Tumski. I first argued against Kurnatowska's concept in 2000[8]; Aneta Bukowska's studies on the first Poznań cathedral church seem to confirm my view.[9] As can be supposed, Poznań's "baptismal font" will, in time, die a natural death, since the European archaeological context speaks for itself with an ever stronger voice, whereas the "mission outpost" concept as proposed by Kurnatowska has poor chance of survival.

The first early-Piast historical monument to draw research attention was that of the ruins on largest of several islands in Lake Lednica. The renowned Polish historian Joachim Lelewel (1786–1861) was the first to interpret the site as "castle" belonging to Boleslaus the Brave. The complex of edifices on the island Ostrów Lednicki (in Polish – *ostrów* being an old word much like "holm", i.e., river or lake islet) has also drawn many years of discussion on the early stage of Christianization in Poland. A no less tempestuous dispute than the one over the Poznań font has been waged around the two recesses discovered in the floor of the chapel of that residential complex. Again, some scholars advocate the view that the structures functioned as baptismal basins[10], with others denying their

---

7   Z. Kurnatowska, "Poznańskie baptysterium", *Slavia Antiqua* 39, 1998, p. 51–69; Z. Kurnatowska, M. Kara, "Początki architektury sakralnej na grodzie poznańskim w świetle nowych ustaleń archeologicznych", [in:] *Początki architektury monumentalnej w Polsce*. ed. T. Janiak, D. Stryniak, Gniezno 2004, p. 47–70.

8   T. Rodzińska-Chorąży, "Co nam mówi architektura murowana?", [in:] *Ziemie polskie w X wieku i ich znaczenie w kształtowaniu się nowej Europy*, ed. H. Samsonowicz, Kraków 2000, p. 370–372.

9   A. Bukowska, *Najstarsza katedra w Poznaniu. Problem formy i jej genezy w kontekście architektury około roku 1000*, Kraków 2013, p. 135–137.

10 T. Rodzińska-Chorąży, "Baptysterium", [in:] *U progu chrześcijaństwa w Polsce. Ostrów Lednicki*, ed. K. Żurowska, Kraków 1994, p. 103–167; eadem, *Zespoły rezydencjonalne...*, p. 106–112; K. Żurowska, "Dwa szkice o architekturze kamiennej Ostrowa Lednickiego", *Modus. Prace z Historii Sztuki* 14, 2014, p. 23–30; Z. Kurnatowska, "Najstarsze ośrodki kultu chrześcijańskiego w Wielkopolsce", [in:] *Miejsca kultu w Wielkopolsce. Materiały*, Poznań 1997, p. 5–20; eadem, "Poznańskie baptysterium", p. 51–69; eadem, *Początki Polski*, Poznań 2002, p. 102–103; eadem, "Początki chrześcijaństwa w Polsce", [in:] *Tu się Polska zaczęła...*, ed. H. Kóčka-Krenz, Poznań 2007, p. 36; J. Górecki, "Głos w dyskusji",

liturgical purpose.[11] What is certain, though, is that the Lednica chapel's recesses cannot be interpreted as mortar mixing bowls, since their cross-shaped form, smooth (gypsum mortar-covered) surface, and modelled edges resemble no construction-related device whatsoever [Fig. 1].

Their function must have been liturgical. Nonetheless, the polemics around their purpose, recently revived by the celebrations of the 1,050th anniversary of Mieszko's baptism in 2016, are again vociferous. To offer an unambiguous conclusion in this regard is not easy, for there are no models directly identifiable in Europe with the structures observed at Ostrów Lednicki. Hence, they ought to be interpreted based on the extensive archaeological, architectonic, and liturgical context. The most similar specimens, in terms of form and situation, are the wall-mounted baptismal fonts of Vrba and Gradac in Dalmatia and in Luni, northern Italy. These may well be the closest analogies and thereby may possibly point the way for further research.[12] Given the current state of research and the comparative material available, it seems that the baptismal function was indeed the case with the recesses found in the Lednica chapel.

The rectangular structure in the rotunda adjacent to the Kraków cathedral church might also have had to do with an evangelization mission and baptismal liturgy.[13] However, the severe destruction of the hollow (which is faced with

---

[in:] *Ziemie polskie w X wieku ...*, p. 412–414; idem, *Gród na Ostrowie Lednickim na tle wybranych ośrodków grodowych pierwszej monarchii piastowskiej*, Poznań 2001, p. 52–57; Z. Pianowski, *Sedes regni principales. Wawel i inne rezydencje piastowskie do połowy XIII w. na tle europejskim*, Kraków 1994, p. 90–91; Z. Pianowski, M. Proksa, *Przedromańskie palatium i rotunda na Wzgórzu Zamkowym w Przemyślu*, Przemyśl 2003, p. 67–79; A. Buko, *Archeologia Polski wczesnośredniowiecznej*, Warszawa 2015, p. 272–279.

11 Z. Świechowski, "Palatium na Ostrowie Lednickim a mity polskiej historii sztuki", *Rocznik Historii Sztuki* 30, 2005, p. 47–56; P. Urbańczyk, "Zagadka Ostrowa Lednickiego", *Kwartalnik Historyczny* 103, 1995, p. 97–108; idem, "Wczesnośredniowieczna architektura polska w kontekście archeologicznym", [in:] *Początki architektury monumentalnej w Polsce*, ed. T. Janiak, D. Stryniak, Gniezno 2003, p. 25–36; D. A. Sikorski, *Kościół w Polsce ...*, p. 119–126; K. Stala, *Architektura rezydencji wczesnośredniowiecznych w Polsce. Próba reinterpretacji dotychczasowych poglądów z uwzględnieniem tła europejskiego*, Kraków 2013, p. 207.

12 K. Żurowska, "Dwa szkice ..." p. 23–30.

13 J. Firlet, Z. Pianowski, "Odkrycie dwu wczesnośredniowiecznych kościołów w rejonie tzw. Bastionu Władysława IV na Wawelu", *Sprawozdania Archeologiczne* 37, 1985, p. 153–167; M. Bober, *Architektura przedromańska i romańska w Krakowie. Badania i interpretacje*, Kraków 2008, p. 31–33; T. Rodzińska-Chorąży, "Zespoły rezydencjonalne i kościoły..." p. 67–83.

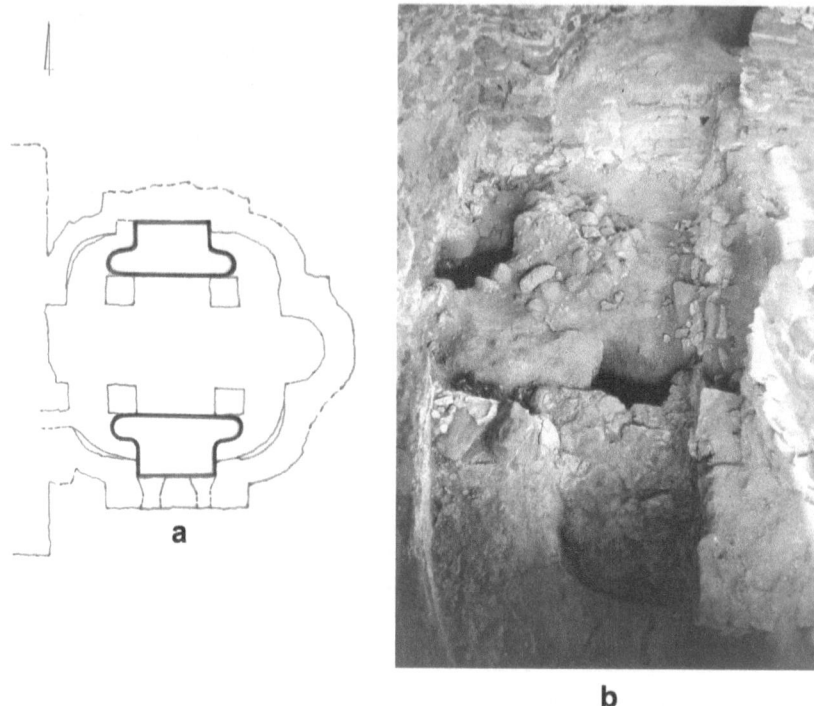

Fig. 1: Ostrów Lednicki, a) the plan of the chapel with two semi-cross depressions (drawing M. Rosół), b) the southern depression, view from the east (photo T. Rodzińska-Chorąży).

sandstone slabs) makes it impossible to identify whether it was once a grave or a baptismal font, albeit the latter option is more plausible. Outstanding in this particular structure are the precisely elaborated rectangular sandstone slabs that face not only the hollow's sides, but also its bottom. Such a method of facing is not to be found in any other known early medieval burial vault, including outside Poland. Hence, the claim that the single-apse rotunda by the northern façade of the Kraków cathedral functioned as a baptistery is not baseless. This being said, we have to humbly accept that there are no unambiguous or explicit interpretations of archaeological finds, nor is there unanimity in assessing the genesis of the material remains presently known to appear in the territory of Poland and associated with the beginnings of Christianization comprehended as a process rather than a single occurrence.

The conversion of the ruler and, most probably, his closest people, informed the ways in which power/authority was manifested. In architecture, the change was expressed in the residences built of stone in some of the central burgs or strongholds (*grody* in Polish) of the Piasts' domain. The findings of the last fifty years tell us that four residential complexes can be associated with the rule of the first dynasts – namely, those of Ostrów Lednicki, Poznań, Przemyśl, and the never-completed project in Giecz (where only the foundations were laid). It is certain that the other strongholds, such as Gniezno, Kalisz, Wrocław, and Kraków also had their residential edifices. However, in the case of the first three their locations have yet to be determined – and as for Kraków, its form has yet to be completely reconstructed. We have to bear in mind that our present knowledge is unsatisfactory and we are still a far cry from being able to synthetically outline the origins of these construction complexes.

It does however seem that the *palatia* in the Greater Poland (Wielkopolska) region – those of Poznań, Ostrów Lednicki, and Giecz – were most probably built at the initiative of Mieszko I[14], whereas the Przemyśl complex can be associated only with Boleslaus the Brave.[15] What these four complexes have in common is the longitudinal building's interior being divided into a number of

---

14 H. Kóčka-Krenz, "Palatia wczesnopiastowskie", [in:] *Średniowiecze w rozjaśnieniu*, ed. K. Skupieński, Warszawa 2010, p. 119–132; eadem, "Palatium poznańskie na tle wczesnośredniowiecznych zespołów rezydencjonalnych", [in:] *Archeologiczne tajemnice palatium i katedry poznańskiego Ostrowa*, ed. M. Przybył, Poznań 2016, p. 21–46; eadem, *Na wyspie Ostrów przy której dziś jest Poznań*, Poznań 2012; T. Rodzińska-Chorąży, Zespoły rezydencjonalne …, p. 18–57, 141–65; K. Żurowska, "Dwa szkice …", p. 30–37; T. Krysztofiak, "Palatium w Gieczu. Archeologiczne podstawy datowania reliktów", [in:] *Lapides Viventes. Zaginiony Kraków wieków średnich. Księga dedykowana prof. Klementynie Żurowskiej*, ed. T. Rodzińska-Chorąży, A. Włodarek, Kraków 2005, p. 293–310.

15 Z. Pianowski, M. Proksa, *Przedromańskie palatium* …, passim; E. Sosnowska, "Analiza porównawcza stratygrafii architektury rotundy i palatium na Wzgórzu Zamkowym w Przemyślu", [in:] *Przemyśl wczesnośredniowieczny*, ed. E. Sosnowska, Warszawa 2010, p. 231–242; T. Rodzińska-Chorąży, "Rekonstrukcja palatium na Wzgórzu Zamkowym w Przemyślu w kontekście form piastowskich zespołów rezydencjonalnych", [in:] *Przemyśl wczesnośredniowieczny*, ed. E. Sosnowska, Warszawa 2010, p. 321–330; A. Bukowska, S. Ristow, "Piasten und Ottonen. Archaologische Forschungen zum Beginn des Hohmittelalters in Polen", [in:] *Das Sakramentar aus Tyniec. Eine Prachthandschrift des 11. Jahrhunderts und die Beziehungen zwischen Köln und Polen in der Zeit Kasimirs des Erneuerers*, ed. K. G. Beuckers, A. Bihrer Wien, Köln, Weimar 2018, p. 307–338.

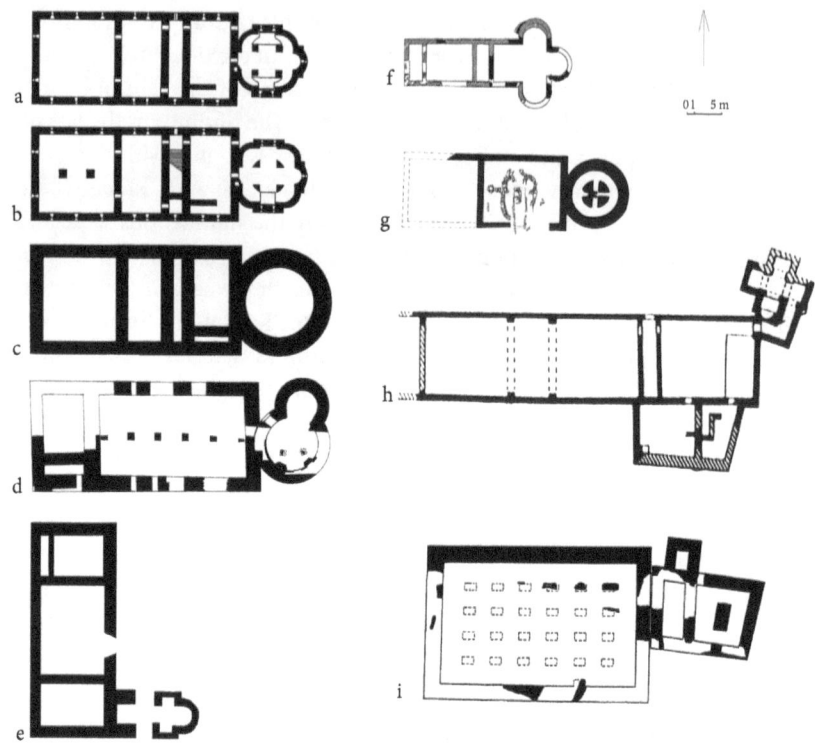

Fig. 2: Early Piast residential complexes and three other examples: a) Ostrów Lednicki I phase, b) Ostrów Lednicki II phase, c) Giecz, d) Przemyśl, e) Poznań, f) Devín (Great Moravia (9th c.), g) Werla (Saxony 10th–11th c.), h) Zürich (after 1000), i) Kraków-Wawel Hill, "Aula of 24 pillars" (by T. Rodzińska-Chorąży).

sections (rooms) in a single-bay arrangement, and the representative building being strictly integrated with the palace chapel [**Fig. 2a-e, i**].

The residences of Ostrów Lednicki, Giecz, and Przemyśl had the two segments merge along the East–West axis, the chapel being situated on the eastern side. The *palatium* of Poznań featured a different arrangement, with the longitudinal axis set north to south, and a chapel adjacent to the south-eastern corner perpendicularly. The projection of the foundations in the Giecz *palatium* appears exceptionally similar to the Lednica complex. In both cases, the divisions of the longitudinal structure's interior are identical, with the same proportions and rhythm, although the *palatium* in Giecz was apparently intended to be somewhat larger than that on Lednica Holm. There are many elements indicating that the design concept of the two complexes may well have been drawn by the same hand.[16]

Each of these *palatia* features a large space which is interpreted as the throne assembly hall. In the Lednica and Giecz complexes, the hall is located in the western segment of the rectangular building; the *palatium* of Poznań has it located centrally, and the one in Przemyśl at the east end, near the chapel. As far as the proportions of the sections/rooms are concerned, the assembly hall in Przemyśl was definitely predominant in the complex, and this was not the case with the *palatia* of the Greater Poland region.

Interestingly, each of the palace chapels had a different form. In Giecz, the original design most probably featured a rotunda with eight niches within the wall's thickness, as may be judged from the extremely wide foundations (3 m).[17] The chapel on Ostrów Lednicki had a Greek cruciform plan, and featured four massive pillars at the center and a circular ambulatory. The Przemyśl complex consisted of a rotunda with one semicircular apse; the two surviving pillars inside it attest that a gallery once existed there, in the form of a balcony or, more probably, the upper story.[18] In Poznań, a rectangular form was used, with a semicircular apse and niches placed within the longer walls in a cross arrangement.[19] While there is no doubt about the palace-chapel function of these central edifices built in Poznań and Przemyśl, the original role of the Lednica chapel is subject to debate. The two symmetrical basin structures situated within its premises, whose function was possibly baptismal, no doubt largely determined the interior's purpose. Thus, we can accept that in the first phase the structure was either a baptistery outright, or a palace chapel equipped with ever so special christening appliances.[20] Since it is hard to find a direct model for either of

---

16 T. Rodzińska-Chorąży, *Zespoły rezydencjonalne* ..., p. 141–164; eadem, "Some Remarks on the Design of two Residential Complexes in Poland from the End of the 10th Century. St. Augustine, Boethius and the Concept of Palatium", *Hortus Artium Medievalium* 24, 2018, p. 271–281.

17 K. Józefowiczówna, "Sztuka w okresie wczesnoromańskim", [in:] *Dzieje Wielkopolski do roku 1793*, ed. J. Topolski, Poznań 1969, p. 136–138, fns. 52 and 55.

18 Z. Pianowski, M. Proksa, *Przedromańskie palatium*..., p. 44; T. Rodzińska-Chorąży, *Zespoły rezydencjonalne* ..., p. 116–117.

19 H. Kóčka-Krenz, "Kaplica wczesnośredniowiecznej rezydencji książęcej w Poznaniu", [in:] *Z badań nad rozwojem architektury średniowiecznej*, ed. K. Stala, II Forum Architecturae Poloniae Medievalis, *Czasopismo Techniczne*, vol. 7A, fasc. 23, Kraków 2011, p. 143–158.

20 K. Żurowska, *Dwa szkice*... p. 23–30.

the two variants across Europe, whether in the formal or functional aspect, the Ostrów Lednicki complex may at present be seen as an original work conceived by its author(s). Let us remark, though, that the closest parallel of the Lednica chapel's form, which combines in its mass and projection the overlapping plans of cross and circle, is the Carolingian episcopal chapel of San Satiro in Milan.[21]

One may conjecture that the *palatia* of the early-Piast rulers were two-storied, both in their secular and sacred sections. This is particularly true for the second stage of the Lednica complex (after its reconstruction around the year 1000) and for the complex in Przemyśl.[22] Moreover, the surviving traces of mortars tell us that at least the chapels had floors made of a gypsum or limestone screed, the whole surface being covered with pale-cream or pale-pink-colored roughcast, as on Ostrów Lednicki. Characteristic of the workshops hired by the early Piasts is also the use of gypsum or screed mortar, virtually without admixtures or contaminations (as, again, on Lednica Holm).[23]

The forms of the early-Piast *palatia* echo with associations with the imperial residential architecture of Ottonian times; traceable are also some distant prototypes from the south of Europe, perhaps even from Byzantium. A single-bay arrangement of the rooms, as especially in the Giecz design and the Lednica edifice, have roots that go back to late antique villas in imperial provinces such as Gallia, Britannia, or Pannonia.[24] The rectangular-shaped representative section, divided into smaller chambers, was first combined with the sacred section located within the axis on a central projection around the middle of the 9th c., in the Great Moravian building locality of Devín.[25] The next complex of

---

21 J. Zachwatowicz, "Architektura przedromańska w wieku X i w pierwszej połowie wieku XI", [in:] *Sztuka polska przedromańska i romańska do schyłku XIII wieku*, ed. M. Walicki, Warszawa 1971, p. 77; T. Rodzińska-Chorąży, "Architektura baptysterium", [in:] *U progu chrześcijaństwa...*, p. 140–167.

22 T. Rodzińska-Chorąży, *Zespoły rezydencjonalne...*, p. 136.

23 J. Skoczylas, "Makroskopowe, petrograficzne badania kamiennych zabytków wczesnośredniowiecznych z terenu Wielkopolski", typescript, IAE Archive, Warszawa 1988, passim; idem, "Budowa geologiczna i surowce mineralne rejonu Jeziora Lednickiego", *Studia Lednickie* 1, 1989, passim; idem, *Użytkowanie surowców skalnych we wczesnym średniowieczu w północno-zachodniej Polsce*, Poznań 1990, passim; idem, *Użytkowanie surowców skalnych w początkach państwa polskiego*, Poznań 1994, passim.

24 K. Żurowska, "Dom biskupi", [in:] *U progu chrześcijaństwa...*, p. 168–182. (While the interpretation of the longitudinal part of the Lednica palatium has changed, the present analysis of the form remains in force).

25 T. Rodzińska-Chorąży, "Veľkomoravská trikoncha na Devine: medzi antikou a stredovekom", [in:] *Počta Vaclavovi Menclovi. Zbornik studii k otazkam interpretacie*

this kind was the imperial *domus* in Werla, Saxony, dating to the 10th c.[26]; however, the sections (rooms) inside it significantly diverge in the layout from the *palatia* designed for Giecz and Lednica. As to the interior layout, the *palatium* of Zürich offers some identifiable analogies; yet its cruciform chapel is situated at the quoin, rather than within the residence's axis.[27] With all these observations, the specific models that were followed or referred to by the architects working for Mieszko and Boleslaus remain unknown; one of them might have possibly been the yet-undiscovered imperial residence in Magdeburg.[28]

What one encounters in Lesser Poland (Małopolska) centered on Kraków, is quite different. The region's integration into the state of the Piasts in the late 10th c. made it (and Kraków above all) a site of intense construction efforts. Unfortunately, the later architectural reconstructions on Wawel Hill have ensured that nothing more than small fragments of walls situated by the western wing of the Royal Castle and the quadrangular building within the present arcade yard can be associated today with the earliest ducal residence.[29] The remains of the ducal curia, dated to the reign of Casimir the Restorer – around the mid-11th c.– are preserved in slightly better condition. The curia building is most frequently envisioned as a two-story assembly hall, its lower level being divided by stone pillars (ever since its discovery the section has been called "the twenty-four pillars hall").[30] The early twelfth-century chronicler Gallus Anonymus reported that King Boleslaus the Bold *ante palatium in curia residebat* while reviewing the

---

stredoeuropskeho umenia, ed. D. Bořutová, S. Ořiško, Bratislava 2000, p. 33–58; eadem, "Wielkomorawski trikonchos w Devinie na Słowacji: analiza formy i funkcji", [in:] *Ars Graeca – Ars Latina*, ed. W. Bałus et al., Kraków 2001, p. 309–322. M. Illáš, "Predrománsky kostol na Devíne", *Historický Zborník* 21, 2011, p. 19–39 revisits the concept of a completely sacral function of the Devin structure.

26 G. Binding, *Deutsche Königspfalzen von Karl dem Grossen bis Friedrich II (765–1240)*, Darmstadt 1996, p. 168–178; P. Feldmann, "Die ottonische Kaiserpfalz Werla", *Harz-Zeitschrift* 34/55, 2002/2003, p. 43–83; M. C. Blaich, M. Geschwinde, *Werla 1 – Die Königspfalz, ihre Geschichte und die Ausgrabungen 1875–1964*, Mainz 2015, passim.

27 G. Binding, *Deutsche Königspfalzen...*, p. 131–137.

28 K. Żurowska, *Dwa szkice...*, p. 30–37.

29 J. Firlet, "Wawelska rezydencja władcy około roku 1000", [in:] *Polska na przełomie I i II tysiąclecia*, ed. S. Skibiński, Poznań 2001, p. 311–324.

30 Z. Pianowski, *Sedes regni principales...*, p. 25–26; M. Bober, *Architektura przedromańska...*, p. 66–69; T. Rodzińska-Chorąży, *Zespoły rezydencjonalne....* p. 46–50; A. Bukowska, "Die Architektur in Wawels in Krakau unter Kasimir dem Erneuerer und ihre Beziehungen in das Rheinland", [in:] *Das Sakramentar aus Tyniec...*, p. 339-358.

tributes from Rus', and his words probably refer to this particular edifice.[31] Master Vincentus (Wincenty Kadłubek) wrote of Boleslaus: *rarus in aula, continuus in castris*, probably picturing this monumental edifice in his mind's eye.[32] It is worth emphasizing that, in the form proposed by archaeologists, its length and width proportions reflect the *sectio aurea*, whereas the extended rectangular projection of the pillars invites associations with a hypocaust system.[33] The assembly hall has a form that is dissimilar to the other, older specimens in the greater Poland region; its origins have been disputed among scholars for a hundred years. However, taking into consideration the hall's proportions and hypothesizing that the lower level's function was one of a heating system – the reception hall as such being placed above it – we have to assume that the designer might have been associated with an artistic milieu where this ancient technological as well as formal tradition was alive. Contrary to the earlier complexes, the Kraków assembly hall was not strictly merged with the sacred structure; scholars have recently identified the function of court church mainly with the basilica situated west of the structure (more on this basilica will be said below). The irregular annex attached to the structure's eastern wall is interpreted by archaeologists as a chapel. The annex was not part of the complex's original concept, and its sacral function is hypothetical.[34]

The palace chapels of the early-Piast rulers were mostly erected on a central plan. Still, apart from the chapel of Giecz, possibly designed as a niche type, and those in Lednica and Przemyśl, the central plan was also characteristic of other early-Piast churches. The earliest church built in Gniezno might have been a rotunda with one apse, though its relics are highly enigmatic.[35] A single-apse rotunda form was definitely applied in the chapel erected in front of the northern elevation of Wawel Cathedral (featuring the above-discussed hollow faced with

---

31 *Galli Chronicon*, ed. A. Bielowski (ser.: Monumenta Poloniae Historica, 1), Lwów 1864, reprint: Warszawa 1960, p. 421.
32 *Mistrza Wincentego Kronika Polska*, trans. K. Abgarowicz, B. Kürbis, ed. B. Kürbis, Warszawa 1974, p. 116.
33 T. Rodzińska-Chorąży, *Zespoły rezydencjonalne* ..., p. 47–50, 160–163.
34 Z. Pianowski, "Dziesiąty kościół wczesnośredniowieczny na Wawelu – kaplica pałacowa pod wezwaniem św. Gereona?", [in:] *Ars sine stientia nihil est. Księga jubeileuszowa prof. Z. Świechowskiego*, Warszawa 1997, p. 211–220; idem, *Sedes regni principales...*, p. 22–25; T. Rodzińska-Chorąży, *Zespoły rezydencjonalne* ..., p. 48.
35 T. Janiak, "Problematyka wczesnych faz kościoła katedralnego w Gnieźnie", [in:] *Początki architektury monumentalnej...*, p. 85–130.

stone slabs)³⁶, in the earliest Saint Benedict Church in Krzemionki (within Kraków)³⁷, and the earliest church in Łekno (in the area known as Pałuki).³⁸ Should archaeological research confirm the dating, the single-apse rotunda adjacent to Saint Gotthard's Church in Strzelin (Śląsk) might possibly be regarded equally old.³⁹

Discussion has also been ongoing over the genesis of the single-apse rotunda form itself. That Bohemian rotundas contributed to dissemination of this layout in the other regions of Central Europe, is a deeply-rooted view.⁴⁰ As for Poland, Mieszko's marriage to the Bohemian Princess Doubravka might be seen as a catalyzer of the adaptation of the form in question in the Piast-ruled country. It does not however seem that imprecise dating of the individual objects, Bohemian as well as Polish, can help confirm this idea. Moreover, it can be supposed that,

---

36 J. Firlet, Z. Pianowski, "Odkrycie dwu wczesnośredniowiecznych kościołów w rejonie tzw. Bastionu Władysława IV na Wawelu", *Sprawozdania Archeologiczne* 37, 1985, p. 153-167; idem, "Wyniki badań archeologicznych w rejonie katedry i pałacu królewskiego na Wawelu (1981-1994)", *Acta Archaeologica Waweliana* 2, 1998, p. 108-109; T. Rodzińska-Chorąży, *Zespoły rezydencjonalne* ..., p. 67-83, 114-118, 136-137.

37 W. Zin, W. Grabski, "Ostatnie odkrycia w rejonie kościoła św. Benedykta na Wzgórzu Lasoty", *Sprawozdania z Posiedzeń Komisji Naukowych PAN*, vol. 9, 1965, part 2: VI-XII, p. 616-621; idem, "Wczesnośredniowieczne budowle Krakowa w świetle ostatnich badań", *Rocznik Krakowski* 38, 1966, p. 57-59; K. Radwański, *Kraków przedlokacyjny*, Kraków 1975, p. 260; J. Czuszkiewicz, "Kościół pw. św. Benedykta w Krakowie w świetle najnowszych badań", [in:] *Architektura sakralna na początkach państwa polskiego (X-XIII wiek)*, ed. T. Janiak, D. Stryniak, Gniezno 2016, p. 85-115.

38 A. M. Wyrwa, "Rotunda łekneńska w świetle dotychczasowych badań na tle architektury wczesnopiastowskiej w Polsce", *Kronika Wielkopolska* 3, 1992, p. 48-64; T. Rodzińska-Chorąży, "Rozważania nad genezą rotund prostych - w świetle nowych odkryć archeologicznych", (ser.: Studia i Materiały do Dziejów Pałuk, 2), Poznań 1995, p. 137-162.

39 T. Kozaczewski, "Rotunda w Strzelinie", *Sprawozdania Wrocławskiego Towarzystwa Naukowego, Architektura*, vol. 8, Wrocław 1956, p. 1-22; Z. Świechowski, *Architektura romańska w Polsce*, Warszawa 2000, p. 232-233; T. Rodzińska-Chorąży, "Rozważania nad genezą...", p. 151-153.

40 A. Merhautova, *Einfache mitteleuropaische Rundkirchen (ihr Ursprung, Zweck und ihre Bedeutung)*, Prague 1970, passim; M. Vančo, *Stredoveké rotundy na Slovensku*, Bratislava 2000, p.passim; idem, *Centrálne stavby veľkomoravskej riše*, Bratislava 2001, passim; L. Konečny, *Románska rotunda ve Znojmé*, Brno 2005 passim; T. Rodzińska-Chorąży, *Zespoły rezydencjonalne* ..., p. 67-83; J. Nawrot, *Kościoły centralne na terenie Czech i Moraw (IX-XIII w.)*, Rzeszów 2013, passim.

apart from the dynastic relationships, the crucial factor for the popularity of the single-apse rotunda model included the parallel conditions in which Central European countries evolved. It is also plausible that the erection of such churches was connected with the progress of missionary efforts. It could be that at the root of the proliferation of the model in question was an archetype shared by everybody, whose ideological significance was decisive in its use. Perhaps such an archetype, common to Central European rotundas with one apse, needs to be traced back among the late antique and early medieval churches of Italy.[41]

Among the early-Piast central edifices we also find the two-apsed rotunda (known as Church B)[42] and the four-apsed rotunda (Blessed Virgin Mary's/ Saint Felix and Saint Adauctus')[43] erected on Wawel Hill. Church B was probably the earliest stone church within the old stronghold of Kraków, as can be judged from its surrounding cemetery[44]; the four-apsed rotunda, most probably furnished with a crypt, could have acted as a reliquary chapel. The peculiar and rare form of both churches has inclined researchers to search for their origins in the architecture of the southern regions of Europe. However, Church B is the edifice that most obviously shows an inspiration related to the Great Moravia area; its only counterpart is Church no. 6 in Mikulčice.[45]

---

41 T. Rodzińska-Chorąży, *Zespoły rezydencjonalne* ..., p. 194–196.

42 S. Kozieł, M. Fraś, *Stratygrafia kulturowa w rejonie przedromańskiego kościoła B na Wawelu*, Wrocław, Warszawa, Kraków, Gdańsk 1979, passim; M. Fraś. S. Kozieł, "Przedromański kościół B na Wawelu w świetle badań archeologicznych w latach 1991– 1992", *Sprawozdania z Posiedzeń Naukowych Polskiej Akademii Nauk*, vol. 37, part 2, 1993, p. 9–10; S. Kozieł, "Badania archeologiczne na Wawelu w latach 1948–1983", *Acta Archaeologica Waweliana* 3, 2006, p. 5–41; Z. Pianowski, "Który Bolesław? Problem początków architektury monumentalnej w Małopolsce", [in:] *Początki architektury monumentalnej...*, ed. T. Janiak, D. Stryniak, p. 277; G. Labuda, "Budowle sakralne na Wawelu w przekazie Jana Długosza z połowy XIII wieku", [in:] idem, *Studia nad początkami państwa polskiego*, vol. 2, Poznań 1988, p. 322–377.

43 K. Żurowska, *Rotunda Wawelska. Studium nad centralną architekturą epoki wczesnopiastowskiej*, (ser.: Studia do Dziejów Wawelu), Kraków 1968, p.1–116; eadem, *Nowe problemy rotundy Panny Marii na Wawelu po odkryciach w latach sześćdziesiątych i siedemdziesiątych XX wieku*, (ser.: Studia nad architekturą wczesnopiastowską. Zeszyty Naukowe Uniwersytetu Jagiellońskiego, Prace z Historii Sztuki, 17), Warszawa, Kraków 1983, p. 7–54); T Rodzińska, *Zespoły rezydencjonalne....*, p. 118–126.

44 S. Kozieł, M. Fraś, *Stratygrafia kulturowa* ..., p. 135.

45 J. Poulík, *Dvě velkomoravské rotundy w Mikulčicach*, Praha 1963, passim; idem, *Mikulčice – sídlo a pevnost knížat velkomoravských*, Praha 1975, passim; M. Vančo, *Stredoveké rotundy na Slovensku*, Bratislava 2000, p. 30–33; idem, *Centrálne stavby veľkomoravskej riše*, Bratislava 2001, passim; L. Konečny, *Románská rotunda ve*

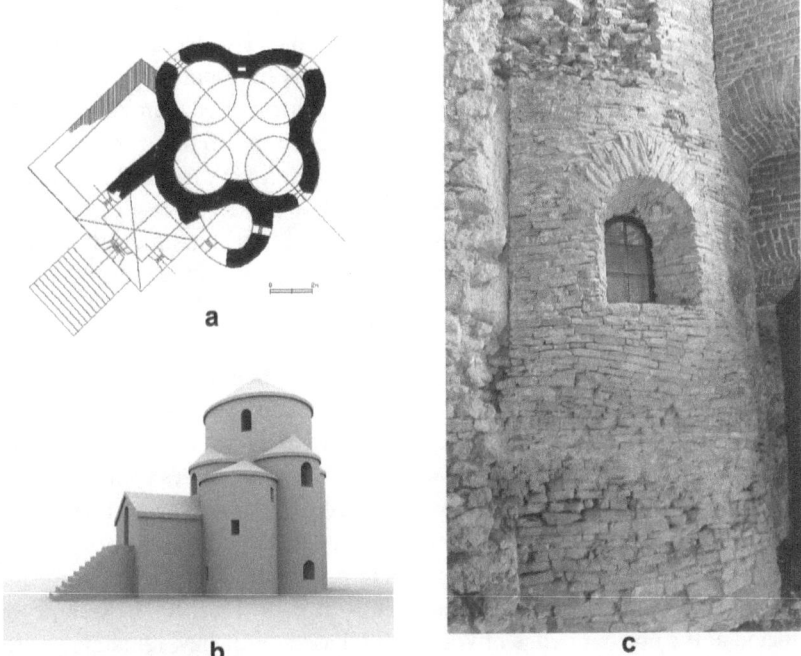

Fig. 3: Kraków-Wawel Hill, tetraconch (St. Mary rotunda): a) the reconstruction of the plan (M. Rosół), b) reconstruction of the form, c) view of the S-E apse (photo T. Rodzińska-Chorąży).

The closest analogy to the Wawel four-apse rotunda is not really Saint Vitus' rotunda in Prague, but rather the Santa Croce Church in Bergamo, this one being a *tetraconch* (possibly, with a crypt) dated to the first half of the 11th c. [Fig. 3a-c].[46]

Znojmě, Brno 2005, p. 385–399; N. Profantová, *Mikulčice – pohřebiště u 6 kostela: pokus o chronologické a sociální zhodnocení*, Brno 2003, passim; L. Galuška, L. Poláček, "Církevní architektura v centrální oblasti velkomoravského státu", [in:] *České země v raném středověku*, ed. P. Sommer, Praha 2006, p. 92–153.

46 G. Zizzo, "Bergamo", [in:] *Itinerari dell'Anno Mille. Chiese romaniche nel Bergamasco*, ed. P. Capellini, G. M. Labaa, Bergamo 1999, p. 63–66; M. C. Miller, *The Bishop's Palace. Architecture and Authority in Medieval Italy*, New York, London 2000, p. 224–226, 251; A. Cardaci, D. Galliana, A. Versaci, "Laser scanner 3D per lo studio e la catalogazione dell'archeologia medievale: la Chiesa di Santa Croce in Bergamo", *Archeologia e Calcolatori* 24, 2013, p. 209–229.

For the latter half of the 11th c., we cannot unambiguously confirm that any buildings existed, whether in Greater or Lesser Poland, which might have functioned as cathedral churches – though historians have not ceased discussing the origins and status of the Bishoprics in Kraków and Poznań before 1000.[47] Actually, the year 1000 is of special importance to the architectural landscape of Poland, for it was then that the Archbishopric in Gniezno and its subordinated episcopal sees in Poznań, Kraków, Wrocław, and Kołobrzeg were created, in each of which a cathedral must have been erected. If their construction (rather than remodeling of an earlier church) commenced after 1000, the founder must have been Boleslaus I the Brave. The extant fragments of walls do confirm that a church existed in Wrocław; its approximate width can be hypothetically determined, but nothing more.[48] The earliest metropolitan cathedral in Gniezno was formed, in turn, into a basilica with a nave and two aisles, with no transept or turrets/towers. It had three apses situated at its east end, and was closed up by a regular wall at the western side. The "Saint Adalbert's confession" was located inside, set along the church's axis [**Fig. 4a**].[49] This reconstruction enables identification of the underlying model within the architectural circle of First Romanesque art – the closest example, in terms of form and proportions, being the San Vincenzo Basilica in Galliano, Lombardy.[50] The cathedral in Kraków was situated at the northern edge of Wawel Hill. Based on the few remaining relics, we may guess that it probably was a basilica with a square-shaped presbytery closed with an apse, with some smaller apses opening toward the transept.[51]

---

47   For a recent summary of the current state of research and related debate, see: D. A. Sikorski, *Kościół w Polsce* ..., p. 130–208.
48   E. Małachowicz, "Przedromański kościół i pierwsza katedra we Wrocławiu", *Kwartalnik Architektury i Urbanistyki* 44, 2000, p. 191–206; P. Rzeźnik, A. Żurek, "Wrocław ok. roku 1000", [in:] *Polska na przełomie* ..., p. 335–352; Z. Świechowski, *Architektura romańska w Polsce*, Warszawa 2000, p. 291–293.
49   T. Janiak, "Z badań nad przestrzenią liturgiczną romańskiej katedry w Gnieźnie", [in:] *Architektura romańska w Polsce. Nowe odkrycia i interpretacje*, ed. T. Janiak, Gniezno 2009, p. 129–174.
50   R. Casanelli, "Un contributo agli assetti presbiterialidi etá ottoniana. Ariberto 'custos' a Galliano (Cantù, Como) e la ricostruzione della basilica di S. Vincenzo", *Hortus Artium Medievalium* 15, 2009, p. 93–206; A. Bukowska, *Najstarsza katedra*..., p. 256.
51   J. Firlet, Z. Pianowski, "Przemiany architektury rezydencji monarszej oraz katedry na Wawelu w świetle nowych badań", *Kwartalnik Architektury i Urbanistyki* 44, 2000, p. 225–236; idem, "Z rozważań nad planem najstarszej katedry krakowskiej", [in:] *Lapides Viventes. Zaginiony Kraków wieków średnich. Księga dedykowana Profesor Klementynie Żurowskiej*, ed. T. Rodzińska-Chorąży, A. Włodarek et al., Kraków 2005, p. 57–66.

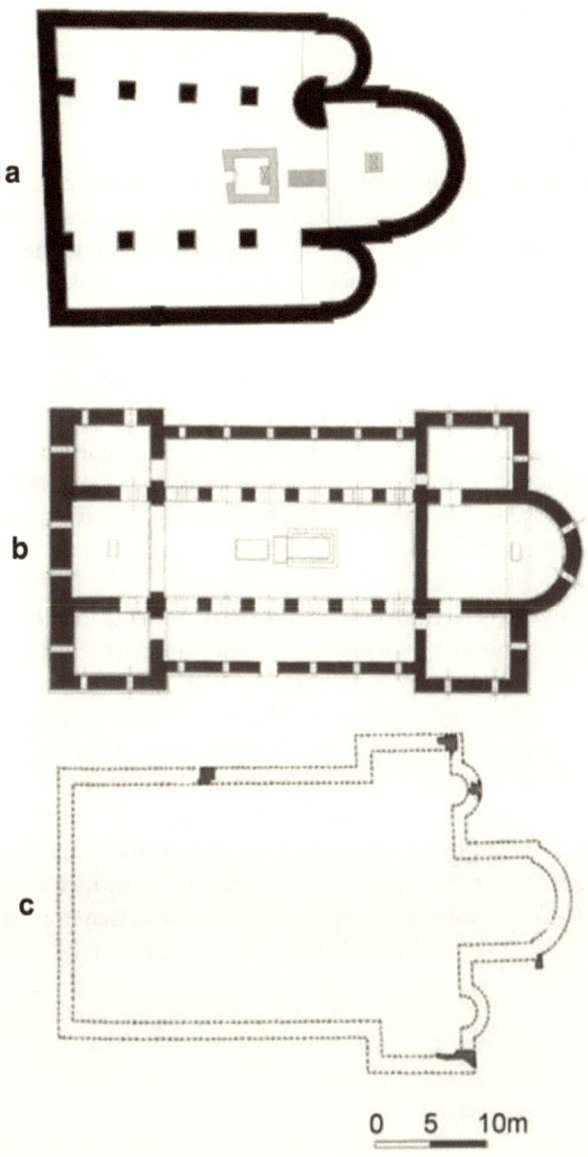

Fig. 4: The cathedrals in Poland after 1000: a) Gniezno (by T. Janiak), b) Poznań (by A. Bukowska), c) Kraków (by J. Firlet, Z. Pianowski).

There is no doubt that the aforementioned single-apsed rotunda equipped with a quadrilateral hollow in the floor functioned in parallel with this particular structure. Nonetheless, the scarcity of available data makes the reconstruction of the layout of the aisle body, or of the form of the western end of the church, impossible [Fig. 4b].

There is no doubt that in terms of size the first cathedral church of Kraków resembled its Poznań counterpart; the relics of the latter have survived relatively well, compared to the other churches in Poland existing around the year 1000. In light of the most recent findings submitted by Aneta Bukowska, it can be stated that the church was a symmetrically laid-out two-choir basilica.[52] Underneath the presbytery, closed up with an apse at the eastern end, was a crypt whose vault was supported on four supports. The western end of the cathedral is its least recognized section, which can be interpreted as a towerless block; otherwise, the western loft might have been highlighted by a four-sided tower along the church's axis. The patterns indicated by Bukowska include the Magdeburg cathedral and, primarily, the Memleben abbey's basilica [Fig. 4c]. The latter example is significant as it was the Memleben Abbot, Unger, who in 1000 was most probably appointed Bishop of Poznań.[53]

Apart from cathedral churches, which speak volumes on the progress of Christianization, monasteries or cloisters were also erected. The location of the earliest hermitage, named *Mestris* in one written record, remains unidentifiable.[54] The five brethren dwelling there died a martyr's death. This incident, dated to 1003, inspired the development of monastic life in the Piasts' lands. However, the next record on a monastery's foundation is dated to 1044 – namely, the Benedictine Abbey in Tyniec near Kraków. According to Jan Długosz's chronicle, the abbey was founded by Casimir the Restorer after his return from exile and the suppression of the political revolt.[55] However, the construction of the church began later, thanks to bestowals from Boleslaus the Bold/Generous and Duchess Judith, consort to Duke Ladislaus Herman, and was probably completed after

---

52 A. Bukowska, *Najstarsza katedra...*, p. 135–246.
53 A. Bukowska, "Przed rokiem 1000? Katedra w Poznaniu, biskup Unger i kościół benedyktyński w Memleben", *Modus. Prace z Historii Sztuki* 8/9, 2009, p. 285–302; eadem, *Najstarsza katedra...*, p. 247–258; D. A. Sikorski, *Kościół w Polsce...*, p. 332–486.
54 G. Labuda, *Szkice historyczne X-XI wieku*, Poznań 2004, p. 183–240; B. Kürbis, "Bruno z Kwerfurtu i początki kultu pięciu braci", [in:] *Polska na przełomie...*, p. 119–120.
55 G. Labuda, *Szkice historyczne...*, p. 241–304.

1100.[56] Relics of the church were discovered in the 1960s, ones which revealed a transeptless basilica featuring a nave and two aisles, the latter divided into rectangular bays, separated by semi-columns closely fit to the internal wall. The western end is reconstructed as a two-tower façade [Fig. 5a].[57] The models for such a basilica are possibly traceable south of the Carpathians, perhaps among the Hungarian basilicas.[58] What we know for certain is that there was a stone-masonry workshop in Tyniec that also operated at Wawel: this attested by details such as the form of the semi-column/stanchion bases and that of the bases found in the crypt of Wawel's Saint Gereon's Basilica.[59]

Known to us are also the relics of three other Benedictine churches dated to the second half of the 11th c. The best recognized one is the church in Mogilno, Greater Poland; King Boleslaus the Bold/Generous endowed the local abbey in 1065.[60] It was a basilica with a short body and a low transept, furbished with two crypts – one under the eastern choir and the other on the lowest level of the massive quadrangular tower situated along the axis, at the west end.[61] The western crypt's layout is peculiar, consisting of four bays vaulted crosswise, with a centrally situated square pillar [Fig. 5b]. The church's design drew from Benedictine basilicas of the Maas River area, such as Hasitere and Celle, which seems legitimate based on the background of the monks residing in the abbey and their close

---

56 M. Graczyńska, M. Kamińska, "Architektura monastyczna w Polsce do końca XI wieku. Nowe spojrzenie", [in:] *Średniowieczna architektura sakralna w Polsce w świetle najnowszych badań*, ed. T. Janiak, D. Stryniak, Gniezno 2014, p. 47–66.
57 K. Żurowska, "Romański kościół opactwa benedyktynów w Tyńcu", *Folia Historiae Artium* 6–7, 1971, p. 49–113; eadem, "Kraków, Tyniec i benedyktyni", [in:] *Artifex doctus. Studia ofiarowane profesorowi Jerzemu Gadomskiemu w siedemdziesiątą rocznice urodzin*, ed. W. Bałus et. al., Kraków 2007, p. 229–231.
58 K. Żurowska, *Romański kościół...*, p. 49–113; I. Takács, *Paradisum plantavit. Bences monostorok a középkori Magyarországon*, Pannonhalma 2001, p. 626; R. Quirini-Popławski, "Parę uwag o adriatycko-węgierskiej genezie stylu kapiteli z klasztoru benedyktyńskiego w Tyńcu", [in:] *Multa et varia. Studii offerti a Marta Marcella Ferraccioli e Gianfranco Giraudo*, vol. 2, ed. F. Cret Ciure et al., Milano 2012, p. 459.
59 K. Żurowska, "Kraków, Tyniec…", p. 229–231; M. Graczyńska, M. Kamińska, "Architektura monastyczna …", p. 53–61.
60 G. Labuda, *Szkice historyczne…*, p. 305–362; L. Wetesko, *Historyczne konteksty …*, p. 176–178; M. Graczyńska, M. Kamińska, "Architektura monastyczna …" p. 51–52.
61 J. Chudziakowa, *Romański kościół benedyktynów w Mogilnie*, vol. 1, Warszawa 1984, passim; eadem, "Opactwo benedyktynów w Mogilnie", [in:] *Benedyktyni tynieccy w średniowieczu. Materiały z sesji naukowej, Wawel-Tyniec, 13–15.10.1994*, ed. K. Żurowska, Tyniec–Kraków 1995, p. 207–220.

a

b

Fig. 5: a) Abbey in Tyniec, the southern wall of the church (photo T. Rodzińska-Chorąży), b) Abbey in Mogilno, the western crypt (photo T. Rodzińska-Chorąży).

contacts with the Diocese of Leodium (Liège).[62] Our knowledge about the first (uncompleted) abbatial church in Lubiń is more limited. Its eastern part, being a three-apse basilica without a transept, similar in form to the Gniezno cathedral, has been recognized.[63] Even more enigmatic are the relics of the edifice unveiled underneath the 12th c. collegiate church in Tum near Łęczyca, which was seemingly a modest single-aisle church with an apse at the eastern end and a tower at the opposite end, and had to do (or, was simply identical) with what is described in the original records as an "abbey of the Blessed Virgin Mary".[64] Hence, in the 11th c. the Benedictine churches erected in the Piast-ruled country featured diverse forms and models, and observed differing traditions.

The architectonic landscape of eleventh-century Poland also featured churches whose original function is unknown. One case in point is Saint John the Baptist's

---

62 K. Żurowska, "Działalność architektoniczna benedyktynów w Wielkopolsce w drugiej połowie XI w.", *Folia Historiae Artium* 6–7, 1971, p. 121–133; eadem, "Kościół opactwa benedyktynów w Mogilnie po badaniach z lat siedemdziesiątych, *Zeszyty Naukowe Uniwersytetu Jagiellońskiego. Prace Historyczne* 89, 1989, p. 27–42; A. Bukowska, "Masyw zachodni w architekturze wczesnopiastowskiej", [in:] *Początki architektury monumentalnej...*, p. 349–361; eadem, "Masyw zachodni benedyktyńskiego kościoła klasztornego w Lubiniu – zagadnienie formy i funkcji w świetle materiału porównawczego", [in:] *Lapides Viventes...*, p. 325–342; Z. Świechowski, "Romańskie bazyliki Wielkopolski północno-wschodniej w świetle najnowszych badań", *Archaeologia Historica Polona* 2, 1995, p. 75–132; M. Graczyńska, M. Kamińska, "Architektura monastyczna...", p. 47–66.

63 Z. Kurnatowska, "Opactwo benedyktyńskie w Lubiniu w świetle badań wykopaliskowych w latach 1978–1983", *Studia i Materiały do dziejów Wielkopolski i Pomorza* 32, 1987, p. 5–23; eadem, "Opactwo romańskie w Lubiniu, Wyniki szczegółowej analizy informacji z badań wykopaliskowych i odkrywek architektonicznych", [in:] *Architektura romańska w Polsce...*, p. 223–250; M. Żurek, "Kościół konwentualny Panny Marii w Lubiniu. Rekonstrukcja kolejnych faz budowy i rozbudowy w XI i XIII w.", [in:] *Opactwo benedyktynów w Lubiniu. Pierwsze wieki istnienia. Materiały z sesji*, ed. Z. Kurnatowska, Poznań 1996, p. 35–57; A. Bukowska, *Masyw zachodni...*, p. 325–342.

64 A. Nadolski, "Łęczyckie opactwo Panny Marii", [in:] *Prace i materiały Muzeum Archeologicznego i Etnograficznego w Łodzi*, 1960, p. 61–83; T. Poklewski-Koziełł, "Kościół łęczycki, czyli budowle romańskie w Tumie. Blaski i cienie u początku tysiąclecia", [in:] *Pokłosie zjazdu gnieźnieńskiego. O początkach kościoła w Łęczycy*, ed. B. Solarski, M. Sęczkowska, Łęczyca 2000, p. 19–28; J. Sikora, "Uwagi na temat tzw. opactwa Panny Marii w Tumie pod Łęczycą", *Kwartalnik Historii Kultury Materialnej* 50, 2002, p. 392–404; M. Graczyńska, M. Kamińska, "Architektura monastyczna ...", p. 47–49.

Church in Giecz, whose form and dating arouse special interest. This single-nave structure had an expanded eastern part which featured a choir elevated above the crypt, crowned with a semicircular apse.[65] The plan of this crypt is unusual, with two symmetric corridors leading to it refracting at right angles and comprising stairwells that led to a transverse section with a niche at the west wall and a quadrilateral main chamber. These elements indicate that the crypt was designed as a place for depositing valuable relics of a saint (regrettably, not identifiable today – but maybe for Bruno of Querfurt).[66] Dated to the first decades of the 11th c., Saint John's Church was in that century's second half remodeled and enriched at its western end, with a massif whose outstanding feature were two massive circular towers.[67] The crypt's form, derived from the corridor-shaped Carolingian crypts, and the forms of the tower massif of a Rhineland or Saxon background, make this church particularly interesting. July 2016 marked the beginning of a new stage in the research into this complex. In 2018, under the nave, the remains of the older building were discovered which can be dated to the second half of the 10th c. Saint John's Church with the crypt, let us add, shows elements present in the architecture of Benedictine complexes, although there is no original record that would allow us to associate this particular church with the Benedictine Order [**Fig. 6a-b**].

---

65 T. Krysztofiak, "Nowoodkryte relikty architektury romańskiej w Gieczu", [in:] *Osadnictwo i architektura ziem polskich w dobie zjazdu gnieźnieńskiego*, ed. A. Buko, Z. Świechowski, Warszawa 2000, p. 75–84; idem, "Giecz", [in:] *Europas Mitte um 1000. Beiträge zur Geschichte. Kunst und Archäologie*, vol. 1, ed. A. Wieczorek, H.-M. Hinz, Stuttgart 2000, p. 464–466; idem, "Wczesnopiastowski kościół p.w. św. Jana Chrzciciela na grodzie w Gieczu w świetle najnowszych odkryć", [in:] *Początki architektury monumentalnej...*, p. 181–198; T. Rodzińska-Chorąży, "Co nam mówi architektura murowana?", [in:] *Ziemie polskie w X wieku...*, p. 361–387; T. Węcławowicz, "Karolińsko-ottoński kościół grodowy w Gieczu p.w. św. Jana Chciciela", [in:] *Ziemie polskie w X wieku...*, p. 420–421.
66 T. Rodzińska-Chorąży, "Krypta kościoła grodowego pod wezwaniem świętego Jana Chrzciciela w Gieczu – analiza formy i funkcji", [in:] *Magistro et Amico amici discipulique. Lechowi Kalinowskiemu w osiemdziesięciolecie urodzin*, ed. J. Gadomski, Kraków 2002, p. 165–185; eadem, "The Church of St. John the Baptist in Giecz as the Evidence of the Relations of the Piast Court with the Rhineland in the 11th Century", [in:] *Das Sakramentar aus Tyniec...*, p. 359–374.
67 T. Krysztofiak, "Ośrodek grodowy w Gieczu w okresie przed i wczesnopaństwowym", [in:] *Gród piastowski w Gieczu. Geneza, funkcja, kontekst*, ed. M. Kara, T. Krysztofiak, A. M. Wyrwa, Poznań 2016, p. 115–154; T. Rodzińska-Chorąży, "Kościół św. Jana Chrzciciela w Gieczu – między przesłaniem a tajemnicą", [in:] *Gród piastowski w Gieczu...*, p. 179–208.

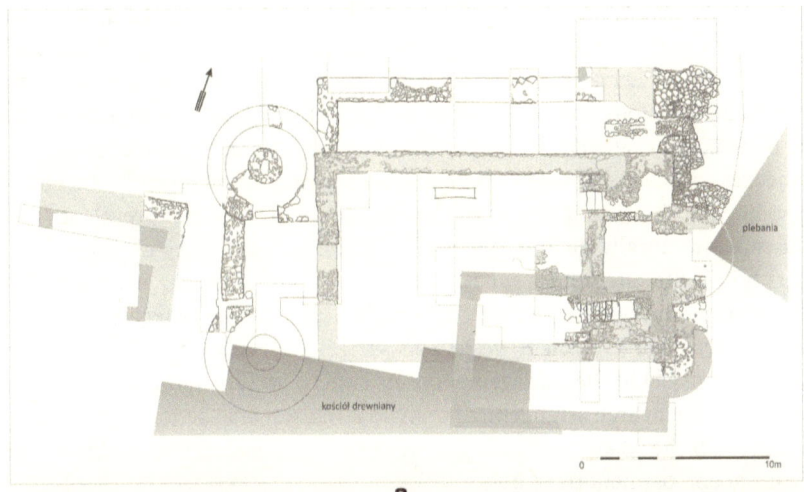

Fig. 6: St. John the Baptist Church in Giecz: a) the plan of the remains with hipothetical form of the earlier church (by T. Krysztofiak, T. Rodzińska-Chorąży), b) aerial view of the eastern part of the church with the crypt (photo T. Siuda).

A similar situation appears with respect to the basilica built in Kraków's Wawel area, at a short distance east of the cathedral.[68] Archaeologists have dated it to the rule of Casimir the Restorer, but it seems that it was founded somewhat later.[69] The functions ascribed to this basilica have included that of a church for the Benedictines settled at Wawel by Casimir; the first and thereafter the second cathedral within the double cathedral church group; more recently the no less hypothetical view that it served as a court church has become prevalent.[70] The church, conjecturally dedicated to Saint Gereon or Saint Mary of Egypt, had a short body with alternating supports, a transept with a gallery in its northern arm, a crypt equipped with four supports beneath the presbytery, and a hard-to-reconstruct three-element western massif [**Fig. 7**]. Its form combines Saxon influence (visible in the arrangement of its eastern section and the body's composition) with an arch arrangement that has its closest association with the crypt in Celles on the Maas, and with the stonework processing the motifs of early medieval embossment from Italy.[71]

---

68 A. Szyszko-Bohusz, "O kościele romańskim odkrytym pod zachodnim skrzydłem zamku na Wawelu", *Sprawozdania z Posiedzeń Komisji PAU*, vol. 24, no. 7, 1919, p. 6; idem, "Z historii romańskiego Wawelu. Pierwsza katedra Krakowska", *Rocznik Krakowski* 19, 1923, p. 1–23; idem, "Wawel średniowieczny", *Rocznik Krakowski* 23, 1932, p. 19–25; idem, "Studia nad katedra wawelską", *Prace Komisji Historii Sztuki*, vol. 8, 1946, p. 107–148; Z. Pianowski, *Sedes regni principales...*, p. 27–28; J. Firlet, Z. Pianowski, "Wyniki badań archeologicznych w rejonie katedry i pałacu królewskiego na Wawelu (1981–1994)", *Acta Archaeologica Waweliana* 2, 1998, p. 110–115; idem, "Przemiany architektury...", p. 213–214; K. Żurowska, "Kraków, Tyniec ...", p. 227–233; idem, "Krakowska bazylika św. Gereona. O recepcji motywów nadmozańskich i śródziemnomorskich w połowie XI wieku", [in:] *Čechy jsou plné kostelů. Kniha k poctě PhDr. Anežky Merhautové*, ed. M. Studničková, Praha 2010, p. 81–95.
69 J. Firlet, Z. Pianowski, "Wawel wczesnośredniowieczny i jego budowle", [in:] *Studia nad dawną Polską*, vol. 3, ed. T. Sawicki, (ser.: Biblioteka Muzeum Początków Państwa Polskiego, 4) Gniezno 2013, p. 42; T. Rodzińska-Chorąży, "Główne problemy związane z formą i interpretacją najstarszych reliktów krakowskiej grupy katedralnej w świetle badań archeologicznych i historyczno-artystycznych", [in:] *Mecenat artystyczny biskupów Krakowskich*, Kraków 2016, p. 55–68.
70 J. Firlet, Z. Pianowski, "Przemiany architektury...", p. 213–214.
71 K. Żurowska, "Kraków, Tyniec...", p. 227–233; eadem, "Krakowska bazylika św. Gereona...", p. 81–95, T. Rodzińska-Chorąży, "Kapitel z krypty bazyliki pod zachodnim skrzydłem Zamku Królewskiego na Wawelu", [in:] *Artifex doctus...*, vol. 1, Kraków 2007, p. 235–243; R. Quirini-Popławski, *Rzeźba przedromańska i romańska w Polsce wobec sztuki włoskiej*, Kraków 2006, p.73-90; idem, "Parę uwag o adriatycko-węgierskiej genezie...", p. 459.

Fig. 7: Kraków-Wawel Hill, St. Gereon Church: the plan and reconstruction by J. Firlet, Z. Pianowski (photos of the details T. Rodzińska-Chorąży).

Yet another identifiable specimen of early-Piast architecture is that of the remnants the first Our Lady's church in Zawichost, whose fragments (the apse) are definitely dated at the last quarter of the 11th c.[72] Conversely, the remains of the church in Kałdus near Chełmno are not clearly identifiable. Its walls and negatives, outlining an extended rectangle with three apses at its east end, do not tell us clearly whether it was an uncompleted basilica or a single-nave church; hence, the dating and function of the structure remain unclear.[73]

***

Given the above remarks, the present-day state of research into Poland's earliest architecture enables some conclusions to be drawn. As far as the period around the year 1000 is concerned, the form of residential complexes of the first Piast rulers distinguishes itself among what is encountered elsewhere in Central Europe, with a concise concept and single-axial layout, and with a diversity in the body shapes of palace chapels. These complexes testify to the dynasty's political ambitions, and prove that the rulers established contacts with various artistic milieu of the Empire (in the broad sense), taking advantage of the services of highly educated architects.

The ducal curia, which was usually situated at the stronghold's highest point, neighbored stone cathedral churches situated within the surrounding settlement and marking the highlights in the area's topography. The close distance between the cathedral and the ruler's residence attests to a strict relationship between secular and the clerical authority, which developed based on the imperial model. The surviving architectural relics suggest that all the episcopal churches were probably basilicas, with a transept definitely existing in two of them. The cathedral of Poznań, the best recognized one, was approximately 40 m long; the lengths of its peers were probably 30 m to 40 m. Given the European sacred

---

[72] D. Wyczółkowski, "Zawichost romański w XI-XIII wieku", [in:] *Architektura sakralna...*, p. 171–82.

[73] W. Chudziak, "Wczesnośredniowieczny zespół osadniczy w Chełmnie", *Acta Archaeologica Pomoranica* 1, 1998, p. 227–235; idem, *Mons Sancti Laurentii*, vol. 1: *Wczesnośredniowieczna przestrzeń sakralna in Culmine na Pomorzu Nadwiślańskim*, Toruń 2003; idem, "Rekonstrukcja bryły wczesnoromańskiej bazyliki z Kałdusa pod Chełmnem na Pomorzu Wschodnim", *Archaeologia Historica Polona* 13, 2013, p. 85–98; idem, "Geneza wczesnoromańskiej bazyliki z Kałdusa na Pomorzu Nadwiślańskim", [in:] *Początki architektury monumentalnej...*, p. 245–256; T. Rodzińska-Chorąży, "Kilka uwag w sprawie metody prezentacji i interpretacji reliktów budowli sakralnej w Kałdusie", [in:] *II Forum Architecturae Poloniae Medievalis*, ed. K. Stala, Kraków 2011, p. 369–380.

architecture of the period, these structures were medium-sized. The research done in the last three decades has shed more light on the genesis of their forms. The inspiration of Saxon architecture, clearly visible in the Poznań cathedral, contrast with elements of a southern provenance, such as the basilica of Gniezno with its central nave and two aisles and no transept or towers. Interestingly, the two cathedrals with such different stylistic features were erected roughly in the same period, at a 50 km distance from each other. This might have been due to the different traditions and experiences contributed to Piast's lands by two Church dignitaries – Unger, the Bishop of Poznań; and Radim Gaudentius of the Slavnik family, Saint Adalbert's brother and the first Archbishop of Gniezno.

The cathedrals, which originally date back to the year 1000, were partly rebuilt or replaced by new edifices in the second half of the 11th c. Their forms of about 1100 testify to a deepening assimilation of the western models from the Empire's territory.[74] One instance confirming this is given by the tower massif appended to the earlier-built body of the Gniezno cathedral.[75] Similarly to the cathedral churches, the best known monastery churches from the latter half of the 11th c. show a diversity of forms. The basilica of Tyniec and the never-built church in Lubiń are transeptless structures with a characteristic three-apse eastern ending. These features render them similar to the Gniezno cathedral in its phase 1 and 2. They share a design type derived from the southern rather than western architecture. The abbey Church of Mogilno appears to have been the first (and not the last) specimen of architecture "imported" from the Maas River region to Piast lands.

An important question with respect to the factors shaping early-Piast architecture concerns the influence of early Bohemian architecture. The artistic relations between the lands of the Piasts and the Přemyslid-ruled country in the latter half of the 10th c. and in the first half of the 11th c. have long been raised in the literature. This issue primarily concerned the central churches: the single-apse rotundas, Church B, or the *tetraconch* at Wawel, the earliest church on Wrocław's Ostrów Tumski island, and the possible association between the pleat-patterned reliefs featured on architectonic details found beneath the cathedral and within Saint Gereon's Church at Wawel, on the one hand, and the decoration of the trunk of the columns in the Prague cathedral's crypt on the other.[76] Exploration

---

74 M. Graczyńska, M. Kamińska, "Katedra Krakowska versus katedra praska – nowa odsłona", [in:] *Architektura sakralna...*, p. 67–84.
75 T. Janiak, "Problematyka wczesnych faz..." p. 85–130.
76 Z. Pianowski, "L'architecture préromane et romane au château royal de Cracovie", *Cahiers de Civilisation Médiévale* 38, 1995, p. 141–163; Z. Świechowski, B. Malik, "Relikty przedromańskiej dekoracji plecionkowej na Wawelu", *Studia Waweliana* 9/10,

of these relationships is a complex task, given the imprecise dating and reconstruction of the monuments under study. There is no doubt that the dynastic relations – primarily, Mieszko and Doubravka's marriage, the background of Adalbert and Radim of the Slavnik family, and the brief rule of Boleslaus the Brave in Prague – are premises indicating that the models and patterns from the land of Bohemia might have been adapted in the territories of Greater and Lesser Poland, especially before 1000. However, the historical monuments we are presently aware of do not permit us to state there was an important impact of early Bohemian architecture on early-Piast structures. The relations between Prague's Saint Vitus's rotunda and the *tetraconch* on Wawel Hill are difficult to define due to their differences, the significant controversies accompanying the reconstruction of these two churches, and their dissimilar function within the strongholds (Saint Vitus's rotunda – Saint Venceslaus's grave church/cathedral; Wawel's *tetraconch* – possibly, a reliquary chapel). The analogy between the cruciform church in Libice and the Wrocław church being hypothetically reconstructed in this form, as shown by some authors, appears to be a misinterpretation, given the condition of the surviving relics.[77] The only specimen one can be more certain about is the aforementioned Church B of Wawel. It is not clear, though, how long the two-apsed Church no. 6 of Mikulčice functioned; nor do we know whether it can be assumed that the builders active at Wawel followed the example of that particular Moravian rotunda, which (hypothetically) might have functioned at the time Church B was erected.

The comparative material quoted by various authors does not allow, in a number of cases, the convenience of proposing/accepting unambiguous opinions regarding the circle of formal and stylistic (inter)dependencies. What can be ascertained, though, is that the earliest architectural works in Poland feature a duality consisting in the coexistence of western and southern forms, with specific models drawn from various artistic milieu. This syncretism obviously

---

2000/2001, p. 195–204; idem, "Relikty przedromańskiej dekoracji plecionkowej na Wawelu", [in:] *Lapides Viventes, Zaginiony Kraków wieków średnich*, ed. T. Rodzińska-Chorąży, A Włodarek, Kraków 2005, p. 83–92; R. Quirini-Popławski, *Rzeźba przedromańska i romańska w Polsce wobec sztuki włoskiej*, Kraków 2006, p.73–85.

77 E. Małachowicz, "Pierwszy kościół i katedra we Wrocławiu", [in:] *Ziemie polskie w X wieku...*, p. 404–410; idem, "Przedromański kościół...", p. 191–206; idem, "Architektura wczesnośredniowiecznych budowli katedry wrocławskiej", [in:] *Początki architektury monumentalnej...*, p. 293–306; P. Rzeźnik, M. Żurek, "Wrocław około roku 1000", [in:] *Polska na przełomie...*, p. 335–352.

resulted from multiple factors, at the fore being the contacts of the ruler and his closest advisors, and the background of the bishops and monks invited to pursue activity in Poland. Also, the position of magnates strengthened: at the end of the 11th c. and in the first half of the following century their role in the shaping of Poland's architectural landscape grew markedly. The so-called testament of Boleslaus the Wrymouth (Bolesław III Krzywousty, 1107–1138) symbolically "liberated" architecture, in the second quarter of the 12th c., from the foundational dominance of a single power center.

Translated by Tristan Korecki

Andrzej Buko

The archaeological discoveries at Bodzia near Włocławek (Kuyavia region) and their significance for Poland's early-medieval history

Abstract: The chapter presents results of the archaeological excavations carried out in 2007–2009 in the village at Bodzia. Among several discoveries the most unique is that of an early-medieval elite cemetery, dated most probably between 980 and 1030. Some members of the early Piast monarchy's social elite probably buried there might be associated with different milieux: Slavic, nomadic, western Scandinavian, and Varangian. Unique for the Bodzia graveyard is also the wealth of monetary finds, one of the largest in Europe, comparing to the total number of graves. The excavations at Bodzia throw light on the social structure of the early Piast state, including the elite groups of Mieszko's advisors and warriors from various cultural zones.

Keywords: archeology, early medieval elites, Slavs, Khazars, Varangians, Mieszko I

The archaeological research conducted in 2007–2009, in an area of the Kuyavia (Kujawy) region to be crossed by the A1 motorway, found features dating to various epochs and periods. Among the several important and significant discoveries, as documented by the Poznań-based Rescue Team of the Institute of Archaeology and Ethnology, Polish Academy of Sciences[1], one is definitely unique: an early-medieval elite necropolis dating to Poland's beginnings. On the slope of a fairly small height, bodies of a small elite population were buried. Some of them must have arrived from outside, and were associated with the Slavic and nomadic cultural environment; others with the western Scandinavian circle (the Baltic zone, as a broad concept); still others, with the Varangian/Ruthenian area. The graveyard is dated to the last decades of the 10th and the early 11th c., most probably between 980 and 1030[2], and thus is chronologically associated with the first Piast monarchy.

---

1   The fieldwork research, carried out in 2007–9, was managed by Iwona Sobkowiak-Tabaka, PhD.
2   A. Buko, T. D. Price, M. Kara, W. Duczko, K. M. Frei, I. Sobkowiak-Tabaka, "A unique medieval cemetery from the 10th/11th century with chamber-like graves from Bodzia

What we find in Bodzia are phenomena for which it would be difficult to find a direct analogy. These include graves arranged into four rows, delineated by rectangular enclosures, numerous construction elements of the like-chamber-grave type known to the north-west of Europe, alongside grave chambers with annexes as characteristic of the nomadic Khazar people. Noteworthy is the "northward" orientation of the dead, which is contrary to what was common practice in Polish territory and Europe at that time. The richly equipped graves, the amounts of coins found in them (unique in comparison with the other cemeteries of the period), and the special places where these coins were deposited, are puzzling. These are but few of the observations that make this burial ground the only of its kind known to date across Europe.

As regards its location, the burial site seems meaningful. The region of Kuyavia is adjacent to the middle stretch of the Vistula River, which in the early Middle Ages connected the Baltic zone with south-eastern Europe and, further on, with Byzantine civilization. For a number of years, the Vistula route has been regarded in the literature as definitely less research-inspiring than western Pomerania (Pomorze) with Wolin island and its legendary Viking settlement of Jomsborg remaining the showcase. Research carried out and the discoveries made in recent years have shown that the importance of the Vistula route in interregional contacts, particularly with Scandinavia, was higher than it had hitherto been believed.[3] There was no coincidence in the fact that east of the territory in question – in the country of the Prussians – a "Danish" locality of Truso had emerged before Poland entered the stage as a country, and lasted there for almost two centuries.[4]

Within the four rows of the burial ground, the bones of fifty-two persons have been identified, among them twelve categorized as male, eighteen female, and eleven children. The gender of nine of the buried humans remains unidentified. That there are more female skeletons identified than male is a fact of interest. In percent terms, 74 % of the bones belong to adults, the remainder of the anthropological material (26 %) being bones of children who died less than fifteen years of age. Most of the skeletons belonged to persons aged forty to fifty; there were

---

(central Poland). Preliminary result of the multidisciplinary research", *Archäologisches Korrespondenzblatt* 43, 2013, p. 423–442.

[3] M. Bogucki, "The Archaeological Context of the Bodzia Cemetery and the Trade Route along the Middle and the Lower Vistula during the Middle and Late Viking Period", [in:] *Bodzia. A Late Viking-Age Elite Cemetery in Central Poland*, ed. A. Buko, Leiden and Boston 2014, p. 9–33.

[4] M. F. Jagodziński, *Truso. Między Weonodlandem a Witlandem*, Elbląg 2010.

none aged above sixty. Research into these findings has produced the image of a cemetery that was used by a rather small community whose average lifespan was up to thirty years. Such short lifetimes fit within the limits accepted for Polish territory of the period. The bodies' heights, as measured for the males (approximately 168 cm) and females (152 cm), can be considered typical, whereas for the men the figure fits within the upper limit of the feature's variability, the lower limit being the case for the women. Anthropological research has revealed evidence of typical pathologies of the buried, such as dental caries, periodontal inflammation, hypoplasia, degenerations/deformations visible on the vertebrae, cancerous findings, and so on. Traces of mechanical damage have been found in three burials: some having been the cause of death, others bearing traces of healing.[5]

Compared to the period's other cemeteries, what one observes in Bodzia is a blend of elements from various cultures and thus, elements of diverse funeral ceremonials, some of them mutually complementary. They are characteristic for the west, north, east, as well as south of Europe in the late 10th and the first half of the 11th c. All this makes many of them not clearly classifiable. Suffice it to say that the same determinants of material culture (such as elements of armament), albeit characteristic for the environment of Poland's northern neighbors, did not necessarily function exclusively in contexts related to Scandinavia.

There is no identifiable direct analogy to the spatial layout of the cemetery, composed of the four rows of graves, a vast majority of which are equipped with enclosures – rectangular or otherwise [**Fig. 1**].

More similarities can be spotted when it comes to analyzing the forms of individual graves. Seen from this standpoint, the significant-sized grave chambers found within or beyond the enclosures attract attention. Their forms are diversified: some resemble a rectangle, others are oval-shaped, trapezoidal, both with and without annexes. They resemble objects defined by expert authors as chamber graves.

A feature that reappears and is consistently observed at the Bodzia cemetery is the depth of the grave pits: they appear much too large compared to what it takes to deposit a corpse. As proposed by Michał Kara[6], this can be attributed to

---

5   A. Drozd-Lipińska, T. Kozłowski, "Analysis of the Skeletal Population from the Cemetery of Bodzia", [in:] *Bodzia. A Late Viking-Age Elite Cemetery in Central Poland*, ed. A. Buko, Leiden and Boston 2014, p. 143–159.

6   M. Kara, "Description of the Cemetery, Organization of the Burial Space, the Burial Rites in the Light of the Cultural and Historical Determinants", [in:] *Bodzia…*, p. 343–411.

Fig. 1: The burial site Bodzia: the graves, rows of graves, and enclosures. Phase 1 graves are marked darker, those of Phase 2 are marked brighter. (After Buko et al. - A. Buko, T. D. Price, M. Kara, W. Duczko, K. M. Frei, I. Sobkowiak-Tabaka, "A unique medieval cemetery from the 10th/11th c. with chamber-like graves from Bodzia (central Poland). Preliminary result of the multidisciplinary research", *Archäologisches Korrespondenzblatt* 43, 2013, p. 423–442).

the funeral customs of the Scandinavians and the Rus' people (large rectangular cavities, some with curved corners) whereas oval pits, some with characteristic niches, are typical of the graveyards of steppe people in eastern territories (the Khazars). This observation remains in line with the context of the equipment of the dead and the cemetery's chronology.

Among the discovered burials, grave D162, the most representative of the entire cemetery, particularly attracts attention. The corpse was deposited in the largest grave chamber of all those identified. The chamber is situated centrally within a rectangular enclosure whose size is approximately 7.6 m x 6.5 m. Peculiar about the grave is its unique situation within the cemetery's space. It may be surmised that the original form of enclosure might have been a palisade fence or a wall made of rectangular lathes, approximately 2 m high. The latter option seems quite plausible as the form is found again in the negatives of beams preserved at the cemetery's lowest level. Worthy of attention is the multiple closing of the enclosure on the eastern side, whose function is unclear, assuming that the grave was to initiate the first row of the burial ground. It cannot thus be precluded that the vault's builders initially intended to construct an entrance to the burial plot at the eastern end. These multipartite enclosure closings visible at the east might be indicative of something resembling an antechamber having originally been situated there, with a pole (possibly, a wooden stele) embedded therein. The main burial was located centrally within the rectangular enclosure thusly constructed.

Adjacent to D162 on the eastern side is the grave of a man with a *langsax* knife, marked E58. While the discovery is unprecedented within Poland, the classical forms of weapons of this type had been disseminated since the Merovingian period, including in the Scandinavian environment.[7] According to Michał Kara, the case in question is a hybrid of a *langsax* (or, possibly, *skramasax*) -type fighting knife and other weaponry (such as sword, sabre, or broadsword), with analogies from the territories of the Balts and Baltic Finno-Ugric peoples from the late 10th and the 11th c. possibly applying to them. The *langsax* of the Bodzia grave was most probably made at one of the workshops situated in the eastern part of the Baltic Sea region.[8]

In terms of our present focus, three other burials (E37 and E856, the latter being a double grave) stand out within the necropolis: the corpses are deposited in an "embryo" position [**Fig. 2**]. Alien to the medieval eschatology in Polish

---

7 W. Hübener, "Die Langsaxe der späten Merowingerzeit", *Acta Praehistorica et Archaeologica* 21, 1989, p. 75–84.
8 M. Kara, "Weapons", [in:] *Bodzia...*, p. 177–196.

Fig. 2: Grave no. E37, containing a body of a woman deposited in an embryo position (photo: K. Waszczuk).

territory, the custom was deeply rooted in the funeral ceremonial of eastern regions of Europe, as widely reflected above all in the burial site of Birka, Sweden.[9] For the grave of a young warrior (E864/I) there are premises allowing us to deem the body's seated position probable.[10]

In this context, apart from the layout of the skeleton bones, the untypical position of the ceremonial sword found by the dead man's head is intriguing [**Fig. 3**]. In Michał Kara's opinion, the sword's surface is covered by an incrusted geometric plait-patterned ornament characteristic of the Scandinavian Mammen style. The distinctive shape of the dace and the pommel enable one to assume that the Bodzia sword has its closest analogy in the specimens identified at the Bengtsarvet graveyard in the Swedish region of Dalarna as well as those from

---

9 A. S. Gräslund, T*he burial customs: a study of the graves on Björkö*, Stockholm 1980.
10 M. Kara, "Description of the Cemetery, Organization of the Burial Space, the Burial Rites in the Light of the Cultural and Historical Determinants", [in:] *Bodzia...*, p. 343–411.

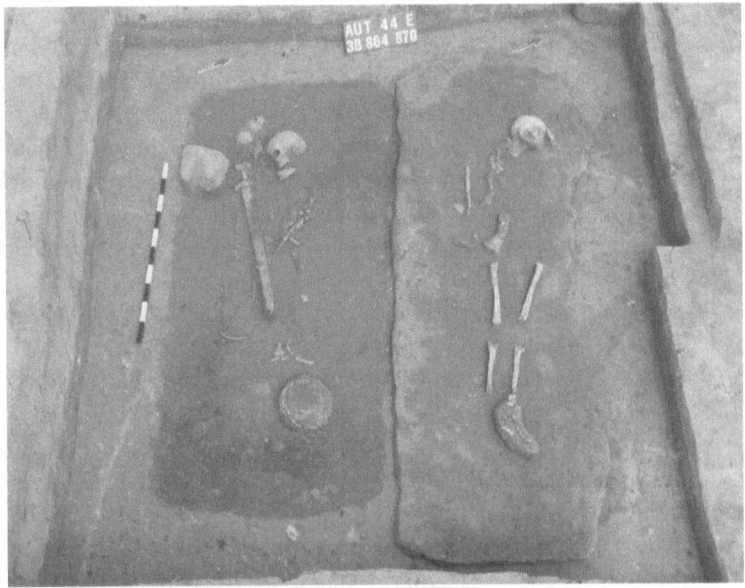

Fig. 3: Grave no. 864/I: details of the bones and sword setup (photo: K. Waszczuk).

Altevatn (Målselv, Norway). Within Polish territory, a parallel specimen was found at the burial ground in the locality of Ciepłe, east Pomerania.[11]

These opinions are shared by Michael Müller-Wille. Having meticulously analyzed the similar finds of swords from the areas of Norway and Sweden, with their telltale decoration of the hilt, silver-incrusted, Müller-Wille eventually concluded that the product found in the graveyard of Bodzia was made in Scandinavia.[12]

Unique for the Bodzia graveyard is its wealth of monetary finds. Totaling sixty-seven coins, whole or fragmentary, the collection is one of Europe's largest (perhaps the largest) in terms of the cemetery's size and the number of thoroughly

---

11 Z. Ratajczyk, "The cemetery in Ciepłe – current research results", [in:] *Scandinaviam culture in medieval Poland*, ed. S. Moździoch, C. Stanisławski, P. Wiszewski, Wrocław 2013; M. Kara, "Weapons" [in:] *Bodzia...*, p. 185–187.

12 M. Müller-Wille, "Das Schwertgrab E864/I aus dem fruhen 11. Jahrhundert von Bodzia, Kujawien", [in:] *"Viator per devia scientiae itinera". Studia nad problematyką okresów przedrzymskiego, rzymskiego, wędrówek ludów i wczesnego średniowiecza*, ed. A. Michałowski, T. Milena, M. Żołkiewski, Poznań 2015, p. 335.

explored graves. Most of these coins are from the territory of the Reich, with England and Scandinavia (eleven pieces each) in second place. Given the context of our interest, let us take note of a consolidated set of three Anglo-Saxon wholepence coins of Canute the Great discovered inside the E851 grave. No such coins have been found in any of the other graves. In the opinion of Stanisław Suchodolski, the Scandinavian coins were not randomly collected among those in wider circulation but purposefully selected by someone having come from England or Scandinavia or by someone who had received them together from their previous owner.[13] The Scandinavian comers hypothesis is not contradicted by the outcome of the strontium isotope content test, which points to the burial's geographical association with the Baltic Zone.[14]

Another unique artefact found within the graveyard is a small cross cut out from a Saxon silver denarius. Although many more finds of the sort have been found for tenth-century Rus'[15], symbols of thess Christian cult tend to be only sporadically discovered in graves within the territory of Poland and other east European countries from that time.[16]

The female dead were buried at the Bodzia cemetery with decorations typical of Slavic women.[17] Yet isotope tests have found that those particular women were not necessarily local. Southern Moravian/Bohemian and Volhynian associations

---

13 S. Suchodolski, "The Obol of the Dead", [in:] *Bodzia...*, p. 322.
14 T. D. Price, K. M. Frei, "Isotopic Proveniencing of the Bodzia Burials", [in:] *Bodzia...*, Table 21.2, Fig. 21.6.
15 A. E. Musin, *Khrist'ianizatsiya novogrodskoi zemli v IX-XIV vekakh. Pogrebalnyi obriad i khrist'ianskiye drevnosti,* Sankt-Peterburg 2002; idem, "Metalicheskiye kresti", [in:] *Drevnosti Semidvoryja I. Srednevekovyi dvukhapsydnyi khram v urochyshche Yedi-Evler (Alushta, Krim): issledovaniya i materiali,* ed. I. B. Teslenko, A. E. Musin, Donetsk 2013.
16 F. Androshchuk, "Symbols of Faith or Symbols of Status? Christian Objects in Tenth-Century Rus'", [in:] *Early Christianity on the Way from the Varangians to the Greeks,* ed. I. Garipaznov and Oleksiy Tolochko, Kiev 2011, p. 78–80; S. Brather, "Pagan or Christian? Early medieval grave furnishings in Central Europe", [in:] *Rome, Constantinople and Newly-Converted Europe. Archaeological and Historical Evidence,* ed. S. M. Salamon, M. Wołoszyn, A. Musin, M. Hardt, M. P. Kruk, A. Sulikowska-Gąska, Kraków, Leipzig, Rzeszów, Warszawa 2012, p. 341; C. Scull, "Chronology, Burial and Conversion: the Case of England in the 7th Century", [in:] *Dying Gods – Religious beliefs in northern and eastern Europe in the time of Christianisation,* ed. C. Ruhmann and V. Brieske, Hannover 2015, p. 78–80; V. J. Sobolev, "Drevnerusskaja pograbal'nya kultura Novogrodskoi zemli: problemy i osobennosti formirovaniya", *Archeologicheskiye Vesti,* 21, 2015, p. 355–357.
17 W. Duczko, "Status and Magic. Ornaments Used by the Bodzia Elites", [in:] *Bodzia...*

are attested by granulation-decorated silver beads found in the graves. Among the other rarely found elements of the corpses' equipment is a padlock, coffin-case ferrules, and a Scandinavian-type knife found in a child's grave.

Who were the dead buried at the cemetery in Bodzia, and what were their functions in the structure of the early Piasts' state? It is in only one case (the third row of the graves) that one can propose a fairly well-grounded guess that the young warrior (E864/I) was associated with the milieu of Grand Prince of Kiev Svyatopolk I (1015–1019), son-in-law of Boleslaus the Brave (Bolesław Chrobry, 992–1025). He was definitely a high-ranking personage, as evidenced by his belt, a luxurious and showy silver-incrusted sword, the (probable) originally seated position of the deceased, and the company of three young women richly equipped for their posthumous journey – one sprinkled with numerous coins deposited together with the warrior in the storied grave chamber, the two other, reposing next to the two corpses. The warrior might have been a relative of the Duke and/or a member of his closest, high-ranking retinue. After the failed episode of attempting to enthrone Svyatopolk in Kiev in 1018, a group of such retinue members found refuge at the Polish court of Boleslaus.[18] The body buried in row 2 of the cemetery (D149), together with a mace-like stick made of oak timber and clad with brown sheet metal, belongs to a man who probably also held a leadership function. The individual buried in the most representative grave chamber no. D162 [**row 1; cf. Fig. 1**] is another conjectural leader.

Along with the supposed leaders, warriors form a clearly identifiable group. This includes the above-mentioned young warrior (E864/I), as well as the man buried in row 1, in a richly-equipped grave chamber – E58, accompanied with the Viking-type long knife (*langsax*), unique throughout Polish territory. In the neighboring row 2, in a large grave chamber with no enclosure, remnants of a man were identified in grave no. E63 having a pick-axe characteristic of the territory of eastern nomads.

But most of the buried individuals remain basically unrecognized/unattributed. Nonetheless, the form and location of their graves and the elements of their rich equipment attest to the high social rank of the buried. Chamber graves cannot in themselves be critical in identifying the provenance of the buried individuals as northern (specifically, Scandinavian): the phenomenon is

---

18 K. Kollinger, "'Jest zaś mogiła jego w pustyni i do dziś dnia; wychodzi zaś z niej smród wielki...'. Próba nowego spojrzenia na okoliczności śmierci i miejsce pochówku Światopełka I", [in:] *Ekskluzywne życie – dostojny pochówek. W kręgu kultury elitarnej wieków średnich*, ed. M. Rębkowski (ser.: Wolińskie Spotkania Mediewistyczne, 1), Wolin 2011.

typical not only of Scandinavia, but extends to a quite large number of cemeteries known from inland Europe.[19] Hence, to properly identify the burials, the results of analyses of stable isotopes and genetic tests are worth referring to.

The strontium isotope tests carried out by Doug Price and Karin M. Frei have found that for row 1 of the cemetery, attributable to the buried are "Baltic" features. In geographical terms, the zones of the appearance of similar indicator values have been confirmed for the north-west of Europe, in the view of the authors. Hence, the dead identified as buried in those graves have been interpreted as aliens – a hypothesis that cannot be precluded in terms of the outcome of the DNA testing done on the human bones. This is primarily true for the Y chromosome isolated for the young warrior (E864/I). In light of the analysis carried out, it is highly plausible that the warrior's male-line ancestors could have been of a Scandinavian descent.[20]

The Bodzia find is inseparable from the context of archaeological discoveries of tenth-century artefacts and/or corpses found across the Greater Poland (Wielkopolska) region. At the threshold of Poland's statehood, differentiation between the territories is clearly recognizable as far as population density and the layout of strongholds are concerned. The state's core, the city of Gniezno, loosely populated in the earlier period, now comes to the fore. The clusters of multi-section strongholds evidenced locally, featuring powerful fortifications and elements of monumental architecture, originally date back – as recent dendrochronological analysis suggests – to the 930s/940s and the latter half of the 10th c. Around what is Gniezno, Poznań, Ostrów Lednicki, or Giecz today, favorable conditions for colonization developed, implying the demographic growth of local populations. Consequently, strongholds were founded densely – in some cases at distances of less than 30 km from one another. Apart from these central places, lower-ranking ones were erected in parallel, being surrounded with a network of newly-developed settlements. Resulting from these processes, settlements and strongholds, initially appearing in south-western Greater Poland, were built during the reign of in Mieszko I (c. 960–992) mostly in the central area of the newly-formed state with Gniezno as its central hub. The most recent dendrochronological findings indicate that all the previously discovered strongholds of the Gniezno area arose between 940 and 1025, in the time of Mieszko and Boleslaus the Brave. In Santok and Międzyrzecz, the fortified centers were

---

19 A. Janowski, *Groby komorowe w Europie Środkowo-Wschodniej. Problemy wybrane*, Szczecin 2015.

20 W. Bogdanowicz, W. T. Grzybowski, M. Buś, "Genetic Analysis of Selected Graves from the Cemetery", [in:] *Bodzia...*, p. 475.

almost entirely rebuilt. With respect to Ostrów Lednicki and Moraczewo, which both can be presumed to have existed before Mieszko's time, their chronological and functional relationships with the other early Piast strongholds call for better clarification.[21]

Apart from the Gniezno zone, the Kalisz Heights area also saw intense construction developments appearing in the state's early period. Altogether twenty-four strongholds have been identified within a 30 km range around Kalisz, this being a rather unusual occurrence. As many as nineteen of these objects functioned in the early Piast period and only one dates back to tribal times. A vast majority of the fortifications found locally were related to fluvial valleys. As has been established, strongholds were built in locations with no earlier-existing early-medieval settlements as well as where some settlements had existed. Researchers tend to associate the cluster of Kalisz strongholds (spanning across two heights and three dells or hollows) with the early stage of the formation. It is believed that the program of their construction was initiated within the circle of the ruler.[22] Characteristically, in the area between the Gniezno Land and its Kalisz counterpart merely a few defensive structures were built. No less interesting are the evident interrelations between the zones in which strongholds had appeared in the pre-state time and those where the structures or objects date to the first Piast monarchy [**Fig. 4**]. These premises, along with the others specified elsewhere[23], are indicative of the formation of the territorial organization of the earliest Piasts at the time.

Archaeology supplies a number of examples attesting to a change that deeply affected the local social and cultural structures, while the new order developed in the land of Gniezno. The actions that implied migration from some of the old strongholds and construction of new ones elsewhere entailed inevitable resettlements. Accepting Zofia Kurnatowska's[24] view whereby the people from the destroyed tribal strongholds in western and southern Greater Poland were

---

21 The settlement changes taking place in Greater Poland during the emergence of the early state have been analyzed by Stanisław Kurnatowski (1994, 1995) and Zofia Kurnatowska (1991, 2000, 2002). (Reference literature included in all the respective publications).

22 G. Teske, "Ze studiów nad osadnictwem grodowym w południowo-wschodniej Wielkopolsce", *Slavia Antiqua* 41, 2000, p. 107–128.

23 A. Buko, "Ośrodki centralne a problem najstarszego patrymonium dynastii Piastów", *Archeologia Polski* 57, 2012, p. 135–161.

24 Z. Kurnatowska. "Proces formowania się państwa gnieźnieńskiego", [in:] *Civitas Schinesghe cum pertinentiis*, ed. W. Chudziak, Toruń 2003, p. 42.

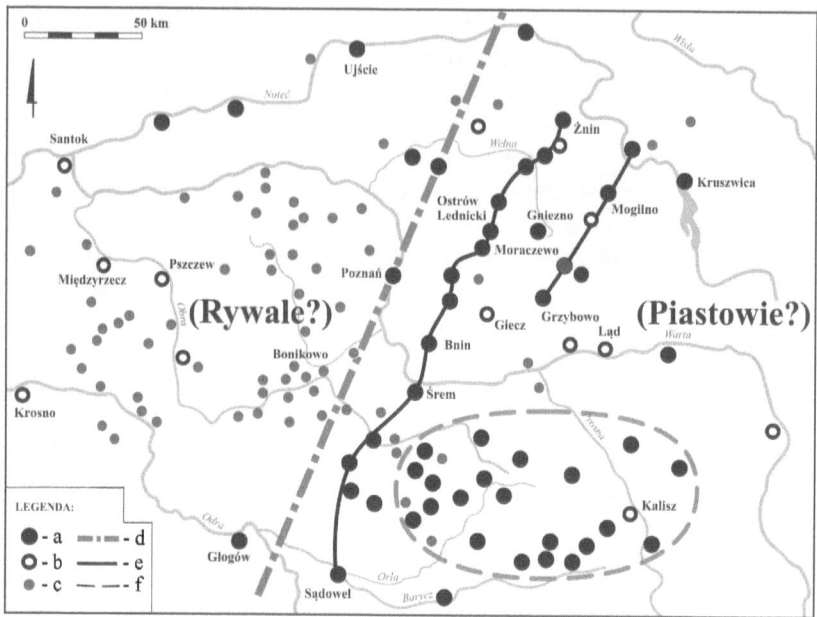

Fig. 4: Two images of strongholds in eastern and western Wielkopolska (Greater Poland): (a) strongholds built under the early Piast rulers; (b) strongholds of a pre-state chronology, surviving after the early-Piast country was established; (c) strongholds of the pre-state period, destroyed or deserted after the Gniezno state emerged; (d) a line delineating two zones of Wielkopolska, prevalently featuring pre-Piast and early-Piast-strongholds, respectively; (e) tightly laid-out Piast-time strongholds situated east of the 'demarcation line' and east of Gniezno; (f) the zone of early-Piast strongholds situated in south-eastern Wielkopolska, in the vicinity of Kalisz (after A. Buko).

forcefully resettled from those areas to Gniezno, the central zone, one cannot avoid the question about the immigrants' relationship with the local settlers of the land of Gniezno. Was the appearance of numerous aliens among them, or perhaps living beside them in newly-formed enclaves, commonly accepted? Or did the demographic changes provoke some conflict previously unknown to the land? For the groups of migrants, was it a journey to a "desired paradise" or, conversely, a violent act committed against them and their relatives?

The example of the stronghold of Grzybowo, built by the Piast rulers in the 920s, seem symptomatic in this context. Regarded as a major fortified center of the Gniezno state, it was formed and developed (for reasons unknown to us) in a previously unsettled area. It is assumed that the instance of Grzybowo was an ultimately failed attempt at creating a new centre and a tradition for the new dynasty. One of the largest early-Piast strongholds, Grzybowo ceased to exist as early as the first half of the 11th c.; continuous settlement appeared in the area once the stronghold was destroyed.[25] Another puzzling thing is that the stronghold of Moraczewo, established not far from Ostrów Lednicki in the early 10th c., succumbed to destruction in mysterious circumstances in the middle of the same century, together with its adjacent open settlement.[26] Assuming that it was the Piasts that had built the stronghold in their own land, who destroyed it – and why?

These examples can serve as a telling confirmation of the argument that it fell to the lot of the Piasts in the land of Gniezno to wrestle – not always successfully – with the problems related to the creation of new forms and zones of settlement. This possibly entailed a disturbance of the established social order, as illustrated by the archaeological data. What one comes across in this respect is a group of strongholds existent since the 9th c. (Giecz being an example), a group of those that ceased existing in the course of the 10th or around the mid-11th c. (Grzybowo and Moraczewo being cases in point), and those emerging from nonexistence as the early Piast state was being formed (Poznań, Ostrów Lednicki, or Gniezno). Noteworthy is the fact that Poznań was situated at the edge of an area that had been almost thoroughly pacified at the time the earliest state entity was emerging.

As a matter of fact, archaeology has at its disposal no instrument which would enable us to precisely trace the inter-ethnic relations in the territory of an emerging state or country along the lines of the definitions and notions applied by contemporary anthropology.[27] At the utmost, one may allege that a chiefdom organization developed by Mieszko I's predecessors was compelled to reinforce and modify the mechanisms of internal control at the same time it was both invading neighboring territories and intensifying the processes of centralizing its power. As a result, the country ruled by Mieszko emerged on the map of Europe. Similar mechanisms, ones discussed in the literature[28], allowed him to

---

25 M. Brzostowicz, *Tradycja i nowy porządek. Mieszkańcy Wielkopolski w obliczu przemian zachodzących w X-XIII wieku* (ser.: Spotkania Bytomskie, 6) Wrocław 2009, p. 30–32.
26 M. Kara, *Najstarsze państwo Piastów – rezultat przełomu czy kontynuacji?*, Warszawa 2009, p. 255.
27 S. Jones, *The Archaeology of Ethnicity*, London, New York 1997.
28 A. Posern-Zieliński, M. Kairski, "Początki państwa w ujęciu antropologicznym", [in:] *Kolory i struktury średniowiecza*, ed. W. Fałkowski, Warszawa 2004, p. 332; P. Urbańczyk, *Władza i polityka we wczesnym średniowieczu*, Wrocław 2000, p. 58–60.

keep a tight rein on the conquered territories and their inhabitants. There is no doubt that the split into "us" (the local people) and "them" (aliens/immigrants) was most clearly visible in the territory of the emerging Gniezno State. The new authority, with its military apparatus of compulsion, must have been committed to efficiently thwart the seeds of potential conflict rooted, for instance, in the diverse background and cultural traditions of the populations inhabiting the territory. In a number of cases this required the Piast elite to quit or modify the previously assumed strategies, as seemingly (and meaningfully) attested by the above-quoted examples of newly-built centers that ceased to exist before the first monarchy expired. It can thus be assumed that, similarly as with many other parts of early medieval Europe[29], the ethnic filiations of the inhabitants of the Gniezno area might have been dynamic and contextual when the state was being formed.

Seen against this background, the role of Kuyavia and Chełmno Land – the region within which the Bodzia graveyard was identified – was still far from final conclusion when the Polish state was being developed.[30] For Kruszwica, the leading center in Kuyavia, research has shown that the early town was built at a relatively late date – namely, in the last quarter of the 10th c. It is believed that the city was built in view of further expansion of the state and Christianization missions progressing toward Pomerania.[31] The necropolis under discussion appeared on the map of the early Piast Poland around the same time.

The phenomena observed in the cemetery of Bodzia have no direct analogy, whether in Poland or in Europe as a whole. This makes them a challenge for archaeologists and medieval historians. But they provide a new quality of knowledge on the complex mechanisms at the foundation of the early-Piast state, its social structure, including the role of aliens who, as the research attests, came from various parts of Europe. Most numerous among them were warriors and merchants: men acquainted with war craft and trade. Similarly as in other countries of the period, they were in the service of rulers; in parallel, they created the rudiments of a new, elite, and "European" society. This is

---

29 W. Pohl, "Conceptions of ethnicity in early medieval studies", *Archeologia Polona* 29, 1991, p. 41; idem, "Archaeology of identity: introduction", [in:] *Archaeology of Identity/ Archäologie der Identität*, ed. W. Pohl, W. Hehofer, Vienna 2010.

30 W. Chudziak, *Zasiedlenie strefy chełmińsko-dobrzyńskiej we wczesnym średniowieczu (VII–XI wiek)*, Toruń 1996.

31 B., W. Dzieduszyccy, "Kruszwicki ośrodek władzy i jego przemiany w XI–XII wieku", [in:] *Lokalne ośrodki władzy państwowej w XI–XII wieku w Europie Środkowo-Wschodniej*, ed. S. Moździoch (ser.: Spotkania Bytomskie 1), Wrocław 1993.

how, in the most general terms, their numerous representation in the Bodzia burial site can be interpreted. The discovery has offered a novel and legitimate basis for studying the forms of the funeral ceremony in early-Piast Poland, the mobility of European peoples in the late 10th/early 11th c., and aspects of the formation of elites in the newly formed country. The graveyard can also be approached as a site of collective memory that was meant to transfer or communicate the values shared by the group of the buried and their living continuators. Viewed against the other cemeteries of the period, the Bodzia site developed into a sign of an identity, singularity, and group coherence, solidified in space and time. The buried, representing the social elite of the early Piast state, formed an ethnocultural group (within the meaning proposed by modern anthropology), assimilated into the local milieu/environment, but cultivating their own specific traditions, at least as far as funeral rituals were concerned. Apart from the features identified above: the "architecture" of the cemetery and the graves with their furnishings, this is most significantly reflected in the northward orientation of the dead, which by the time the cemetery functioned had at best become, in late-tenth-century Poland and Europe, a reminiscence of the far past. It is interesting that a similar (N–S) layout of the buried is observable for a bi-ritual elite warrior burial site in the locality of Ciepłe in the Pomerania region. The equipment discovered there is indicative of the Scandinavian origin of the dead deposited there.[32] Yet in Scandinavia, in the period concerned, such orientation of dead bodies was already a relic of the past. Is this to mean that a tradition so remote was "locally" resumed at some point, as a "historical" discriminant or ethnocultural sign of the limited in quantity population?

The burial site in Bodzia is an expressive testimony of crucial episodes in the earliest history of Poland as a state. The permanent presence of local as well as foreign traditions at this critical and sensitive moment, when the framework of the early Piast state was being created, is an undisputable aspect in this context. Also, the argument gains legitimacy whereby Mieszko I, the actual founder of Poland as a state, albeit himself of a local, Greater Poland-based ethnic substrate, made use of broad organizational resources in his country-forming activities, through involving in these projects elite groups of advisors and warriors from various cultural zones. This formed a particular synthesis of European

---

32 Z. Ratajczyk, "The cemetery in Ciepłe – current research results", [in:] *Scandinaviam culture in medieval Poland*, ed. S. Moździoch, C. Stanisławski, P. Wiszewski, Wrocław 2013, p. 346.

experience, as incisively documented by the discoveries made at the Bodzia site. Together with new settlers, as archaeologically identified for various regions of the country, they formed a colorful ethnocultural mosaic that implies a qualitatively new, demographically and culturally complex, settlement-related picture of the country governed by the first Piast rulers.

Translated by Tristan Korecki

Part II: Modern Myths

Igor Kąkolewski

The roads by which Christianization proceeded in the history of Poland and in the Poles' culture of memory – new research perspectives and modern myths

Abstract: From the long-term perspective, Christianization presents a complex phenomenon that exceeds well beyond the "prologue" to the history of Polish statehood in the late 10th c. Indeed, it seems more befitting to speak of "processes of Christianization" (in the plural), ones that comprise the manifold civilizational evolution of religious, cultural, and social life. The Christianization of the early Piast period was but an introduction to the more complex religious and cultural transformations occurring over the subsequent decades, centuries, and epochs. In the first part of his chapter the author discusses how Christianity in Polish history from the mid-10th c. until the 20th c. was confronted with differing sets of questions and challenges. In the second part, using the methodology of culture of memory studies, he attempts to analyze the collective imaginings of the connections between the origin of the state and the beginnings of Christianity in Poland and other East European countries – as well as the myths of "beginnings", "continuation", "renewals" and "rebirths" of statehood in modern cultures and politics of memory.

Keywords: processes of Christianization, Baptism of Poland, communist politics of memory, foundation myths, process of secularization

Christianization's manifold course on Polish lands in the European context

The matter of "Christianization" can be viewed from two perspectives – one involving a shorter, and the other a longer time-period. In the first perspective the process of Christianization pertains to the introduction and strengthening of the foundations of the new religion and the associated ecclesiastical institutions, which in the case of the early Middle Ages were closely connected with the formation of state structures. This perspective is predominant in the works of the authors whose research we present in the first part of our volume.

From the long-term perspective, Christianization presents a complex phenomenon that extends beyond the strict "prologue" to the history of Polish statehood. Thus, taking into account the broader historical context, it seems more befitting to speak of "processes of Christianization" (in the plural), ones that encompass the manifold civilizational transformations comprising religious, cultural, and social life. The processes of Christianization so conceived occupy a larger frame than Christianization in the early Middle Ages, understood as the process of accepting, spreading, and internalizing basic Christian values. The Christianization that took place in the early Piast period was therefore but an introduction to the more complex cultural transformations of Christianity occurring over the following decades, centuries, and epochs. Having been ingrained with conventional periods in European and Polish history, we often neglect to bear in mind that, in its various epochs, Christianity (as is also the case with the world's other great religions) confronted sets of questions and challenges that, in differing historical contexts, could well have given rise to responses and solutions other than the ones arrived at – or to similar ones that nonetheless, because of the differing context and the plexus of circumstances, could well have yielded divergent results.

At the same time, in any such comprehensive grasp we must not ignore the significance of the "de-Christianization" processes that accompanied the development and expansion of Christianity, which nevertheless were not a mere reaction negating the Christian value system, but rather a component of a broader civilizational process in which the religion dominant in a given culture (or: with pretentions to predominance) encounters more or less complex contestation on the part of another value system. Such contestations can swell in time from a marginalized counter-culture to the stature of the main and officially dominant cultural current – remaining, however, in dialectic dependence and strict reference to the religious values it negates. Indeed, in its beginnings, Christianity was in just such a situation and thus had to pass through similar processes as it competed with differing belief systems.

Let us endeavor to observe in the long-term perspective the processes of Christianization in the history of Poland in the broader European context.[1] For from this vantage point we may contend that the Polish state, over the past millennium, passed through **three general phases of Christianization processes**.

The first phase is strictly connected with the founding myth of early-Piast statehood and the acceptance of baptism in the Latin rite by Poland's first historical ruler, Mieszko I (c. 960–992), in the early part of the second half of the 10th

---

[1] The considerations presented here expand on my reflections included in: I. Kąkolewski, "Specyfika procesów chrystianizacyjnych w historii Polski w kontekstach historii powszechnej", *Kwartalnik Historyczny* 122, 2015, p. 775–783.

c. The meager amount of source materials permits us to form merely a hypothetical reconstruction of the initial stages of society's Christianization in the period that immediately followed. A similar process, and one somewhat better documented in written sources, unfolded on the territories of the Poalabian Slavs and western Pomerania (Pomorze) from the 10th to the 12th c. Late-medieval sources from Lithuania and the state of the Teutonic Order in Prussia (lands not Christianized until the 13th/14th c.) confirm that the spread of Christianity was necessarily a lengthy process, one prompting waves of "pagan reactions" and fostering the encrusting of some pre-Christian customs with new forms of Christian piety.[2] As a result, this could bring about the emergence of syncretic forms, ones only formally Christian, whose substratum of age-old beliefs required considerable time to be eliminated.

In this regard Christianity in Poland from the mid-10th c. proceeded in a similar context to that in other countries of "younger Europe",[3] i.e., in those areas of Central and Eastern Europe which in the preceding epoch had not been under the civilizational influence of the Roman Empire, and which in the Middle Ages were a theater for the introduction of two rites – the Latin and Byzantine-Slavonic. What was characteristic for Polish lands in the first phase of development, lasting until the mid-14th c., was the gradual ascendance of Christianity in the Latin rite, which was then stabilizing its influence initially as the religion exclusively of the ruling elite, and in time embracing broader circles within society. In analyzing the process of Christianity's spread in this phase, we must not however ignore the moment of religious plurality, i.e., the parallel, long-term existence of mutually interacting and competing Christian and pre-Christian religions and value systems.

The beginning of **the second phase of Christianity's spread** in Polish lands can be dated to the mid-14th c. and may be labeled "Christianization in a Christian multi-confessional and religious multi-cultural setting". This phase

---

2 In reference to the territoires of the Teutonic Order in Prussia see: M. Biskup et.al., *Państwo zakonu krzyżackiego w Prusach. Władza i społeczeństwo*, Warszawa 2009, p. 48–175 with rich subject literature.

3 The notion of "younger Europe" was introduced into Polish historiography by Jerzy Kłoczowski to describe people and states that entered the circle of Christian civilization around the year 1000, both through baptism in the Latin rite (Bohemia, Poland, Hungary, Denmark, Norway, Sweden, Croatia), as well as the Byzantine rite (Bulgaria, Kievan Rus', Serbia) – see: J. Kłoczowski, *Europa słowiańska w XIV-XV wieku*, Warszawa 1984 and idem, *Młodsza Europa. Europa Środkowo-Wschodnia w kręgu cywilizacji chrześcijańskiej średniowiecza*, Warszawa 1998.

was strictly connected with the change in the Kingdom of Poland's borders and their literal reorientation, first in consequence of Casimir the Great's (Kazimierz III Wielki, 1333–1370) incorporation of Red Ruthenia (after 1340), and not long thereafter owing to the Polish-Lithuanian union (1386). As a result of this, the borders of Polish crownlands, followed by those under Jagiellonian rule in the Polish-Lithuanian union, began to encompass sundry religious and confessional communities that, on the one hand, had to work out a *modus vivendi*, and on the other to secure state protection. The type of multicultural and multifaith model that then took shape resulted from the fact that also communities adhering to Judaism (Jews and Karaites) and Islam (Tatars) were granted religious and self-government privileges.[4] Above all, however, that model coalesced from the multiconfessional character of Christianity. At the close of the Middle Ages in lands inhabited mostly by Polish-speaking population the overwhelming majority of people were Catholics; conversely, the huge majority of people living in the Grand Duchy of Lithuania were Orthodox Ruthenians. Besides, in Poland's south-eastern crownlands there was a small, albeit influential group of Armenians who adhered to Monophysitism.

The mutual relations, co-existence, as well as the interaction of these groups along with the relations of state structures to each of the groups individually, became from that moment elements of complicated culture-forming processes (that included Christianization) across the lands of the Polish-Lithuanian state. These processes were bolstered by the course of the Reformation in the 16th c. – more precisely, by the "two reforms of Christianity", Protestant and Catholic – that redefined Christianity in early-modern Western Europe.[5] At the same time, from the close of the 14th c. Christianization (in the strict meaning) was underway in the Latin rite in Lithuania proper, whereas on the vast territories of the Grand Duchy of Lithuania the expansion of Catholicism was curbed by the successes of Protestantism and the defensive posture of the Orthodox Church in the 16th c. All of the phenomena mentioned here made a lasting imprint on Christianity and its cultures in the multi-cultural Polish-Lithuanian Commonwealth.[6]

---

4 See recently: *Under a common sky. Ethnic groups of the Commonwealth of Poland and Lithuania*, ed. M. Kopczyński, W. Tygielski, Warszawa, New York 2017.

5 J. Delumeau, *Naissance et affirmation de la Réforme*, Paris 1965; idem, *Le Catholicisme entre Luther et Voltaire*, Paris 1971; both monographs were translated into Polish and published under a shared title: *Reformy chrześcijaństwa w XVI i XVII w.*, vol. 1: *Narodziny i rozwój reformy protestanckiej*, vol. 2: *Katolicyzm między Lutrem a Wolterem*, Warszawa 1986.

6 I. Kąkolewski, "Toleranz oder Tolerierung. Das Problem der Toleranz von Christen gegenüber Juden in Polen-Litauen vor dem Hintergrund des Alten Reiches vom 16. bis

As a result of the changes underway from the mid-14th c. in the multi-ethnic Polish-Lithuanian state, new vital challenges appeared – ones existent only marginally during the early stages of Christianization in Poland. They were related to the cohabitation of differing Christian confessions and their approach to the neighbors who practiced the non-Christian religions of Judaism and Islam. By the second half of the 16th and early 17th c. the confessional-ethnic composition of the Polish-Lithuanian Commonwealth now counted only 40–50 % of the Polish-speaking population, foremost Catholic, although with a significant (especially in political and cultural life) percentage of Protestants. Among the many other groups the most numerous were the Ruthenians (approximately 30–40 %), initially faithful in the majority to the Orthodox Church, although following the Church Union of Brest in 1596 adherents of Greek-Catholicism (i.e., the Uniate Church) became over time plentiful, as did the dynamically growing Jewish population, which in the mid-18th c. amounted to 7 % of the Commonwealth's population.[7]

The processes of Christianization in this multicultural and multiconfessional situation demanded the elaboration of new mechanisms for neutralizing potential or existing conflicts. And here we come to the matter of religious tolerance or rather toleration and the widespread image of the former Commonwealth as "a state without stakes" during the 16th and early 17th c. in a Europe otherwise wracked with religious wars. This image[8] is still predominant in some popular publications that portray the Commonwealth of Both (or many) Nations as a unique arcadia – the cradle of the Warsaw Confederation of 1573, which

---

zur Mitte des 17. Jahrhunderts, [in:] *Frühneuzeitliche Reiche in Europa/Empires in Early Modern Europe*, Wiesbaden 2016, p. 189–202 and idem, "Tolerancja reglamentowana? Koncepcje tolerancji chrześcijan wobec Żydów w Rzeczypospolitej na tle Rzeszy Niemieckiej w XVI i I połowie XVII", *Czasy Nowożytne* 28, 2015, p. 11–23.

7 A. Teller, I. Kąkolewski, "Paradisus Iudaeorum? 1569–1648" [in:] *Polin: 1000 Year History of Polish Jews*, ed. B. Kirchenblatt-Gimblett, A. Polonsky, Warszawa 2014, p. 86–125; idem, "Rzeczpospolita wielu narodów, wyznań i kultur", [in:] *Pod wspólnym niebem. Rzeczpospolita wielu narodów, wyznań i kultur. Wystawa Muzeum Historii Polski. Zamek Królewski w Warszawie 3 V – 31 VII 2012*, ed. I. Kąkolewski, M. Kopczyński, Warszawa 2012, p. 41–50.

8 Popularized by the title of Janusz Tazbir's book, which was, however, quite often read without thorough understanding of the contents of this outstanding historian's work – see the last Polish edition of the book: J. Tazbir, *Państwo bez stosów: szkice z dziejów tolerancji w Polsce XVI i XVII w.*, Warszawa 2009 and in English: idem, *A state without stakes. Polish religious toleration inthe 16th and 17th centuries*, New York 1973.

preceded with its originality other historic European documents declaring religious peace.

However, the panorama of confessional relations across early-modern Central and Eastern Europe reveals a dynamic similar to that in Poland-Lithuania, along with a similar type of religious toleration – for instance, in Transylvania in the mid-16th and in the early 17th c. in the Habsburg Kingdom of Hungary, not to mention the specific kind of toleration in Ottoman Empire. Indeed, it is the latter that should be deemed "a state without stakes" in the early modern period. Islamic civilization generally – in how it stressed the affiliation of Muslims, Jews, and Christians as "people of the book" – should be presented more as tolerant than Christian civilization in Europe during the period of religious wars and confessional divisions in the 16th c.[9]

It seems that one of the most important causes as to why the above-mentioned regions of Central and Eastern Europe attained a comparatively high level of religious tolerance, was their telltale type of multi-culti, something hardly to be found in Western Europe in that period. The centuries-long tradition of multi-confessional and multi-religious cohabitation in "younger Europe", whose cultures remained diverse i.a., because of the longstanding divisions and mutual influences of Eastern and Western Christianity, fostered, by way of compromise, the institutionalized cohabitation of divergent ethnic and religious groups – both Christian and non-Christian. In specific situations that tradition could also generate tensions and conflicts – however, in the early modern period this generally occurred on a smaller scale than in the western half of the continent.

Characteristic here for the divergent paths and fates of Christianity's development (and at the same time, for the long-term processes of Christianization) was ever the vibrant interaction between the cultures of the Orient and the Occident. This became an important factor at the moment when on the westernmost areas of Europe at the close of the 15th c. the process of the Reconquista ended, together with the expulsion of the remaining Jewish and Muslim communities

---

[9] J. Lecler, *Histoire de la tolérance au siècle de la Réforme*, vol. 1–2, Paris 1955 and Polish edition: *Historia tolerancji w wieku reformacji*, vol. 1–2, Warszawa 1967; H. Schilling, "Die 'acceptation de la diversite' im Europa der frühen Neuzeit und im Rahmen der europäischen vergleichenden Perspektive" [in:] *Ausgewählte Abhandlungen zur europäischen Reformations- und Konfessionsgeschichte*, ed. L. Schorn-Schütte, O. Mörke, Berlin 2002, p. 32–47; J. Berenger, *Tolérance ou paix de religion en Europe centrale: 1415–1792*, Paris 2000; Polish edition: idem, *Tolerancja religijna w Europie w czasach nowożytnych*, Warszawa 2002, extensive considerations on Transylvania and Hungary in chap. 2 and 5, and a brief reflection on the Ottoman Empire, p. 232.

from the Iberian Peninsula – and when simultaneously in the East the Ottomans power successfully continued its expansion into Europe.[10]

The consequence of this in the lands of the Polish-Lithuanian state was, on the one hand, the shaping in the early modern epoch of Sarmatism[11], which was a synthesis of influences from the East and West – and on the other the necessity of a state elite ever more dominated by the Catholic Church to co-operate with adherents to Orthodoxy – especially the Cossacks – in the aim of defense against the Ottomans and Tatars. It was the delegalization of the Orthodox Church as a result of the Union of Brest in 1596 and the none too successful expansion of the Uniate Church (which tried to replace Orthodoxy) that became one of the causes of the increasingly strong dissatisfaction of the Commonwealth's Orthodox population and one of the components of the outbreak of the great Cossack uprising in 1648. The latter event is treated in Polish historiography as the first serious symptom of the lengthy crisis of the Polish-Lithuanian state, soon worsened during the Swedish Deluge, i.e., the temporary (1655–1657) occupation of huge parts of the Polish-Lithuanian Commonwelath by the Swedes, who were perceived in the Commonwealth as adherents of Lutheranism and enemies of Catholicism. This, in turn, led to an intensified hostility toward Protestantism among society's Catholic majority. The first clear manifestation of this was the Sejm's 1658 legalization of expelling from the Commonwealth members of the radical Protestant group (already subject to odium on the part of the main Protestant currents) – the Polish Brethren (Arians).[12]

The generally amicable co-existence of various confessions and religions in the Commonwealth until the mid-17th c. was influenced by its unique social structure. Owing to the situation of a state and society made up of estates, certain ethno-religious groups, such as Jews and Armenians, attained a position similar to that of social estates that were guaranteed their traditional privileges and freedoms, and this in turn created the basis for the development of policies of toleration characteristic for the pre-modern period. Here it bears stressing

---

10 Compare recently on this subject: B. J. Kaplan, *Divided by Faith. Religious Conflict and the Practice of Toleration in Early Modern Europe*, Cambridge MA, London 2009.

11 See: recently M. Faber, "Das Westliche des Sarmatismus," [in:] *Sarmatismus versus Orientalismus in Mitteleuropa. Sarmatyzm versus Orientalizm w Europie Środkowej*, ed. M. Długosz, M. Faber, P. O. Scholz, Berlin 2012, p. 67–92, as well as a monograph: idem, *Sarmatismus. Die politische Ideologie des polnischen Adels in der frühen Neuzeit*, Wiesbaden 2018.

12 W. Kriegseisen, *Between State and Church: Confessional Relations from Reformation to Enlightenment: Poland-Lithuania-Germany-Netherlands*, Frankfurt am Main 2016.

that the dominant conception of religious toleration in the early-modern period in Christian Europe evinced a decidedly pragmatic character, in line with the Latin meaning of *tolere* as "to suffer" – hence, to suffer those who differ in faith until the moment they convert to the single true religion or confession. This understanding of "toleration" – predominant at the very least among the moderate, concerning religious matters, intellectuals in the period of "confessional hatred"[13] – recalled the conception of toleration postulated in earlier epochs by certain authorities of the Christian world vis-à-vis the adherents of non-Christian religions. For, in theory at least, what obliged was the principle passed down by Saint Augustine and Gregory the Great: *credere non potest homo nisi volens*.

This postulate spoke not of forcible conversion (which was permissible only vis-à-vis heretics, i.e., dissenters, those who had departed from the main current of Christian doctrine), but of patiently "awaiting" the conversion of non-Christians. Later Saint Thomas Aquinas stated that it is essentially not a good thing if cults exist that are based on mistaken beliefs, although they may be tolerated on behalf of avoiding a greater evil, or for obtaining a greater benefit. A similar manner of thinking existed in Poland's multicultural setting in the late Middle Ages, and was upheld by legal minds from the Academy in Kraków, among whom we most readily flash on Paweł Włodkowic. In the epoch of the Renaissance and the Reformation, in turn, this irenic attitude was presented by various Polish and Western-European humanists who postulated the introduction of the doctrine of shunning violence not only toward non-Christians, but also toward Christian dissenters. Moreover, a similar manner of thinking is contained in other legal acts of so-called limited or "piecemeal" toleration in Europe in the 16th c. In the German territories this concerns the Peace of Augsburg of 1555 and the conclusions of the Peace of Westphalia of 1648 that pertained to religious matters. In Transylvania it concerned the decisions of the parliament in Torda in 1569, and in the Polish-Lithuanian Commonwealth the Warsaw Confederation of 1573. In France, of course, we think of the Edict of Nantes of 1598, and in Hungary the conclusions of the 1606 Treaty of Vienna.[14]

As we see, the markedly similar problems that Christianity, and particularly its intellectual elite, confronted all throughout its history, met with similar responses and proposals for action that, for reasons of the divergent cultural context of the given epoch, could however lead to solutions and outcomes diverging from those arrived at during earlier epochs.

---

13 W. Sobieski, *Nienawiść wyznaniowa tłumów za rządów Zygmunta III-go*, Warszawa 1902.
14 I. Kąkolewski, *Toleranz oder Tolerierung...*, p.17.

In the whole of early-modern Latin Europe, including the Polish-Lithiuanian Commonwealth, a deepening of the impact of Christianity was brought about by cultural phenomena elicited by the Reformation. One of the most important such phenomena was that of introducing vernacular languages to the Protestant liturgies and expanding the possibility of catechism in those languages also in non-Protestant confessions thanks to the great "media revolution" of the 16th c. – namely, print.[15] This is confirmed by the publishing explosion of translations of Protestant Bibles into Slavic languages, and by the abundant religious literature in all the main currents of confessional Christianity in the Commonwealth. The question of introducing national languages to the liturgy and as a primary instrument of catechism in Central and Eastern Europe had however appeared much earlier – in the course of early-medieval Christianization in the 8th c., as well as during the missions of Cyril and Methodius in the 9th c., whose efforts led to the formation of the Slavic-Byzantine rite. Initially, the position of the Latin Church in the matter was divided, as the words of Pope John VIII from 880 testify:

> Nor is there any violation of the true faith and its teaching in conducting Holy Mass in the Slavonic language, nor in reading the Holy Gospel and the lessons of the Old and New Testaments in that language [...] For He who created the three main languages – Hebrew, Greek, and Latin – also created all other languages for His greater glory.[16]

During the Reformation, therefore, the postulates that had been tabled in Central and Eastern Europe in the course of the early medieval missions returned: the vernacular language in the liturgy and the translation of the Bible were to be employed as core instruments for spreading the truths of the faith. The second postulate was also characteristic i.a., for late-medieval radical movements bent on reforming religious life both in Western Europe (Wycliffism) and in Central and Eastern Europe (Hussism) – those unfulfilled pre-reformations. These movements expressed the dissatisfaction of reformers not only with the monopoly of the representatives of the hierarchical Church on access to the Holy Scripture, but also with the progress of Christianization among the broad masses. However, faced with the lack of suitable mass-media in the pre-Reformation period, the postulate of spreading the truths of the Christian faith mainly via vernacular languages proved impossible to carry out.

---

15 J. Burkhardt, *Das Reformationsjahrhundert. Deutsche Geschichte zwischen Medienrevolution und Institutionenbildung 1517–1617*, Stuttgart 2002.

16 *Cyryl i Metody – apostołowie i nauczyciele Słowian. Studia i dokumenty*, ed. J. S. Gajek, L. Górka, part 2, Lublin 1991, p. 94–96.

The deficits having appeared in the medieval phase of the process of Christianization were to be compensated by other efforts in the scope of the early-modern "dual reforms of Christianity", which in German historiography are typically labeled "confessionalization" (*Konfessionalisierung*).[17] At issue here is the diverse spectrum of efforts fostering the deepening of Christianization across broad sections of society. These efforts were undertaken in the period between the mid-16th and the mid-17th c., and included religious disciplining, the introduction of new ecclesiastical rites, and the internalization of redefined theological concepts. The key role in initiating and carrying out said confessionalization – most plainly seen in the Protestant countries, but also in those where Roman Catholicism maintained its dominant position – was played by the structures of state power that pressed the modernization of social life as a whole via the given country's officially recognized confession.

The model of confessionalization created by German historians, as applied to various countries of Latin Europe, emphasizes the decisive influence of the state in the sphere of ecclesiastical policy and its monopolistic pursuit to maintain its dominant place in being recognized as the official Christian confession, along with the "homogenization" of confessional relations in the given country. Hence the proposals tabled by some researchers to shift the end of the "epoch of confessionalization" to the period either side of the year 1700, as per the revocation of the Edict of Nantes in 1685 in France, the stabilization of Anglicanism's dominance in the years 1688–1707 in England, and the expulsion of Lutherans from the territories of the Archbishopric of Salzburg in 1731.[18] When viewing the confessional relations in the Polish-Lithuanian Commonwealth from this perspective, the model of confessionalization lends itself to interpreting a series of key historical events and processes connected with the expansion of Catholicism and the reaction it elicited – from the Union of Brest in 1596, the confessional

---

17 Of the hundreds of works on the subject, first of all, classic works need to be mentioned: E. W. Zeeden: *Konfessionsbildung. Studien zur Reformation, Gegenreformation und katholischen Reform*, Stuttgart 1985; W. Reinhard, "Konfession und Konfessionalisierung in Europa", [in:] *Bekenntnis und Geschichte. Die Confessio Augustana im historischen Zusammenhang*, ed. idem, München 1981, p. 165–189; H. Schilling, *Konfessionskonflikt und Staatsbildung. Eine Fallstudie über das Verhältnis von religiösem und sozialem Wandel in der Frühneuzeit am Beispiel der Grafschaft Lippe* (ser.: Quellen und Forschungen zur Reformationsgeschichte, 48), Gütersloh 1981.

18 W. Reinhard, "Zwang zur Konfessionalisierung? Prolegomena zu einer Theorie des konfessionellen Zeitalters", *Zeitschrift für Historische Forschung* 10, 1983, p. 257–277, here p. 262.

aspects of the Khmelnytsky Uprising in 1648, and the expulsion of Arians in 1658, to the tragic events connected with the violence in Toruń in 1724 that was directed against local Protestants and supported by Catholic structures of state power. The attempt to apply the model of confessionalization to analysis of the socio-cultural processes underway in the Commonwealth removes the odium of uniqueness from the Polish-Lithuanian state, in which – over the course of the 17th and 18th c. – the domination of the Roman Catholic Church became ever more pronounced, at the same time as symptoms of religious intolerance became stronger.[19]

A similar type of "confessionalizing" practices will stretch on in Europe, and all the way to the Enlightenment, which redefined the role of religion and the Church within the state. This in turn will also pose one of the most significant components of the process of secularizing the public sphere, whose genesis lies with the cultural transformations commenced in the 18th c. In all certainty a fundamental role in the secularization of European culture was played by the modern formula for toleration, which differed from the above-mentioned concept of pragmatic toleration ("suffering") that was characteristic for the early-modern epoch. The concept of "dogmatic toleration"[20] that was taking shape with the Enlightenment and then spread in the 19th and 20th c. relegated matters of faith to the private sphere, and thus posited the complete separation of Church and state, neutrality, and worldview pluralism, along with the equal rights of all religions. Moreover, this could also extend to agnostic views, freethought, and outright atheism.

Atheism – at least in the official version of social life – had been a marginal phenomenon in the epochs of pre-modernity. The term "atheist" in European languages long meant "godless" and was associated with sundry moral transgressions.[21] It was not until around the year 1700 that the first attempts, ones not entirely unequivocal, at the systematization of anti-theistic views were made. In the Commonwealth this was taken up by Kazimierz Łyszczyński[22], who

---

19 An extensive discussion of the above mentioned study in: W. Kriegseisen, *Between state and church...* as well as in: idem, "Between Intolerance and Persecution: Polish and Lithuanian Protestants in the 18th century", *Acta Poloniae Historica* 73, 1996, p. 13–27.
20 This term is used in the work quoted above and in J. Berenger, *Tolérance ou paix de religion...*
21 I. Kąkolewski, *Melancholia władzy. Problem tyranii w europejskiej kulturze politycznej XVI stulecia*, Warszawa 2007, p. 232n, 239–244.
22 A. Nowicki, "Sprawa Kazimierza Łyszczyńskiego na Sejmie w Warszawie w świetle rękopisu Diariusza Sejmowego, znajdującego się w Wojewódzkim Archiwum

was subsequently burned at the stake, and by Father Jean Meslier[23] in France. The permission, and later the sheer fashion in certain milieu for freethought and views hostile to Christianity, began in the 1840s to expand from the narrow circle of intelectuals as a result of the systematization of the anti-theistic and anti-Christian worldviews carried out by Ludwig Feuerbach, who wielded significant influence i.a., on the doctrines of Marx and Engels, but also on rightist ideologies that can be subsumed under social Darwinism.[24]

In the Enlightenment we may seek the origins, and in the 19th and 20th c. the full flowering, of **the third phase of the processes of Christianization**. We may succinctly characterize this phase as Christianization in a setting of Christianity having lost its monopoly as the dominating religion in individual countries in Europe, and the intensification of secularizing processes in social life. Here the question arises as to the qualitative differences between the phenomena of secularization and de-Christianization. The latter term, in my opinion, should be mainly reserved for deliberate actions undertaken mainly in state systems that absorbed radical twentieth-century ideologies aimed at liquidating or reducing the role and influence of Christian Churches along with the traditions and value system of Christianity.

Such a policy of "state atheism", implemented top-down as a carefully devised program of "state atheization", was characteristic above all for the Soviet Union from the mid-20th c. in various degrees of intensity, as well as in the USSR's satellite countries in various periods (and in such kindred states as – in Europe – Albania). The prefiguration of the ideologized policy of "de-Christianization" can be discerned over a century earlier in the radical phase of the French Revolution in 1793, at the moment when battle was declared against the traditions of Christianity in the promotion of the Cult of Reason.[25] Nonetheless, it should not be identified with the advancing (from ca. 1800) manifold process

---

Państwowym w Gdańsku", *Euhemer* 4, 1963, p. 23–39; and idem, "Ateizm Kazimierza Łyszczyńskiego", [in:] *Wykłady o krytyce religii w Polsce*, Warszawa 1965, p. 51–68.

23 G. Katschnig, "Der Radikale und sein Zensor. Über das editoriche Verhältnis zwischen Jean Meslier und Voltaire", [in:] *Kultursoziologie. Aspekte, Analysen, Argumente. Wissenschaftliche Halbjahreshefte der Gesellschaft für Kultursoziologie*, ed. W. Geier, E. Kalbe, vol. 22, 2012, p. 53–64; G. Mager, *Das Wissen des Jean Meslier. Über die wahre Entstehung der Aufklärung*, München 2006.

24 The reader can find the latest discussion on the genesis of the modern concept of atheism in the comprehensive monograph by M. Ruse, *Atheism. What Everyone Needs to Know*, Oxford 2015.

25 See among others: N. Aston, *Religion and Revolution in France, 1780–1804*, London 2000; *Die Kirche in der Gegenwart. Die Kirche zwischen Revolution und Restauration*, ed. R. Aubert, J. Beckmann, P. J. Corish, R. Lill, Freiburg/Breisgau, Basel, Wien 1971;

of secularizing society, which had a much broader scope and meaning. In this context it is also difficult to distinguish atheism, as an attitude toward religion, from religious indifference. However, both attitudes in today's mainstream, particularly in western European culture, seem dominant.[26]

Unreflectively equating atheization and secularization is a mistake, one that nonetheless often appears not only in scholarly works, but also in the slogans of ultraconservative Christian milieu that have adopted defensive positions vis-à-vis modern Euro-Atlantic civilization's typical attitudes and values resultant from contemporary multiculturalism – ones structurally and substantially different from the multiculturalism of the early-modern epoch. In the case of today's Europe, this is caused by complex post-colonial processes (migrations)

J.-P. Bertaud, *Alltagsleben während der Französischen Revolution*, Freiburg, Würzburg 1989, p. 66–97.

26 On the situation of the increase of people describing themselves as agnostics or atheists in contemporary Europe described as "Post-Christian Europe" – see an extensive study on the subject: P. Jenkins, *God's Continent: Christianity, Islam and Europe's Religious Crisis*, Oxford 2005; idem, *The Christian Revolution in The Next Christendom: The Coming of Global Christianity*, Oxford 2002; and Ch. Taylor, *A Secular Age*, Harvard 2007. According to the 2010 Eurobarometr public opinion poll 51 % of citizens of EU Member States responded positively to the question "I believe there is a God", 26 % "I believe there is some sort of spirit or life force" whereas 20 % "I don't believe there is any sort of spirit, God or life force", while 3 % refused to answer. The percentage of respondents that answered affirmatively to the question "I don't believe there is any sort of spirit, God or life force" was highest in the Netherlands (30 %), France (40 %), Estonia (29 %), Sweden (34 %) and the Czech Republic (37 %). In turn, a study conducted in the years 2008–2009 by the Gallup Institute demonstrates that the question: "Is religion important in your daily life?" was answered affirmatively by a majority of respondents living in countries with a high percentage of Muslims: Kosovo, Turkey, Bosnia and Herzegovina (range 90 %-77 %). Compared to that, the percentage of positive answers (respectively 86 %-75 %) is exceptionally high in Poland and Malta (dominance of Roman Catholicism), as well as in orthodox Romania, Macedonia and Cyprus (84 % -76 %). It is exceptionally low in traditionally protestant Scandinavian countries and Estonia, and among post-communist countries in the Czech Republic (range 21–16 %). Russia, in turn, together with the majority of other post-Soviet republics and countries of the Eastern Bloc remains in the 30 %-49 % range, where also the majority of Western European countries (except Italy and Portugal-each around 72 %) places itself [electronic resource] available at: https://en.wikipedia.org/wiki/Religion_in_Europe#cite_note-4. A slightly more diverse picture of the Poles' level of faith is presented by the 2015 CBOS' profiled research, [electronic resource] available at: http://www.cbos.pl/SPISKOM.POL/2015/K_029_15.PDF.

and globalization – i.e., the long-term homogenization of world culture to which (ironically) the missionary expansion of Christian Churches indirectly contributed over the past centuries. As a result, today's Christianity around the world – just as on the Old Continent – is gradually being deprived of its culturally privileged position. This is because in the political sphere and public space of individual states, Christianity began to lose its position together with the process of secularization in the period of intensive modernization in the 19th and 20th c.

The fundamental element of the processes of secularization and modernization in this period is that of the consistent policy of the separation of Church and state began by the Josephine reforms in Austria in the late 18th c. In the 1870s that policy was carried out in a comprehensive way i.a., in the large, newly created states in the center of Europe: the Kingdom of Italy and the German Empire, the latter being in opposition to the Roman Catholic Church within the framework of *Kulturkampf*, whose primary objective was to curtail the manifold influence of the Vatican and the Church hierarchy on the structures of the modern, secularizing state. We need at once note, however, that in Polish cultural memory *Kulturkampf* crystallized almost exclusively as the policy of Germanizing Poles in the Prussian partition.[27] Later, following WWI, in the newly created nation-states of Central and Eastern Europe, including Poland, the full separation of Church and state could be sanctioned only at the moment of laying the foundations of modern legislation. A doubtlessly normalizing function existed in the concordats Pope Pius XI agreed with those states in the 1920s, and which regulated their relations with the Catholic Church.[28] Interwar Poland, similarly as other states of Central and-Eastern Europe that emerged after 1918, inherited a multicultural legacy from its earlier epochs. However, multiculturalism in nation-states in the interwar period – structurally different than the pre-modern multiculturalism of estate societies, as well as the postcolonial, secularized multiculturalism that emerged in Western Europe in the wake of WWII – functioned in the context of the modernizing and ever more secularized societies of the modern epoch.

---

27 M. Borutta, *Antikatholizismus. Deutschland und Italien im Zeitalter der europäischen Kulturkämpfe*, Göttingen 2011; *Kulturkampf in Europa im 19. Jahrhundert*, ed. Ch. Clark, W. Kaiser, Leipzig 2003. In Polish historiography, see recently: G. Kucharczyk, *Kulturkampf: Walka Berlina z katolicyzmem* (1846–1918), Warszawa 2009, as well as the classic monograph by J. Krasuski, *Kulturkampf. Katolicyzm i liberalizm w Niemczech XIX wieku*, Poznań 1963.
28 See: M. Banaszak, *Historia Kościoła katolickiego*, vol. 4: *Czasy najnowsze 1914 – 1978*, Warszawa 1992, p. 16–88.

It is difficult, however, to accept the one-sided view in the 19th and 20th c. Christianity was deemed to be a system remaining exclusively in opposition to modernization and the violent transformations of the epoch of industrialization. Such a one-sided appraisal is undercut e.g., by the formation of new forms of piety inspired by none other than the process of modernization, or the social reform movements initiated within various currents of Christianity in Europe (and the United States) over the period of subsequent breakthroughs in the industrial revolution. In German historiography there even appeared the label "the second age of confessionalization", meant to define the entire scope of transformations in the sphere of religion and its sociotechnical instrumentalization by the modern state apparatus in the "long" 19th c.[29] In the early 1960s, in turn, an important moment conducive to modernizing the structures of the Catholic Church, and at the same time to deepening the modern process of Christianization, came with the reforms of the Second Vatican Council, with its expansion of the role of laypeople in the life of the Church and, last but not least, the ending of the monopoly of Latin by introducing national languages to the liturgy.[30]

Thus, the history of the Poles – a nation without a state in the period of the partitions (1795–1918) – provides interesting and by no means ambiguous examples. This is because some representatives and milieu of the Catholic Church in Poland were playing the role of both irredentists and modernizers of social and economic life. Providing testimony to this is the activity of a long list of iconic figures, if only to mention the priests Piotr Ściegienny and Piotr Wawrzyniak.[31] In the 20th c., in turn, during WWII as well as during the People's Republic of Poland, there is no way to overlook the contribution of representatives of the Catholic Church and its traditional values in the efforts to restore independence and lend support to the great social protest movement born in 1980 and its demands for reform that was *Solidarność*, which contributed hugely to the processes of transformation in the final decade of the 20th c. An active role in the political processes within the states of the Eastern Bloc was also played by

---

29 L. Hölscher, *Geschichte der protestantischen Frömmigkeit in Deutschland*, München 2005; idem, *Atlas zur religiösen Geographie im protestantischen Deutschland zwischen der Mitte des 19. Jahrhunderts und dem Zweiten Weltkrieg*, vol. 1–4, Berlin 2001.
30 M. Banaszak, *Historia Kościoła katolickiego...*, p. 183–190..
31 W. Djakow, *Piotr Ściegienny. Ksiądz-rewolucjonista*, Warszawa 1974; Cz. Łuczak, *Ks. Piotr Wawrzyniak (1849–1910)*, Poznań 2000.

oppositionist circles associated with the Protestant Churches in the former East Germany, and with the Catholic Church in Hungary.[32]

Today, when in the main currents of Christianity, and especially in the Catholic Church, debates are being waged over traditional values and the voices of Tradition and of Reform clash with each other, it seems worth recalling the origins of Christianity as a religion and a value system that challenged the existing traditions and that radically reformed the petrified order. However, hearkening to Christianity's beginnings was always inconvenient, both for the Church's establishment and the adherents of the Christianity's later traditions...

Myths old and new: imagining the beginnings and the rebirths of statehood

Alongside the concept of the drawn-out processes of Christianization from the perspective of history in the first degree (i.e., analysis of events and processes), what also seems justified is to examine the topic of Christianization from the vantage point of history in the second degree – i.e., via analysis of cultures of memory. This concerns the collective imaginings of the connections between the origin of the state and the beginnings of Christianity in its lands – as well as the role in constructs of the "beginnings", "continuation", "renewals" and "rebirths" of statehood that was played (and is played) by social memory concerning the baptisms of the first historic rulers of the given state. The venerable writings that created such memory, together with modern historiography as shaped in the 19th c., whose objective was (and is) the intergenerational conveying of memory of the past (both in mythologized and scholarly form), remain an important instrument of state policy and of shaping and reinforcing group identities. Their fundamental element is that of the conviction of the need for the continuity and endurance of the state to which the given community belongs. In this situation both premodern historical writers as well as modern historians were and often remain hostages, as it were, to state ideologies in the way they present (or mythologize) in their works the births, demises, and continuation of the given state.[33]

---

32 See among others: E. Neubert, "Kościół i opozycja w NRD", *Raporty Fundacji Konrada Adenauera*, vol. 18, 2011, [electronic resource] available at: http://www.kas.de/wf/doc/kas_21828-1522-8-30.pdf?110204164926.

33 I expand here on my deliberations presented in: I Kąkolewski, "Nigdy nieumierające ciało państwa, czyli o trwałości toposu reborn statehood w europejskiej kulturze politycznej", *Kwartalnik Historyczny* 125, 2018, p. 483–498.

Both foundation myths[34], connecting as they do the story of the given state's genesis with the beginnings of the religion dominant within it, as well as the collective imaginings of rebirths and the continuation of the state (after a period of its collapse), have played and do play a key role in the process of legitimizing the authorities and creating collective identities. Traditional myths of the rebirths of states have adopted the formula of conveying – i.e., *translatio* – the former tradition of statehood to the newly arisen state entities. Alternately, they have adopted the formula of *renovatio*. The best known example in European history of an ideologized *translatio* and *renovatio* of the state was that of the imagined succession of the Roman Empire's statehood during the Middle Ages and modernity. The concept of *translatio imperii*, whose roots reach back to the Biblical vision of "the four kingdoms" in Daniel chap. 2, later modified by Saint Jerome, received new raiment together with the *renovatio* of the Roman Empire via the imperial coronation Charlemagne (768–814) in 800, and thereafter with the coronation of Otto I the Great (936–973) in 962 and the shaping of the Holy Roman Empire over the subsequent centuries – from the close of the 15th c. informally, and from the 17th c. officially named as the Holy Roman Empire of the German Nation.

Matters were similar in Eastern Europe even earlier, where in Byzantium, and later the Muscovite state, we see that the medieval and early modern idea of a Christian empire was connected with the conveying and continuation of the Roman Empire in the form of a "second" and then "third Rome". Besides, the ideological reflections and the overtures to the continuation of the western half of the Roman Empire, following its collapse in 476 (a date universally accepted both in modern historiography and the European culture of chronological

---

34 I use here the term "foundation myth" in a broader meaning than the literary definition, which defines myth as an expanded narrative stemming from oral tradition, which is about supernatural or historically unpredictable characters or events that persist and evolve throughout culture through their constant transformations and reinterpretations. From the point of view of research on memory cultures, also historical characters and events can acquire mythical character thanks to transformations and reinterpretations, especially if they serve ritual or ceremonial purposes strengthening the sense of identity and of belonging to a certain community. The close connection between myth and ritual is emphasised in various contexts by the British School of Social and Cultural Anthropology, see: R. A. Segal, *Myth: A Very Short Introduction*, Oxford 2004; as well as my remarks in: I. Kąkolewski, "Krzyżacy jako metafora. Pamięć o wojnie 13-letniej w obchodach jubileuszy inkorporacji Prus Królewskich do Korony Polskiej w epoce staropolskiej" [in:] *Johann Daniel Tietz vel Titius, Całkowite poddanie ziem pruskich na rzecz Polski. Die gänzliche Ergebung der Lande Preußen an Polen*, ed. I. Kąkolewski, Chojnice 2017, p. 72.

memory), were also clear in the conceptual and propaganda motives accompanying the imperial aspirations of the Western European powers: sixteenth-century Spain, seventeenth-century France and England, and in the early 19th c. across Europe in the Napoleonic system. In a certain sense this also concerns the German Empire created in 1871, which directly drew upon the idea of the succession of the Holy Roman Empire.[35]

The subsequent turn of the 19th c. – i.e., the rising wave of nationalism across Europe – also gave rise to the Franco-German dispute over whether Charlemagne was a Frenchman or a German (*Charlemagne* or *Karl der Grosse*). Later, in Nazi Germany, the official propaganda reluctantly referred to him as the "unifier of German tribes" with regard to the bloody campaigns he led in the aim of converting the Germanic Saxons to Christianity.[36] However, the overtures arising after 1871 in Germany to the traditions of the medieval and early modern Holy Roman Empire (of the German Nation), as well as the compromised construct of the "First" and "Second Reich" after 1933 in the Nazi "Third Reich" (which was to last for a thousand years), ceased to play (especially after 1945) any significant role in the German culture of memory.

Components of the tradition of *translatio* regarding the *Imperium Romanum* may also be found in today's European Union, as well as in attempts to create a transnational continental identity. Although the republican/democratic concept of European unity is a phenomenon qualitatively new, its architects – along with pan-European intellectual milieu – also regularly make mythologized overtures in line with the formula *translatio imperii*. One historiographical example of this involves the search for a prefiguration of the European Union in the Holy Roman Empire.[37] Besides, in politics of memory we have the Charlemagne Prize (German: *Karlspreis*, since 1988 *Internationaler Karlspreis zu Aachen*), awarded

---

35 Among many attestations of the viability of the notion of *translatio imperii*, in German Reich after 1871 it was confirmed by the iconographic interior design of the chapel inside the Imperial Castle in Poznań — the last building of castle-like character in Europe erected for royal purposes, whose construction was finished in 1910, see: I. Kąkolewski, "Miasto symboli. Poznań w epoce zaborów", [in:] *Ziemia obiecana. Miasto i nowoczesność. Wystawa Muzeum Historii Polski, Warszawa 26 września – 6 grudnia 2015*, Warszawa 2015, p. 81–96.

36 K. F. Werner, *Karl der Große oder Charlemagne? Von der Aktualität einer überholten Fragestellung*, München 1995, [electronic resource] available at: http://publikationen.badw.de/010605828.pdf.

37 See for instance: G. Schmidt, "Das Alte Reich und die Europäische Union – ein Versuch", [in:] *Vorträge der Geisteswissenschaftlichen Klasse 2010–2011*, ed. M. Vielberg, Erfurt 2013, p. 79–98.

in Germany since 1950 to outstanding individuals and institutions for their merits in promoting peace and unity in Europe. At the same time, ever more popular in public discourse is the construct of Charlemagne as "the father of united Europe" and "the patron of the European community".

It seems that in "younger Europe", whose territories were found outside the direct influence of the Roman Empire and early Christianity, a greater role than in Western Europe in the shaping of collective, multi-generational cultures of memory continues to be played by founding myths that conjoin the origins of states with the introduction of Christianity in their lands. Strictly connected with the founding myths of statehood are especially the introduction of Christianity in the Latin rite and the conclusion of the early phase of Christianization in the 10th and the early 11th c. by the laying of the foundations of the Church's organization among a portion of the states of Central and Eastern Europe, like in Bohemia of Wenceslaus I (921–935) and mostly his two successors, Poland of Mieszko I and Boleslaus the Brave (Bolesław Chrobry, 992–1025), and Hungary of Stephen I the Great (997–1038). Over the course of the subsequent millennium, these myths went on to play a key role in the continuation of the statehood of Hungary and Bohemia/Česko, having been shaped during the close of the early Middle Ages.

Contributing to this was also the canonization of rulers who carried out the decisive phase of Christianization, thereby becoming the Christian patrons of statehood, which fact was expressed in the later Middle Ages in the political constructs of those countries – i.e., "the Crown of Saint Wenceslaus" and "the Crown of Saint Stephen". In a certain sense a similar function was performed (despite the discontinuity in the medieval history of Rus') by the cult of Saint Volodimer for the Orthodox Rus' world, and thereafter for Ukraine and Russia. In fact, Volodimer the Great (980–1015) was not the founder of Kievan Rus' statehood, but he was the ruler who – thanks to his decision of Christianization of Rus'– together with his two successors carried out the crucial step in consolidating old Rus' statehood. In this regard the history of Poland seems to be an exception for neither of the first two Piasts who went about introducing and strengthening the institutional bases of Christianity was ever canonized – indeed, the role of the early patron of the Polish state fell to Saint Adalbert (Wojciech), the Bishop of Prague, who had come to Poland at the invitation of Boleslaus the Brave and soon thereafter was murdered during his evangelizing mission among the pagan Prus.

The elevation, in today's culture of memory among Poles, of the founding myth of their state, whose key element is the construct "the Baptism of Poland" by Mieszko I as the symbolic beginning of Polish statehood, was nevertheless born realtively late. The decisive moment in the way it was shaped came in the 19th c. and remains strictly tied to the overall shape of processes underway in that century pertaining to the emergence of modern national consciousness and nation-states, along with – what is highly relevant – historicism in the fine arts.

One of the first manifestations of the grand place the events of 966 came to enjoy in the modern Poles' memory was the building in 1835–1841 of a mausoleum in the Poznań Cathedral for the first Piasts, one constructed in Byzantine style and financed by Count Edward Raczyński, who had obtained the permission of King of Prussia Frederick Wilhelm III (1797–1840). This "Golden Chapel", with monumental figures of Mieszko I and his son Boleslaus the Brave, created by the German sculptor Christian Daniel Rauch, is one of the most marvelous artefacts of historicist art from that time in Europe.[38] The further development of the myth of "the Baptism of Poland" fell to the second half of the 19th c. – to the period of the dynamic expansion of history in modern Europe's public spaces and of the "invented tradition".[39] This left behind a wealth of examples of monumental paintings devoted to the topic[40], and which in subsequent decades were spread far and wide owing to the development of printing graphic art. The best known example is that of *The introduction of Christianity, AD 965*, the painting by Jan Matejko (1889) from his series *The history of civilization in Poland*. Noteworthy is the fact that the artist gave up his original idea for the painting's title – *The baptism of King Mieczysław*. In the end, and in accord with his typical manner of compiling many historical themes, Matejko decided to portray (besides the scene he imagined of Mieszko's baptism) the introduction of "Western Civilization" in the lands of the Polanians, together with the arrival of the Bohemian Princess, Doubravka, which happened in 965.[41]

The myth of "the Baptism of Poland in 966" gained a new dimension in the national culture of memory following "the rebirth" of an independent Polish state in 1918. In the interwar period the myth of Poland's rebirth began to be treated in strict connection with Poland's original founding myth, and this was recalled i.a., during the 20th anniversary celebrations of the new Polish statehood

---

38 Z. Ostrowska-Kłębowska, "Pomniki", *Dzieje Poznania*, vol. 2, 1793–1918, ed. J. Topolski, L. Trzeciakowski, Poznań 1994, p. 539.
39 *The Invention of Tradition*, ed. E. Hobsbawm, T. Ranger, Cambridge 1983.
40 Currently, the largest collection of paintings devoted to this theme can be seen in Gniezno at the Museum of the Origins of the Polish State.
41 B. Ciciora, A. M. Wyrwa, *Zaprowadzenie chrześcijaństwa w Polsce. Krótkie studium obrazu Jana Matejki „Zaprowadzenie chrześcijaństwa R.P. 965"*, Dziekanowice, Lednica 2013.

in 1938. Ultimately the popularization of "the Baptism of Poland in 966" as the founding myth was completed by the millennium celebrations culminating in 1966, which witnessed an intense rivalry between the communist authorities and the Catholic Church. This kind of overture to distant fragments of history and the creation of modern founding myths regarding statehood was not, however, something unique to Poland, but in a certain sense was typical for both Europe's "older" and especially its "younger" countries in the epoch of the blossoming of nation-states.

Glancing at the map of Europe in the year 1000 and then 1,000 years later permits us to follow over that period a wealth of cases of the collapse and disappearance of states and to connect them with cases of continuation and the "rebirth" of states whose genesis reaches back to the early Middle Ages. Even if in the latter case what was most concerned was not a genuine "rebirth", but rather qualitatively altogether new nation-states, ones that were mythologized for the needs of current state propaganda. Thus, as a result of WWI and the resulting collapse of the Habsburg and Russian empires, a series of new states could emerge in Central and Eastern and South-Eastern Europe, ones which in the sphere of the politics of memory would search for their roots by hearkening to the traditions of medieval statehood. The question for the modern, say, Polish or Lithuanian historian concerns the matters of "ethnic *translatio*" and the social imaginings of the continuation of the "reborn" states of Poland and Lithuania in 1918 after the more than century-long partitions.[42]

A similar ideological need was part and parcel of the reconstruction of the states of Central and Eastern Europe in the framework of the Eastern Bloc after WWII, which brought about further territorial changes. Thus for instance, the shifting of Poland's western borders in 1945 to the Oder and Neisse Rivers evoked the need to create and popularize in the People's Republic of Poland the ideology of the "Recovered Territories", in overture to the tradition of Piast Poland. This tendency was reinforced by underlining the thousand-year traditions of statehood within the framework devised by the communist authorities for mass-scale

---

42 See on this subject the exquisite essays by A. Nikžentaitis, "Unie polsko-litewskie w kulturach pamięci Litwy", [in:] *Od Horodła do Horodła: Unia horodelska – dzieje i pamięć (1413–2013)*, ed. I. Kąkolewski, P. Kondraciuk, M. Kopczyński, Zamość, Warszawa 2013, p. 103–117; and idem, "Zapomniany drugi – Litwini w Rzeczypospolitej Obojga Narodów", [in:] *Pod wspólnym niebem. Rzeczpospolita wielu narodów, wyznań i kultur…*, p. 63–74; A. Bumblauskas, "Konstytucja 3 maja a amnezja historyczna Litwy i Polski", [in:] ibidem, p. 75–85.

celebrations in 1966 of "1,000 Years of Polish Statehood" that was to counter the Catholic Church's celebrations of the "Millennium of Baptism of Poland". However, even the communist authorities, despite their initial efforts to determine earlier dates and events in order to compete with Mieszko's baptism, ultimately accepted the year 966 as the symbolic beginning of Polish statehood. It seems that especially the state program commemorating "1,000 Years of Polish Statehood", which surpassed in scale the jubilees observed in other countries both before and after the fall of the Iron Curtain with its the rich program of observances and accompanying gatherings, like no other project in politics of memory gave the events from 966 their final status as the founding myth of Polish statehood.[43]

We could cite more such cases when the politics of memory of postcommunist states called upon the mythological, medieval roots of their "reborn" statehood. The demise of Soviet supremacy from 1989 in the states of the Eastern Bloc and later the collapse and transformation of the imperial structures of the multi-national USSR and the Federation of Yugoslavia in the early 1990s, created new opportunities in politics of memory for myths of the rebirth and *translatio* of statehood from distant corners of history.[44] Particularly interesting here are the competing jubilees celebrating the 1,150 years of statehood in modern Russia, especially in the context of the way "the Baptism of Rus'" in 988 is imagined, as worked out by Tsarist Russia's culture of memory in the 19th c. This finds expression i.a., in the remarks for the Russian and American media of President Vladimir Putin, published in the press as "Russia and Ukraine will one day be together again" during the G20 summit in Saint Petersburg in 2013:

> Regardless of what happens, regardless of which direction Ukraine goes, one day we shall again meet together. Why? Because we are one nation [...]. We have a shared Kievan baptismal font, shared historical roots, shared fates, and a shared faith. We have kindred cultures, languages, traditions, and mentality [...] part of Ukraine was found

---

43 See: B. Noszczak, "History as a tool in the state's struggle against the Catholic Church during the celebrations of the 'One-Thousand Years of the Polish State' (1956–1966/1967)" [in:] this volume; idem „*Sacrum*" czy „*profanum*"? - *spór o istotę obchodów Milenium państwa polskiego (1949–1966)*, Warszawa 2002.

44 Regarding the competitively celebrated jubilee of the 1,150th anniversary of statehood in contemporary Russia and Ukraine, see the extensive analysis by V. M. Tkachenko, "Nepodil'na spadshchina Davn'oï Rusi (pro svjatkuvannja 1150-richja zarodzhennja rosijs'koï derzhavnosti)", *Problemi vsesvitn'oï istoriï* 1, 2016, p. 24–49. An English version of this text is included in this volume.

in the hands of various countries lying to the west of its territory, and throughout all those years the Ukrainian nation was forced to suffer hardships. It was in a slave-like, humiliating position.⁴⁵

At the same time the main thrust of today's Ukrainian historiography remains in conflict with Russia's current neo-imperial historical narrative. From the Ukrainian perspective, the recognition of Kievan Rus' as the beginning of Russian history would essentially be tantamount to recognizing Norman England as the beginning of the USA's statehood. Thus, today's Russian-Ukrainian quarrel over the Russian vis-à-vis Ukrainian character of Kievan Rus' recalls to a degree the more than century earlier Franco-German debate over Charlemagne and his state and "nationality" that asked *Charlemagne or Karl der Grosse*? This does not, however, rule out the possibility, similarly as in the case of the Carolingian state, for two nations: the French and the Germans. Indeed, the construct of the beginnings of Kievan Rus' may also be deemed a founding myth of more than one state.⁴⁶

In drawing to a close, let me voice several conclusions that, at first glance, may seem paradoxical. It seems that the deepened processes of modernization and secularization of the states and societies of Western Europe, and also the slow demise of nation-states in step with the intensification of the integration in the founding states of the European Union, have brought about a weaker need for "millennial" founding myths, as well as the myth of Christianization as an act of pivotal significance for the given state. And this is so even if certain Western lands, riding the wave of new nationalisms, are marked by pursuits to recreate vanished statehoods (Scotland, Catalonia, Flanders, Lombardy) and thereby hearken to the medieval roots of their statehood. Besides this, the integrational processes of the EU carry within them the need of creating a new type of identity rather more continental than national, and this in turn fosters the reconstruction of the mythology connected with the *renovatio* of Carolingian Europe, and also the Holy Roman Empire.

Moreover, the "rebirth" of the states of Central and Eastern and South-Eastern Europe at the close of the 20th c. have been accompanied (namely, in those countries with a less secularized culture, or those reacting to earlier,

---

45 [Electronic resource] available at: http://www.polskieradio.pl/5/3/Artykul/924641, Putin-Rosja-i-Ukraina-kiedys-znow-beda-razem-jestesmy-jednym-narodem.
46 K. Wóycicki, "Okiem narratologa: Unia horodelska w kulturze pamięci państw sukcesorów dawnej Rzeczypospolitej", [in:] *Od Horodła do Horodła…*, p. 131–145.

top-down efforts by communist rulers to de-Christianize their countries) by returns to national founding myths in which the link between the beginnings of statehood and Christianity is emphasized. This is plain especially in those states in which the Christian religion and Church institutional structures remain instrumentalized for political objectives, including historical policy and the politics of identity.

Taking into account the strict link in state founding myths of the constructs of the foundations of statehood and the Christianization of the country, the history of "younger Europe" may seem – although it is an optic illusion resulting from the meanders and telltale workings of cultures of memory – longer than that of the states of "old" Western Europe. Indeed, so measured, the history of Poland and Russia as states can loom as being longer than that of England with its symbolic date for the beginning statehood being 1066 with the Battle of Hastings (and the meaning, in this connection, of the crown of Edward the Confessor in the obligatory to this day coronation rite of the kings of England). The same is even more apt for Italy, unified not until 1861–1870, where the beginnings of Christianity are not connected with the beginnings of statehood in today's cultures of memory. The matter appears similar in today's Germany culture of memory as shaped after 1945, with its feeling of discontinuity in German history – both regionally and on the state scale.

In the case of the more nationalized and decidedly less secularized culture of memory in today's Poland, the imaginings of the millennial continuation of the Polish state – despite the discontinuity due to the partitions and occupations – were strengthened as a result of the official politics of memory of the state and the Church during communist times, especially in the 1960s. Particularly after the changes to Poland's borders after 1945 and the ethnic homogenization of the population, the second founding myth of statehood (after that of Piast Poland) also underwent erasure – namely, the Jagiellonian myth, which was strictly connected with the Christianization of Lithuania, which event was eagerly described in the Polish culture of memory as a "missionary" role on the part of Poland. Hence in the typical attitude of today's Poles the over one-thousand-year continuity of Polish statehood, as resting on the founding myth of "the Baptism of Poland", does not seem to raise any doubts.

This found full expression in the resolution of the Polish Sejm of December 22, 2015 to name the year 2016 "The 1,050th anniversary of Baptism of Poland": "The Chamber expresses the hope that the celebrations of the anniversary will be an occasion for reconciliation and the rebuilding of the Polish national community". At the same time, and despite the lack of any evidence in the historical sources, the acceptance of baptism by the first historical ruler of Poland was dated to "Easter Vigil, April 14, 966". Voting in favor of the resolution were 413 deputies hailing from all the parties represented in the Polish Parliament, without a single abstention or vote against.[47]

Translated by Philip Earl Steele

---

47 The draft resolution prepared by PiS (the governing party *Prawo i Sprawiedliwość*) emphasised that "The baptism of the ruler of Polanians and of his court, and, in consequence, the baptism of Poland took place on the Easter Vigil, on April 14, 966. This act was of decisive importance for the process of uniting the Polish tribes under Piast rule and of shaping the Christian identity of our Nation (...) The Sejm pays tribute to the memory of this groundbreaking act in Polish History, i.e., the baptism of Duke Mieszko I" [trans. K. Jamrog]. The Document also refers to the words of John Paul II: "Poland entered the circle of Western Christianity and began to build its future on the foundations of the Gospel. From that moment on we became a full member of the European family of nations with all of the consequences. With all the other nations of Europe we are the co-creators, and, at the same time, the heirs of a rich culture and history" [trans. K. Jamrog]. This echoes the celebration of the "Sacrum Millennium Poloniae" from 1966 as an expression of mass resistance to the communist authorities, [electronic resource] available at: http://docplayer.pl/14402537-Rok-jubileuszu-1050-lecia-chrztu-polski.html.

Philip Earl Steele

Homo religiosus: the phenomenon of Poland's Mieszko I

Abstract: The chapter describes the primary set of interpretations of Mieszko I's acceptance of Christianity in 966 that predominated in Polish historiography until the very recent past. The author shows that these interpretations reflect a deep bias toward scientism, as preserved in the former Soviet Bloc by Marxist strictures. These interpretations are then deconstructed, with a new case being built on a broad, comparative basis that stresses the role of empirical religiosity, something almost entirely rejected and/or ignored by all but the most recent Polish scholars. The author concludes by arguing that Mieszko's acceptance of baptism stands as one of the clearest examples in medieval Europe not only of the role of empirical religiosity – but of empirical religiosity having been the primary motive for a ruler's conversion.

Keywords: Mieszko I's baptism, Christianization, paganism, empirical religiosity, conversion

The full significance of Mieszko I's (c. 960–992) decision to adopt Christianity in 966 has generally evaded Polish historiography. This is understandable regarding recent generations of Polish scholars, as the dogmas imposed during the country's communist period had the effect of preserving the rationalist skepticism which Jacob Burckhardt, for instance, had applied in the mid-19th c. toward understanding the conversion of Constantine the Great.[1] That reductionist approach, often labeled "scientism" in Poland, dismisses the etiological power of religious beliefs and motives in history's dynamics – and it was deeply criticized in Western scholarship roughly a century ago.[2] Yet as the medieval historian Richard Fletcher observed already a decade into the post-Cold War era, "This line of argument has held some appeal for historians of a Marxist inclination, of whom a few may still be encountered in remote places".[3] Indeed, "path dependency" being what it is, the materialist paradigm in historical research that

---

1 J. Burckhardt, *Die Zeit Constantins des Grossen*, Basel 1853.
2 Cf. C. Odahl, *Constantine and the Christian Empire*, London, New York 2013, p. 285–286.
3 R. Fletcher, *The Barbarian Conversion: From Paganism to Christianity*, Oackland CA 1999, p. 238.

was enforced during the Soviet Bloc's existence continues to influence much of Polish historiography to the present day. [4]

True, the impact of Mieszko's decision for Poland's subsequent history has been rightly (albeit variously) stressed all along, but the reasons many historians (and untold hosts of teachers) have cited as underlying that decision are fundamentally misguided. For beyond their lack of comparisons to other rulers' conversions and the crisp clarity that can bring, they also have tended to ignore both the powerful hold of paganism as a "political program" seeking *pax deorum*, and above all the selfsame nature of Christianity's attractiveness for the pagan ruler. As Stanisław Trawkowski wrote in 1993, offering an early breath of fresh air, "For decades the positivist proclivities of the critical school [in Poland] confined the interests of historians of the Church to its organizational development, leaving the realm of religious experiences and attitudes aside".[5]

Nonetheless, no breakthrough was soon in coming. One telling example is provided by Gerard Labuda who in 2002 published the biography *Mieszko I*. In the subchapter entitled "On the transition from the pagan cult to the Christian" Labuda wrote: "What is most difficult to determine is the state of the religious mindset of the Polanians and other Polish tribes in the mid-10th c., during the period when they were discarding the polytheistic pagan cult and adopting the monotheistic, Christian worldview".[6] The matter is undeniably difficult, and yet in what follows Labuda makes no attempt whatsoever at an answer.

The primary objectives of this paper are: to offer non-Polish readers a sense of recent main stream Polish historiography concerning Mieszko I; to critically discuss the major materialist explanations of his baptism; to present the scope and sway of "empirical religiosity"[7] in early medieval Europe and how, in its pagan form, empirical religiosity lent itself as a bridge to Christianity; and to highlight,

---

[4] The relative isolation of national scholarly communities, as a result of the structural realities of the Soviet Bloc, of course compounded this problem. Cf. here professor K. Modzelewski's comments in his work, *Barbarzyńska Europa*, Warszawa 2004, p. 466–467; see also: M. Sághy, "Medieval perspectives after the fall", *Annual of Medieval Studies at the CEU* 15, 2009, p. 171–175. See also: footnote 72.

[5] S. Trawkowski, "Początki Kościoła w Polsce za panowanie Mieszka I", [in:] *Polska Mieszka I*, ed. J. M. Piskorski, Poznań 1993, p. 54. *Nota bene*: all translations of Polish-language sources are my own.

[6] G. Labuda, *Mieszko I*, Wrocław 2002, p. 217.

[7] For this term I am indebted to R. Fletcher, *The Barbarian Conversion...*, p. 6–8.

on a comparative backdrop, the strikingly religious nature of Mieszko's choice to adopt Christianity.

* * *

What are the reasons traditionally cited in Polish historiography for Mieszko's baptism?[8]

The most prominent stresses the dire threat posed by the Ottonian Empire – traditionally presented in Polish historiography as the "German" reason. This line of argument holds that Mieszko adopted Christianity in order to rob the newly resurrected (962) Holy Roman Empire of the pretext to crusade against his pagan realm - that baptism was "the better part of valour".[9] Further underlining the anti-German motive behind Mieszko's decision, his baptism is nonetheless said to have been received "from Bohemian hands".

The second explanation highlights the material and civilizational benefits Mieszko sought in joining Christendom. Apart from the application of "modernization theory", in the openly Marxian version characteristic for Polish historiography (particularly in the 1950s and 1960s), this argument makes the case that Christianization was to facilitate the "feudalization" then incumbent upon Poland's Piast dynasty.

The third interpretation stresses the purely diplomatic-political dimension and motivation of Mieszko's baptism. The purported motive of the Polanian ruler to accept Christian faith was here to overcome "the lowly stature of the pagan in the diplomatic protocol of the period".[10]

The fourth argues that Mieszko I, in establishing himself as a Christian ruler, aimed to strengthen his throne in line with the doctrine of "the divine right of kings" as importantly laid down by Saint Paul: "Everyone is to obey the governing authorities, because there is no authority except from God and so whatever authorities exist have been appointed by God" (Romans 13: 1).[11]

The fifth argues that, in introducing a new, uniform religion for the peoples ("tribes") within his expanding realm (as well as for the neighboring peoples he yet intended to conquer), Mieszko sought to foster and facilitate their sense of unity – in accord with the principle *religio vinculum societatis*.

---

8   These reasons are critically discussed and treated at greater length in my book: P. E. Steele, *Nawrócenie i chrzest Mieszko I*, Warszawa 2005, 2nd expanded edition: Warszawa 2016.
9   N. Davies, *God's Playground*, vol. 1, New York 1982, p. 63.
10 G. Labuda, *Mieszko...*, p. 103. Cf. below p. 213n.
11 All Biblical quotations in this chapter are from *The New Jerusalem Bible*.

As we shall see, these interpretive views[12] fall either within a materialist paradigm or focus exclusively on geopolitics and sociotechnics. None of them stands up to criticism.

* * *

The argument concerning the threat from the "German" Empire disregards the facts from the period of Mieszko's reign – nevertheless it deeply meshed with Poland's post-WWII anxieties over German revanchism vis-à-vis the "Recovered Territories", which in 1945 the Allies had ceded to Poland from Germany. Thus, postwar Poland's renewed presence along the Oder River's right bank was buttressed by a state policy of extolling the Piast presence there in the early Middle Ages. The German menace (*Drang nach Osten* – i.e., the aggressive "Drive to the East" – in fact, a phrase coined not until the mid-19th c.) was likewise transposed all the way back to the days of Mieszko I.

However, the sources on the rule of Emperor Otto I the Great (936/962–973) make clear that the thrusts of his foreign policy hardly concerned the east. Most apt would be to subsume them under "Drive to the South" for especially over the final dozen or so years of Otto's life (which precisely coincides with the first dozen or so years of Mieszko's reign), it was Italy that consumed virtually all of the emperor's time and efforts. Indeed, shortly after his intense entanglements with Pope John XII in Rome in 961–963, and then with Pope Leo VII in 964 and early 965, Otto simply moved to the Eternal City, and remained there with his court for six years, from 966 to 972. This imperial *Drang nach Süden* goes far in explaining why we have such scant Ottonian sources on the lands ruled by Mieszko during Otto I's life.[13]

---

12 There are others, as well, including the notion that Mieszko's baptism (treated, mistakenly, as part of his marriage contract with the Bohemian princess Doubravka) was meant to break the Bohemian-Polabian alliance. However, why the Piasts would have to forsake the religion of their ancestors and risk losing the favor of their gods, though pagan Polabian Slavs could pact with Christian Bohemia, goes unexplained: D. A. Sikorski argues the same in his book *Kościół w Polsce za Mieszka I i Bolesława Chrobrego*, Poznań 2011, p. 101–103.

13 For instance, Liudprand, who served at Otto's court, in conversation with Basileus Nicephoros in Constantinople in 968, vaguely alludes to "Slavic peoples" under Otto, ones he claimed were mightier than Peter, king of the Bulgarians (*Embassy* – 16), but adds nothing more. We may nonetheless assume that Liudprand must have had in mind Mieszko and the Polanians, then the mightiest of the Slavs allied with Otto I. I rely on: *The Complete Works of Liudprand of Cremona*, trans. P. Squatriti, Washington DC 2007. The infamously selective Widukind (who omitted Italy from his accounts, never mentioned a single pope, wrote not a word about the creation in 968 of the

The source that has misled many historians into accepting the existence of a purported German threat to Mieszko's Poland was provided by Thietmar, the Bishop of Merseburg, in his *Chronicle*, written from 1012 until his death in 1018.[14] There, in Book II, chap. 9 he reports on matters from the year 963: "Gero, the margrave of the Eastern March, subordinated to the supremacy of the Emperor the Lusatians, Selpoli – and also Mieszko together with his subjects".[15] However, beginning with professor Labuda shortly after WWII and extending to Tomasz Jasiński in Poznań today, this passage has been shown to be a mistake on Thietmar's part.[16]

Archbishopric in Magdeburg, and devoted a whopping 47 chapters of Book III [viz. 23–69] to the otherwise marginal figure and Saxon outcast Wichman) did mention Mieszko twice by name in Book III (where, in chapters 66–69, he recounts the battles that Wichman, commanding Polabian warriors, waged with Mieszko), but only in passing. Moreover, despite working on his *Res gestae saxonicae* until 973, Widukind neglects to note Mieszko's baptism: though he does refer to Mieszko as both king (*Misaca rex* – III 66) and as an ally of the emperor (*amicus imperatoris* – III 69). I rely on: *Res gestae saxonicae. Die Sachsengeschichte*, Ditzingen 1980.

14 I rely on the outstanding scholarly Polish edition of his work: Thietmar, *Kronika Thietmara*, ed. M. Z. Jedlicki, Kraków 2005.
15 Ibidem, p. 25.
16 See: the paper by T. Jasiński published to commemorate the 1,050[th] anniversary of Mieszko's baptism "Chrzest Polski", [electronic resource] available at: *http://chrzest966.pl/chrzest-polski/: "On the basis of [Thietmar's] information, scholars [...] accepted that ca. 963 Mieszko I was defeated by margrave Gero and compelled to receive baptism. We would have to assent to this mistaken view if *The Deeds of the Saxons* written by Widukind at the time of the events in question had not survived. For it turns out that Thietmar's brief note is no more than a summary of four chapters of *The Deeds* (65–68) [...] and contains several serious errors [...] When we examine Widukind's account we find out that he describes Gero's defeat of the Lusatians, but mentions nothing of Mieszko and his subjects [...]. Nor is this the end of the matter, as yet a further important [contemporary] source is silent [about Mieszko] – namely, the continuation of the Chronicon of Regino. This source was completed in December 967 [...] and was written on the occasion of the coronation [...] of the young Otto II, December 25, 967. For this reason, the author of the work tasked himself with enumerating all the marvelous deeds and conquests of the Ottonian dynasty. The defeat or even subjugation to the emperor's rule of Mieszko's realm, one of the most important in the region (I refer scoffers to Ibrahim ibn Yakub) would have been a diadem in the Chronicon's narrative. And yet we find nothing of the kind here. Rather, all we may read for the year 963 is: "The Slavs who were called Lusatians were subjugated". Thus we have two contemporary sources interested in listing the conquests of Otto and his subordinates, each of which is silent about any dependence whatsoever of Mieszko on the empire, against the single mention

The problems with the purported German threat run deeper still. Otto I – in addition to his many internal wars to crush rebellions – warred against such members of Christendom as West Francia, Bohemia, and Italy. Moreover, Christian and pagan countries were known to form military alliances[17], as in the highly relevant case of the Bohemian-Polabian alliance lasting into the mid-960s, and somewhat later the alliance with the Polabian Slavs which Emperor Henry II (1002/1014–1024) targeted against the Christian realm of Mieszko's son, Boleslaus the Brave (992–1025). Baptism hardly shielded a Christian realm from attack by fellow-Christians in the Middle Ages. We have a telling example from the year 972, when Margrave Hodo of Lusatia warred against Mieszko on the Oder River. Importantly, Mieszko's army won that battle, which fact makes the image of Mieszko as a Slavic ruler cowering to the Germans all the more untenable. And this was naturally put to good use in postwar Poland's commemoration of the Battle of Cedynia.[18]

The Polabians, that kaleidoscopic hodge-podge of pagan Slavs living between the Oder River and the Elbe[19], despite their inability to form a united polity, managed to throw off one attempt at subjugation after another (as famously in 983) made by the Empire or its German margraves, and to overthrow and kill a would-be Christianizer of their own (Gottschalk, † 1066)[20], and to thereby remain both pagan and independent for two full centuries after Mieszko's baptism.[21] If

---

Thietmar made 50 years after events, and this in a passage containing a series of errors arisen in the course of summarizing earlier sources [...]". Cf. D. A. Sikorski, *Kościół w Polsce* ..., p. 98–101, where (though he omits the Chronicon from his analysis) he concludes it is unclear who should be given priority – Widukind or Thietmar; cf. also J. Strzelczyk, *Mieszko Pierwszy*, Poznań 1992, p. 81–96.

17 There are too many examples to list, though among the more colorful is the alliance of 892 between the apostate Vladimir of Bulgaria, pagan Hungarians, and Arnulf, would-be Holy Roman Emperor, against Christian Great Moravia – cf. Liudprand, *Retribution*, Book I, p. 56. Another involves the Emperor of East, Nikephoros, who in 969, according to Nestor, pacted with the pagan ruler of Kiev, Svyatoslav, against Christian Bulgaria – cf. *The Primary Chronicle*, [in:] *Medieval Russia's epics, chronicles, and tales*, ed. S.A. Zenkovsky, Dutton 1963, p. 59.

18 Cf. B. Noszczak, "History as a tool in the state's struggle against the Catholic Church during the celebrations of the One-Thousand Years of the Polish State (1956–1966/1967)", [in:] this volume.

19 In Polish, "Łaba" – hence the Polish terms "Połabie", meaning "beyond (past) the Łaba" and "Słowianie Połabscy", i.e. Polabian Slavs.

20 For a brief description of Gotschalk's fascinating career, see: P. E. Steele, *Nawrócenie...*, p. 126–127.

21 Cf. J. Strzelczyk, *Słowianie Połabscy*, Poznań 2002.

the fragmented Polabian Slavs could accomplish this, all the while buffering, as it were, the Piast dynasty from the German territories of the Empire, the same could only have been vastly easier for Mieszko and his successors. Had only the Piasts wished.

This whole point is moot for even better reason: the leading Polish scholars have rejected it (though not Polish textbooks and popularizing publications).[22] For instance, in 1988 Labuda wrote: "Our historiography is rife with the conviction that Mieszko was baptized in order to deprive the Germans of a pretext to invade Polish lands [...] [But this premise is] of course made up out of thin air [...]. Mieszko's baptism neither protected his country from [German] expansion nor could it deprive the Germans of a pretext to do so".[23] In 1992, Jerzy Strzelczyk emphasized that:

> in 965–966 the 'German problem' was not in all probability perceived by Mieszko I as a genuine threat, and in spite of the unquestionable qualifications of the statesman, ones which we shall not deny Mieszko I, he probably did not possess the gift of clairvoyance, so he could not have known how relations between Poland and Germany were to develop in the future. What is more [...] the relations between Poland and Germany up until the death of Mieszko I, and even during the first decade of his successor's reign, were altogether correct – even somewhat more than correct.[24]

---

22 Cf. K. Ożóg, who explains Mieszko's decision to adopt Christianity entirely in the context of external relations, especially vis-à-vis Ottonian Empire, in his book: *966. Chrzest Polski*, Kraków 2016, p. 82–88. However, in the summer of 2016, Ożóg made a sharp about-face from his book in comments to the press: "At the bottom of all this is an act of faith, the act of Mieszko's conversion from the pagan faith to the true Christian faith"; "Mieszko [...] became a believer, he genuinely came to believe", [electronic resource] available at: https://www.youtube.com/watch?v=4kg9ZQG_oOQ A more nuanced argument, albeit one that also focuses on external relations, is found in A. Nowak, *Dzieje Polski*, vol. 1: *do 1202. Skąd nasz ród*, Kraków 2014, esp. p. 80–81. Cf. the comment by D. A. Sikorski: "It's easy to agree with Gerard Labuda when he states that the search for external motives frees one from having to address the reasons for which Mieszko himself wished to become a Christian", *Kościół w Polsce...*, p. 103.

23 G. Labuda, *Studia nad początkami państwa polskiego*, Poznań 1988, vol. 1, p. 452.

24 J. Strzelczyk, *Mieszko...*, p. 118–119. Among the many matters then giving evidence to Poland and Germany's "altogether correct" relations is Mieszko's marriage (after his first wife Doubravka's premature passing in 977) to Oda, the daughter of Dietrich of Haldensleben, Margave of the Northern March. In yet further refutation of Mieszko's purported anti-German policy, it was only Oda and her two sons with Mieszko (namely, Lambert and Mieszko Jr.) who were included in Mieszko I's "final will and testament", *Dagome Iudex* (i.e., it makes no mention of Boleslaus the Brave).

He further adds that "we simply should accept the fact that a thousand years ago there were no fundamental clashes of interest between Poland and Germany".[25] What also speaks volumes about the current approach of Polish historiography to the *Drang nach Osten* thesis is that Dariusz A. Sikorski does not even deign to discuss it in his magisterial work from 2011 *Kościół w Polsce za Mieszka I i Bolesława Chrobrego*.[26] Lastly, archaeology also confirms a dearth of Ottonian interaction with Polanian lands at that time.[27]

Now let us examine the sub-thesis concerning Mieszko's purportedly cunning reception of Christianity "from Bohemian hands". We foremost need stress that until 973, some seven years after Mieszko's baptism, there was no independent Bohemian Church. For until the founding of the Bishopric of Prague[28], the Bohemian Church was administered by the Bishopric of Regensburg, such that conducting missionary work was beyond the Bohemians' competence. As Władysław Abraham long ago recognized, "Christianity could have been brought to Poland from Bohemia only through the Germans, for in Bohemia itself it had not yet become sufficiently rooted. And that there could have existed a clergy capable of autonomous missionary activity is highly doubtful".[29]

In fact, there is now a general, albeit tentative consensus in Polish scholarship that Rome was the most probable provenance of the Christianizing mission to

---

25 Ibidem, p. 201.
26 D. A. Sikorski, *Kościół w Polsce...*, see chapter 3.1: "Chrzest Mieszka I: Przyczyny". Much the same may be said of Roman Michałowski's pivotal analysis, "Chrystianizacja monarchii piastowskiej", [in:] *Animarum cultura: studia nad kulturą religijną na ziemiach polskich w średniowieczu*, ed. H. Manikowska, W. Brojer, Warszawa 2008 – which most closely follows mine from 2005 regarding empirical religiosity (*Nawrócenie...*), and which will be discussed later in this text.
27 M. Bogucki, "Intercultural relations of the inhabitants of Polish territory in the 9th and 10th centuries", [in:] *The Past Societies: Polish lands from the first evidence of human presence to the early Middle Ages*, vol. 5: *500 AD – 1000 AD*, ed. P. Urbańczyk, Warszawa 2016, p. 235, states: "The territory of present-day Poland was separated from Ottonian Germany by Bohemia and the lands inhabited by Polabian Slavs, which is why interactions with Germans were rather insignificant until [...] the process of Christianization began. This is reflected in the small amount of [...] archaeological findings which might be connected with this cultural circle. The few older [Ottonian] items [...] had made their way to Polish lands mainly through Great Moravia and/or Bohemia".
28 The year 973 is the traditional date. However, the Bishopric in Prague in fact began to function not until several years later with the consecration of Bishop Dietmar/Thietmar in 976. See: D. A. Sikorski, *Kościół w Polsce...*, p. 327–328.
29 Taken from: S. Trawkowski, "Początki Kościoła..." p. 53.

Mieszko's Poland.[30] This view is buttressed *inter alia* by the fact that Poland's amazingly swiftly erected first bishopric (in Poznań) did not fall under the purview of the Archbishopric Magdeburg, created in 968.[31] Moreover, had the Church in the Empire been the vehicle for Mieszko's baptism, Bishop Thietmar most certainly would have known and not have ascribed the matter to the influence of Mieszko's Bohemian wife Doubravka. Nor does the name of the first bishop on the Polanians' territories – Jordan – at all suggest Bohemia (or Saxony), but rather Italy. Nonetheless, one can only conjecture about the probable papal mission to the Piast realm in the 960s.[32]

But first, none of the preceding is meant to belittle the role of the Bohemian princess Doubravka, who must have been influential – particularly after her husband's conversion, in the course of teaching him the practices of the Christian faith. We shall say more about this later. For now, however, the early annals inform us that *Dubrovka venit ad Misconem* in 965[33] – a year before

---

30 In 1992 Anzelm Weiss summed up the problem as follows: "After many years of discussion on the beginnings of Christianity and Church organization in Poland, certain facts are generally accepted. Among them are: that Mieszko I and his subjects by their own will consented to baptism; the connections of that ruler with Rome; and the independence of the early Polish Church's organization from the German metropolitan. Consequently, the Bishops Jordan and Unger are regarded as directly subordinate to the Holy See on the grounds that they were missionary bishops". Ks. A. Weiss, *Biskupstwa Bezpośrednio Zależne od Stolicy Apostolskiej w Średniowiecznej Europie*, Lublin 1992, p. 157. On the most recent scope of this discussion cf. D. A. Sikorski, "O nowej koncepcji okoliczności powołania biskupa Jordana", [in:] *Ecclesia. Studia z Dziejów Wielkopolski* 9, 2014, p. 7–20. The conception in question (tabled initially by Tomasz Jasiński in several papers; later by Wojciech Jasiński) argues that Pope John XIII appointed Jordan an exempted bishop – not a missionary bishop.

31 In 1920 the German scholar P. Kehr presented a thesis, soon expanded upon by A. Brackman and W. Mollenberg, which today is essentially uncontested among both Polish and German scholars. This concerns two questions important for us; namely that Jordan, from 968 the first bishop in Piast Poland, was not subordinate to Archbishopric in Magdeburg, and that the German Metropolitan in Magdeburg (established in 968) made no claims to suzerainty over lands to the east of the Odra, that is, to territories included within Mieszko I's realm (Cf. K. Buczek, *Pierwsze Biskupstwa Polskie*. Kraków 1995, a reprint of Buczek's original work from 1938). See also: M. Hardt, "Magdeburg and the Beginnings of the Archdiocese of Poznań", [in:] this volume.

32 See: P. E. Steele, *Nawrócenie...*, 2nd ed., 52–54. The matter involves Liudprand's description of Pope John XII's machinations, and a possible mission to Gniezno analogous to that of Zacheus'.

33 Cf. *The Old Holy Cross Annals*, Latin manuscript from the early 12th c., copied from the no longer existing *Annales Regni Polonorum deperditi*.

Mieszko's baptism, which the annals ascribe to the year 966. The accounts of both Thietmar and the anonymous Monk from Lido, author of the early 12th c. *Gesta principum Polonorum* or *Polish Chronicle*[34], traditionally called *Gallus Anonymus's Chronicle*, also give this sequence – first marriage, then baptism. "The unbelieving husband is sanctified through his wife" (I Cor. 7:14). Indeed, the marriage of a Christian princess to a pagan ruler was an altogether standard vehicle and *topos* for Christianity's spread following the demise of the Roman Empire.[35]

Examples run from the classic story of the first King of the Franks Clovis († c. 511) and Clotilda, to Ethelbert († 616) and Bertha in Kent, Edwin († c. 633) and Ethelburg in Northumbria, past Pribina († 861) of Nitra and his Bavarian wife, to Mieszko and Doubravka, and on to their daughter Świętosława, who married the pagan King of Sweden Eric († c. 995). In that case, however, Eric never did convert – although his son with the Piast princess did. We know him as the first Christian King of Sweden Olaf Skötkonung (c. 995–1022).

And this is the point I have in mind: hopes no doubt being what they were on the part of the Bohemian bride, her family, her *adiutor fidei*, etc., the conversion of her pagan husband was neither stipulated in the marriage contract[36] – nor was

---

34 Nearly a decade ago Tomasz Jasiński established that the author known since the 16th c. as "Gallus Anonymus", and who wrote the *Polish Chronicle* at the court of Boleslaus the Wrymouth in the years c. 1112–1116, is one and the same as the author of *Translatio Sancti Nicolai* (written between 1102 and 1108), who describes himself as a monk from the Benedictine monastery in Lido, near Venice. Interestingly, *Monachus Littorensis* (as the author of the *Translatio* is known, and who may have come from Slavic Dalmatia) stated that he had been in Tours. Jasiński explains that this is how his Latin acquired certain stylistic features that inclined scholars to identify him as a Frenchman. Cf. T. Jasiński, *O pochodzeniu Galla Anonima*, Kraków 2008 and *Gall Anonim – poeta i mistrz prozy*, Kraków 2016, p. 163–182; also M. Eder, "In search of the author of *Chronica Polonorum* ascribed to Gallus Anonymus: a stylometric reconnaissance", *Acta Poloniae Historica* 112, 2015, p. 5–23.

35 It would seem that the marriage of Poland's Jadwiga to the Grand Duke of Lithuania Ladislaus Jagiełło in 1386 and the baptism of the Lithuanian ruler has created a *topos* of its own. Cf. A. Nowak: "[...] the Bohemian Duke Boleslaus could not marry his daughter to a pagan" – in: "My, Polanie..." p. 54–59.

36 In fact, the Monk from Lido *vel* Gallus Anonymus does make this suggestion (Book I, chap. 5), though he immediately thereafter contradicts himself, citing first marriage then baptism, as do the surviving annals and Bishop of Merseburg Thietmar, who more fully describes Doubravka's committed, post-marital efforts to persuade her husband (Book IV, chap. 55–56). About the resistance of Polish historians to accepting Thietmar's account of Doubravka's role, D. A. Sikorski writes that this "results from

it fully assured. In the case of Clovis, we need recall, Clotilda's efforts took at least three years (if we accept the traditional 496 as the year of Clovis' conversion) and as many as 15 years if we accept the more likely date of 508.[37] Even so, such cases involved Church missions. Clovis was encouraged to adopt Catholicism by the Frankish Bishops Remigius and Avistus.[38] Ethelbert's conversion drew not only from Bertha and her confessor Liudhard – but also from the mission Pope Gregory the Great sent to Kent, as headed by Augustine. Edwin's conversion, in turn, as we know from the Venerable Bede, involved the persuasion not only of Ethelburg and her confessor Paulinus, but also that of the pagan high priest Coifi – and above all a visitation by a "spirit" who, in line with the precepts of empirical religion, promised Edwin that, in exchange for obedience to the Christian God, "you should become king, crush your enemies, and enjoy greater power than any of your forebears, greater indeed than any king who has ever been among the English nation".[39]

There remains a list of further matters to be refuted within the case made for the Bohemian provenance of the evangelical mission to Mieszko's Poland, for instance, by pointing out that Cosmas of Prague failed to ascribe Poland's Christianization to Bohemia. Perhaps the most important of them is linguistic. For it was long held that 75 % of the earliest ecclesiastical vocabulary in Polish drives from Czech language[40] and, furthermore, that the relevant terms – *kościół* (church), *ksiądz* (priest), *ołtarz* (altar), *msza* (Mass), etc. – had been borrowed during the reign of Mieszko I from the Bohemian clergy then hypothesized to have been evangelizing Piast lands. However, as I pointed out in my book (2005), even well into the second half of the 13th c. the Czech and Polish languages could hardly be distinguished. Sources from the 11th and 12th c. treated the language of Bohemia and Poland (and other parts of Slavdom) as one and the same, labeling it simply "Slavic". Among the many such examples is Adam of

---

the habit of always treating the conversion of rulers in political categories: either they accepted baptism under the duress of external forces, or after minute calculation of gains and losses", *Kościół w Polsce...*, p. 98.
37 Cf. I. Wood, *The Merovingian Kingdoms 450–751*, Harlow 1994, p. 48.
38 Ibidem, p. 41–49. Wood does not, however, give credence to the purported teaching role of a third churchman, Vedast of Arras.
39 Bede, *Ecclesiastical History of the English People*, Book II, chap. 12, London, New York, Ringwood, Toronto, Wairau Road 1991, p. 127. The riveting story of Coifi ("the classic case of the poacher turned gamekeeper" – R. Fletcher *The Barbarian Conversion...*, p. 123) is in Book II, chap. 13.
40 E. Klich, *Polska terminologia chrześcijańska*, Poznań 1927.

Bremen, who in his work *Gesta Hammaburgensis ecclesiae pontificum* (written in the years 1075–1080) stated that Poles and Bohemians "differ neither in appearance nor in language".[41] The Bohemian chronicler Cosmas, writing shortly before the year 1120, several times refers to "the Slavic language" as one shared by the Slavs.[42] The Monk from Lido similarly suggested a shared Slavic language in the *Polish Chronicle*, written just a few years earlier.[43]

The breakthrough in Polish historiography on the Bohemian provenance of Polish ecclesiastical terminology came a year later, with the publication of a brief paper by Dariusz A. Sikorski and its subsequent expansions.[44] In a nutshell, Sikorski has demonstrated that only 13.5 % of the ecclesiastic terms in Polish have an unequivocal or probable Czech origin (5 % and 8.5 %, respectively). Moreover, the author proved that it is impossible to show that any of those 13.5 % were borrowed during the reigns of Mieszko I and his son Boleslaus the Brave: "the hypothesis that the Czech genesis [of Polish language's ecclesiastical vocabulary] began in the missionary phase (10th and 11th c.) can no longer be maintained".[45]

***

Let us proceed with the interpretation that Mieszko chose to be baptized in anticipation of "civilizational" and material benefits, and that Christianity allowed the feudalization of Polish lands to take place.

The purported "civilizational advancements" for which Mieszko is said to have rejected the gods of his people and their guardianship over the Piast dynasty

---

41 Adam of Bremen, *History of the Archbishops of Hamburg-Bremen*, trans. J. Tschan, New York 2002, Book II, chap. 21, p. 65.

42 Cosmas of Prague, *The Chronicle of the Czechs*, Washington DC 2009, Book I, chap. 23, 31, and 40, p. 73, 84, and 102.

43 Cf. "in the city of Gniezno [originally, 'Gniezdno'], which in Slavic means the same as 'nest' [gniazdo]", at the very beginning of Book I; and "vessels known in Slavic as 'cebry' [buckets, pails]" in Book II, Gall Anonim, *Kronika polska*, ed. R. Grodecki, Wrocław et al. 1996.

44 D. A. Sikorski, "O czeskiej proweniencji polskiej terminologii kościelnej", [in:] *Przemyślidzi i Piastowie – twórcy i gospodarze średniowiecznych monarchii*, Poznań 2006, p. 101–106; D. A. Sikorski, "Najstarsza warstwa terminologii chrześcijańskiej w staropolszczyźnie – próba weryfikacji teorii o czeskim pochodzeniu", [in:] *Wielkopolska – Polska – Czechy: Studia z dziejów średniowiecza ofiarowane Profesorowi Bronisławowi Nowackiemu*, Poznań, 2009, p. 347–370; see especially his book: D. A. Sikorski, *Początki Kościoła w Polsce. Wybrane problemy*, Poznań 2012, p. 223–272; also *Kościół w Polsce...* p. 283–285.

45 D. A. Sikorski, *Początki Kościóła w Polsce...*, p. 272.

seem to result rather from ahistorical assumptions and the paradigm of progress as the driving force in history. On the one hand it is enough to recall what paltry inroads literacy made under the rule of the first two Piasts. After all, with the single exception of Mieszko's final will and testament *Dagome Iudex* (which survived in the form of a summary compiled in the Roman Curia c. 1080), not a one of our sources is of Polish authorship.[46] And that fact extends all the way to the early-twelfth-century's *Polish Chronicle*, which was also written by a foreign author. The majority of contemporary sources relating to the early Piasts was compiled on the territories of the Holy Roman Empire and are sprinkled with Arabic, Czech, Ruthenian, Greek, and other works.[47]

Secondly, Ibrahim ibn Yakub, writing on the eve of Mieszko's baptism, left us with a description of Mieszko's "state administration" that is altogether impressive. He reports that Mieszko (the "king of the north") ruled over "the most extensive of the Slavic countries", and that he possessed "three thousand men in armor [...] and one hundred of them means as much as ten hundred others". Ibn Yakub also explains how Mieszko collected taxes in order to make monthly payments to his soldiers, adding that Mieszko taxed his soldiers for each child they fathered, and that later, when the child (whether male or female) was given in marriage, Mieszko gave the father a considerable wedding present.[48]

What, more broadly, must be borne in mind is that Western Europe and the Church's "soft power" knows no lower ebb than the 10th c.[49] There is no solid

---

46 In fact, it need be surmised that *Dagome iudex* was drafted by the Bishop of Poznań, Unger, who may have been a Saxon (and probably served for a time as the abbot in Memleben), or maybe (as his name seems to indicate) a Hungarian. Cf. D. A. Sikorski, *Początki Kościóła w Polsce...*, p. 186–194.

47 Worth recalling in this vein is the crude "denar of Mieszko", which, along its rim, misspells his name thus: "OCZLTM" (scholars explain this must be read backwards, as "MTLZCO"— sic!). In fact, many numismatists now believe the denar was minted during Boleslaus the Brave's reign, and refers to his son, Mieszko II – which, if true, would place the civilizational advancement theory in even greater doubt. Cf. J. Strzelczyk, *Mieszko Pierwszy...*, p. 202–203; for an image of the denar see: [electronic resource] available at: http://www.denary.com.pl/denar-mieszka-lamberta-01.html.

48 On the basis of the translation by T. Kowalski, *Relacja Ibrāhīma Ibn Jakūba z podróży do krajów słowiańskich w przekazie al-Bekrīego* (Pomniki dziejowe Polski. Seria 2/1. Wydawnictwa Komisji Historycznej. Polska Akademia Umiejętności, 84), Kraków 1946.

49 There simply was no dazzling light of civilization shining from the Christian West to Mieszko's realm. The Carolingian renaissance was already long over. It was only on the eve of the baptism of Mieszko that the papacy found a new defender for itself in the person of Otto I, crowned Emperor in 962, then in its infancy. However, his title was

ground for suggesting there were potential "civilizational advances" of a kind that could, in the near-term, justify the risk Mieszko must have perceived as part and parcel of apostasy to the Slavic gods.[50] Dariusz A. Sikorski recently added in this vein that neither could the Ottonian political system have loomed before Mieszko as something coveted, as something superior to his own system:

> Mieszko's closest examples of Christian rulers did not give him any bases for believing that the functioning of the new religion [could strengthen his power]. The German throne, although in practice hereditary, was nevertheless elective. Rebellions against the lawful Christian ruler were hardly a rarity, and thus from Mieszko's perspective the bases of the power of Christian rulers were not at all that different from those he knew as a pagan in his own Polanian backyard.[51]

The material benefits Mieszko is supposed to have counted on must also be questioned – foremost for the reason that, following his baptism, Mieszko ended the trade in his realm's hitherto greatest export commodity. Just recently, Mateusz Bogucki published a breakthrough in this matter. It concerns the presence of Arab coins in Greater Poland (Wielkopolska) – and above all their sudden disappearance. Archeologists have discovered a huge amount of these coins – dirhams, as they are known – dating to the 10th c. Beginning in the 930s these dirhams were ever more numerous. It seems there was a votive ritual involving the burial alongside one's homestead of approximately 1 %, as it is estimated, of one's earnings from trade with Arab buyers, ones primarily from the east (Baghdad). That is, differently than one might otherwise assume in thinking of Ibrahim ibn Yakub and his service to the caliph in Cordoba, there are relatively few dirhams from Muslim Spain. At that time the main commodity in trade with the Arabs in Central and Eastern Europe was that of slaves. We can also assume that the trade in slaves brought great wealth to the rising Piast dynasty.[52]

Indeed, the mid-10th c., when the vast network of strongholds was being built in the Greater Poland region, is the period when that trade reached its zenith. Large quantities of the dirhams found date to the 930s, as I have noted, and even larger quantities to the 940s, 950s and 960s, at which point they all but disappear

---

at that time "hopelessly lacking the splendor that Charlemagne had lent it in the year 800" – J. Strzelczyk, *Mieszko Pierwszy...*, p. 31.
50 As Clovis (according to Gregory of Tours) explained to Bishop Remigius, "There remains one obstacle. The people under my command will not agree to forsake their gods" – cf. *The History of the Franks*, London 1983, Book II, chap. 31, p. 144.
51 D. A. Sikorski, *Kościół w Polsce...*, p. 105.
52 Cf. P. Urbańczyk, *Mieszko Pierwszy tajemniczy*, Toruń 2012, p. 121–125.

from Greater Poland, i.e. directly after Mieszko's baptism. It is hard to imagine that this timing is a mere coincidence. Rather, what seems most probable is that Mieszko accepted the Church's ban on slavery and ended the practice in his realm as a result of Christian teaching.[53] And there may be a case of sociotechnics here, as well: that is, in the eyes of many in his realm Mieszko may have seemed a liberator, as having issued an "emancipation proclamation", so to speak.

We need bear in mind that slavery was not successfully forbidden in every Christianized country. The case of America again presents itself. But the more appropriate case here is of course Bohemia in the 10th c. For as we know from the *Vitae* of Saint Adalbert (as well as from the illuminated cathedral doors in Gniezno), the slave trade went on apace in Prague, where it left Adalbert at wit's end – and ultimately drove him to flee his Bohemian flock.[54] In Mieszko's Poland things took a radically different course, where – in startling defiance of our modern economic thinking – trade in the realm's most lucrative export good seems to have been abandoned.[55]

Finally on this point, it was back in 1993 that Stanisław Trawkowski, in a paper notable for its focus on the religious dimension of Mieszko's conversion, scorned the Marxian thesis long seriously regarded. He wrote:

> We may dismiss out of hand the majority of conjectures on the internal political reasons behind Poland's baptism that were declared in the 1950s and early 1960s, including that at issue was introducing the Church to Poland because it was an institution engaged in the flourishing of the socio-economic feudal system, whose development lay in the interests of the Polanian social elite with Mieszko as its leader. [...] [After all] the feudalization of socio-economic relations in Poland occurred not until the 13th–14th c. Even so, it did not lead to the creation of feudalism as the state system.[56]

As Karol Modzelewski put it in 2004:

> [...] the term [feudalism] was at bottom a masking device, a kind of extortion that Polish medieval historians paid half a century ago in their game of hide-and-seek with the guardians of the compulsory ideology. If we are to understand feudalism as it is

---

53 M. Bogucki, "Intercultural relations of the inhabitants of Polish territory in the 9th and 10th c.", [in:] *The Past Societies...*, p. 236–245.
54 Cf. *Święty Wojciech w polskiej tradycji historiograficznej: antologia tekstów*, ed. G. Labuda, Warszawa 1997.
55 Trade with Arabs in other goods, albeit on a vastly smaller scale, did of course continue, as we note in the case of Mieszko's gift in 985 to young Emperor Otto III – namely, a camel: Thietmar, *Kronika....*, Book IV, chap. 9, p. 60.
56 S. Trawkowski. "Początki Kościoła w Polsce..." p. 55.

grasped in today's medieval studies in the West, then we must state that Eastern Europe never did experience feudalism.[57]

***

The next thesis we wish to discuss is that Mieszko, "mired in the mistakes of paganism"[58], decided to accept the Christian faith in order to overcome his lowly status of a pagan ruler in the contacts with the Emperor's court or other European Christian hubs of power.

This argument draws on the case of Duke of Bohemia Bořivoj I (c. 870–889) who, together with his wife Ludmila, are revered as Bohemia's Christianizing couple. The story in question, found in the *Legend of Christian*[59], concerns how Bořivoj was humiliated for his paganism and made to sit on the floor in the banquet hall of Svatopluk I (870–894), the ruler of Great Moravia, during a feast enjoyed by the Christian elite. No less than Saint Methodius himself then scolded Bořivoj, imploring him to turn away from paganism – which the Bohemian ruler subsequently agreed to do. On the basis of this analogy, a range of Polish historians contend that Mieszko I opted for baptism as a way to secure greater prestige among the rulers of Christian Europe.[60]

Well, let us deny Mieszko neither vanity nor arrogance, but we must again reflect on the gravity of rejecting worship of the Slavic gods. We hardly need ask if Mieszko abandoned the venerable religion of his people and their forefathers, if he cut down the sacred groves only to frequent Europe's Christian capitals and/or to invite Christian rulers to Gniezno. All we know of his travels abroad is that he was twice (perhaps three times) summoned to the Emperor's court in Quedlinburg and nothing more. Simply put, with the thesis that Mieszko was really a European – and/or found himself "entangled in a vast and complex

---

57 K. Modzelewski, *Barbarzyńska Europa*…, p. 453–54. It must be stressed, however, that the feudalization thesis in its vulgar Marxist form in fact persisted into the 1980s: cf. J. Wyrozumski, *Historia Polski do roku 1505*, Warszawa 1984, particularly chapter IV, "Early Polish feudalism (from the mid-10th to the end of the 12th c.)", p. 80–115. Concerning the post-communist period, Henryk Samsonowicz is among the dwindling number of scholars who have continued this tradition (albeit in less vulgar form) see: H. Samsonowicz, *Dzień chrztu i co dalej*…, Warszawa 2008, p. 72–73 and chap. 7: "The economy and the time of baptism", p. 93–112.
58 Gall Anonim, *Kronika polska*…, Book I, chap. 5.
59 Cf. J. Bažant, N, Bažantová, F. Starn, *The Czech Reader: History, Culture, Politics*, Durham NC 2010, p. 17–19.
60 G. Labuda, *Mieszko*…, p. 103. Cf. M. Barański, *Mieszko I i Bolesław Chrobry*, Warszawa 1999, p. 17; see also: H. Samsonowicz, *Dzień chrztu*…, p. 62–63.

system of feudal and courtly values and behaviors incumbent upon representatives of the imperial elite"[61] – we completely lose sight of the fact that at the time of his baptism Mieszko I ruled over an entirely pagan country – and that his ambitions, clearly seen in the historical record, were directed toward the conquest of surrounding pagan territories.

***

We can just as summarily dismiss the still popular view that Mieszko opted for Christianity in order to make his subjects more obedient on the basis of Saint Paul's teaching.[62] Let us admit that in countries with a Christian establishment and society, the Pauline doctrine carried certain advantages for rulers, although regicide and rebellion were never something unknown in Christian Europe – and that most certainly goes for Otto I, against whom not only a range of dukes rebelled, but even his own son, Liudolf (952–954). Nonetheless, in the lands ruled from Gniezno and Poznań in 966 there was a pagan establishment and a pagan society. How was Paul of Tarsus to have swayed them? Clearly, this line of reasoning is absurd on its own terms. This explanation ignores two other important facts – namely, that pagan convictions of the sacred also "embraced the institution of kingly leadership"[63], and, again, that political realities in Christian countries hardly bespoke the spell of Paul's teaching.

"On the basis of his knowledge that the German elites were Christian", Dariusz A. Sikorski writes, "[Mieszko] could not conclude that a society of Christians gathered in the hand of a single ruler was not at risk of internal conflicts and local separatisms. As we know – and as Mieszko most certainly did, too – Christian countries were no less assailed by internal conflicts than was his own realm".[64] Jerzy Strzelczyk points out: "In the short-term the adoption of Christianity [....] must have meant (as the Christianizers must have been aware) a dramatic splintering of society, which, after all, not at once and not as a whole let itself be converted to the new religion".[65] Indeed, inasmuch as Mieszko I perceived the potential advantages of the Pauline teaching for the Christian monarch (which is far from certain), by no means could he have hoped to reap such advantage during his own reign, but rather only during that of his prospective Christian

---

61 J. Banaszkiewicz, "Mieszko I i władcy jego epoki", [in:] *Civitas Schinesghe: Mieszko I i poczatki państwa polskiego*, ed. J. M. Piskorski, Warszawa 2004, p. 95.
62 G. Labuda, *Mieszko I...*, p. 107. Cf. a popular outline history of Poland: M. Bogucka, *Dawna Polska: Narodziny, Rozkwit, Upadek*, Warszawa, Pułtusk 1998, p. 30.
63 Cf. K. Modzelewski, *Barbarzyńska Europa* ..., p. 402.
64 D. A. Sikorski, *Kościół w Polsce...*, p. 104.
65 J. Strzelczyk, *Mieszko...*, p. 124.

successors.⁶⁶ He himself could only expect insurrection. That is, insofar as he did not count on Providence – a matter which we shall take up below in our discussion of empirical religiosity.

***

Finally for this portion, let us consider the thesis that Christianity was to have been a tool in Mieszko's aim of uniting his own people and the surrounding Slavic tribes into one great state – that his introduction of a foreign, religion was to have been a "unifying factor".⁶⁷

This supposition raises profound doubts. Why should Mieszko have expected to find it easier to wield power over his pagan subjects, let alone subjugate neighboring Slavic tribal territories of Pomerania (Pomorze), Mazovia (Mazowsze), Lesser Poland (Małopolska), and Silesia (Śląsk) as an apostate whose rule had to mean not only the submission of their leaders, but also the eradication of all they considered sacred?⁶⁸ In line with any socio-technical use of religion, it would have been far more logical for Mieszko to have striven to unite his own and neighboring peoples as one of them, a Slav faithful to the Slavic pantheon then universally worshipped⁶⁹ in the Slavic (!) language, and not as a defector

---

66 Z. Dalewski makes a point worth noting: "The breakdown of the first [Polish] kingdom [in the 1030s], along with the later collapse of Bolesław the Bold's monarchial rule [1079], clearly prove that – regardless of the external factors that hindered the Piasts' royal ambitions – the idea of the Divine anointment of royal power did not enjoy many adherents in eleventh-century Poland". See: Z. Dalewski, "Publiczny wymiar kultu w chrystianizowanej monarchii piastowskiej" [in:] *Animarum cultura...*, p. 60.

67 Cf. J. Strzelczyk, *Mieszko...*, p. 122; S. Trawkowski, "Początki Kościoła...", p. 55–6; R. Michałowski, *Zjazd Gnieźnieński: religijne przesłanki powstania arcybiskupstwa gnieźnieńskiego*, Warszawa 2005, p. 98; A. Nowak, *Dzieje Polski...*, p. 83; G. Labuda, *Mieszko...*, p. 107.

68 Cf. S. Trawkowski, "Początki Kościoła..." p. 66: "The destruction of public places and fixtures attached to the pagan cult was an obligation of the Christian ruler, as explained by Saint Augustine. The destruction of idols made by human hands and of places pagans deemed sacred was at the same time, from the viewpoint of Christians in those days, an exorcising of the country and its populus from the power of demons".

69 Although far too few details of pagan worship among the Slavs (and other medieval European peoples) are known, suffice it here to stress four matters. The first concerns what Karol Modzelewski, building on Reinhard Wenskus, demonstrated in his magisterial work *Barbarzyńska Europa* – namely, the astounding similarity of the (completely independent from each other) descriptions of pagan worship recorded by both pagans and Christians alike – from Tacitus to Thietmar, Adam of Bremen, and Helmold – that encompass Germanics, Slavs, and Balts. Secondly, we also have the fact of identical names such as Swarożyc and Swaróg for Slavic gods from east to west across Slavdom

or invader bent on toppling their gods and bringing an end to the world they knew.⁷⁰ The example of the Empire's Christianizing encroachments into Polabian territories shows how arduous a task this was.⁷¹ Let it also be recalled that it took more than 500 years for Christianity to overcome paganism as it spread beyond

---

(from the Rus' to the Polabian Slavs) – cf. A. Szyjewski, *Religia Słowian*, Warszawa 2003. Thirdly, Polish archeologists today write of a material and symbolic culture so homogenous throughout Polish lands in the pre-Christian period that they are unable to identify "territorial political organizations". This homogeneity includes burial customs, and leads to the conclusion that "pre-state Poland was a large ethno-historical region, relatively uniform in terms of language and culture, whose people cultivated similar lifestyles shaped by similar experiences [...]" – see: professor P. Urbańczyk, Preface [in:] *The Past Societies: 500 AD – 1000 AD*, ed. M. Trzeciecki, Warszawa 2016, p. 15–16. Fourthly, I see no reason to assume the existence of divergent gods among the Polabian Slavs on the basis of Bishop Thietmar's remarks in the famous passage in Book VI, chap. 23–25, where he writes, "There are as many shrines, and as many images of idols are worshipped by the pagans, as there are districts in this country". For as is clear in this passage taken as a whole, he is describing a religious hierarchy having a pantheon (re: his description of Świarożyc and the other gods at the high temple in Radogoszcz) that is "worshipped among all the pagans" – along with a lower system of local and household gods that would seem to echo that of the Romans' lares and manes.

70 I argued this point in the first edition (2005) of my book *Nawrócenie...* It was restated by D. A. Sikorski in the 2011 and 2013 editions of his *Kościół w Polsce...*, p. 104: "One may nonetheless ask whether in fact the consolidation of conquered peoples was the primary aim of Christianization, or if it would have been better – from Mieszko's perspective – to impose on all conquered peoples a unified, pagan 'Gnieznan' religion that no doubt would not have differed essentially from the putative local cults, and hence would have been sufficiently similar that subjection to it would not have elicited important resistance. If Mieszko had indeed wished to employ Christianity as a platform for ideologically unifying the inhabitants of the lands he ruled over, then we have to conclude that he was able to construct a political vision a century into the future, for we can hardly suspect Mieszko to have naively assumed that the process [of Christianization] would yield results within the foreseeable future. [...] Here it is rather the results of Christianization seen from the perspective of two or three centuries that compel us to state that the new religion ultimately gave rise to such a shared ideological platform. However, we cannot treat the results of actions [...] as their cause". Cf. the discussion by Jerzy Dowiat concerning pagan syncretism in Slavdom, especially the example of multi-faced gods (Trzygłów, Światowid), whose statues are conjectured to have represented the deliberate creation of a "shared platform", a case best known in Rus', among the Polabian Slavs, and in western Pomerania: J. Dowiat, *Chrzest Polski*, Warszawa 1958, p. 24–29 and 59–60.

71 Cf. J. Dowiat, *Chrzest...*, p. 56: "And that's precisely how it was in the Polabian part of Slavdom, where paganism reigned until the 12th c., despite the fact that those lands

the Roman *limes* to Scandinavia.⁷² Thus, not only does this thesis fly in the face of Polabian Slavs' case – and not only does it violate historical methodology by flattening time: it also betrays a striking absence of sociological thinking.

* * *

Having set the above explanations aside, we are faced with the apparent recklessness of Mieszko's decision to adopt Christianity. Around 966 he was already a powerful ruler of the Polanians, after all, and was under no compulsion – whether external or internal – to tear down his people's *Irminsul*, the pillar holding up their world. On the contrary, Mieszko should best have sought to employ a syncretic form of Slavic paganism in extending his dominion – all the more so, as we have no information, whether written or archeological, about the presence of any Christians whatsoever in Polanian lands prior to Mieszko's baptism.⁷³ Not so much as a single errant Irish monk.⁷⁴ Every bit as important to remember is the

---

had entered into various German dioceses a couple centuries earlier. How precious little the mission inspired from outside meant!"

72 Of course, a comparative approach in regard to the beginnings of the early-Piast state or pre-Christian religions was not completely lacking in Polish historiography before 1989. See i.a.: the 6-volume publication by H. Łowmiański, *Początki Polski: z dziejów Słowian w I tysiącleciu n. e.*, vol. 1–6, Warszawa 1963–1985; cf. also A. Gieysztor, *Mitologia Słowian*, Warszawa 1982 (1st edition) and the new expanded post mortem edition, editorially prepared by A. Pieniądz and with a foreword by K. Modzelewski, Warszawa 2006.

73 There is in fact a set of three pottery shards from Podebłocie (c. 100 km south of Warszawa) discovered in the 1980s in a phase of settlement dating to the 7th and 8th c. Some scholars see on fragments 2 and 3 the Greek letters *IXCH*, which they have interpreted as an acronym for *I(sus) Ch(ristos) N(ika)*. One counter-interpretation – that the marks are not even letters, but rather the imprints of twigs – was ruled out by specialist examinations in 1998. Moreover, the clay of one of the shards was found to be of Mediterranean origin. It is hypothesized these objects may have belonged to a trader or slave. Cf. A. Buko, "Chrześcijanie i poganie: o problemach interpretacji odkryć archeologicznych związanych z początkami chrześcijaństwa na ziemiach polskich", *Slavia Antiqua* 57, 2016, p. 14–18.

74 About the intentions of certain Irishmen to start missions among the Slavs see: R. Fletcher, *The Barbarian Conversion…*, p. 142; 153. As for Polish lands, in the late 9th c. Saint Methodius may have had missionary contacts extending just north of the Carpathians to the "ever so powerful pagan ruler seated in Visle" (*Pannonian Legend*). Cf. R. Michałowski: "At the moment when Mieszko I received baptism, the region extending from the Warta to the middle Vistula was unspoiled pagan territory. Never before then – whether in Antiquity or in the early Middle Ages – had Christianity reached those lands. And even if missionaries, ones completely unbeknownst to us, did make their way to the region, their activity left no trace", *Zjazd Gnieźnieński…*, p. 91.

fact that in the 960s the Piast realm was surrounded by pagans literally from all sides. The Polabian Slavs to the west, the Pomeranian tribes to the north, the Balts to the northeast, the neighboring Mazovians to the east, and the Varangians farther to the east – they were all pagan. Silesia, between pagan Greater Poland and Christian Bohemia, was still an unevangelized no man's land[75] – and Ottonian Empire's "angle of repose", as stressed above, was southward.

So what convinced Mieszko to carry out an *autogolpe*, as it were? "The baptism of new peoples was not the result of political transformation, but rather its beginning", Karol Modzelewski stresses: "Baptism entailed a societal coup d'état. It struck at the foundations of the traditional system of European tribes, demolished it, and set the path toward establishing a new order".[76] "For the barbarians", Modzelewski adds, "the death of the gods signified the end of their world".[77] Indeed, the gamble Mieszko took may seem outright foolhardy.

The history of medieval Europe, after all, is littered with examples of pagan rulers who, for varying reasons, adopted and strove to institute Christianity only to be killed or banished by their own people. The Venerable Bede gives us two such cautionary tales from seventh-century Britain. The first concerns King of the East Angles Earpwald (624–c. 627 or 632), who, having barely commenced the evangelization of his people in 627, was murdered by one Ricbert, after which "the province relapsed into heathendom".[78] The second instance is that of King of the East Saxons Sigeberht II the Good (c. 653–c. 661). In 653 he began "to convert his people to the Faith of Christ and baptize them". Only a couple years

---

75 Cf. D. A. Sikorski, *Początki Kościoła…* p. 11–104, especially "Conclusions", p. 102–104, where we read: "Our sources certainly do not indicate in any convincing way that the southern lands of [today's] Poland were part of the Přemyslids' state in the 10th c. […] There is no unequivocal trace of the presence of Bohemian regiments in the strongholds of southern Poland, nor are there traces of Bohemian exploitation of those territories – we do not possess even the flimsiest of premises [to postulate otherwise]. The character of what traces of Bohemian provenance we do find permits us to deem them no more than traces of mutual trade contacts, which – given the direct proximity – is not only understandable, but entirely obvious. […] Inasmuch as the dependence of Poland's southern lands on the Bohemian bishopric is not at all a tenable likelihood, there is no need in further reflections to treat it as a fact that can influence interpretations […] of the beginnings of the Church in Poland."
76 K. Modzelewski, *Barbarzyńska Europa…*, p. 454.
77 Ibidem, p. 460.
78 Bede, *Ecclesiastical History…*, Book II, chap. 15, p. 132–133.

later, however, "at the instigation of the Enemy of all good men, the king was murdered by his own kinsmen".[79]

A third such example pertains to Harald Klak († c. 852), who was placed on the Danish throne in 819 by Emperor Louis the Pious (814–840). Seven years later, in 826, Harald, together with his family and retinue, traveled to Louis's court in Ingelheim near Mainz and was baptized. As we know from Ermoldus Nigellus, a contemporary courtier to the Emperor, Harald's godfather was Louis himself: Empress Judith stood beside Harald's wife. Following his christening, all the powers of Heaven and Earth on his side, Harald returned to Jutland together with Saint Ansgar to evangelize the Danes. They began with the construction of the country's first church in the bustling trade city of Hedeby. However, the new religion was not to the Danes' liking and Harald was soon driven out of the country.[80] He seems to have lived in exile in Frisia for the next 20-some years.[81] The Danes, meanwhile, returned to their pagan gods – and for another 6 or 7 generations. All the way until the conversion of their ruler Harald Gormsson (†c. 986) about 965.

Other examples, ones which come after the reign of Mieszko I, but nonetheless further refute the tenet that the adoption of Christianity secured the convert-ruler's throne, include: Gottschalk, the would-be Christianizer of Polabian Slavs (killed in 1066); and Mindaugas (1236–1263), first and only King of Lithuania, who was crowned by Pope Innocent IV in 1253 and killed, together with his two sons, 10 years later when Christianity was violently rejected.[82] It was not until nearly a century and a half later (1386) that Lithuanian Grand Duke Jogaila (1377–1434) was baptized.

We also know cases when the convert-ruler himself rejected Christianity and reverted to paganism, having become convinced that the new religion was either

---

79 Ibidem, Book III, chap. 22, p. 178–180.
80 Cf. *Vita Ansgari*, chap. 7 written by Bishop Rimbert of Hamburg and Bremen ca. 875, [electronic resource] available at: https://sourcebooks.fordham.edu/basis/anskar.asp; and Adam of Bremen, *History of the Archbishops...*, Book I, chap. 15, p. 21–22.
81 Intriguingly, in all three of these cases we see royal sponsorship of baptism from abroad. Earpwald, Bede tells us, was persuaded by King Edwin of Northumbria; Sigbert II, in turn, was won over to Christianity by King Oswy of Northumbria. Harald, caught up in a "game of thrones" going back at least to 812, was enthroned by Louis the Pious. Among the many other such cases is that of the Bohemian ruler Bořivoj, who was sponsored by Svatopluk I of Great Moravia. Of course, the Bohemians swiftly forced Bořivoj to flee Bohemia, though Svatopluk soon restored him to the throne.
82 For a discussion of Mindaugas, see: P. E. Steele, *Nawrócenie...*, p. 139–141.

ineffectual and/or unable to quell the wrath of the abandoned pagan gods. One such example is again from the Venerable Bede, who describes an event from 665 when a plague that had begun to rage among the East Saxons prompted their neophyte King Sighere († c. 668) to lapse into paganism: "For the king himself, together with many of the nobles and common folk, loved this life and sought no other, **or even disbelieved in its existence** [bold - Ph.S.]. Hoping for protection against the plague [...], they therefore began to rebuild the ruined temples and restore the worship of idols".[83] Similar events reflecting the grip of empirical religion took place throughout Europe, and include the ultimately failed Swedish mission of Saint Ansgar, who – after Harald Klak's expulsion from Denmark – crossed the sea northward and, beginning in Birka in 829, pursued the evangelization of the Swedes, initially with marked success. However, as Władysław Duczko has argued, a series of comets in 837 prompted the Swedish folk to expel the Christianizers (along with King Anund, as he had permitted the mission) and to reassert the worships of their gods.[84] The case of the Slavs in Pomerania in the third decade of the 12th c. provides several other examples. We know of them thanks to Ebo and Herbordus, the mid-twelfth-century biographers of Bishop Otto of Bamberg, "the Apostle of Pomerania", the lapses in question having been led by pagan priests.[85]

Rejections of Christian proselytization need also be borne in mind. Bede mentions the case of King of Mercia Penda († 655), who chose to remain a pagan, even though in 653 his son Peada († 656), agreed to baptism "together with his companions and thegns and all their servants" and began a Christianizing mission

---

83 Bede, *Ecclesastical History...*, Book III, chap. 30, p. 200.
84 Cf. W. Duczko, *Moce Wikingów*, Warszawa 2016.
85 "The wicked priests, when in a certain year men and beasts suffered illness and death owing to the changes in the temperature, declared that this calamity was sent by the gods, and, with the consent of the people, they had broken down the bells and had begun to destroy the church of the blessed martyr Adalbert."; and further "It happened, moreover, that a great mortality occurred in the town, and, when the [pagan] priests were questioned by the people, they said that they had met with this calamity because they had put away their idols, and that all of them would die suddenly if they did not try to appease their ancient gods by sacrifices and the accustomed gifts. In consequence of this declaration a public assembly was forthwith held, the idol images were sought out and the profane, idolatrous observances and ceremonies were performed again by the people, and the middle portions of the Christian churches were destroyed", *The Life of Otto Apostle of Pomerania 1060–1139*, New York 2007, p. 155, 110.

with the help of four priests.[86] One also thinks of the Polabian chiefs, often vacillating over whether "to be or not to be" Christian.[87] For instance, Thietmar of Merseburg presents the Obotrites' ruler Mstivoj (†995) as a pagan, although he mentions that Mstivoj kept a Christian chaplain named Aviko in his retinue.[88] Adam of Bremen describes Mstivoj's son Udo as "a bad Christian", although he adds that Udo did send his son Gotschalk to the abbey in Luneburg for his education.[89] Despite that schooling, in 1029 Gotschalk apostatized – only to reconvert in the 1040s and become the would-be Christianizer of Polabian Slavic territories.[90]

The most riveting rejection of Christian proselytizing is that of Radbod (†719), the Frisian ruler. As the *Vita Vulframni* tells us, literally seconds before he was to be christened, Radbod – standing but a single step from the baptismal font, no doubt wearing a white gown, *alba vestis* – asked Bishop Wulfram where his (pagan) ancestors, the kings and nobles and leaders of the Frisian people, were – in heaven or in hell? Wulfram is reported to have replied:

> it is certain that the multitudes of his elect are at the house of God, but on the other hand, your predecessors, the leaders of the Frisian people, who passed away without the sacrament of baptism, have certainly received the sentence of damnation. However, whomever henceforth believes and is baptized, will rejoice with Christ eternally.

This crystallized matters for Radbod, who at once knew he could not sever his ties with his ancestors. He then turned about and left – remaining a pagan until his death in 719.[91] The case of Radbod is compelling because of its eschatological component, something we comparatively seldom encounter in the history of medieval Europe's conversion. Among the better known examples, one flashes on the case of *translatio* in Jelling, where the Danish ruler Harald Gormsson, who had converted ca. 965, reburied his pagan father Gorm the Old († 958) in a nearby church (something Clovis, by way of contrast, did not do, leaving his pagan father Childeric forgotten in his tomb in Tournai).[92] We may well also recall the words spoken in 627 by one the "chief men" at King Edwin's court

---

86   Bede, *Ecclesastical History*..., Book III, chap. 21, p. 177–178. Bede lists the priests as Cedd, Adda, Betti (who were English), and Diuma, an Irishman.
87   See: C. Lübke, "Between Reception and Aversion: The earliest traces of Christianity among the Polabian Slavs", [in:] this volume.
88   Thietmar, *Kronika*..., Book III, chap. 18, p. 51.
89   Adam of Bremen, *History of the Archbishops*..., Book II, chap. 66, p. 100.
90   Ibidem, p. 100–101.
91   Radbod also appears in Bede, *Ecclesastical History*..., Book V, chap. 9–10, p. 280.
92   Cf. I. Wood, *The Merovingian*..., p. 44: "For a Merovingian, whose dynasty originated with a sea-monster, rejection of previous beliefs must have been particularly hard."

in Northumbria, who, during the court's debate on whether or not to accept Christianity, waxed poetic with a yearning to know what comes after death:

> Your Majesty, when we compare the present life of man on earth with that time of which we have no knowledge, it seems to me like the swift flight of a single sparrow through the banqueting-hall where you are sitting at dinner on a winter's day with your thegns and counsellors. In the midst there is a comforting fire to warm the hall; outside the storms of winter rain or snow are raging. This sparrow flies swiftly in through one door of the hall, and out through another. While he is inside, he is safe from the winter storms; but after a moment of comfort, he vanishes from sight into the wintry world from which he came. Even so, man appears on earth for a little while; but of what went before this life or of what follows, we know nothing. Therefore, if this new teaching has brought any more certain knowledge, it seems only right that we should follow it.[93]

But we must at once remind ourselves of the words Edwin's pagan high priest Coifi shared immediately before then, as they bespeak the empirical religiosity we shall now turn to:

> Your Majesty, let us give careful consideration to this new teaching; for I frankly admit that, in my experience, the religion that we have hitherto professed seems valueless and powerless. None of your subjects has been more devoted to the service of our gods than myself; yet there are many to whom you show greater favour, who receive greater honors, and who are more successful in all their undertakings. Now, if the gods had any power, they would surely have favoured myself, who have been more zealous in their service. Therefore, if on examination you perceive that these new teachings are better and more effectual, let us not hesitate to accept them.

* * *

There is, to be sure, a greater multiplicity of types of kingly conversions and rejections of conversion than I have given above. After all, there were the syncretists like Redwald (†624), ruler of the East Angles, who "tried to serve both Christ and the ancient gods, and he had in the same shrine an altar for the holy sacrifice of Christ side by side with a small altar on which victims were offered to devils".[94] Another is the father of the King of Hungary Stephen

---

> In Clovis's case the sharpness of the break seems to have been remarkable. It can be gauged by a comparison between Childeric's burial at Tournai, and his son's interment in the Church of the Holy Apostles in Paris. Further, Childeric's grave was apparently forgotten about; the horse burials which surrounded it were already cut into in the sixth century by secondary inhumations. Clovis and his descendants did not protect the tombs of their pagan ancestor." Childeric's grave was rediscovered in 1653.

93 Bede, *Ecclesiastical History...*, Book II, chap. 13, p. 129–130.
94 Ibidem, Book III, chap. 15, p. 133.

the Great (997–1038), Gejza (†997), to whom Thietmar of Merseburg referred as *Deuvix* and wrote that after he had been baptized, "he nonetheless made offerings not only to Almighty God, but also to sundry false pagan idols. And when his bishop rebuked him for this, [Gejza] declared to him that he was rich and powerful enough to allow himself to do so".[95] There were also other cases and forms of apostasy, including the Bulgarian ruler Vladimir-Rasate (889–893) and Kievan Grand Prince Svyatoslav I (c. 963–972) who, despite his mother Olga's conversion to Christianity in 957, remained a staunch pagan to his death; and of course those who were baptized by force of arms, particularly in the context of Charlemagne's Saxon wars and the Baltic crusades beginning in the late 12th c.

But the point to stress is what a rocky, uncertain road Europe's Christianization was. Its process as understood from the vantage point of a millennium later, is that Christianity spread via centrifugal, all-but inevitable forces – again, ones that focused on the tactic of "get the king". Most Polish historians are wont to portray conversion as virtually inescapable and always having been rationally calculated, neglecting the myriad different paths Christianity's erratic advance took and ignoring the many risks and setbacks it suffered throughout the period from the 5th to the 11th c.

* * *

The enormous role of empirical religiosity in the conversion of Europe is most starkly displayed in two areas. The first concerns the myriad "showdowns" staged by priests and missionaries, during which the earthly power of the Christian God was demonstrated to be superior to that of the pagan gods. The second, which is even more relevant for our considerations of Mieszko I's decision in the year 966, concerns the scores of cases when the Christian "pitch" made to the medieval pagan ruler laid stress above all – and usually exclusively – to the promise of strengthening his rule and realm.

But first, let's examine the "religious mindset", which Gerard Labuda failed to address concerning Mieszko's Poland. What most easily can be evaluated is the presence of magical thinking. As Karol Modzelewski has shown, across "barbarian" Europe – from Antiquity to the Middle Ages – the many pagan peoples, when gathered at their public assemblies (*wiec* in Polish – cf. *thing*) relied on astonishingly similar divination rituals to discover the will of the gods and win their favor for the tribe's worldly safety, health, prosperity, etc. Indeed, "In matters giving rise to doubts, it was necessary to turn to the gods for guidance – that is, to reach out to oracles. There can be no doubt but that divinations were

---

95 Thietmar, *Kronika…*, Book VIII, chap. 3, p. 219.

the link conjoining pagan cultic practices with the decision-making mechanism at the *wiec*[96], Modzelewski stresses.

Przemysław Urbańczyk, in one of his recent books focusing on Mieszko I, presented the nature of such empirical religiosity (which he calls "practical paganism") as follows:

> Whereas in pre-Christian religions it was of utmost importance to perform prescribed rituals intended to succor the favor of the gods and/or one's ancestors, Christianity, in turn, laid stress to an internal conviction that was made manifest in obligatory participation in highly ritualized activities. Simply put, the difference between practical paganism, whose adherents expected a specific and swift "payment" for having performed ritual activities, and Christianity – based on obeying an ethical code and on devotion that points to a distant, posthumous reward – must have been rather difficult to comprehend for early-medieval converts. We may therefore suspect they maintained an altogether mercantile approach to the new God and treated the duties imposed by the Church as the means to obtain due 'payment' for having fulfilled the requirements of the new faith.[97]

The corollary to *do ut des* is: be sure you are imploring the most powerful and/or most concerned god. Hence both our upcoming showdowns, and the pitches made to pagan rulers. For it was none other than empirical religiosity that offered pagans the easiest and most direct bridge to initiation into Christianity.

However, the scope of pagan empirical religiosity was foremost collective. It was tantamount to a political program, one based in religious categories of thought that centered on assuring a people's temporal *pax deorum*. "For the tribe was a community whose bond was conceived in sacral categories", Modzelewski writes, "[…] Cultic practices connected with the *wiec* and with war rested on the conviction that the gods take part in all the activities of tribal institutions".[98] By all reckoning the conception of the community's sacral identity betrayed virtually nothing akin to notions of personal salvation and individual heavenly reward: instead, it focused on achieving and maintaining earthly security for

---

96 K. Modzelewski, *Barbarzyńska Europa...*, p. 384.
97 P. Urbańczyk, *Mieszko...*, p. 206.
98 K. Modzelewski, *Barbarzyńska Europa...*, p. 402. Cf. "The gods were always present at the *wiec* as the guarantors of the sacral peace and as the source of inspiration for the people gathered. [The gods] were behind the *wiec*'s every decision. The role that was played at the *wiec* by pagan priests and oracles offers telling testimony to the unseverable tie between the tribe's politics and decision-making and the pagan *sacrum*", p. 397.

the tribe.[99] This is what is meant by "empirical religiosity" – a kind of collective "prosperity gospel", as it were.

The showdowns we shall now briefly discuss are of course a *topos*. As such it bears repeating that they portray not real events, but the mindscape – which is not a whit less important. They have their basis in the Torah – specifically, in the showdown waged by Moses and Aaron against the Egyptian priests and sorcerers found in Exodus 6–8.[100]

There is almost no end to analogous descriptions in the history of Christianity. They extend from Lactantius' account in *De mortibus persecutorum* – where the presence of Christians during divinations conducted by Diocletian's *haruspices* prevented them from reading the entrails (and prompted the Emperor to launch the Great Persecution); to that of Sulpicius Severus in his life of Saint Martin – where the sacred pine tree the pagans agreed to fall "miraculously" missed Martin; to the even more dramatic eighth-century story of Saint Boniface and the Oak of Donar; and to Widukind's account (Book III, chap. 65) of the Christian missionary Poppa carrying the glowing-hot piece of iron without injuring his hands, whereby he convinced King Harald Gormsson to convert. What these dozens of stories bespeak is none other than the "religious mindset" existing among pagans, for whom empirical demonstrations of superior supernatural power (or: tales of such demonstrations) were the linchpin in converting them to Christianity.

The same goes for the pitches made to pagan rulers to convert to Christianity. *Hoc signo victor eris* was the promise made ever and again during Christianity's expansion out from the Roman world. Richard Fletcher has cited literally scores of examples[101] – both far too many to list here, and far too many to ignore any longer in Polish scholarship on Mieszko I. These pitches were made by popes, missionaries, Christian wives to their pagan husband-rulers, and Christian kings to pagan ones. They range from Bishop Avistus explaining to Clovis that baptism would make his weapons even more powerful[102] – to that

---

99 This matter is discussed more fully in: P. E. Steele, *Nawrócenie…*
100 The passage in 7:10–12 distills the point: "Moses and Aaron went to Pharaoh and did as Yahweh had ordered. Aaron threw down his staff in front of Pharaoh and his officials, and it turned into a serpent. Then Pharaoh in his turn called for the sages and sorcerers, and by their spells the magicians of Egypt did the same. Each threw his staff down and these turned into serpents. But Aaron's staff swallowed up theirs".
101 R. Fletcher, *The Barbarian Conversion…*, i.a., p. 97–129; 242–248; 515–519.
102 See: D. Shanzer, I. Wood, *Avistus of Vienne: Letters and selected prose*, Liverpool 2002, Epistula 46, p. 362–369.

of Methodius, who told Bořivoj, "When you abandon idols and the demons dwelling in them, you will become the lord of your lords, and all your enemies will be subjugated to your rule, and your descendants will multiply daily, like an enormous river, into which various streams flow".[103] They include even the anonymous author of the early-twelfth-century *Polish Chronicle*, who underlined for Duke Bolesłaus the Wrymouth (1107–1138) and his heirs the blessings Boleslaus the Brave had received for his devotion to Christ and His Church: "God lifted his head in glory and thus in everything [Boleslaus] fared well and prosperously. And as far as Boleslaus was pious in matters concerning God, all the greater was his glory in things mundane".[104] Nor does even the ringing "Dirge on the death of Boleslaus"[105] say anything at all about the ruler's heavenly reward.

There is a persistent premise at work throughout much of Polish historiography on both Mieszko's and other rulers' conversions, one that makes invisible the role of empirical religiosity. Let us return yet again to the case of the Bohemian Duke Bořivoj, often cited in the literature, for perhaps nowhere is this premise revealed more conspicuously. After all, the passage about Bořivoj's shame in not being permitted to eat at the table is immediately followed by the passage containing Methodius' pitch to Bořivoj's empirical religiosity – notwithstanding which, Polish scholars ignore it, opting to see only the issue of wounded pride[106]. This is all the more puzzling as there are literally scores of parallel pitches known from the early Middle Ages – and merely a few similar shame stories[107]. Moreover, those few are greatly outnumbered by counterexamples of pagan rulers being "wined and dined" by Christian ruler-proselytizers.[108] Thus, the fact that some Polish scholars discern here only the issue of "the lowly stature

---

103 From "Legenda Christiani" [in:], *The Czech Reader*..., p. 18.
104 See: *Kronika Polska*..., chap. 11 (cf. chap. 9).
105 Ibidem, chap. 16.
106 Cf. G. Labuda, *Mieszko*..., p. 103–104; J. Banaszkiewicz, "Mieszko I..., p. 90–91; A. Pleszczyński, *The birth of a stereotype: Polish rulers and their country in German writings c. 1000 AD*, Leiden 2012, p. 29.
107 E.g., that found in *Conversio Bagoariorum et Carantanorum*.
108 Again, one thinks of Earpwald, persuaded by King Edwin of Northumbria; Sigbert II, won over to Christianity by King Oswy of Northumbria; and Harald, lionized by Louis the Pious – along with the inveterate pagan Svyatoslav I, who – according to Nestor – was courted by the Byzantine emperor Nikephoros (in 968) and then 3 years later by Tzimiskes who even allowed the Kievan ruler to swear by his pagan gods.

of the pagan in the diplomatic protocol of the period" discloses a pronounced flaw in the optics at work.

This approach is typically accompanied by another, one that outright justifies the relevant scholars in ignoring the religious aspects behind early-medieval conversions at large. Thus, some Polish historians submit that acceptance of baptism by hitherto pagan rulers involved "personal spiritual conversion", "personal motives", "personal convictions", and thoughts on "eternity", "eschatology", and "the salvation of the soul"[109] – and that as these matters supposedly lie outside the realm of historical methodology, they must be left aside.[110] Those who apply a more anthropological paradigm while discussing myths and narratives about early Piasts and their realm belong to a clear minority.[111]

These conclusions, most especially the first, hardly bring accolades to Polish scholarship. For just as with the leap toward making Mieszko a modern religious cynic, the leap toward ascribing him with a "personal spiritual conversion" and wishes for heavenly reward in 966 violates our methodologies by removing Mieszko from his own time and "zip code". Mieszko must be viewed in his own context, and not that of Paul on the road to Damascus or Mary of Egypt in Jerusalem. Close examination of "getting the king" in early-medieval Europe plainly reveals that issues of sin and the need for redemption, along with the promise of reward in the life hereafter, were seldom ever used as motivating factors in converting pagan rulers: throughout the *Barbaricum* it was the demonstration and/or promise of earthly power and prosperity that was pitched to them and led to conversion. Moreover, such conversion was treated collectively, decided at the court, the *wiec* or the *thing*, and adopted as a political program designed to secure *pax deorum*.

Mieszko, as a pagan Slavic ruler of his time, acting within a culture that was inextricably political and religious, chose the more powerful god to safeguard his rule and his realm.

This idea has in fact been developed by some Polish medievalists in recent years. Notable are the papers published by Roman Michałowski and Zbigniew

---

109 These are terms used i.a., by A. Nowak, *Dzieje Polski*..., p. 85–86; idem, "My, Polanie...", p. 56; D. A. Sikorski, *Kościół w Polsce*..., p. 98; P. Urbańczyk, *Mieszko*..., p. 206, 234; and many others.
110 Cf. D. A. Sikorski, *Kościół w Polsce*..., p. 105.
111 See: J. Banaszkiewicz, *Podanie o Piaście i Popielu. Studium porównawcze nad wczesnopośredniowiecznymi tradycjami dynastycznymi*, Warszawa 1986 (2nd edition 2010) and his: *Polskie dzieje bajeczne mistrza Wincentego Kadłubka*, Wrocław 1998. See also: A. Gieysztor, *Mitologia Słowian*..., passim.

Dalewski in 2008 in *Animarum Cultura*. Writing of Mieszko, Michałowski stressed that the Piast dynasty's choice of Christianity was meant "to secure divine blessings together with all consequences – political and existential, temporal and eternal", adding more generally about the conversion of Europe's pagan rulers that, "At issue was not merely sociotechnical cunning and securing for oneself the greatest number of allies. The main issue lay elsewhere: which religion, it was asked, will more effectively win the favor of the heavens?".[112] Dalewski, in turn, elucidated the role empirical religiosity played during the reign of Boleslaus the Brave and its "pagan-leftover" collective form: "In this regard, it seems the difference between Christianity and pagan beliefs did not have a fundamental character. In both cases the predominant role fell to the public cult. Its proper fulfillment was to guarantee prosperity and protection by the sacral powers".[113]

As I argued in the first edition of my book (2005)[114], there is very solid ground for holding that, following his conversion, Mieszko's empirical "religious mindset" went on to reinforce him in the conviction that he had chosen the more powerful God. This in all likelihood began as soon as 967, when, in renewed fighting, Mieszko defeated a member of the Saxon House of Billung, Wichman and the Polabian forces he led, Wichman himself falling in that battle. It is easy to picture Mieszko, having experienced the favor of Providence, kneeling on the battlefield and offering thanks to his new God. Victories like this continued on to the end of his reign in 992, by which time he had at least tripled the size of the Piast realm. Mieszko's sense of accomplishment must have been great, and indeed, he clearly expressed his gratitude to his new God in his final will and testament, the above mentioned *Dagome iudex*.

Mieszko's understanding of Christian theology of course grew over the 26 years of his life following baptism in 966. We may well surmise, in line with what Thietmar and the author of the *Polish Chronicle* had to say about Doubravka, that his Bohemian wife truly did instruct him in Christian belief and practice. This was no doubt also the case with his subsequent wife, Oda who grew up in the monastery of Kalbe, near the Milde River in the north of Magdeburg. The same obviously goes for Bishops Jordan and Unger. Both Bruno of Querfurt[115] and Thietmar of

---

112 R. Michałowski, "Chrystianizacja...", p. 36; 14.
113 Z. Dalewski, "Publiczny wymiar...", p. 54.
114 See above footnote 32 and the similar opinion by R. Michałowski, "Chrystianizacja...", p. 16–17.
115 In his famous letter to Henry II written in 1008, Bruno refers to the happier days of Polish-German relations, and cites Mieszko's efforts to "convert the pagans" – see the

Merseburg[116] describe Mieszko as a committed Christianizer of his expanding realm, and additional sources allow us to discern several examples of medieval piety in Mieszko from the period after his conversion. For instance, that in 973, when having to leave his son Boleslaus at the imperial court in Quedlinburg, Mieszko sent a large locket of the boy's freshly cut hair to the Pope. And when, having been shot in the arm with a poisoned arrow, he was "miraculously" saved thanks to the intercession of Saint Udalryk, after which he sent a silver arm to the saint's grave in Augsburg.[117] And when, having grown old and sensing the approach of death, he bequeathed in *Dagome iudex* his entire realm to Saint Peter.

The last thing I must say – while leaving out much more[118] – is that the sheer temerity we have depicted in Mieszko's conversion is all the more remarkable when we glance at the ever so different origins of Christianity among Poland's neighbors and peoples elsewhere across Europe.

Among the Bohemians, for instance, as we know from the *Annals of Fulda*, 14 of their princes were baptized in 845. Nonetheless, the Christianizing career of Bořivoj and Ludmila began not until the 880s, and that process did not become earnest until half a century later, under Duke Boleslaus I the Cruel (935–972). And yet the first bishopric in Bohemia was not functioning until the late 970s – some 130 years after Bohemia's initial baptisms. Even so, Saint Adalbert (the second Bishop of Prague) still had the Bohemians for pagans. So, a very sputtering venture, despite the fact that the Bohemians found themselves with contiguous Christians neighbors west, south, and east.[119] Moreover, the example Bohemia is altogether normal. It is the case of Mieszko that is so extraordinary.

English translation (based on the edition in the ser.: Monumenta Poloniae Historica. Series nova, 4/3, Warszawa 1973, p. 97–106), [electronic resource] available at: https://apps.carleton.edu/curricular/mars/assets/Bruno_of_Querfurt_Letter_to_Henry_II_for_MARS_website.pdf. Cf. W. Falkowski, "The Letter of Bruno of Querfurt to King Henry II", *Frühmittelalterliche Studien* 43, 2009, p. 417–438.

116 See: Thietmar, *Kronika…*, Book IV, chap. 56 and 57, p. 83.
117 Cf. D. A. Sikorski, *Kościół w Polsce…*, p. 302–304.
118 I am unable to discuss here the recently debated question among Polish archeologists, "to what degree did Mieszko pursue the Christianization of his people?" Suffice it to say that Przemysław Urbańczyk, in several recent works, has argued forcefully that the label "Christianizer" suits Bolesław Chrobry – but not Mieszko. Andrzej Buko has just as forcefully countered, and it is he with whom I side. Cf. P. Urbańczyk, "Jak (s) chowano pierwszych polskich chrześcijan?", *Funeralia Lednickie* 17, 2014, p. 129–142; and A. Buko, "Chrześcijanie i poganie…" p. 13–51.
119 Cf. P. Sommer, D. Třeštík, J. Žemlička, E. Doležalová, "The Christianisation of Bohemia and Moravia", [in:] *Annual of Medieval Studies at the CEU* 13, 2007, p. 153–163.

After all, the mission to the Swedes, briefly mentioned above, began some 170 years before King Olaf Skötkonung was baptized in about 1000. The baptism of Denmark's Harald Gormsson came nearly 140 years after Harald Klak's. Christianity had also long made inroads among the Rus' before Volodimer the Great's (980–1015) baptism in 988. Close contacts with Constantinople reached back more than a century by then. What is more, Volodimer's own grandmother Olga had become a Christian and was baptized in Constantinople in 957 – and as the regent of Rus', no less. Nothing whatsoever of the kind can be said of the Piasts before Mieszko.

Glancing further afield and deeper into time, the King of the Franks Clovis ruled over a land having a largely evangelized population and a developed ecclesiastical structure. Ethelbert of Kent, in turn, handed over to Augustine a church still standing from Roman times.

In sharp contrast to these cases, Mieszko introduced Christianity among the Polanians on utterly virgin soil and surrounded by pagans. At his own will, at a time of strength and stability, and with no obvious "ulterior" motives. The case of Mieszko's "acceptance of baptism" stands as one of the clearest examples in medieval Europe not only of empirical religiosity – but of empirical religiosity having been the primary motive for a ruler's conversion.

Mikołaj Banaszkiewicz

Searching for the meaning of the Russian way. The ideological setting of the 900th anniversary celebrations of the Baptism of Rus' (1888)

Abstract: The chapter presents the ideological setting of the 900th anniversary celebrations of the Baptism of Rus', which were held in 1888 in Kiev. This was the first event in the history of Russia to commemorate on a state-wide scale the baptism of Vladimir the Great in 988. The celebrations in 1888 were thoroughly ecclesial, rather than official and state-run. However, the event ought not to be rashly depreciated due to the absence of Tsar Alexander III and the bureaucratic elite of the Russian Empire. Analysis of the anniversary's debates reveals an inherent identity dilemma that reflects the ambiguous (inter)dependencies between the Empire and the Nation. From the standpoint of the celebration's organizers and the opinion-forming periodicals, both conservative and liberal, the Russian Empire was the legitimate successor and bearer of the Kievan Rus' heritage and legacy. The issue remains essential in contemporary Russo-Ukrainian relationship.

Keywords: Baptism of Rus', anniversary celebrations, Russian identity, politics of memory, memory studies

Conceptual assumptions

In spite of the enormous theoretical effort and the appearance of a number of valuable empirical studies, memory studies have not yet taken advantage of the full rights the discipline is entitled to as a recognized sub-domain of historical science. Donald R. Kelley, the author of a fundamental synthetic monograph on the development of historiography, classifies memory studies as "a form of conjectural history, more valuable for synthesis than for analysis". Skepticism with regard to researching into collective memory by means of standard historical methods, Kelley explains, arises because cultural memory is but the "flickering" of a "faulty" flame: it is simply a "residue of innumerable traces", and a "repository of many mythical creations".[1] This chapter is a far cry from sophisticated

---

1 D. R. Kelley, *Frontiers of History. Historical Inquiry in the Twentieth Century*, New Haven 2006, p. 225, 241–242.

conceptual studies that could overcome resistance so motivated. Rather, my intention is to show that a memorological tack in the analysis of source material does not in fact betray features of speculative reasoning: instead, it contributes added value to detailed considerations of the history of ideas.

This chapter focuses on the ideological setting of the 900th anniversary celebrations of the Baptism of Rus', which were held in 1888 in Kiev.[2] This was the first event in the history of Russia to commemorate the adoption of Christianity carried out on a state-wide scale; no such initiative had ever been undertaken in the previous centuries. Specifically, the celebrations were thoroughly ecclesial, rather than official and state-run. However, the event ought not to be rashly depreciated due to the non-attendance of Tsar Alexander III (1881–1894) and the bureaucratic elite of the Russian Empire[3], though it is true that the political prestige of the event was severely affected (also in terms of how it was viewed abroad). Nonetheless, this in nowise affected the course of the public debate related to the jubilee. Viewed from our present perspective, the teleological tone of the disputes held on that occasion may cause irritation. All the visions expressed as part of the debate accepted Russia's following her historic path as an obvious thing, though the course and the end point of the journey were outlined in diverse ways. The search for guideposts in the past, ones that would protect Russia from diverting from the path, reflected the need to anchor the then-current strivings regarding universal values, as well as to actualize "eternal" ideals. Vivisection of the anniversary's debates reveals an inherent identity

---

2   The organizational aspect of the celebrations and their underpinning political concept is dealt with in the (unpublished) candidate thesis by A. I. Buslaev, *Imperske jubilei tysiatelete Rossii (1862 god) i deviatisotletie kreshenia Rusi (1888 god): organizacia, simvolika, vospriatie obshchestvom*, Moscow 2010. For a change, the *opus magnum* of the American researcher of the semiotics of the Russian authorities, where the jubilee is approached rather summarily, adds nothing to the issue, see: R. S. Wortman, *Scenarii vlasti. Mify i ceremonii russkoj monarhii*, vol. 2: *Ot Aleksandra II do otrechenija Nikolaja II*, Moscow 2004, p. 332–333 (original ed.: R. S. Wortman, *Scenarios of Power. Myth and Ceremony in Russian Monarchy*, vol. 2: *From Alexander II to the Abdication of Nicholas II*, Princeton 2000). For an extensive material documenting the preparations and course of the celebrations, see: *Prazdnovanie devjatisotletija kreshchenija russkogo naroda v Kieve*, Kiev 1888 (a publication of the Kiev Spiritual Academy).

3   The highest-ranking representative of the state administration who attended the celebrations was Konstantin Pobedonostsev (1827–1907), Ober-Procurator of the Most Holy Synod and *éminence grise* at the imperial court. The dignitary's letters to the monarch are a valuable historical source in this respect; see: K. Pobedonostsev, *Pis'ma Pobedonosceva k Aleksandru III*, Moscow 1926, p. 178–192.

dilemma that reflects the ambiguous (inter)dependencies between the Empire and the Nation, a factor of extreme importance in the history of Russia.[4]

I am confident that memory studies may contribute a large number of new findings that will allow us to better recognize the socio-political and socio-cultural dimension of phenomena under study, thus enriching the image offered by political history and the history of ideas (in their classical form). Such findings cannot, however, bring about the expected benefit if they are treated as a replacement tool devised to obtain at a pre-assumed result. The reinforced manner of narration tells one to describe the Russian state as a possessive governor of souls that fervently and unrestrainedly tampers with the memory of its subjects. Apart from an excessively convoluted perspective (hegemonic intents being implicitly assumed, ethical premises for "memory-generating" activity being precluded), a weak point of this descriptive method is in how it bestows demiurgic characteristics upon the power and authority of Russia in all epochs (i.e., timelessly).[5]

This trend can be exemplified by the essay of Konstantin Tsimbaev that deals with anniversary jubilees *en bloc* in the land of Tsars. What we can learn from it is that in the 19th c. the historical jubilee became a convenient propaganda instrument that the authorities took advantage of for purposes of legitimization. Carefully staged and directed, not only did the jubilee form the idea of the country's heroic past amongst the masses, but it also suggested that there was no need whatsoever for any systemic political change. Its impact was incomparable to any of the cyclical folk festivities, the court or religious celebrations,

---

4   As a contemporary Russian historian puts it, "'The History of Russia' is a pretty vague notion – as the name of the school/university subject and as the domain of knowledge [...] it would be appropriate to understand the history of Russia as a history of a certain territory within which a number of state and political formations existed over the centuries, whereas the area and limits of the territory have varied by historical period. ... the phrase 'national history' is only applicable with regard to the history of Russia in a rather conventional manner"; after A. Kamieński, "Współczesna rosyjska historiografia Rosji i światowa nauka historyczna. Integracja jako bieg z przeszkodami", [in:] *Humanistyka krajowa w kontekście światowym. Doświadczenie Polski i Rosji*, ed. J. Axer, I. Sawieliewa, Warszawa 2011, p. 142–143.

5   Assumed here is an automatic transposition of certain representations of memory to human acting or, putting it bluntly, politics with respect to memory into a political change. The question in what ways such effect on individual and collective entities is actually exerted, is left aside. Cf. the remarks of Pieter Vermeulen and Richard Crownshaw in a panel discussion on the prospects of memory studies, *Dispersal and redemption: The future dynamics of memory studies – A roundtable*, ed. P. Vermeulen et al., *Memory Studies* 5, 2012, p. 231–232, 235.

or even the events celebrated by any of the Empire's nations. As it manifested itself across the spheres of life, the event equally involved the power elite, various social strata, religious communities, and professional corporations. The driving force behind all the jubilee feasts and ceremonies rested with administrative structures. Both the preparations and the celebrations were managed by the official instances (primarily, the Ministry of the Imperial Court). Representatives of associations – artistic, scientific, or other – were assigned auxiliary functions at the very most. The dates deserving commemoration, the celebration sites, and the methods of celebrating were determined in a top-down fashion. Consumers were consigned the role of passive viewers – and since they were subject to prior selection anyway, attendance and related matters were in fact not voluntary.[6]

The basic doubt following from the above is based on the axiomatic (though left implied) assumption of the omnipotence of Russian authority or government. Putting this in stricter terms, it is about the latter's ability to mold the historical awareness of Russian subjects. Such a view stems from unintentionally mistaking intentions for reality, based on a mythologized idea of Russian autocracy. Hence, whereas the collective description of the Russian jubilees cannot be accused of fallaciousness, the impression cannot be resisted that suppression of the question of the efficiency of the authorities' efforts deprives this description of explanatory power. I myself deem this efficiency none too high, since there was no uniform Russian collective identity prevalent in the latter half of the 19th c. The quite evident ideological polarization characteristic of "reformed" Russia (which began with the time of the "Great Reforms" whose symbolic caesura was 1861 – the year serfdom was abolished) jeopardized the capacity to unrestrainedly model worldviews and attitudes among the Tsar's subjects by a central decision-making body. The ideas of the longed-for socio-political order were directly stimulated by the professed ethical ideals, which in turn were related to one of the great identity projects offered by the most popular ideological currents in their

---

6   K. N. Tsimbaev, "Rekonstrukcija proshlogo i konstruirovanie budushchego v Rossii XIX veka: opyt ispol'zovanija istoricheskih jubileev v politicheskih celjah", [in:] *Istoricheskaja kul'tura imperatorskoj Rossii: formirovanie predstavlenij o proshlom*, ed. A. N. Dmitriev, Moscow 2012, p. 475–476, 482–485. The author considers the 100th anniversary of the city of Petersburg, celebrated in 1803, to have been the first all-Russian jubilee in the broad sense, whilst he sees the 100th anniversary of Alexander Pushkin's birth (1899), which opened an "anniversary craze", as the first such jubilee in a strict sense.

various ramifications (conservatism and liberalism, with various admixtures of nationalism; revolutionary radicalism; and so on).[7]

The temptation to mix and thereby contaminate the then-competing identity projects – in order to view, on the spot, a panorama of intellectual life in prerevolutionary Russia in all its diversity – is strong indeed. However, this would distort the image by depriving it of certain telltale features. The benefit offered by the analysis of discourses using memory-studies categories is basically about imaging the ideological identifications of the collectivity under study.[8] Public opinion, in the modern sense, appeared in prerevolutionary Russia only in the second half of the 19th c. and, encompassing a rather small group, formed society's avant-garde. The press, subjected from the mid-1860s onwards to repressive censorship (in lieu of the previous preventative procedure), was the mouthpiece of the endeavors of the group's various strata. In the absence of a parliament and the legalized activities of political parties, press organs served as the broadest forum for the exchange of thoughts. Hence, it is newspapers, magazines, and other periodicals that offer us the most reliable source of information on the ideas circulating within public opinion (rather than those being the deposit of a narrow intellectual elite). The message-creating milieu represented various political traditions, each of which had woven its own story about Russia, and each of which drew on the memory of its constitutive values and their "carriers". The character of the periodical publications of the time confirms the argument that memory's function is not limited to the epistemological aspect, which ensures "access" to the past, but is prescriptive as well, as it informs about the obligations the favored past imposes upon remembering individuals.[9] Nevertheless, the existence of a moral obligation and the promise of its fulfilment are not decisive in

---

7 Cf. O. J. Leontieva, "Memorialnyj povorot v sovremennoj rossijskoj istoricheskoj nauke", *Dialog so vremenem* 50, 2015, p. 81. For the same author's selective (and disputable) description of some identity projects, see: idem, "Istoricheskaja pamjat' i obrazy proshlogo v kulture poreformennoj Rossii", [in:] *Dialogi so vremenem: pamjat' o proshlom v kontekste istorii*, ed. L. P. Repina, Moscow 2008, p. 636–681.

8 I find apt the following generalizing remark of a Polish scholar: "The competing interpretations of sites of memory often crystallize social conflicts and thus are related to the problem of power/authority; the rivalry for a possibility to push through a certain reading of the past sets the framework of group adherences, thereby concerning the processes of exclusion and inclusion."; Cf. K. Kończal, "Bliskie spotkania z historią drugiego stopnia", [in:] *Pamięć zbiorowa jako czynnik integracji i źródło konfliktów*, ed. A. Szpociński, Warszawa 2009, p. 220.

9 Cf. R. Poole, "Memory, history and the claims of the past", *Memory Studies* 1, 2008, p.152.

terms of the capacity to influence the real world of politics. What is, then, the rationale behind my conviction that this was possible for Russia?

This chapter refers to a research proposal put forth by Olga Malinova, a Russian scholar specializing in the "macropolitical identity" of Russians. Inspired by Pierre Bourdieu's sociological considerations, Malinova opts for analyzing the formation of identity so described with the use of symbols or a "the politics of symbols" (*simvolicheskaja politika*). The latter, in Malinova's concept, is an inherent part of real politics, one that focuses on creating ways to interpret social reality and on attempts to make them a dominant message. The primary advantage of such an approach is that it places in the research field a variety of entities participating in/contributing to the political process, rather than just the power elite. What this practically entails is a refocus from the legitimation of a political/constitutional order to other dimensions of politics. This approach makes one take a different look at politics: namely, politics becomes a domain of actors competing against one another in the public space to give meaning to the phenomena being described, and to reinforce such meanings in society's memory. Further, the approach in question appreciates the limitations of social engineering: although it is the elite that creates the meanings, the same elite has to submit (at least rhetorically) to the meanings that have been broadly accepted by society. Moreover, importance is attached to the mechanisms of politics. Literacy with respect to this topic helps understand why some methods of interpreting reality take root whilst others get rejected; the social context of constructing meanings and of their circulation amongst other ideas comes to the fore. Lastly, agencies of the state do not have the exclusive right to pursue politics in respect of symbols. The state is privileged indeed, as it exercises control over the distribution of resources (material and other). All the same, there is an unmanaged area called the public space, and it can be taken advantage of by non-state creators of meanings.[10]

---

10 V. N. Efremova, "O nekotoryh teoreticheskih osobennostjah issledovanija simvolicheskoj politiki", [in:] *Simvolicheskaja politika*, vol. 3: *Politicheskie funkcii mifov*, Moscow 2015, esp. p. 60–1, 63. For a proposal (complementing the above concept) based on approaching ideology not only as a cohesive system of ideas and convictions but also as other symbolic forms gifted with a meaning, see: O. Malinova's contribution to a discussion panel on the symbolic space politics: O. Malinova, "Sovremennye tendencii razvitija simvolicheskogo prostranstva politiki i koncept ideologii", *Polis. Politicheskie issledovanija* 4, 2004, p. 40–41. The concept in its essence is presented in a monograph by the same scholar, see: idem, *Konstruirovanie smyslov: Issledovanie simvolicheskoj politiki v sovremennoj Rossii*, Moscow 2013.

From the standpoint of a scholar researching the politics of symbols, official festivities and ceremonies are primarily functional as they maintain or outright create the identity of a group or community. Hence, it is impossible for one to perceive them in terms of submission to prejudice, or yielding to the commands of a "tradition", or as manifestations of irrational thinking. A state-held jubilee is not really, and not only, an instance of "the invention of (a) tradition" in line with Eric Hobsbawm's concept[11], but primarily a symbolic construct that carries an ideological message (meanings) that varies over time. When approached as a tool for the politics of symbols, a holiday or festival has its limitations, rooted in its inherent "instability"; this renders it peculiar vis-à-vis the "stable" symbols – such as the flag, national anthem, currency, legal system, architecture, and/or phenomena of folk culture. Overall, neither the state nor national symbolism is an invariable entity – on the contrary, each undergoes more or less radical revisions. A feast-as-a-symbol is unstable as it occurs rarely and can easily be ignored; the sense or meaning it carries is inconstant. On the other hand, such a feast expresses identity with a particular intensity, rather than forming a background for ordinariness and everyday reality. Thus, a state-run feast and, specifically, a jubilee may shape social reality, but only so when non-administration entities have got involved in giving it a purpose and meaning(s).[12]

The Baptism of Rus' as a determinant of the Russian path: the visions from the late 19th c.

Let us now see what follows from this angle of analysis for the ideological entourage of the 900th anniversary of the Baptism of Rus'. Below are five interpretative proposals that became predominant in the public space at the time. I describe them in a detailed manner, for I deem it important to show the specific features of the period's journalism and political commentaries, ones that took delight in comprehensive structures. My other focus is methods of persuasion, which, in turn, enable one to drill deeper down into the recipient's/consumer's intellectual profile. For that purpose, I have selected the most opinion-forming periodicals, for reading any of these meant identifying oneself with a given political outlook

---

11 *The Invention of Tradition*, ed. E. Hobsbawm, T. Ranger, Cambridge 1992.
12 V. N. Efremova, "Gosudarstvennye prazdniki kak instrument simvolicheskoj politiki", [in:] *Simvolicheskaja politika, vyp. 2: Spory o proshlom kak proektirovanie budushchego*, Moscow 2014, p. 74–77.

and worldview.[13] Thus, there are the conservative-nationalist dailies: *Moskovskie Vedomosti* (run by Sergey Petrovskij); *Novoe Vremja* (with Alexei Suvorin, the most famous nationalist in prerevolutionary Russia, as the editor-in-chief); and, *Grazhdanin* (edited by Prince Vladimir P. Meshcherskij, a friend of Alexander III) – the latter two magazines were published in Saint Petersburg. The liberal profile[14] was represented by the monthlies: *Vestnik Evropy* – the then-oldest Russian magazine with a liberal bias, run from the beginning (1866) by Mikhail Stasjulevich; and, *Russkaja Mysl'*, a Moscow-based monthly published from 1880 and (unofficially) edited, in the period of our interest, by Viktor Goltsev. This "short list" neglects the illegal press published by the anti-systemic opposition who denied land of Tsars its legitimacy. Verifying the individual statements proposed in the texts under discussion based on the current state of research is not part of my present purpose; hence, I will not add any polemical notes whatsoever.

I should start my presentation with an essay published in *Moskovskie Vedomosti*, whose author(s) derives the primacy of the Russian constitutional model over those of the other Christian countries from the Baptism of Rus' in the Eastern rite. The newspaper editors ascribe the greatness of the Russian Empire to the unswerving loyalty observed over the consecutive centuries by the nation of Rus' with respect to Kievan Grand Prince Vladimir the Great's (980–1015)[15] conversion to Christianity in 988. Further on, one can read that standing by the "moral and spiritual obligation" imposed through the adoption of faith from the

---

13 This particular circumstance will protect me, I suppose, against the methodological charge raised by a memory studies critic who claimed that recipients/consumers (readers, viewers) of a specific broadcast/mass medium form no coherent group, and hence one should rather refrain from assuming their susceptibility to the medium's content or message; Cf. W. Kansteiner, "Finding Meaning in Memory: A Methodological Critique of Collective Memory Studies", *History and Theory* 41, 2002, p. 193–194.
14 It was to my astonishment that I have encountered an attempt at discrediting liberalism on the grounds of philosophy: according to one author, liberalism allegedly neglects the link occurring between history and the duties and obligations of citizens, with respect to the other members of a political collectivity; see: J. Thompson, "Apology, historical obligations and the ethics of memory", *Memory Studies* 2, 2009, p. 196–197.
15 *The form *Vladimir* is used here as it is the transcription of the most common linguistic form used in Russian language. In the remaining texts in this volume the form *Volodimer* is used (editor's footnote).

Eastern Church had become the guarantee of power and happiness.[16] The grace of God had protected Russia and her inhabitants against the fate shared by the Western world, something inherent to it since the very beginning. The division of the Roman Empire into two parts, the article explained, dichotomized the European idea of state and statehood. The consequent misfortunes stemmed from, on the one hand, the collapsed prestige of imperial power, which could no longer resist the military strength of the barbaric peoples – and on the other, from the inordinately growing importance of the Roman depositary of faith. The appearance on the stage of the new "potentate", the Pope, had entirely revealed the fiction of autocracy, which is ultimately based upon strength.

The conflict between clerical authority and secular authority was predominant in Western Europe in the Middle Ages, the publicist argued, readily adding that the consequences had extended to his own day. In his view, the immemorial dispute between the two superpowers had undermined the authority of each of them in the perception of their respective subjects; what is more, the unrestrained methods of discrediting the opponent had a demoralizing impact on those who observed the struggle. The division of the Western Church and the war of religion came as a direct result of the contradicting interests of the Papacy and the Empire. However, in historical perspective, yet another element turned out to be more important: the people, whose support was sought by both parties, began aspiring to play an autonomous political role. This, in turn, created thorough confusion, and inefficient efforts were taken to rearrange it with use of the contractual principle in the form of a Constitution. The strengthening of the democratic ideals, according to the author, would inevitably lead to a rejection of monarchy and the emergence, in lieu of it, of a republic with its characteristic "chaotic polyarchy". To the author's mind, this scenario had all along been made part of the logic of the development of the Western Church; resulting from its having transformed into a "theocratic empire", the latter, paradoxically, had challenged the monarchic principle.[17]

This gloomy image of relations in Catholic/Protestant Europe is juxtaposed by the *Moskovskie Vedomosti* article with an idyllic image of secular and clerical authority in the East. Here, the editors reassured readers, power was exercised

---

16 The Metropolitan of Kiev, who hosted the ceremony, presented the case in the same terms; see: "Beseda skazannaja vysokopreosveshchennym Platonom, mitropolitom kievskim, v den' prazdnovanija 900-letnego jubileja kreshchenija Rossii, 15-go ijulja 1888 goda", *Zhurnal Ministerstva narodnogo prosveshchenija* 258, August 1888, p. 66–67 [with separate pagination for the section "Sovremennaja letopis'"].
17 "Torzhestvo pravoslavija", *Moskovskie Vedomosti* 194, 15th (27th) July, 1888, p. 1.

with a heavy hand by the *basileus*, in the spirit of the first Roman Emperors. Thus, the Eastern Church resisted the temptation the Roman Bishops otherwise yielded to as they compromised on the teachings of Christ. Not only did the Orthodox Church recognize the monarch's prerogatives, but it also rendered the ruling individual sacred, thus contributing to a reinforcement of the image of the ruler as a defender of the Apostolic Orthodox Church.

The daily newspaper reassured its readers that this description accurately rendered the relations prevailing in Byzantium, from which they were transferred to the territory of Rus'. Much time had passed, indeed, before the Byzantine model took real shape on Rus'sian soil. It was a matter of fact, the author further argued, that Orthodoxy had contributed to the development of autocracy and autarchy in this particular territory, which further led to the appearance of an "All-Russian Empire". Whereas monarchy and papacy were destroying each other in the West, the Tsar and the Orthodox Church supported each other in Russia, strengthening their mutual and respective authority in the eyes of their subjects. Nowhere else was respect and admiration toward authority and power as strong, the readers were told. Hence, the contractual principle did not apply in the specific Russian conditions where there was no basic premise for a constitution – namely, hostility between the ruler and the ruled. Russia owed this situation to her Orthodox religion, which had protected her against the "canker of constitutionalism and parliamentarianism" that triggered the revolutions which shook Western Europe. Russia might endure only as an Orthodox country. After all, this was what her role was all about: without having accepted Baptism in 988 according to the Eastern rite, "the true teaching of Christ" would have perished amidst the vagrant Christians and heretics.[18]

The constant belief in the anniversary-related conservative journalistic writings was that what the Russian state owed to its Orthodox baptism was a spiritual enlightenment related to the civilizational privileges offered by Christianity, along with the superpower or imperial position it had achieved and reinforced on the political map of the world.[19] The *Novoe Vremja* daily presented the most complete argumentation in this respect. Every single constituent of the excellence and splendor of Russia – the citizenship of her natives (*sic!*), national

---

18 Ibidem, p. 1–2.
19 This conviction was expressed in even more radical terms in an oration delivered by the Ober-Procurator of the Most Holy Synod [K. Pobedonostsev] before a solemn meal: "She [i.e., the Orthodox Church] is the only one to have helped us become Russians". Cf. "K 900-letiju kreshchenija Rusi", *Pravoslavnoe obozrenie* 2, August 1888, p. 747.

independence, and political powerfulness, was primarily rooted in Byzantium, the editors found. In their view, the dependence between the Eastern Roman Empire and the land of Tsars was not really one of bequeather and heir – rather, it was a master and disciple relationship.

The editorial openly polemicized with the critics of Byzantinism who saw in it nothing more than a "heartless formalism and lifeless ceremoniality". The author put the negative attitude toward the Byzantine heritage down to the Russianness that had been deformed under the influence of alien and outlandish ideas. The state of Constantine I the Great (306–337), he went on to explain, represented the pinnacle of the achievement of Ancient Rome, neatly combining a great cultural acquisition with the best of social and political organization patterns. The author placed emphasis on how christened Russia had benefited from the international opportunity: the country could follow the example of its "teacher" without fear of becoming politically dependent, for Byzantium showed a weakness that heralded a collapse already in the 10th c. This circumstance protected the lands of Rus' from the fate the other Slavs were doomed to share. In the concept of this nationalistic publicist, "national initiative/genius" (*nacional'naja samodejatel'nost'*) in the domains of spirituality and culture (something which drew its stimulation to act from the opportunity to grasp Christianity and imbibe civic wisdom from the books written in the Old Church Slavonic language) had proved crucial in this regard. The situation of those who encountered Latin on their way, which in the longer run doomed them to a loss of national independence, had proved incomparably worse.[20]

The argument of the destructive influences of Catholicism was reinforced in the eyes of readers through the contradictory remark on the state-forming role of Orthodoxy. Contrary to what was argued in *Moskovskie Vedomosti*, the Petersburg daily's editorial, rather than focusing on political/structural issues, portrayed the Orthodox Church as a "guardian of Russian statehood and national self-reliance". The reader was reassured that the Church fulfilled this function also in the most dire moment in the country's history, i.e., during the period of Tatar/Mongolian bondage. In their consistent support of the secular authorities, down through the centuries the ecclesial structures helped to overcome all the historical difficulties and create a superpower that was to be "a pillar of strength for the entire Slavonic world". The Western Slavs, by way of contrast, could not count on similar support. Resulting from their direct contact with

---

20 "Devjatisotletie pravoslavnoj Rusi", *Novoe Vremja* 4445, 15th (27th) July 1888, p. 1.

European civilization, they became no stronger: on the contrary, they turned into a "pariah, never being allowed to take a place equal to that of the other nations".[21]

It is by no means a matter of coincidence, the author goes on, that Orthodoxy's confessors are the only ones to enjoy an independent political existence, in contrast to Western Slavdom, which is thoroughly subordinated to mightier organisms. One may only be liberated from dependency through establishing closer terms with the Orthodox confession, i.e., ultimately, Russia herself. Decisive in this regard was the necessity that was instinctively felt by the Slavs themselves and noticed by their enemies. Orthodox Russia, never repudiating her own Slavonic face, and seriously treating the rights and obligations of a Slavic empire – a Russia that refuses to disown herself – ought to be ready to fulfil whatever she is tasked to fulfil, in spite of her enemies.[22]

The Baptism of Rus' was the event that determined the historic mission of the Russian Empire: this interpretation (which permeates through the aforementioned texts) was most fully manifested in the jubilee writings of the newspaper *Grazhdanin*. Here again we can read that the acceptance of Byzantine Christianity set the path for the successors of Vladimir. The fall of Constantinople in 1453 was not tantamount to annihilation of the faith in its pure form, as the editorial explained, referring to the concept of Moscow as the "Third Rome". Muscovy survived as the only sovereign Orthodox kingdom, whilst the East and the West both fell to the "equally horrid rule" of the Pope and the Sultan. Thus, Russia was ascending the historic stage as the successor of Byzantium – and as the defender of the Orthodox world against the violence of the Latin West and the Mohammedan East.

Awareness of this mission was quite apparent already in the 15th c.: as evidence supporting his argument, the publicist referred to some excerpts of Rus'sian *letopises* or the famous message from the Pskov monk Philotheus to Tsar Vasili III (1505–1533) (the eschatological dimension of which, let us add straight away, has many a time been replaced by a doctrinal interpretation of expansion, embellished with religious clichés). He added to all this the *bylinas* about Il'ja Muromtsev, the hero of folk culture: having learned of the conquest of Constantinople, he immediately travels there to set the city free. The latter example was meant to testify to the task of liberating the Greek-Slavonic world by Russia as being deeply rooted in the common awareness of the populace.

---

21 Ibidem.
22 Ibidem.

Wide-ranging justifications were cited to support this argument. They included attempts at deriving the genealogy of the House of Rurikovich from Roman Emperor Augustus (27 BC–14 AD), along with taking over from Byzantium the two-headed eagle as the national emblem. Moreover, the legend of the regalia purported that it had been forwarded to Kievan Grand Prince Vladimir II Monomakh (1113–1125) by Byzantine Emperor Constantine IX Monomachos (1042–1055). Another legend was about the sending of a *klobuk* (demon) by the Constantinopolitan Patriarch Philotheus to Novgorod. Lastly, the Muscovite Princes' succession rights to Byzantium, as derived based upon the Rurikovichs' kinships due to Grand Prince of Moscow Ivan III's (1462–1505) marriage to Zoe Palaiologina, fraternal niece of the last Byzantine Emperor Constantine XI Dragases (1449–1453), was touched upon. The *Grazhdanin* journalist reminded his readers of these dubious arguments not in order to demonstrate the legitimacy of the current pretenses of the Russian Empire: his focal concern was to convince the reader that the Baptism had had far-reaching political consequences. Ever since, the entire Rus'sian nation had apparently considered "the solution of the Eastern question as a task imposed by Providence".[23]

The chapter characterized the history of Rus'/Russia as incessant struggle with the West and with papism. Defense of the faith and of political autonomy required the Rus'sian rulers to inhibit aggression – as was the case, e.g., with the "crusade" of King of Poland Stephen Báthory (1576–1586) in 1579. The *Smutnoe vremja* (Time of Troubles 1598–1613), which came not long afterward, also called for being overcome. With the granting of the patriarchate, the messianic idea (liberation of the subdued Slavs) began to take real shape. Pan-Slavism, the expression of this idea, had emerged as early as the 16th c., the publicist argued. The fact that Serbia, Bulgaria, Romania, and Montenegro had all become established as entities/actors proves that Russia had partly fulfilled its mission. The author went on to state that for the Eastern question to be properly solved, the path of the ancestors, who marched forward under the banner of Orthodoxy, must be followed. The foundation of the concept that had been implemented with success over the last three centuries – i.e., Russia's leadership in the Orthodox world – had been laid on the banks of the Dnieper nine hundred years ago, the author concluded.[24]

---

23 "Pravoslavie i slavjanskij mir (Po povodu 900-letija kreshchenija Rusi)", *Grazhdanin* 195, 15th (27th) July 1888, p. 11.
24 Ibidem.

Yet the impression that a chorus of mutually complementary conservative and nationalistic voices completely filled the public space with its sound is false. The liberal press was declaring a less thunderous, but no less momentous message. This message was expressed, however, with use of social and cultural categories, and thus was a far cry from the above extremely politicized concepts.

The analysis published in *Vestnik Evropy* proves extremely characteristic in this respect. The monthly sympathized with other periodicals in their evaluation of the importance of the Baptism of 988, apparently comparable with the recognition of Christianity as the public religion of the Roman Empire. Nonetheless, the cooption of Rus' into the "family of historical nations" did not translate into the country's social order, the commentator remarked bitterly. There was no coincidence in the fact that Russia was celebrating a jubilee of her christening for the first time. But even with serfdom abolished, the liberal author opined, the intellectual and moral standard of the masses in nowise attested that nine centuries had passed since the moment of joining Christian civilization. The skeptical commentator was imbued with optimism because of the pace of change – and believed that, with time, the overall ignorance, obscurantism, and demoralization would be overcome. Critical remarks were also uttered with regard to the omission of the "tribesmen" (Old Believers and the "sectants"), conflicted as they were with the Orthodox Church, about which no comment whatsoever was made by the right-wing press.[25]

A polemical position against the nationalistic vision was the most emphatically expressed in the monthly *Russkaja Mysl'*. The jubilee appeared to its editors as a great festival of Russian culture. Russia had become part of the Christian world and hence belongs to Europe, the commentator explained. The Baptism separated Eastern Slavdom from Asia much more efficiently than geographical barriers, such as the Ural Mountains or the Caspian Sea, could ever have done. Christianity had protected the nation from "mental stagnation", for the Asian progressive movement was implemented only through rapacious raids and onslaughts. The intermediacy of Byzantium had enabled Rus' to enter into contact with ancient civilization and ensure for herself a contribution to future intellectual development – and in the first international solidarity in the history of humankind.

---

25 "Iz obshchestvennoj hroniki" ["Kanun tysjacheletija hristianstva v Rossii – Rech' o. Iakova Novickogo – Itogi pervyh devjati vekov, i zadachi poslednego veka"], *Vestnik Evropy* 8, 1888, p. 862–863, 866.

This solidarity, the publicist explained, extended to the shared intellectual and moral effort of the nations. It would have not existed in a pre-Christian epoch, and was only rendered feasible owing to the teachings of the immortality of the soul – that of individuals and whole nations. The spiritual vitality of all the christened nations is evidence of this observation: while many of them have ceased existing as political entities, none of them has died an organic death in the image of so many a savage nation. This rule had been reconfirmed in the history of Rus'. The Mongolian yoke that was borne for two centuries left no stigma on the soul of the Rus'sian tribe, remaining merely an alien mechanical oppression which severed the bonds of Eastern and Western Rus', but never upset its national and historic foundation. As the author reassures us, Rus' had never lost the sense of solidarity that binds the confessors of Christianity, the latter being anchored in recognition of the spiritual equality of people, the right of individual nations to exist, and acceptance of a common repository of moral notions and ideas. "Solidarity" is thus not one of interests, as an "ethical bond of existence" (*nravstvennaja svjaz' byta*) is the actual point.[26]

These apparently abstract considerations of a liberal publicist were meant to extirpate the argument voiced by the right-wing commentators of the Baptism, who, as we could see, used the differing systems of organizing spiritual/clerical authority to draw the conclusion of a fundamental discord between the moral ideals (and the constitutional and legal, political and social arrangements based thereupon) of Orthodoxy's followers and the universe of Western values. The Moscow monthly's contributor intended to prove that the theory of cultural-and-historical types, with Romano-Germanic civilization perceived as the most pernicious enemy of Slavdom – a view that enjoyed success at the time – was inadequate. The article strongly opposed the perception of Prince Vladimir's decision as a resolute act of withdrawal from Europe: in fact, he claims, the Baptism attested to the strife for incorporation into the Christian world.

The author accused his adversaries of attaching excessive significance to the East's rejection of the primacy of papal authority, though the moral principles taking root in the country, equivalent for the Christian faith in both of its versions, was an incomparably more important aspect. Both Veliky Novgorod in the north and Kiev in the south opted for getting on more friendly terms with Europe, with the spiritual sphere remaining autonomous. The seclusion of Rus',

---

26 "Vnutrennee obozrenie" ["900-letie kreschenija Rusi – Istoricheskaja sud'ba russkoj kul'tury – Dvukratnoe vlijanie Kieva v ee istorii"], *Russkaja mysl'* 8, 1888, p. 153–154.

which followed later on, came as a consequence of occurrences having nothing in common with the acceptance of Christianity. To the author's mind, the theories of Russia's self-existence, which were developed in his time, glorified the source of the misfortunes: coerced by the Horde's invasion, the country closed itself off to external influences. This particular stage in its history resulted in a withdrawal compared to where Europe was; even the cultural impact of Byzantium was blocked. Hence, it was not a peculiarity of the Orthodox religion compared to Catholicism that drew the lands of Rus' back from the West: the actual reason was the standstill stemming from the Mongol invasion, the author emphasized.

The conclusion of this liberal argumentation was not at all pessimistic. The author found with relief that the Baptism of Rus' had not been completely negated: Grand Prince of Kiev Vladimir's deed had found its worthy successors in the reforms of Emperor of Russia Peter the Great (1682–1725), which broke down the destructive impact of the isolation shared by the Great Rus'sians. The Reformer-Emperor reinstated Rus'sian-European unity, based on a community of beliefs, intellectual development, and moral principles. Such a conclusion reversed the perspective assumed by nationalist circles, but it did fit into the dispute between Russian Occidentalists and their opponents. A genuine controversy must have arisen because of something else – namely, an explicit remark that in the 10th c. as well as in the late 17th/early 18th c. South-Rus'sians contributed to "the enlightenment" of the Great-Rus'sian nation, which in the latter case came as a result of the integration of Little Russia (Rus' Minor) into Muscovy in the middle of the 17th c.[27]

The identity dilemma faced by a member of the Russian imperial community

As already mentioned, the celebrations were not a state affair: the hosts and highest-ranking participants were the hierarchs of the Orthodox Church. This being the case, it is worth determining who else celebrated the jubilee, and for whom it was a genuine experience. This apparently banal question implies two basic problems that are in the field of interest of the history of ideas and second-degree history. First, the contributors/attendees must have approved of the view that the Russian Empire was the legitimate heir of Kievan Rus'; thus, there appeared two hypostases of one and the same historic entity. Second, these men must have felt part of the *civitas imperii* (for our present purpose, let us consider

---

27 Ibidem, p. 157–159.

the imagined or real character of the community negligible), thereby considering themselves patriots, conscious citizens of their motherland[28] named Russia. Let us now try and deal with the challenge.

The dispute over the inheritance of Kievan Rus' led to the crystallization of two identities: the dominant Great-Rus'sian (Russian) and Little-Rus'sian (Ukrainian). The controversy began in the middle of the 11th c. and it is not surprising that it only grew stronger in the 19th c., when modern national identities were being forged and the mythologies fertilizing them emerged. The rivalry for the "Kievan succession" was the key element of the nation-building process in Eastern Europe. As we saw above, the liberal commentary was the only one to have alluded to the contribution of Southern Rus' to the Christianization effort – even though the role the author "assigned" to it was auxiliary. Because even today, some 130 years after the nationwide celebration of the Baptism of Rus', the issue remains essential, it does call for attention. From the standpoint of the celebrations' organizers and the leading newspapers or magazines (whose message was targeted at the "Orthodox" members of the imperial community), the Russian Empire was the legitimate successor and bearer of the Kievan heritage and legacy.

The case was demonstrated on two planes: religious (the ecclesial metropolis transferred from Kiev, via Vladimir-on-the-Klazma, to Moscow) and historical/ideological (the Rurikovich family ruling the country uninterruptedly, the center of grand-princely power being consecutively moved from Kiev to Rostov, Suzdal, Vladimir and, lastly, to Moscow). The adherents of the Ukrainianness of Kievan Rus' mostly raised territorial, ethno-demographic, social, and institutional arguments. Both visions were embedded in realities that were unknown to the period under description, but conformant to the canonical national history, which included the territorial, ethnic, and political integrity of Rus'sian territory.[29] In a somewhat simplified way, it can be said that these

---

28 Rather than subjects, the *cives boni* – good citizens, aware of their rights and obligations – are meant in this regard. Cf. R. Koselleck, "Patriotyzm. Racje i granice pewnego nowożytnego pojęcia", trans. J. Merecki, [in:] idem, *Dzieje pojęć. Studia z semantyki i pragmatyki języka społeczno-politycznego*, Warszawa 2009, p. 238–239.

29 The diagnosis is confirmed here whereby "The different national memory discourses are essentially based upon intensive transnational communication processes. Hence, analysis of the origins and impacts of the shared/divided and parallel sites of memory offers considerable cognitive potential. It often enables to better understand the logic and motivation behind individual as well as collective action in a neighbourhood context, compared to 'empirical' study of a 'real' dimension of bilateral history."; see: M. G. Müller, "Historia transnarodowa, historia wzajemnych oddziaływań i (po)dzielone

realities formed a modified projection of the North-South conflict – i.e., the one between Vladimir-Suzdal Rus' and Halych-Volhynian Rus'. Each of those organisms followed its own statehood-building scenario, even if they referred to the same heritage in the religious and cultural dimension. Both built a monarchical system, but the models they followed were different (Great Rus' was primarily formed by Byzantium and Tatar/Mongol influence, as neatly pointed out by the right-wing journalism). And they belonged to different civilization circles – their attitude toward the Horde's yoke and to the "Latinism" having reinforced the dichotomy.[30]

The nineteenth-century episode in the conflict for the sole right to the Christian heritage of Rus' (Ruthenia)[31] manifested itself, most of all, in pushing through the only true story of the moment of departure: after all, any *longue durée* must have begun somehow, somewhere. The national context implicated the imperial narration in an apparently unsolvable trouble in this particular aspect as well: the imperial identity, it turned out, had lost the quality of organizing principle.

The question of how adequate were the ideological constructions endorsed in the Russian public space in regard to the tenth-century realities of Rus' has so far been kept in the background. German historian Hans Henning Hahn warns us against readily giving a negative reply. As he notes, the nationalization of history, inventing the past, and describing it in novel categories – all this being typical of the 19th c. – does not at all imply that group or collective identities had been deprived of the national element before; while clearly not exhausting these

---

miejsca pamięci. Tradycja i wyzwania metodologiczne", trans. J. Górny, [in:] *Historie wzajemnych oddziaływań*, ed. R. Traba, ass. ed. B. Dziewanowski-Stefańczyk, Warszawa 2014, p. 44.

30 An argument proposed by a connoisseur of the period has been invaluably helpful to me, see: J. Pelensky, "The Contest for the Kievan Inheritance in Russian-Ukrainian Relations: Origins and Early Ramifications", [in:] idem, *The Contest for the Legacy of Kievan Rus'*, New York 1998, p. 1–20.

31 A cognitively fascinating operation would be to confront the above-discussed projections with the ideas of Rus' elites as recorded in the early literary pieces, which were analyzed (years ago) by a Polish medieval, see: A. Poppe, "How the Conversion of Rus' Was Understood in the Eleventh Century", *Harvard Ukrainian Studies* 11, 1987, p. 287–302; idem, "Two Concepts of the Conversion of Rus", [in:] *Proceedings of the International Congress Commemorating the Millennium of Christianity in Rus'-Ukraine, Harvard Ukrainian Studies* 12/13, 1988/1989, p. 488–504.

identities, such element did exist.[32] Klaus Zernack, the author of a fundamental comparative synthetic study of the histories of Poland and Russia, was inclined to recognize that medieval and modern national consciousness are substantially convergent. The essential difference is recognizable with respect to the catchiness of the national idea, which in the Middle Ages was confined to the elites (including religious ones, which is particularly important in regard to Rus'). In any case, Christianization was critical to the shaping of this formation.[33]

The most recent Russian historiography has developed a current whose representatives put into question the national narrative with regard to Kievan Rus'. They advocate the theological (rather than political) character of the statehood of that time, which is apparently confirmed by linguistic research – to be more specific, analysis of the phraseology used to describe the capital city of Kiev. An additional argument in favor of this statement is the use of the geographical criterion (a specified area being inhabited) as a discriminant of identification, which was used by the authors of early chronicles.[34] The national perspective is reproached for giving preference to the diachronic associations of socio-political formations within a given territory, whilst marginalizing the synchronic associations between the collectivities neighboring each other. Thence, not only chronology is affected (as the time span vanishes), but so is the precision of imaging the real relationships between the individual territories. Denationalization of the history of Rus' would enable to show, in a new light, the land's/country's cultural affinity between the 9th and the 13th c., its interregional contacts, and – at last – ponder over how legitimate it is to identify the Old Rus' with Eastern Europe.[35]

To celebrate the 900 years of the Baptism of Rus' called for identifying oneself with Russianness to a degree much higher than what was guaranteed by one's attachment to imperial patriotism from before the era of nationalisms. Unconditional acceptance of the constitutional model (autocracy/autarchy) or

---

32 H. H. Hahn, "Mniejszości narodowe a narody stanowiące większość w XIX wieku. Kilka podstawowych przemyśleń na temat powstawania tożsamości zbiorowej", trans. J. Kałążny, [in:] idem, *Stereotypy – tożsamość – konteksty. Studia nad polską i europejską historią*, Poznań 2011, p. 159.
33 K. Zernack, *Polska i Rosja. Dwie drogi w dziejach Europy*, trans. A. Kopacki [orig.: *Polen und Russland. Zwei Wege in der europäischen Geschichte*, Berlin 1994], Warszawa 2000, p. 62–63. The author's actual intention is unveiled through the remark that "nations tend to reciprocally constitute one another in their political awareness"; Cf. ibidem, p. 66.
34 See: I. Danilevskij, "Drevnerusskaja gosudarstvennost' i narod Rus': vozmozhnosti i puti korrektnogo opisanija", *Ab Imperio* 3, 2001.
35 V. Aristov, "Chto novogo v Kievskoj Rusi?", *Ab Imperio* 1, 2015, p. 484–486.

declared loyalty to the ruling dynasty no longer sufficed. Alexander III openly implemented a Russification line, his understanding of Russification was different from the concept which prevailed in the first half of the 19th c., with the focus on administrative unification and favoring acculturations (Poland having been a contrary case in point). The "Great Reforms" of the 1860s, which promoted the idea of an "imperial nation" – essentially, a state ethnocultural nationalism – brought about a fundamental change. Propelled by the intent to act in defense of the Empire's unity, what Russification did in this particular case was to reinforce the ancillary status of non-Russians. Thus, paradoxically, state nationalism weakened (rather than strengthened) the Empire, as it devastated the political space within which various nationalities (ethnicities) had so far coexisted. One could not, essentially, become an irreproachable citizen without being Russian (the Great Reforms period, opening the opportunity for Russia to move closer to Europe, did promise to turn the people into citizens); becoming Russified had no effect on the equalization of status. The universality of the category of "citizen of the Empire" proved fictitious.[36]

Nonetheless, it should not be believed that Russian nationalism adopted only from-above or top-down forms. On the contrary, the take-over of nationalist discourse by authoritative factors was a fateful conceding of the imperial idea to the benefit of the Nation-State idea which was promoted in the circles of the nineteenth-century Russian intelligentsia.[37] What this particularly meant was the rejection of the old system of legitimization, quitting the primacy of social stratification based on estates, and the sanctioning of a political messianism of the hitherto-incapacitated collective entity. Initially, nationalism stood up against the traditional state structures, and it was only with time that it was absorbed into the *arcana imperii*. This required that imperial patriotism be adjusted

---

36 "Dilemma stabilnosti i progressa: imperija i reformy, XIX vek", *Ab Imperio* 3, 2015, p. 233–235.

37 The statement of Michael Karpovich, one of the founding fathers of *Russian studies* in the United States, namely: "The nineteenth-century Russian intelligentsia was much more highly resistant to the 'virus of nationalism' compared to West European intellectuals; hence, the weakness of the nationalistic current in the Russian thought. They were never preoccupied with the destiny of the Empire or the lot of a nation-state; never have they professed its 'cult'", can only be seen as a historiographic curiosity. Cf. M. M. Karpovich, "Nacionalizm: N. Ja. Danilevskij, M. N. Katkov, K. P. Pobedonoscev, K. N. Leont'ev", [in:] *Lekcji po intellektualnoj istorii Rossii (XVIII – nachalo XX veka)*, Moscow 2012, p. 216–217 [a lecture delivered at the Harvard University in the 1950s, tape-recorded].

beforehand. Out of the dispute between Slavophiles and Occidentalists, dating back to the Romanticist era and recurring every now and then, two models of the nation emerged: one coincided with identification with the Rus'sian ethnos, while the other did not attach the decisive importance to ethnic identification. In their "pure" form – as intellectual constructions – both models fostered the empowerment of subjects. As a modern society was taking shape, nationalism appeared as a surrogate of the autonomy of the estates (orders) with respect to the authorities, which was part of the West European tradition.[38]

Reading the anniversary pieces of journalism *Anno Domini* 1888 leaves no doubt that various views on the nation manifested themselves in the Russian public space. This, in my view, proves that analysis of the source material with a focus on demonstrating the rivalry between the alternative identity projects has been a legitimate idea. The discussions held at the time basically reveal exclusivity in the conservative/nationalist(ic) approach, in contrast to the inclusivity of the liberal approach. Clearly, it was the latter that could attract non-Rus'sian elements to Russianness – which could have occurred, had the approach been sanctioned officially. The liberal stance referred to the sense of relationship with the universal social and cultural values of Europe, whilst perceiving the history of Russia as moving circuitously in the direction set by European civilization. The conservative idea, demonstrating the singularity of Russia, ascribed the country's position to its titular nation only. The defeat of ethnocultural nationalism, clinched by the Revolution of 1917, in nowise inclined the idea's followers (and their successors) to revise their views. A patriotism that would have been founded upon historical and sociocultural community was never tested in the Russian Empire. These two versions of prerevolutionary patriotism have not been buried together with the land of Tsars: they have recently squared off again.[39]

* * *

Mindful of the warning offered by critics of memory studies, who mistrust the cultural homogeneity of the recipients of an ideological message and the tectonics of identity constructions, we cannot be certain what the readers of the

---

38 Compare: A. Renner, "Izobretajushchee vospominanie: Russkij etnos v rossijskoj nacionalnoj pamjati", [in:] *Rossijskaja imperija v zarubezhnoj istoriografii. Raboty poslednih let. Antologija*, ed. P. Bert, P. S. Kabytov, A. I. Miller, Moscow 2005, p. 437–439, 445, 448, 463.

39 An argumentative introduction to further study of these issues is provided by the essays: V. A. Tishkov, "Chto est' Rossija i rossijskij narod" and A. I. Miller, "Nacija kak ramka politicheskoj zhizni", published as part of: *Nasledie imperij i budushchee Rossii*, ed. A. I. Miller, Moscow 2008.

Russian press – the "good citizens" of the Empire – particularly felt in the jubilee days of 1888 while pondering the path Russia had made. We can however be sure that many of them shared the longing to sense the meaning of the path, the one contained in the continuity of shining years, both past and those to come. Nevertheless, as Hannah Arendt has pointed out, there is no continuity without a testament (i.e., tradition) indicating where to look for the treasure, and what the real value of the treasure is.[40] As long as memory of the treasure persists, there are stories to tell. The story, or tale, about the Russian path continues to have new narrators and new listeners. Moreover, it is ever rekindled by these same motifs – which is why one observes that the Russian identity dilemma of the late 19th c. has yet to come to a definitive conclusion.

Translated by Philip Earl Steele

---

40 H. Arendt, "Preface: The Gap Between Past and Future", [in:] eadem, *Between Past and Future. Six Exercises in Political Thought*, New York 1961, p. 5.

Bartłomiej Noszczak

History as a tool in the state's struggle against the Catholic Church during the celebrations of the One-Thousand Years of the Polish State (1956–1966/1967)

Abstract: In 1956 the Catholic Church in Poland initiated a program of preparations for the upcoming 1,000th anniversary of the baptism in 966 of the first historic ruler of the Polish state, Mieszko I of the Piast dynasty. The program of the *Sacrum Poloniae Millennium* was seen by the communist authorities as a challenge to the state and the communist party. Thus, in 1957 preparations began for a rival state jubilee, one designed to overshadow the Church's celebrations and to regain the upper hand in the fight for "the hearts and minds". The chapter analyzes the genesis, development, and implementation of the Polish state's project for the One-Thousand Years of the Polish State that culminated in the celebrations in 1966. The communists' goal was to demonstrate the "progressive" achievements of the Polish nation over the past thousand years, with particular emphasis on the "achievements" of the 20 years of the People's Republic of Poland, which were to entail a kind of antidote to the Church's celebration of the Millennium.

Keywords: Baptism of Poland, anniversary celebrations, communist propaganda, politics of memory, memory studies

One-Thousand Years vs. the Millennium – the beginnings of the confrontation

In the second half of the 1940s, following the communist authorities' liquidation of the political and armed opposition in Poland, the Catholic Church was the sole legally acting entity which resisted the political system that had been imposed by force. For this reason the Church became the object of wide-ranging and long-lasting repressions aimed at subordinating it to the state.[1] A similar model of state policy toward Christian Churches and religious organizations was instituted in the wake of WWII in all the countries of Central and Eastern Europe

---

1 Concerning state policy toward religious confessions, see: A. Dudek, *Państwo i Kościół w Polsce 1945–1970*, Kraków 1995; A. Dudek, R. Gryz, *Komuniści i Kościół w Polsce (1945–1989)*, Kraków 2006; B. Noszczak, *Polityka państwa wobec Kościoła rzymskokatolickiego w Polsce w okresie internowania prymasa Stefana Wyszyńskiego*

subjected to the Kremlin's dictate. The crowning, as it were, of this process in Poland came with the internment of the Primate, Stefan Wyszyński, the highest-ranking clergyman of the Catholic Church in Poland, in September 1953, and the resulting oath of loyalty to the Polish People's Republic (PRL)[2] submitted by members of the country's Episcopacy in December that same year. What saved the Church in Poland from completely losing its subjecthood was the relative liberalization of the socio-political system that at least from late 1954 began to foster the decomposition of party-state structures and was important in unleashing, in a large portion of society, a spirit of defiance toward the system.[3] Thanks to this process the Church also began to shake off the restraints that had been imposed by party-state apparatchiks.[4] It was in this atmosphere that in May 1956 Cardinal Wyszyński, still interned, created a program of preparations for the Church in regard to the upcoming 1,000th anniversary of "Poland's Baptism"[5], as in the

---

1953–1956, Warszawa 2008; Z. Zieliński, *Kościół w Polsce 1944–2007*, Poznań 2009; J. Żaryn, *Dzieje Kościoła katolickiego w Polsce (1944–1989)*, Warszawa 2003.

2 PRL – *Polska Rzeczpospolita Ludowa*, the official name of the Polish state from 1952 to 1989 (until 1952 it had retained the pre-war name, *Rzeczpospolita Polska*). The term *Polska Ludowa* (People's Poland) was also then used. These names were to stress that post-war Poland was a state in which power rested with the working people of the cities and villages. Communist propaganda treated the *Manifest Polskiego Komitetu Wyzwolenia Narodowego* of July 22, 1944 as the founding act of People's Poland. See: footnotes 31 and 55 below.

3 M. R. Bombicki, *Polski Październik '56. Początek drogi*, Poznań 1993; P. Codogni, *Rok 1956*, Warszawa [undated]; T. Kisielewski, *Październik 1956 punkt odniesienia. Mozaika faktów i poglądów. Impresje historyczne*, Warszawa 2001; P. Machcewicz, *Polski rok 1956*, Warszawa 1993; E. Makowski, *Poznański Czerwiec 1956. Pierwszy bunt społeczeństwa w PRL*, Poznań 2001; A. Paczkowski, *Strajki, bunty, manifestacje jako „polska droga" przez socjalizm*, Poznań 2003; *Październik 1956. Pierwszy wyłom w systemie. Bunt, młodość i rozsądek*, ed. S. Bratkowski, Warszawa 1996; *Poznański Czerwiec 1956*, ed. S. Jankowiak, A. Rogulska, Warszawa 2002; Z. Rykowski, W. Władyka, *Polska próba. Październik '56*, Kraków 1989.

4 A. Dudek, *Państwo i Kościół...*, p. 35–36; B. Noszczak, "Duchowieństwo wobec komunizmu, pt. 1", *Przegląd Powszechny* 5, 2005, p. 90–93; idem,"Duchowieństwo wobec komunizmu, pt. 2", *Przegląd Powszechny* 6, 2005, p. 52; idem, *Polityka państwa...*, p. 301–303; J. Żaryn, *Dzieje Kościoła...*, p. 133–135.

5 J. Michalska, "Śluby Jasnogórskie. Powstanie tekstu i przewiezienie go na Jasną Górę", Warszawa, 30 V 1993". [in:] *Kardynał Wyszyński. Losy więzienne*, ed. P. Raina, Warszawa 1999, p. 210; B. Noszczak, "Okoliczności powstania Jasnogórskich Ślubów Narodu Polskiego", *Przegląd Powszechny* 7–8, 2007, p. 37–38; M. Okońska, *Z misją do Komańczy*, Warszawa 2006, p. 5–6.

Polish culture of memory it is customary to dub the acceptance of baptism in 966 by the first historic ruler of the Polish state, Mieszko I (c. 960–992) of the Piast dynasty. In Wyszyński's intention, the jubilee *Sacrum Poloniae Millennium* was to unfold in three stages. The first involved the Catholic faithful submitting the vow known as *Śluby Jasnogórskie Narodu* (in August 1956), next came the *Wielka Nowenna Narodu przed Tysiącleciem Chrztu Polski* (1957–1966), and then the jubilee *Rok "Te Deum" Narodu* (1966).

The *Śluby Jasnogórskie* (hereafter: Jasna Góra Vows) primarily concerned social and ethical matters: the protection of life, marital fidelity, inviolability of the family, the Catholic upbringing of children and the young, and the struggle against social ills. Another of the vows involved expanding the Marian cult. The vows were a response to the tribulations of living in Poland in that period, ones that had arisen i.a., because of the traumatic experiences of WWII and the policies of the communists after 1945. Inspired by these vows, Catholics were to be defiant toward the policies of the country's rulers over the period that the *Wielka Nowenna* (hereafter: the Great Novena – each of its nine years was dedicated to fulfilling a given Jasna Góra Vows) was to groom society for a dignified celebration of the *Rok "Te Deum" Narodu* (hereafter: the Nation's *Te Deum* Year).[6]

The *Sacrum Poloniae Millennium* celebrations were negatively evaluated from the beginning by the first secretary of the Central Committee of the Polish United Workers' Party (hereafter: PZPR) Władysław Gomułka, who came to power on the wave of socio-political changes sweeping Poland in October 1956. In Polish historiography and culture of memory, the political upheaval which then occurred is known simply as October '56.[7] The changes in political, social, economic, and cultural life introduced on this wave ostensibly bespoke a loosening of the state's oppressiveness. One of the manifestations of this "thaw", as it is otherwise known, was the Gomułka team's release of Primate Wyszyński that month. In fact, this and related measures were tactical and provisional.

---

6 A. F. Dziuba, *Przesłanie społeczne kardynała Stefana Wyszyńskiego Prymasa Polski*, Warszawa 2004; J. Kowalski, "Dogmatyczne i moralne aspekty Jasnogórskich Ślubowań Narodu" [in:] *Maryja Matka Narodu Polskiego*, ed. S. Grzybek, Częstochowa 1983, p. 171–188; B. Noszczak, *Sacrum czy profanum? – spór o istotę obchodów Milenium polskiego (1949–1966)*, Warszawa 2002, p. 83–84. E. Suchcicka, "Odnowienie oblicza polskiej ziemi przez naukę zawartą w Ewangelii w nauczaniu Prymasa Tysiąclecia w okresie Wielkiej Nowenny", *Studia Prymasowskie* 3, 2009, p. 208–209; K. Turowski, "Zagadnienia społeczne w Ślubowaniach Maryjnych", *Homo Dei* 6, 1957, p. 915–919.

7 For a cross-section review of these matters see: J. Eisler, *"Polskie miesiące" czyli kryzys(y) w PRL*, Warszawa 2008.

They helped solidify the "new" regime, which trumpeted its renunciation of the "period of errors and distortions", as the years of Stalinism were defined in the party's newspeak. Thus, Gomułka's political course soon grew ever more severe, and this also concerned relations between the state and the Church. Nonetheless, Gomułka's team did not return to the Stalinist models for fighting the opposition. After 1956, extreme repressions were replaced by milder methods of administrative, fiscal, and propaganda pressure.

The program for the celebrations of the *Sacrum Poloniae Millennium*, created by Primate Wyszyński was seen by the new authorities as a challenge to the PRL and the expression of a policy directed against the state. The communists were afraid the Church would monopolize the jubilee celebrations, something which could tarnish their image, or perhaps even wreak political havoc. Despite the communists' experiments to foist atheism and secularization on a society in which the majority identified with Catholicism, the millennium of Mieszko's baptism could not be belittled – much less ignored altogether. Thus, the symbolic date of 1966 at minimum risked weakening the communists' efforts to marginalize the place and role of the Church in Poland. Gomułka's team was uncertain how to celebrate this alien (to the communist holiday calendar) anniversary. They therefore searched for a fitting approach towards the upcoming Church jubilee, so as not to suffer political loss and damage to their image. Soon the preparations for a rival state jubilee were begun, one designed to overshadow the Church's celebrations and to regain the upper hand in the fight for "the hearts and minds". In the aim of the power apparatus, its own celebrations of the One-Thousand Years were to entail a kind of antidote to the Church's Millennium (the terms Millennium and One-Thousand Years, written in this chapter in capital letters, refer to the separate jubilee celebrations of the Church and the state, respectively).

The origins of the concept of the One-Thousand Years of the Polish State

In the wake of October '56, the first activities related to the celebration of the thousand years of the state were taken up by the scientific community. The professor of archaeology and director of the Institute of the History of Material Culture of the Polish Academy of Sciences (PAN), Witold Hensel, in a letter from June 14, 1957 to the Scientific Secretariat of the First Department (Social Sciences) of PAN, called attention to the waning dynamism of research into the beginnings of the Polish state that followed the founding of the institute. Hensel then added that, in the face of the upcoming anniversary of the millennium of Poland's Baptism, the scientific community had to undertake appropriate preparations.[8]

In response to Hensel's initiative, on June 19, 1957 the First Department of PAN decided to establish a special committee for matters related to celebrating the thousand years of the Polish state. Three months later the committee decided that the climax of the celebrations should be in 1965, which, however, was not to exclude the organization of associated events, whether before or after that date.[9] The next step was made on October 23, 1957 when the authorities of the First Department of PAN decided to address PAN's secretary of science, prof. Henryk Jabłoński, with a request to establish a nationwide committee for the celebrations of the millennium having its own budget.[10]

In early 1958, the Political Bureau of the Central Committee of the PZPR decided that the preparations for the state jubilee would be organized over the years 1960–1965. It was argued that the period of 960–965 was when the most intense formation of Polish statehood took place. The communists were well aware that the Church planned the main celebrations of the Millennium of Christianity in Poland for 1966. Hence, the initial preference of the authorities for organizing the celebrations already in 1965 was intended to upstage the Church's jubilee. Besides, the proposal that 1965 should be the culmination of the celebrations, as mentioned above, had already been tabled by the scholarly community associated with PAN.[11]

Gomułka's team was aware that for two years the Church had been preparing Poles for the baptismal anniversary, and that the state had not taken any countermeasures. Thus, the state power apparatus, monitoring the progress of the program of the Great Novena being implemented by the Church, decided to move as swiftly as possible to develop and implement its own project for

---

8 T. P. Rutkowski, *Nauki historyczne w Polsce 1944–1970. Zagadnienia polityczne i organizacyjne*, Warszawa 2007, p. 368–369. In fact, this was Hensel's second Millennium initiative; already in 1946 he had drawn attention to the need to scientifically prepare for the anniversary of the millennium of Poland's Baptism. This idea began to be implemented in 1949–1953 as part of the archaeological work of the Management for Research on the Origins of the Polish State, see: B. Noszczak, *Sacrum czy profanum?...*, p. 29–30; T. P. Rutkowski, *Nauki historyczne...*, p. 146–147.
9 T. P. Rutkowski, *Nauki historyczne...*, p. 369.
10 Ibidem, p. 370.
11 Archiwum Akt Nowych (AAN), Biuro Polityczne Komitetu Centralnego Polskiej Zjednoczonej Partii Robotniczej (BP KC PZPR), V/60, Notatka w sprawie obchodów Tysiąclecia Państwa Polskiego, Warszawa 1958, no page numbers.

celebrating the anniversary of the state's 1,000 years. In accordance with this premise, at the meeting of the Political Bureau on February 13, 1958, the decision was made to establish, by the Nationwide Committee of the Front for National Unity[12] (OK FJN) and the Council of State, the Committee for the Preparations of the Celebrations of the One-Thousand Years of the Polish State (KPOTPP). Shortly thereafter, the Sejm adopted a resolution that unanimously declared the period 1960–1966 to be a celebration of the One-Thousand Years of the Polish State (TPP). In the propaganda tone that was characteristic of those years, the decision was explained thus:

> The celebrations of the One-Thousand Years will remind us of the glorious history of the construction and development of the first states of the Piasts; they will show the heritage of creative political thought that over ten centuries strengthened the community of the nation and unified its efforts to defend the Homeland, and later to fight for its liberation. [...] The celebrations of the One-Thousand Years should multiply the strength of our nation in building socialism and strengthen the Polish People's Republic. They should increase the importance and enhance the role of Poland as a spokesman for the peaceful aspirations common to all nations. The celebration of the One-Thousand Years will highlight the participation of our nation in the general progress of humanity, and testify to our place and role in Europe. [...] they will become a sublime manifestation of the community of the entirety of Polish society gathered in the Front for National Unity, tighten the bond of brotherhood between society in Poland and our countrymen around the world. [...] they will give us new strength for the further development of our People's Homeland.[13]

On the basis of the adopted resolution, the State Council[14] formally established the KPOTPP, whose chairman was the President of the Polish Academy of Sciences, the eminent Polish philosopher prof. Tadeusz Kotarbiński. Its

---

12 The Front for National Unity was a socio-political institution founded in 1952 (until 1956 it functioned as the National Front) which included political parties, trade unions, and other social organizations in the PRL. It was subordinate to the PZPR and pursued its political goals. The Front participated in conducting the elections to the Sejm and national councils (it presented the only lists of candidates), and was the patron of statewide and local social campaigns. The FJN's activities were managed by the Nationwide Committee (its chairman was usually the chairman or deputy chairman of the Council of State).

13 "Uchwała Sejmu o Obchodach Tysiąclecia", *Trybuna Ludu*, 26 II 1958.

14 From 1952 to 1989 the Council of State was one of the highest organs of state power in the PRL. It was empowered with competencies matching that of the Sejm (e.g., the right to issue decrees with the power of a parliamentary act).

committee included many scholars – mainly medievalists.¹⁵ Due to the nature of the jubilee, scholars representing the field of history were to play a particularly important role in the celebrations. It was also deemed necessary to set up specialized committees to prepare and develop specific issues. In line with this approach, the following were to be created: an Archaeological Committee; a Historical Committee (within its framework the Subcommittee of Linguistics and the Subcommittee on Art History operated); a Scientific Cooperation Committee; the Popularization Committee; the Committee on Museums and Exhibitions; and the Local Initiative Coordination Commission. On April 4, 1958 the Presidium of the KPOTPP decided to extend the composition of the Committee and officially appoint the above-mentioned specialized committees within its framework.¹⁶ In connection with the celebrations of the Thousand Years, local committees also undertook activities within their purview.¹⁷

The most advanced work was conducted by the Archaeological Committee. Its plans envisaged concentrating excavations in the main centers of early Piast Poland: Czermno, Gdańsk, Giecz, Gniezno, Kołobrzeg, Kraków, Kruszwica, Międzyrzecz, Opole, Poznań, Santok, Szczecin, Wolin, Wrocław and the Wały Śląskie ("Silesian Ramparts"). As part of the work of the Archaeological Committee, it was also planned to deepen cooperation in

---

15 "Pełny skład komitetu: Komitet Przygotowawczy Obchodów Tysiąclecia", *Życie Szkoły Wyższej* 13/4, 1958, p. 120–121.

16 "Z prac przygotowawczych do obchodu Millenium", *Życie Szkoły Wyższej* 13/5, 1958, p. 117–118. Concerning the scientific preparations (especially that of historians) for the celebrations of the One-Thousand Years of the Polish State (TPP), see: W. Hensel, "Z przygotowań do polskiego Tysiąclecia", *Z Otchłani Wieków* 4, 1958, p. 225–229; A. Gieysztor, "W sprawie badań związanych z Tysiącleciem Państwa Polskiego", *Kwartalnik Historyczny* 65, 1958, p. 707–717; T. Manteuffel, "Prace badawcze historyków w ramach obchodów Tysiąclecia Państwa Polskiego", *Kwartalnik Historyczny* 65, 1958, p. 947–948; W. Hensel, "Archeologia w pracach przygotowawczych do obchodów Tysiąclecia Państwa Polskiego", *Kwartalnik Historyczny* 65, 1958, p. 948–951; J. Deresiewicz, "W sprawie problematyki milleniowej [sic!]", *Kronika Miasta Poznania* 1958, p. 6–10; W. Hensel, "O polskim Tysiącleciu", *Życie Szkoły Wyższej* 13/13, 1958, p. 27–32; W. Hensel, "Archeologia w pracach przygotowawczych do obchodów Tysiąclecia Państwa Polskiego", *Wiadomości Archeologiczne* 26, 1959, p. 85–89.

17 "Z prac przygotowawczych do obchodu Millenium", *Życie Szkoły Wyższej* 13/5, 1958, p. 118; also see: AAN, BP PZPR, V/60, Sprawozdanie Prezydium Komisji Przygotowawczej Obchodów Tysiąclecia Państwa Polskiego i powołanych przez Prezydium Komisji Problemowych, Warszawa 13 II 1958.

the field of scientific research with archaeologists from Czechoslovakia, the German Democratic Republic, and the Union of Soviet Socialist Republics (USSR). The committee considered it important to publish the results of the new archaeological research within the *Millennium Poloniae Monumenta Archeologica* series.[18]

In addition to its core tasks, the Museum and Exhibition Committee, in turn, which partially acted as the committee of the Ministry of Culture and Art, submitted a plan to build permanent "monuments of the Thousand Years" by erecting new edifices (the National Library and Music Academy in Warsaw; the Silesian Library in Katowice; the National Museum and Opera in Kraków; the National Museum in Poznań), as well as the reconstruction of historical buildings destroyed during WWII (the Royal Castle in Warsaw and the Pomeranian Dukes' Castle in Szczecin). However, due to the costs related to this concept, the Presidium of the KPOTPP chose to build only one of the proposed objects from the state funds in the Thousand Year jubilee (namely, the National Library), without excluding the possibility of building the others from local funds. The Museum and Exhibition Committee also proposed the organization of historical exhibitions in 1960 in Kraków, Poznań, and Warsaw.

A wide scope of work was enjoyed by the Local Initiative Coordination Committee, which selected applications to KPOTPP from all over the country regarding the forms for commemorating the 1,000th anniversary of the Polish state. By 1960, voivodeship administration bodies together with local Front for National Unity (FJN) committees had adopted resolutions that outlined the plan for the celebrations, recommending at the same time that lower level, local government authorities develop their own, similar programs. Tasks that were supposed to bring economic and cultural benefits to the Poles were at the forefront. Among them was the construction of the so-called Thousand-Year Schools[19]

---

18 G. Zalewski, "Nad czym pracują komisje Komitetu Przygotowawczego Obchodów Tysiąclecia", *Rada Narodowa* 28, 12 VII 1958, p. 12. More fully on the project for scholarly works from the field of history concerning the TPP, see: T. Manteuffel, "Prace badawcze...", p. 947–948.

19 The "Thousand-Year Schools" – or rather "the school-monument to the One-Thousand years of the Polish State" – was the term used in the PRL for school buildings erected from budgetary and social resources as part of the educational program implemented as part of the TPP project. In total, from 1960 to the early 1970s, 1,417 "Thousand-Year Schools" were built.

and support by national councils for scientific societies, institutions, and departments, etc.[20]

During the meeting of the Presidium of the Nationwide Committee of FJN and KPOTPP in Warsaw on June 7, 1958, the concept and state of preparations for the celebration of the Thousand Years was discussed.[21] It was emphasized that the main idea of all the works undertaken was to hearken to "the best patriotic and progressive traditions of the Polish nation". Worth stressing here is that, in the language of communist propaganda, the adjective "progressive" was used to define all those processes and phenomena that were approved by the doctrine of Marxism-Leninism. The emphasis of these traditions was to give the celebrations of the One-Thousand Years a "deeply up-to-date, educative ideological content understandable for millions".[22,23]

A dozen or so other speakers also took part in the discussion. Among them was Władysław Gomułka himself, who pointed out that works related to the celebration of the TPP should take into account the achievements of Poland's entire history and extract from them what was creative and served the development of the nation and the country. Speaking of the scope of archaeological research, the secretary of PZPR stressed the need to focus mainly on the "Recovered Territories", the phrase used during the PRL for the post-German areas that had been granted to Poland during the Allies' conference in Potsdam in 1945. In this way, their "ancient Polishness", Gomułka stressed, could be accentuated even more forcefully.[24]

Extremely telling for shaping the ideological content of the state celebrations of the TPP was the close of the meeting on June 7. After the discussion an appeal was made to the nation regarding the celebration of the 550th anniversary of the Battle of Grunwald, and a Coordination Committee of the Grunwald Celebrations at KPOTPP was established. It was responsible for the celebration of the anniversary of the Battle of Grunwald, i.e., the victory of the Polish-Lithuanian armies

---

20 On the role of FJN committees in the preparations for the TPP celebrations, see: J. Kalinowski, "Rola Komitetów FJN w przygotowaniach do Obchodów Tysiąclecia", *Trybuna Ludu*, 26 IV 1958.

21 "W przygotowaniach do 1000-lecia Państwa Polskiego powinny wziąć udział miliony ludzi naszego kraju", *Trybuna Ludu*, 8 VI 1958.

22 A. Zawadzki, "Sięgnijmy do sławnych kart polskiej myśli postępowej", *Rada Narodowa* 24, 14 VI 1958, p. 5–6. Also see: "Posiedzenie Prezydium Ogólnopolskiego Komitetu FJN w sprawie obchodów Tysiąclecia", *Życie Szkoły Wyższej* 13/7/8, 1958, p. 156.

23 This quotation and all following quotations from non-English sources were translated into English by the translator of the chapter.

24 *W przygotowaniach do 1000-lecia…*, p. 3.

on July 15, 1410 over the forces of the Teutonic Order in Prussia. This event held great importance in the historical consciousness of many generations of Poles, having become a metaphor of ongoing Polish-German relations. During WWII the Germans were also aware of this, and thus destroyed, for instance, the Grunwald Monument in Kraków (unveiled on the 500th anniversary of the battle in 1910). The Polish side, including the Polish communists, deliberately referred in its propaganda to Grunwald symbolism. It is not by accident that July 15 was chosen as the date for the swearing-in of the units constituting the nucleus of the Polish People's Army[25] fighting from 1943 alongside the Red Army. In turn, the choice to add the Coordinating Committee for Preparations for the Grunwald Celebrations to the group of Committees summoned for the preparation of the celebration of the TPP was a revealing symptom of the communist politics of memory for two reasons. First, it signaled that the communist authorities, in organizing commemorations on a large scale, would also try to introduce other jubilees, selected in accordance with the current line of party-state propaganda and without any direct cause-and-effect relationship with 966. Secondly, the anti-German tone (targeted specifically at West Germany) that was encoded in the project for the Grunwald celebrations was symptomatic, as the culmination was to fall on the 550th anniversary of the battle in 1960.[26]

The final concept of the One-Thousand Years of the Polish State and the accompanying celebrations

On February 12, 1960, the Council of State accepted the framework program of the TPP celebrations developed by KPOTPP for 1960–1966, indicating that it was in line with the "ideological-political conception and direction set for the preparatory works and the celebrations of the Thousand Years in the solemn

---

25 The so-called Polish People's Army was the widely used, albeit unofficial name of the Polish armed forces created in 1943–44 in the USSR, and of the PRL's Polish Army of 1944–1989.
26 Among the many publications concerning the importance of the Battle of Grunwald in Polish and German cultures of memory, including in the context of the jubilee celebrations of 1960, see: O. M. Olivier, "Bitwa pod Grunwaldem. (Nie)udane mity zwycięstwa" [in:] *Polsko-niemieckie miejsca pamięci*, vol. 1, ed. R. Traba, H. H. Hahn, ass. ed. M. Górny, K. Kończal, Warszawa 2014, p. 270–287; S. Dyroff, "Grunwald w historiografii i tradycji niemieckiej i polskiej" [in:] *Wojna, pamięć i tożsamość. O bitwach i mitach bitewnych*, ed. J. M. Piskorski, Warszawa 2012, p. 130–146.

resolutions of the Council of State and the Sejm of the PRL in February 1958".[27] The program of the TPP celebrations adopted by the Council of State[28] stated that the 1966 jubilee should contribute to expanding knowledge about the past of the nation and stimulate interest in its history, so that it would be "a source of emotional involvement in everything progressive and creative in Poland".[29]

The draft of the KPOTPP's resolution emphasized that in the years 1960–1966 many historical anniversaries were present, ones which significantly impacted the history of the Polish nation and which were to constitute the pivotal points of the celebrations of the TPP. These were, in order: the 1,000th anniversary of "Poland's appearance on the stage of history"; the 550th anniversary of the Battle of Grunwald; the 600th anniversary of the Jagiellonian University (founded in 1364)[30]; several anniversaries related to the "national-liberation struggle of the Polish nation"; and last but not least, in 1964 the 20th anniversary of People's Poland.[31] The celebrations of other anniversaries related to the development of Polish culture, the political history of the nation, and the jubilee celebrations of individual cities and settlements were to be complemented in the local sphere with the central points of the TPP celebrations. In the aim of the KPOTPP, they were an important factor in deepening patriotism by making society aware of the traditions of the given city or region – and in the "Recovered Territories", of the Polish past of these areas, their historical role in the first centuries of the existence of the state, and their struggle to maintain Polishness there in later periods.

The celebrations of the One-Thousand Years of the Polish State (TPP), as intended in the concepts of their creators, were also to become an opportunity to recall Poland's contribution to world culture and science. This was the purpose of the celebrations connected with the 600th anniversary of the Jagiellonian University, during which the intention was to remind both Poland and the world of the University's most prominent professors and pupils, as well as to show the contribution of other centers of scientific life in Poland to the achievements of global science.

---

27 "Program obchodów Tysiąclecia zatwierdzony przez Radę Państwa", *Trybuna Ludu*, 14 II 1960; also see: J. Hejno, "Rady narodowe w obchodach Tysiąclecia Państwa Polskiego", *Rada Narodowa* 17, 23 IV 1960, p. 3–4.
28 *Obchody Tysiąclecia. Informator*, ed. A. Kiełpiński, Warszawa 1962, p. 11–12.
29 "Program obchodów Tysiąclecia zatwierdzony przez Radę Państwa", *Trybuna Ludu*, 14 II 1960.
30 U. Perkowska, *Jubileusze Uniwersytetu Jagiellońskiego*, Kraków 2000, p. 201–202; T. P. Rutkowski, *Nauki historyczne...*, p. 374–375.
31 See: footnote 2.

The draft resolution of the KPOTTP stated that the aim of the above was to popularize the traditions of the Polish nation which had made a significant contribution to the struggle of other nations to break "the bonds of feudalism and national oppression", especially the struggles of "progressive trends in Polish uprisings against backward pursuits" and "the cooperation of Polish patriots and revolutionary forces in Russia and solidarity campaigns of all Europe's progressive forces".[32] The events of the January Uprising of 1863–1865, important for the Polish culture of memory, in the post-war situation were of a particularly sensitive nature. For the January Uprising was one of the two largest pro-independence and anti-Russian uprisings in the era of the partitions of Poland (1772/1793/1795–1918). Therefore, it was the intention of those who determined the communist propaganda to celebrate in 1963 the 100th anniversary of its outbreak by stylizing it, in accordance with the current ideology, as not only an independence struggle, but also a "revolutionary-progressive" struggle in the Marxist understanding. It was decided that the contribution of the Polish nation to national liberation and social struggles in the world would be showcased, as would the traditions of the Poles' participation in the struggle for American independence, in the French Revolution, the Spring of Nations, the Paris Commune, the October Revolution, the civil war in Spain, and "everywhere that progressive forces of the Polish nation fought 'For both our freedom and yours'".[33]

The final part of the KPOTPP document discusses the program for the celebrations of the 20th anniversary of People's Poland. In order to properly prepare this anniversary, it was decided that a wide range of scientific and popularizing works would be developed, ones aimed at fully showing the achievements of Polish society after 20 years of work building a new system, as well as the differences between the Second Polish Republic (that is, Poland in the interwar period, 1918–1939) and the "achievements" of People's Poland. This anniversary was closely related to another jubilee, one very important for the communist apparatus – namely, 1965's 20th anniversary of the "liberation". In the language of communist propaganda the Red Army in 1945 had liberated Poland from German occupation, though in reality it only brought Poland's enslavement to the USSR.[34] Of course, 1945 also saw the incorporation of the Recovered Territories into Poland. Therefore, 1965 was to be solemnly celebrated both in Poland and

---

32 "Program obchodów Tysiąclecia zatwierdzony przez Radę Państwa", *Trybuna Ludu*, 14 II 1960.
33 Ibidem.
34 A. Skrzypek, *Mechanizmy autonomii. Stosunki polsko-radzieckie 1956–1965*, Pułtusk, Warszawa 2005; idem, *Mechanizmy klientelizmu. Stosunki polsko-radzieckie 1965–1989*,

by Polonian communities abroad in order to emphasize the ties between those lands and the rest of Poland.

During the plenary sessions of the Nationwide Committee of FJN in Warsaw (February 20, 1960), the 7-year period of the celebrations of the TPP was officially opened (1960-1966).[35] After the Council of State approved the program of the TPP's celebrations, the Political Bureau of the Central Committee of the PZPR dissolved the KPOTPP[36] (December 13, 1960) and appointed in its place the Scientific Committee of the Celebrations of the One-Thousand Years of the Polish State (KNOTPP) at the Nationwide Committee of FJN, which continued to operate in reliance on the auxiliary committees' work.[37] This body included a group of eminent scholars who guaranteed a high substantive level of scientific and popular-science works related to the TPP.[38]

The One-Thousand Years of the Polish State celebrations, 1960-1965

In 1960, ceremonial inaugurations of the One-Thousand Years of the Polish State (TPP) took place all over Poland: March 23 in Gdańsk, March 26 in Białystok, April 4 in Kraków, April 28 in Warsaw, May 28 in Poznań, June 5 in Kruszwica, and July 10 in Opole.[39] Their program was enriched with various forms of celebrations, as well as with a variety of themes referring to historical events which the communist authorities tried to incorporate into an appropriately interpreted vision of Poland's past.

Pułtusk, Warszawa 2008; idem, *Mechanizmy uzależnienia. Stosunki polsko-radzieckie 1944-1957*, Pułtusk 2002.

35 *Rada Narodowa* 10, 5 III 1960, p. 4-8; T. Kotarbiński, "W przededniu obrachunku Tysiąclecia", *Argumenty* 10, 6 III 1960, p. 3-5; also see: "Uchwała Plenum OK FJN", *Rada Narodowa* 10, 5 III 1960, p. 8.

36 A. Paczkowski, *Gomułka i inni: Dokumenty z archiwum KC 1948-1982*, Warszawa 1986, p. 127.

37 "Struktura organizacyjna Komitetu Naukowego Obchodów Tysiąclecia Państwa Polskiego" [in:] *Obchody Tysiąclecia...*, p. 8-10.

38 Tadeusz Kotarbiński became the KNOTPP's chairman. On the composition of the presidium see: "Struktura organizacyjna Komitetu Naukowego Obchodów Tysiąclecia Państwa Polskiego" [in:] *Obchody Tysiąclecia...*, p. 8-10). The KNOPTT no longer had any representatives of the Sejm and the FJN, see: T. P. Rutkowski, *Nauki historyczne...*, p. 373.

39 *Trybuna Ludu* from: 24 III 1960; 27 III 1960; 5 IV 1960; 29 IV 1960; 29 V 1960; 6 VI 1960; 11 VII 1960.

In order, these were: the 550th anniversary of the Battle of Grunwald (1960); the 40th anniversary of the Third Silesian Uprising (1961)[40]; the 1,000th anniversary of Gdańsk (1962); the 100th anniversary of the outbreak of the January Uprising (1963); the 20th anniversary of the Polish People's Army (1963); the 600th anniversary of the founding of the Jagiellonian University (1964); and the 20th anniversary of People's Poland (1964–1965). These central ceremonies were accompanied by hundreds of other smaller events of a scientific, popular-science, cultural, artistic, or sports nature.

These celebrations involved a considerable outlay of efforts and resources. There were mass spectacles that combined historical references and folk elements, with the former often verging on historical provocation aimed primarily at the Federal Republic of Germany. For instance, during the celebration of the 550th anniversary of the Battle of Grunwald, a monument was unveiled on the site of the battle that presented knightly faces directed west, while the museum located there boasted a collection of urns gathered from many battlefields where Poles had fought against Germany down through the centuries.[41]

The historicism of the anniversary celebrations was not accidental – indeed, the entire focus on the past that characterized the celebrations of the TPP was deliberate. It was combined with immediate political goals that above all were to undergird the thesis about Poland and its "crowning" – the PRL, which was now leading the eternal struggle against the manifold threats from Germany. In the language of the state's propaganda, Germany was defined using a range of adjectives bespeaking this threat: "Germanic", "Teutonic", "imperialist", "fascist", "Nazi", "militaristic", "revisionist", etc. This style was supposed to confirm the rights of Poland to the "Recovered Territories" and the Piasts' legacy. In this aspect, the celebrations of the TPP contained elements of nationalism that were appropriately dispensed by the communist apparatus and directed primarily against the Federal Republic of Germany[42], and in particular "West German revisionism".[43]

---

[40] The last of the three Silesian uprisings against Germany (1919, 1920, 1921), the aim of which was to conjoin Upper Silesia to the reborn Polish state as a result of WWI. The third Silesian Uprising (from May 2/3 to July 5, 1921) ended with the joining of the most industrial part of Upper Silesia to the Second Republic of Poland.

[41] W. Mierzwa, *Grunwald pole bitwy*, Warszawa 1986.

[42] M. Zaremba, *Komunizm, legitymizacja, nacjonalizm. Nacjonalistyczna legitymizacja władzy komunistycznej w Polsce*, Warszawa 2001, p. 307–310.

[43] The term used in the propaganda of the PRL in relation to the foreign policy of the Federal Republic of Germany, accusing that state of seeking to change the international

Jubilee events were accompanied by the mass mobilization of society. The historical celebrations turned into great manifestations with the participation of tens or even hundreds of thousands of people. Official state data stated that some 200,000 people took part in the manifestation at Grunwald (July 17, 1960).[44] Celebrations commemorating the 40th anniversary of the outbreak of the Third Silesian Uprising (June 4, 1961) in the amphitheater at the foot of the Monument to the Uprising on Mount Saint Anna were watched by approximately 170,000 people.[45]

The program of the central celebrations of historical anniversaries was rich, diverse, and generally attractive for attendees. Often the program went beyond strictly historical subject matter. Each jubilee celebration was a pretext to manifest not only the noble past of Poland, but also to cast the present in a positive, uncritical light (with hope for a bright future). A special role in this mass-scale historical "education" (it in fact had more in common with indoctrination) was ascribed to young people, who were mobilized to take part in jubilee celebrations. For the jubilee of the Battle of Grunwald a Grunwald Jamboree (*Zlot Grunwaldzki*) was organized for July 1–17, 1960 that was attended (it need be added, obligatorily and despite the summer holiday), by about 30,000 youths belonging to four organizations affiliated with the PZPR: the Polish Scouting Association, the Socialist Youth Union, the Union of Rural Youth, and the Association of Polish Students.[46] Young people not only provided the celebrations of the TPP with great numbers, something ever so important in the state's clash over image (and prestigious) with the Church, but they also made various kinds of vows and commitments that connected them with the PRL. Besides those at the Grunwald celebrations, similar such vows also took place during the celebrations of the 1,000th anniversary of Gdańsk and the 600th anniversary of the Jagiellonian University.

---

situation of Germany and to "revise" the Polish border on the Oder and Lusatian Neisse Rivers as established during the Potsdam conference in 1945.
44 "Wielkie uroczystości na Polach Grunwaldu", *Trybuna Ludu*, 18 VII 1960.
45 "W 40. rocznicę walk ludu śląskiego o połączenie z Macierzą", *Trybuna Ludu*, 5 VII 1961.
46 "Rozpoczyna się Zlot Grunwaldzki", *Trybuna Ludu*, 2 VII 1960; "Już 15 tysięcy uczestników zlotu przybyło na Pola Grunwaldzkie", *Trybuna Ludu*, 3 VII 1960; "Pierwsza niedziela pod zlotowymi namiotami", *Trybuna Ludu*, 5 VII 1960; "Oddział reprezentacyjny sił zbrojnych w uroczystościach grunwaldzkich", *Trybuna Ludu*, 6 VII 1960; "Dzień przyjaźni i pokoju na Zlocie Grunwaldzkim", *Trybuna Ludu*, 7 VII 1960; "Uroczystości w całym kraju", *Trybuna Ludu*, 15 VII 1960; "Wielki zlot młodzieży zakończony", *Trybuna Ludu*, 18 VII 1960.

The events of the TPP were attended by members of the highest party and state authorities, political and social activists at the local level, veterans of the Polish workers' movement, delegations of the Polish People's Army, Polonia organizations, etc. The rank of the TPP celebrations was also testified to by the presence of guests and foreign delegations (civil and military), mainly from countries of the Eastern Bloc.[47]

The historical aspects of the TPP were conveyed in the years 1960–1966 by numerous scientific and popular-science publications, scientific sessions, conferences, exhibition congresses, academies, etc. In general, such examples were directly related to the anniversaries of specific important historical events that had been entered into the 7-year calendar of the central celebrations of the TPP. Some of the scientific events related to the state jubilee were of international and high-level scientific importance.[48]

The power apparatus made sure that the jubilee events stressed the Polish past of the "Recovered Territories". This was no doubt the criterion that guided the selection of anniversaries such as the 550th anniversary of the Battle of Grunwald, the 40th anniversary of the Third Silesian Uprising, the 1,000th anniversary of Gdańsk, and the 20th anniversary of the PRL. In this case, history served as an argument to justify joining these areas to Poland in 1945. Overtures to the recovered lands appeared during the TPP in many of the official speeches of politicians, Gomułka himself included. This was fostered by quasi-religious events during which various declarations, promises, and vows were made.[49] In this way the communists created their own counterweight to the Church's concept of the Jasna Góra Vows, which gathered and mobilized the faithful around the implementation of a religious program.

---

47 See: "Obchody 20-lecia Ludowego Wojska Polskiego", *Trybuna Ludu*, 11 X 1963.
48 For instance, beginning on May 6, 1964, a three-day international scientific conference was hosted in Kraków. Its theme was "The history of the University of Kraków against the background of the history of universities in Europe". The conference gathered many world-renowned scholars, among them were the President of the International Committee for the Study of the History of Universities, prof. Sven Stelling-Michaud from Geneva, and the secretary general of that committee, prof. Jacques Le Goff from Paris. About this and accompanying conferences see: *Obchody Tysiąclecia...*, p. 26.
49 On the quasi-religious character of communism and communist holidays in the PRL, see: M. Kula, *Religiopodobny komunizm*, Kraków 2003; P. Osęka, *Rytuały stalinizmu. Oficjalne święta i uroczystości rocznicowe w Polsce 1944–1956*, Warszawa 2007; P. Sowiński, *Komunistyczne święto. Obchody 1 Maja w latach 1948–1954*, Warszawa 2000.

A perfect illustration of this phenomenon was the oath made by youth at the site of the Battle of Grunwald on July 17, 1960. It was preceded with a speech delivered by Władysław Gomułka. In that speech the "party priest" emphasized the "deep, creative, and peaceful influence of socialism", thanks to which Poland had taken the road of "friendship and good-neighborly cooperation" with other communist states.[50] After this speech, tens of thousands of young people gathered on the battlefield of Grunwald then vowed their unity in the "service of the nation, socialism, and peace"; the will to marshal all their forces while at work and school under the ideological leadership of the PZPR; their readiness to struggle against "backwardness and ignorance" (which in the party newspeak were *de facto* synonyms for the Church); and lastly their commitment to "join forces in vigilance against the enemies of socialism". The vows ended with the declaration: "Our youth, our enthusiasm and knowledge, our best feelings for the cause of socialism forever connected to You, O People's Republic, in service do we lay down".[51]

In 1963, the communist state authorities tried to popularize the date 963, to which the Saxon chronicler Widukind in his *Res gestae Saxoniae* fixed the first mention of Mieszko I and his dominion. This was designed to tactfully supersede the date of Mieszko's baptism in 966, and thus allow the communists to underline the secular character of the celebration of the TPP. In addition, that date pointed to earlier interest in Poland outside of Slavdom, and also showed the political role that the early-medieval Polish state had begun to play in Europe in the mid-10th c. In this way, a link was made with how the state was established via a long-lasting fight for its reconstruction in the 19th and early 20th c., as waged by "national liberation movements" (here, the loose association with the anniversary of the January Uprising in 1863 was important) and thereafter continued by the workers' movement.[52]

The ideologization and use of history for current political aims accompanied all the central celebrations of the TPP associated with the commemorations of anniversaries. The degree of intensity of this phenomenon became greater, the closer in time the date being celebrated was. The culmination took place in 1964–1965, when the 20th anniversary of People's Poland was celebrated as part

---

50 "Przemówienie na uroczystości 550 rocznicy zwycięstwa pod Grunwaldem wygłoszone na Polach Grunwaldzkich 17 VII 1960" [in:] W. Gomułka, *Przemówienia 1960*, Warszawa 1961, p. 279–285.
51 "Wielkie uroczystości na Polach Grunwaldu", *Trybuna Ludu* 18 VII 1960.
52 From an interview with prof. Witold Stankiewicz, conducted by the author of this paper, Warszawa, Feb. 22, 2000.

of the national jubilee. It was based on the belief in the unique character of the "people's state" promoted by the communist rulers. This was expressed in the propaganda slogan: "The PRL – the crowning of the thousand-year history of the Polish state".[53] In connection with the jubilee, the OK FJN called for mass participation in the "social acts" that were to commemorate the 20th anniversary of People's Poland.[54] The supreme task in these celebrations was to inculcate society with recognition of the "significance of the historic breakthrough that has occurred in the fate of the nation and the state since the manifesto of the PKWN [the Soviet-sponsored Polish Committee for National Liberation of July 22, 1944][55] as well as of the achievements attained in the course of socialist construction".[56] The 20th anniversary of People's Poland was to show Poles the surpassing importance of friendship and alliance with the countries of the Eastern Bloc, and to develop the idea of deeper and wider work among young people, along with a sense of social discipline and care for the nation-wide interest.

The premises of the 20th anniversary of the PRL are perfectly illustrated by the statement of Gomułka, who on July 21, 1964 during an academic session at the Congress Hall of the Palace of Culture and Science in Warsaw emphasized the "sublimeness" of July 22, 1944 in Polish history. In his opinion, it marked not only the rebirth of the country to an independent life in the new borders from

---

53 The resolution adopted in 1964 regarding the participation of PAN in the celebrations of the 20th anniversary of People's Poland stated: "Historical events, whose anniversary we will celebrate in a decisive manner, influenced the formation of socio-economic relations and the political system, and consequently the culture and contemporary art of Poland. Demonstrating this influence and examining the social processes implied by the establishment of people's power in Poland should constitute a contribution of the social sciences to the jubilee celebrations". (C.f. *Obchody Tysiąclecia...*, p. 25).

54 "Odezwa Ogólnopolskiego Komitetu Frontu Jedności Narodu", *Rada Narodowa* 7, 15 II 1964, p. 3.

55 The Polish National Liberation Committee was established in Moscow on July 20, 1944. It was a usurpatory, provisional authority that served as a communist government on the Polish lands then liberated from German occupation. On July 22, 1944, the PKWN's manifesto was proclaimed in Chełm, which constituted the political program of the new authorities (this date was the symbolic beginning of People's Poland and thus was celebrated as the state holiday, the Day of Poland's Rebirth). The Polish National Liberation Committee organized its own administration, a police apparatus, and expanded the army; it fought against the legal institutions of the Polish Underground State by means of terror. On December 31, 1944, it was renamed the Provisional Government of the Republic of Poland.

56 A. Zawadzki, "Front Jedności Narodu w obchodach XX-lecia Polski Ludowej", *Rada Narodowa* 7, 15 II 1964, p. 8–9.

the Bug to the Oder and Lusatian Neisse Rivers, but also a turning point in the thousand-year history of the state and its socio-economic development. It was also the date of the Polish nation's start toward "a new life, toward a better, just social system – toward socialism".[57]

The state's turn to the past led to the fact that scholars played a significant role in celebrating the TPP, above all historians and archaeologists. During the celebrations of the TPP, three large congresses and scientific conferences devoted to Poland's past took place. From June 21–23, 1960, at the Staszic Palace in Warsaw, a scientific conference was held on the beginnings of the Polish state, organized by the Polish Academy of Sciences and the KNOTPP. Alongside historians and archaeologists, representatives of other scientific disciplines also took part in these deliberations – among them were: art historians, ethnographers, linguists, and conservators. Many scholars from Czechoslovakia, East Germany, Hungary, and the USSR were in attendance.[58]

The 1st International Congress of Slavic Archaeology took place in Warsaw over September 14–18, 1965. The deliberations gathered over two-hundred foreign participants (delegations arrived from: England, Austria, Belgium, Bulgaria, Czechoslovakia, France, East Germany, West Germany, Hungary, Italy, the Netherlands, Norway, Romania, Switzerland, Sweden, the USSR, and Yugoslavia) and just as many Polish participants.[59] The chairman of the Congress's organizing committee and its presidium was prof. Witold Hensel.[60] The 1st International Congress of Slavic Archaeology was the first in the history of archaeological research on the Slavic past to make such a comprehensive attempt to discuss the achievements and further development of Polish science. The intention of the scholars was for the deliberations to serve "progressive scientific thought" and the rapprochement between scholars representing differing ideological attitudes and directions of scientific thinking.[61] The subject matter of the proceedings was

---

57 "Przemówienie na akademii w Warszawie z okazji XX-lecia PRL" [in:] W. Gomułka, *Przemówienia, lipiec 1964–grudzień 1966*, Warszawa 1967, p. 7–8.
58 "Sesja naukowa PAN poświęcona początkom Państwa Polskiego", *Życie Szkoły Wyższej* 13/7/8, 1960, p. 230–231; "Sesja o początkach Państwa Polskiego", *Trybuna Ludu*, 22 VI 1960.
59 A. Gieysztor, "Ludy i kultury słowiańskie w starożytności i średniowieczu", *Życie Warszawy*, 5 X 1965.
60 "Skład Komitetu Organizacyjnego i Prezydium I Międzynarodowego Kongresu Archeologii Słowiańskiej", [in:] *I Międzynarodowy Kongres Archeologii Słowiańskiej, Warszawa 14–18 IX 1965*, vol. 1, Wrocław, Warszawa, Kraków p. 6–7.
61 Ibidem, p. 11.

broad, which, in the intention of the organizers, was to help in the review of the topics then pursued in many countries in the field of archaeological and historical Slavic studies.[62] The Congress consolidated the conviction that, along with Mediterranean archeology, Slavic archeology was at that time at the forefront of the archaeological sciences. Moreover, the role of Polish and Soviet scholars in this field was brought into relief. It was also made clear that many scholars from non-Slavic countries (especially English, French, and Italians) were also interested in this area of research.[63]

The final large scientific conference of the TPP was organized on November 23 and 24, 1966 in the halls of the Royal Castle on Wawel. This was a scientific conference devoted to the thousand-year history of Poland. It summarized the achievements of Polish science during the TPP celebrations from 1960 to 1966. PAN and the Jagiellonian University (Kraków) were the organizers of the conference. Besides the scholars, the representatives of the highest state and party authorities attended.[64] During the conference, Prime Minister Józef Cyrankiewicz took the floor, stressing that the Kraków conference was a summary of the achievements of historical science related to the Thousand Years. Cyrankiewicz also discussed the role of historiography in national history and pointed to the danger of harnessing it for political purposes (sic!), and by way of example he cited Germany. This statement resounded with exceptional cynicism in the context of TPP celebrations, the essence of which consisted in the use of the past by the communist state as a tool for the political struggle against the Church. In his speech, Cyrankiewicz stated that the historical experiences of the Eastern European nations had been transformed into a common policy that "constituted an impassable barrier" for "revisionist" tendencies. During the session, the participants of the session listened to papers devoted to pivotal issues from the history of Poland and the course of the TPP celebrations.[65]

---

62 *I Międzynarodowy Kongres Archeologii Słowiańskiej, Warszawa 14–18 IX 1965*, vol. 1–7, Wrocław, Warszawa, Kraków 1968–1972
63 A. Gieysztor, "Ludy..."
64 "Sesja naukowa na Wawelu", *Trybuna Ludu*, 24 XI 1966. A review of the session: T. P. Rutkowski, *Nauki historyczne...*, p. 441–443.
65 These were in turn the papers by: prof. Henryk Jabłoński, "The contribution of Polish science to the celebration of the One-Thousand Years of the Polish State"; prof. Bogusław Leśnodorski, "The Difficulty and Value of the Polish State"; and doc. dr Feliks Tycha, "Social forces in the historical process of Poland". For more on this topic see: *Sesja naukowa na Wawelu...*; on the content of these papers, see: "Zakończenie sesji na Wawelu", *Trybuna Ludu*, 25 XI 1966.

The Letter of the Polish Bishops and the State-Church confrontation, 1965–1966

During the millennial confrontation, Gomułka's team used history as a tool to fight against the Church, as he did in the conflict that occurred in connection with the "Letter of the Polish Bishops to Their German Brothers in Christ's Pastoral Office", which was handed to the German episcopate on November 18, 1965.[66]

During the debates of the final, fourth session of the Second Vatican Council, Polish bishops sent 56 letters to the world's episcopates, the World Ecumenical Council, and the Orthodox Patriarch of Constantinople, Athenagoras. They were in the form of a notification about the upcoming celebrations of the Millennium of Poland's Baptism. The bishops asked for prayer of behalf of the Millennium, stressed the religious and historical ties of the Polish Church and the Church in various countries, highlighted both its joyful and painful experiences, and invited the addresses to take part in the Millennium celebrations in Poland.

The Polish Bishops' Letter in 1965 had both religious and moral as well as political significance. Ahead of its time, it flew in the teeth of the Cold War status quo binding in Bonn-Warsaw-Moscow relations. Bringing up the then controversial and at the same time delicate problem of relations between the PRL and West Germany, the Polish bishops, over the heads of the politicians, sought to reconcile the two nations and, at variance with the geopolitical conditions then, placed Poland in the realm of Western civilization. Contrary to the official state-party interpretation of history then binding in Poland, the hierarchs presented their own historiosophical analysis of Polish-German relations in their Letter. The most important place was occupied by recent history, in particular WWII with its consequences for both nations. The bishops noted that as a result of those events, mutual relations between Poland and Germany were "heavily burdened". These relations were further burdened by the "flashpoint" in the form of Poland's western border on the Oder and Lusatian Neisse Rivers. Despite this "situation all but hopelessly burdened with the past", the members of the Polish

---

66 The circumstances behind the creation of the Message have not yet been thoroughly clarified. See: J. Rydel, "Nowe elementy mozaiki. Nieznane niemieckie dokumenty dyplomatyczne o Liście Biskupów z 1965 roku", *Więź* 1, 2011, p. 101–110. E. K. Czaczkowska, *Kardynał Wyszyński*, Warszawa 2009, p. 471–472; E. Gigilewicz, "Orędzie biskupów polskich do ich niemieckich braci w Chrystusowym urzędzie pasterskim", [in:] *Encyklopedia katolicka*, vol. 14, ed. E. Gigilewicz et al., Lublin 2010, p. 751–752.

Episcopate appealed for dialogue.[67] The bishops also presented in their Message the premises and implementation of the program for the Great Novena. In their intentions, the upcoming celebrations of the millennial jubilee year (1966) were to become an opportunity for Poles and Germans to examine their conscience and forgive each other's guilt.[68]

All this posed a difficult intellectual challenge for the laity and people of the Church in Poland and West Germany, who were not yet ready to seek mutual understanding. The effects of the hecatomb of WWII were still strongly felt in Poland. On the other hand, a significant part of German society (including Catholics) could not get over the post-war loss of their lands in the east, nor forget about the painful experiences connected with the *Flucht und Vertreibung*, for which Poles were deemed co-responsible.[69]

The communist power apparatus in Poland did not see (or did not want to see) the Christian aspect of the bishops' letter and deemed it a political gesture

---

67 The Vatican, November 18, 1965, see: "Orędzie biskupów polskich do ich niemieckich braci w Chrystusowym urzędzie pasterskim", [in:] P. Raina, *Kościół w PRL. Kościół katolicki a państwo w świetle dokumentów 1945–1989*, vol. 2: *Lata 1960–1974*, Poznań 1995, p. 361.

68 Ibidem, p. 362. Although he signed the Message, Primate Wyszyński was reserved about the possibility of Polish-German reconciliation. For instance, during a conversation with Minister Kazimierz Kąkol in Choszczówka (Oct. 12, 1979) he was to have said: "I adhere to the precept that we must never fight on two fronts. The Germans can never be believed", c.f. B. Noszczak, "Spotkanie kierownika Urzędu do Spraw Wyznań Kazimierza Kąkola z prymasem Wyszyńskim (Choszczówka, 12 X 1979)", *Zeszyty Historyczne* 169, Paris 2009, p. 153. For more on the topic of Cardinal Wyszyński's attitude toward Germany and the Germans, see: E. K. Czaczkowska, *Kardynał Wyszyński...*, p. 469–470.

69 In 1965, the editor-in-chief of "Würzburger Kirchenzeitung", Fr. Helmut Holzapfel, in a letter to Alfonso Erb, wrote: "All the greater consternation is caused by the hatred to Poland, evisceral as it is among German Catholics, as well, as so many letters have convinced me. Anti-Semitism has been legally banned among us [in Germany], and so anti-Polonism runs all the more wild", c. f. B. Kerski, T. Kycia, R. Żurek, "*Przebaczamy i prosimy o przebaczenie*". *Orędzie biskupów polskich i odpowiedź niemieckiego episkopatu z 1965 r. Geneza, kontekst, spuścizna*, Olsztyn 2006, p. 16. On December 5, 1965, the *Greetings of the German Bishops to their Polish Brothers in the Episcopate's Mission, and a reply to the letter of November 18, 1965* were published. This document was more balanced in tone than the Polish Message. The German hierarchs did not explicitly support the inviolable and final character of Poland's western border. This stance disappointed the Polish bishops, see: "Communiqué of the Polish Episcopacy, Rome, Dec. 5, 1965 r." [in:] *Orędzie biskupów polskich...*, p. 25–26.

unnecessary and detrimental to the raison d'état of the PRL. The team of the First Secretary of the Central Committee of the PZPR, who was aware of the loss of the field in the struggle against the Millennium that he had inspired, used the Letter as a convenient excuse for a massive political and propaganda strike against the episcopate and its program of celebrating the great jubilee of Polish Christianity. Referring to historical examples – primarily ones related to the crimes committed by the Germans on Poles during WWII – the communist rulers sought to undermine not only the rank of the Letter, but also accused the Church of acting to the detriment of Poland and the Poles.

Making avail of the anti-German moods in December 1965, the communists initiated the largest propaganda campaign against the Church in the history of the PRL. Its purpose was to drive a wedge between the episcopate and Primate Wyszyński on the one hand, and the lower clergy and laity on the other. Having an important place in this new round of the anti-Church campaign were references to history.

The "Notes and proposals in connection with the Polish bishops' letter addressed to the German bishops", prepared by the Administrative Department of the Central Committee of the PZPR, included a propaganda action plan that was to condemn the Church's attitude as "anti-national" and "anti-socialist", and also as conducive to German "revisionism". An important aspect of the anti-Church campaign was to show the Church's alleged falsification of the history of Poland.[70]

The involvement of scholars, especially party members, in anti-Church propaganda was for many of them, especially among the younger generation, an opportunity to emphasize their support for the authorities, something which opened the way for a future career. Such opportunism sometimes caused conflicts among party activists, especially on generational lines. The state's policy was also criticized by some of the academic staff associated with the Church.

In the last ten days of December 1965, representatives of the local state administration began talks with deans, parish priests, and parish administrators about the Letter of the Polish Bishops. During those talks historical themes related to Polish-German relations were brought up.[71] In light of the assessments of the

---

70 "Protokół z posiedzenia Komisji KC d/s Kleru w dniu 30 XII 1965 r.", [in:] *Tajne dokumenty...*, p. 166. Also see: AAN, BP KC PZPR, XIA/179, Protokół nr 23 posiedzenia BP KC PZPR z 8 XII 1965. On various aspects of the anti-Church policy against the Message see: A. Dudek, *Państwo i Kościół...*, p. 185; P. Madajczyk, *Na drodze...*, p. 130–131; T. P. Rutkowski, *Nauki historyczne...*, p. 436–441.
71 P. Raina, *Kardynał Wyszyński. Orędzie biskupów a reakcja władz*, Warszawa 1995, p. 61–62.

Administrative Department of the PZPR Central Committee of March 1966, the campaign had achieved its goal. The Letter was critically assessed by 53 percent of parish priests; 25 percent of them did not take a clear position on this matter, and 22 percent attempted to defend the Message. These results were considered a significant achievement. It was also noted that there was a considerable distance between the lower diocesan clergy and the episcopate.[72] The general surprise and indignation of Poles over the Letter was also noted by the secret political police.[73]

Poland's communist rulers, hoping to divide the episcopate and undermine the position of Primate Wyszyński, inspired talks that were held from January 27 to February 5, 1966 with the bishops in the presidia of the provincial national councils. Summarizing their results, it was stated that the bishops defended the content and "positive effects" of the Letter. They often expressed astonishment, indignation, or sharp protest over the untrue interpretations aired by the authorities, the printed press, radio, and television regarding the intentions of the document.[74] Therefore, in the subsequent months the state focused its propaganda attacks on the person of the Primate.[75]

During the meeting of the Nationwide Committee of the Front for National Unity in Warsaw on January 14, 1966, Władysław Gomułka took the floor.[76] The First Secretary of the PZPR's Central Committee stressed that the Message had deep political content and accused the episcopate of a policy aimed at attacking Poland. In his speech, Gomułka for the first time officially pointed to the Church's effort to juxtapose its program of celebrating the Millennium to the state's concept of the celebration of the One-Thousand Years of the Polish State.[77]

The communists analyzed the situation related to the "millennial clash" between the state and the Church on an ongoing basis and, depending on the

---

72 "Ocena rozmów z proboszczami i administratorami parafii na temat 'Orędzia' sporządzona przez Wydział Administracyjny KC PZPR z marca 1966 r", [in:] *Tajne dokumenty…*, p. 206–211.
73 AAN, KC PZPR, 237/VII/5295, Opracowanie Departamentu IV MSW z 17 XII 1965 r., p. 53–64.
74 "Ocena rozmów z biskupami sporządzona przez Wydział Administracyjny KC PZPR w lutym 1966 r". [in:] *Tajne dokumenty…*, p. 173, 174.
75 A. Friszke, "Sprawozdanie Głównego Zarządu Politycznego WP z akcji propagandowo-odczytowej na wsi, rozmów z klerem oraz Sztafet Tysiąclecia, maj 1966", *Więź* 2, 1994, nr 2, p. 154.
76 "Przemówienie na plenarnej sesji Ogólnopolskiego Komitetu Frontu Jedności Narodu, 14 I 1966 r". [in:] W. Gomułka, *Przemówienia. Lipiec 1964–grudzień 1966*, Warszawa 1967, p. 398.
77 Ibidem, p. 401–403.

unfolding of events, they nimbly altered the program of the TPP's celebrations to effectively compete with the Millennium. An important role in this was played by history. The Press Office of the Central Committee of the PZPR paid attention to the new situation caused by the Message, which required supplementing the TPP's program with new elements in the form of national content and themes.[78] In connection with the fact that the main Church celebrations of the Millennium were to take place at Jasna Góra on May 3, 1966, the 175th anniversary of the May 3 Constitution[79], it was considered harmful if, in the opinion of part of society, the Church and the post-war political émigrés sympathetic with the Polish authorities residing in exile in London "were considered the heirs, advocates, and defenders of the traditions of May 3".[80] In the opinion of the Polish historian Marcin Zaremba, for the party authorities the rivalry with the Church was a conflict for nationalist legitimacy: that rivalry was to declare who – the Church or the communist party – was the heir of the national tradition.[81]

In this situation, the members of the Press Bureau of the Central Committee of the PZPR proposed shifting the TPP's center of gravity from the Day of Poland's Rebirth (July 22) to Labor Day (May 1). The celebrations commemorating the anniversary of the May 3 Constitution were to take place on May 1 and combine two traditions – namely, the workers' and peasants' Labor Day and the celebration of the TPP. On December 22, 1965, at the meeting of the Secretariat of the Central Committee of the PZPR, it was decided to organize the main celebrations of the TPP on May 1 and July 22, 1966.[82]

---

78 M. Zaremba, *Komunizm...*, p. 318–319.
79 The anniversary of the adoption of the Constitution of May 3rd, 1791, which became a symbol of independence aspirations in the historical consciousness of Poles, was aimed primarily at the domination of Poland by Russia. Its celebration was forbidden during the partitions of Poland (1772/1793/1795–1918). May 3rd Constitution Day was introduced to the official calendar of national holidays only after Poland regained its independence, and was then solemnly celebrated in 1919–1939. During WWII, it was made illegal by both the German and Soviet occupiers. Following anti-communist demonstrations on May 3rd, 1946, it was replaced by the holiday of May Day (Labor Day), which the communists gave the status of a public holiday. In 1951, the May 3rd Constitution Day was officially banned in Poland by the communist authorities.
80 M. Zaremba, *Komunizm...*, p. 318–319.
81 Ibidem, p. 318.
82 Ibidem, p. 319.

The celebrations of the One-Thousand Years of the Polish State in 1966

The entire jubilee year of 1966 was marked by a state-inspired conflict with the Church.[83] With the help of the administrative apparatus, the communists sought above all to reduce the number of people participating in the Church's celebration of the Millennium. As part of this struggle there was also a "fratricidal" fight for Polish culture of memory. It was not a coincidence that the subsequent central Church ceremonies also contained in their programs various kinds of presentations (lectures, sessions, readings, etc.) by historians who offered their audiences a picture of history (primarily the history of the Church in Poland) free from the ideological pressure of the communist state. On the other hand, the Gomułka regime, which at the same time was holding its own secular events, presented an alternative picture of Poland's past, one that accentuated secular threads and eliminated or criticized the otherwise unquestionable millennial oeuvre and contribution of the Church to political, cultural, and social life.

The state events in the jubilee year were appropriately synchronized with Church undertakings and they lasted a certain time before and after their completion. This activity was spread over the entirety of 1966 and part of 1967.[84] The goal of the state authorities was not only to draw Poles away from Church events, but also to show the traditions and achievements of the Polish nation in the past thousand years, with particular emphasis on the "achievements" of the 20 years of People's Poland.[85]

From the meeting of the Party and Government Commission for the TPP celebrations of March 29, 1966, the state authorities coordinated efforts to create a program of secular celebrations aimed not only at organizing events designed

---

83 *Milenium czy Tysiąclecie*, ed. B. Noszczak, Warszawa 2006; *Milenium kontra Tysiąclecie – 1966*, ed. K. Białecki, S. Jankowiak, J. Miłosz, Poznań 2006; *Millennium polskie. Walka o rząd dusz*, ed. C. Wilamowski, Warszawa 2002; B. Noszczak, *Sacrum czy profanum?...*, p. 163–164. P. Raina, *Kardynał Wyszyński. Konflikty roku milenijnego 1966*, Warszawa 2000; S. Wyszyński, *Zapiski milenijne. Wybór z dziennika „Pro memoria" z lat 1965-1967*, Warszawa 2001; *Zapomniany rok 1966. W XXX rocznicę obchodów Milenium Chrztu Polski*, ed. L. Mażewski, W. Turek, Gdańsk 1996. On the Millennium synthesis, see: D. Gucewicz, "Polski rok 1966. Ku syntezie obchodów polskiego tysiąclecia", [in:] *Czas próby. Kościół katolicki w okresie PRL*, ed. W. Polak, A. Czwołk, S. Galij-Skarbińska, Toruń 2017, p. 155–156.
84 "Protokół z posiedzenia Prezydium Komisji Partyjno-Rządowej ds. Uroczystości Tysiąclecia w dniu 15 III 1966 r.", [in:] *Tajne dokumenty...*, p. 215.
85 Ibidem, p. 221.

History as a tool in the state's struggle against the Catholic Church 267

to paralyze and pull the faithful away from Church celebrations, but also aimed at showing the Poles' "traditions and the achievements of our nation over the last 1,000 years, with particular emphasis on the achievements of the twentieth anniversary of the Polish People's Republic".[86] A framework record of the TPP celebrations in 1966 was created by the Administrative Department and the Propaganda and Agitation Department of the Central Committee of the PZPR (a scenario of preparations was presented for Gomułka's approval on April 5), which was based on proposals presented by the State Commission for the TPP Celebrations, which met on March 24. The culmination of the celebrations was the July 22 celebration organized in the capital of Poland. The plan from December 1965 to include the Labor Day was abandoned. Besides, many other events were also planned for the calendar of state celebrations.[87]

Over April 9–16, 1966, Church ceremonies took place in the first historical capital of Poland – Gniezno, which inaugurated the celebration of the Nation's *Te Deum'* Year. At that same time (April 16) a patriotic manifestation took place in the city, one which launched the central ceremony of the state celebrations of the One-Thousand Years of the Polish State and the 21st anniversary of the crossing of the Oder and Lusatian Neisse Rivers by the soldiers of the First and Second Polish People's Army. This last anniversary was a propaganda farce; not only was it not a "round" anniversary, but it had never been celebrated so solemnly.

On that day, leading representatives of the state authorities, headed by Poland's Marshal Marian Spychalski, a member of the Political Bureau of the Central Committee of the PZPR, came to Gniezno.[88] After the official opening of the ceremony, he delivered a speech emphasizing the independence traditions of Greater Poland (Wielkopolska, the region centered on Poznań), the development of the "Recovered Territories", the contribution of the inhabitants of Wielkopolska to the construction of the "Thousand-Year Schools", and the increase in the standards of living and culture. The next part of the Marshal's speech was devoted to the Church. Spychalski argued that it was conducting a political fight and strove to oppose the state with its Millennium celebrations.[89] He also stressed the danger of German "revisionists" and stressed the commitment of the communist states

---

86 C.f.: T. Krawczak, *Centralne władze…*, p. 16.
87 Ibidem, p. 16–18.
88 "Manifestacja patriotyczna w Tysiącleciu Państwa Polskiego. Wielki dzień Gniezna", *Życie Warszawy*, 17 IV 1966; "Rozpoczęcie tegorocznych uroczystości Tysiąclecia Państwa Polskiego", *Trybuna Ludu*, 17 IV 1966.
89 "Przemówienie tow. Mariana Spychalskiego", *Trybuna Ludu*, 17 IV 1966.

to "fight for peace". The culmination of the state ceremonies in Gniezno was the announcement of the foundation act of the monument of Mieszko I and his son and successor, as well as the first King of Poland from the Piast dynasty, Boleslaus the Brave (Bolesław Chrobry, 992–1025).

Thus it was in Gniezno that, for the first time, the open and "institutional" clash between the state and the Church in the year of the millennium jubilee took place. From that moment on, this phenomenon was indeed a permanent element of the jubilee celebrations of 1966. The response to the successive central celebrations of the Church at various bishopric seats was that of state counter-celebrations. Over the following months of 1966 and 1967, this paradigm, as played out by the communist authorities in Gniezno, was repeated from one location to the next. The celebration of the Church's festivities were limited as much as possible by means of oppressive measures – e.g., through obstruction of the roads pilgrims took, not allowing days off or other types of leave, additional classes at schools and colleges, shrill public speeches by the authorities against the Church and Primate Wyszyński, etc. Behind-the-scenes harassment and sowing of chaos was conducted by the Security Service, i.e., the PRL's secret political police. At the same time, the authorities tried to draw the Catholics away from participating in Church celebrations through attractive programs in the mass media, cultural events, various entertainment spectacles, sporting events, etc. It was also important that the narrative of the Church's people at the Millennium celebrations met with the counter-narrative of the people in power.

Illustrating this phenomenon were the celebrations in Katowice, the most important goal of which was to weaken the turnout and importance of the central Millennium celebrations at Jasna Góra (May 3, 1966). In order to counteract the Millennium in the Katowice voivodeship, the state authorities planned the erection of the Silesian Insurgents Monument in the region's capital. The pretext was the 45th anniversary of the outbreak of the Third Silesian Uprising. The local press reported this investment and prepared the Silesians for a big rally combined with the act of laying the cornerstone for the future monument.[90]

No doubt what additionally impacted the reduced attendance at Jasna Góra was the fact that May 3 was a working day, about which superiors demanded discipline – and it also fell in the period of intense farm work. On the same day in Katowice, during the large state ceremony, the cornerstone for the construction of the Silesian Insurgents monument was ceremonially laid, along with an urn

---

90 Ł. Marek, *"Kler to nasz wróg". Polityka władz państwowych wobec Kościoła katolickiego na terenie województwa katowickiego w latach 1956–1970*, Katowice 2009, p. 388.

containing soil taken from 21 battlefields. Representatives of the highest party-state authorities came to the city. The Katowice ceremonies were reported to have drawn up to 700,000 people.[91] If we are to believe the official data, this would be the record for the whole year of the great jubilee. The local press reported that it was "a powerful manifestation, constituting an integral part of the central celebrations of the 1,000th anniversary of the Polish state".[92] The construction of the monument lasted over a year, with its ceremonial unveiling taking place on September 1–2, 1967.

An important component of the anti-Church policy of the Gomułka team in 1966 was also the traversing all across Poland of the "Thousand-Year Relays". Two of them set off on April 16. The first one went from Chełm Lubelski to Kołobrzeg along the combat trail of the First Polish People's Army. On May 6 the relay forked: one tine went further on to Kołobrzeg, whereas the second pressed on to Siekierki. The second relay race set off from Bogatynia to Szczecin along the border of the Oder and Lusatian Neisse Rivers. A day later (April 17) the next two relay races were begun – from Białystok to Gdańsk and from Lublin to Zgorzelec (following the route of the Second Polish People's Army). On May 1 another relay race set off from Kruszwica to Zgorzelec. All of them were to finish their routes on May 8 and May 9 (the last date was celebrated in the PRL, as in the entire Eastern Bloc, as V-Day, commemorating the end of WWII in Europe). Altogether, the "Thousand-Year Relays" wound through sixteen provinces, 104 major cities, and some 8,000 towns and villages.[93]

About 150,000 people (including 20,000 soldiers), mostly youth, participated in the relay marches. They were organized into over 2,000 teams that represented various socio-political organizations, sports clubs and associations, schools and workplaces, self-defense units, and military units. These formations crossed certain sections of the routes by foot, on bicycles, motorcycles, cars, on horseback, and even on horse-drawn wagons.

At the 640 rallies and gatherings, 89 jamborees, and 850 concerts that took place on the occasion of the "Thousand-Year Relays", about 3 million people took part (according to official state data, which were doubtlessly inflated).[94] At the various stages of the relays, accompanying events were included in the programs for the May 1 celebrations. On the days of the celebration of the 21st anniversary

---

91 Ibidem, p. 392.
92 Ibidem, p. 391.
93 "Główny Zarząd Polityczny WP: Sprawozdanie z akcji propagandowo-spotkaniowej na wsi, rozmów z klerem oraz Sztafet Tysiąclecia, maj 1966", Więź 3, 1994, p. 93.
94 Ibidem, p. 94.

of the victory over Germany, the ceremony of finishing the relay race in Gdańsk, Kołobrzeg, Szczecin, and Zgorzelec was combined with the decoration of veterans of the Polish People's Army.[95]

The various teams on the relay routes carried "Relay Books" containing an appeal having the character of a political declaration.[96] This appeal was read at rallies. It was also signed by representatives of the local authorities, socio-political organizations, youth organizations, and the army, all of which declared their support for its theme. After the end of the relay, all such books were placed in regional museums located at the destinations of the "Thousand-Year Relay Race". Playing a huge role in these relays were manifestations that hearkened to Polish history, especially to events of a patriotic and anti-war character. These manifestations took place at the official stages and sub-stages along the routes.

In the conditions of the time, the "Thousand-Year Relays" were a relatively attractive form for the centrally-controlled demonstration of society's patriotism and political involvement. In many regions they played an inspiring role in making commitments and boosting volunteerism. They fostered the popularization of Poland's past (especially its military traditions), showcased the "achievements" People's Poland had attained in its 20 years, and the idea of "people's defense". The relays demonstrated the organizational efficiency of the party's local rungs, as well as of the administrative authorities, military staffs and other institutions. They also elicited initiative and the significant activity of the population in small towns and across the countryside.

The nationwide propaganda campaigns undertaken by the Polish People's Army in the spring of 1966 constituted the most massive political campaign in small towns and villages since 1956. The aim of Gomułka's team was for them to be an expression of society's trust and support for the policy of the state authorities of the PRL. They were to testify to the condemnation of German revisionists and the "anti-national" activities of a portion of the episcopate, as well as to contribute to the weakening interest and participation of a large part of society in the Church's Millennium celebrations. Precise definition of how well these objectives were met requires further research.

The celebrations of the TPP organized in the small town of Cedynia, located on the Oder River, were of special significance. In January 1945 there was fighting near the town with the participation of Polish Army troops, as a result of which it was possible to force the Oder, and then launch the offensive on Berlin. After

---

95 "Sztafety Tysiąclecia na mecie", *Trybuna Ludu*, 9 V 1966.
96 "Apel Sztafet Tysiąclecia", *Trybuna Ludu*, 17 IV 1966.

the post-war borders were established, Cedynia became the westernmost town of Poland. It is here that some historians located the first battle specifically mentioned in the historical sources on Poland. For it was at Cedynia in 972 where the troops of Mieszko I fought against an army commanded by the German nobleman Hodon, nota bene against the wishes of Emperor Otto I (962–973), who maintained good relations with the Polanian ruler. After WWII, the authorities of the PRL, as part of the policy legitimizing Poland's rights to the "Recovered Territories" and the new western border on the Oder and Lusatian Neisse Rivers, stylized the clash of 972 as the "first border battle with Germany" within the (purported!) "thousand-year" struggle of Poles against the Germanic *Drang nach Osten*. In 1966, a massive patriotic demonstration was organized at the probable site of the battle. During it, the appeal was read out of the "fallen victors" from Cedynia, as well as from other battles between Poles and Germans – including Grunwald in 1410 and Berlin in 1945. At the permanent exhibition of the Regional Museum in that jubilee year, artefacts were shown from archaeological excavations carried out at the battlefield of Cedynia. The town was also visited by participants of mass TPP events, including the Thousand-Year Relay.[97]

The central celebrations of the TPP jubilee were celebrated by the Gomułka team as planned on July 21–22, 1966 in Warsaw. On the Day of Poland's Rebirth (22 July), a great military parade, a youth manifestation, and a sports parade took place in Warsaw – these were the culminating events of the final year of the TPP celebrations.

---

97 B. Brzostek, "PRL: propaganda czy polityka historyczna?" [in:] *Polityka czy propaganda. PRL wobec historii*, ed. P. Skibiński, T. Wiścicki, Warszawa 2009, p. 57–86; P. Migdalski, *...w tej strażnicy Rzeczypospolitej. Rejon Pamięci Narodowej Cedynia-Gozdowice-Siekierki*, Szczecin-Poznań 2007; Ł. Polniak, *Patriotyzm wojskowy w PRL w latach 1956–1970*, Warszawa 2011. It is also worth mentioning that during the ceremonial celebration of the millennium of the Battle of Cedynia in 1972, the Monument of Polish Victory over the Oder was erected on the hill near Cedynia. This was to associate the clash in 972 with battles in 1945. In addition, Cedynia's two historicizing mosaics depicting battle scenes show the Germans in stereotypically dark costumes. (P. Migdalski, "Obchody tysiąclecia bitwy pod Cedynią w 1972 r. w świetle prasy regionalnej", [in:] *Prasa jako źródło do dziejów Śląska i Pomorza w XIX i XX w.*, ed. E. Włodarczyk, J. Nowosielska-Sobel, Szczecin 2005, p. 159–182). Owing to these propaganda efforts, the relatively minor clash of 972 in Cedynia became a "foundation myth" in the historical consciousness of Poles – similar to the half-legendary battle in the Teutoburg Forest waged in 9 AD between Germanic tribes led by Arminius and Roman legions in the German culture of memory. P. Migdalski, D. Mellies, "Bitwa w Lesie Teutoburskim i bitwa pod Cedynią. Bitwy w służbie narodowych mitów fundacyjnych", [in:] *Polsko-niemieckie...*, vol. 3, p. 107–124.

On Plac Defilad in downtown Warsaw, the largest display of armed forces in the PRL's history was reviewed by representatives of the highest party and state authorities, as well as by guests from abroad. The show was opened by an air parade, followed by a parade with a representative company of the Polish Army, its branches in historical uniforms, carrying battle standards. There were students from the military academies, mechanized armies, and a motorcycle column. After that, there was a parade of youth from all over Poland and a procession of athletes who concluded the central celebrations of the One-Thousand Years of the Polish State.[98]

In the second half of 1966, the conflict over the anniversary of Poland's Baptism waged between the state authorities and the Church slowly ebbed. Due to the superabundance of events in 1966, the Church transferred the Millennium celebrations in the following cities to the next year: Sosnowiec, Łódź, Tum, Kamień Pomorski, and Kołobrzeg. Then, too, state counter-celebrations were held.[99] For both sides, the time then came for summing up the profits and losses of the over nine-year Millennium campaign.

Summary

The term "politics of memory" was of course unknown and not used in the 50s and 60s. Despite this, the mechanism for "managing history" by Gomułka's team (in line with the operating logic of the PRL, the first secretaries of the Central Committee of the PZPR had a decisive influence on almost every aspect of the state policy)[100] does offer certain analogies with today's understanding of this kind of political activity.[101] However, it must be stressed that the decisions of

---

98   Z. Zamencki, "Wielka defilada wojskowa i imponująca parada młodzieży", *Trybuna Ludu*, 23–24 VII 1966.
99   Ł. Marek, *Kler to nasz wróg*..., p. 397–398. M. Trąba, *Kościół nie da się zagrodzić łańcuchami... Uroczystości milenijne w Sosnowcu (20–21 maja 1967)*, Katowice 2007; S. Wyszyński, *Zapiski*..., p. 245–246.
100 J. Eisler, *"Siedmiu wspaniałych". Poczet pierwszych sekretarzy KC PZPR*, Warszawa 2014.
101 More on this topic: *A European memory? Contested histories and politics of remembrance*, ed. M. Pakier, B. Stråth, New York 2012; *Damnatio memoriae w europejskiej kulturze politycznej*, ed. R. Gałaj-Dempniak, D. Okoń, M. Semczyszyn, Szczecin 2011; *Geschichtspolitik in Europa seit 1989. Deutschland, Frankreich und Polen im internationalen Vergleich*, ed. E. François, K. Kończal, R. Traba, S. Troebst, Göttingen 2013; *Kommunismusforschung und Erinnerungskulturen in Ostmittel und Westeuropa*, ed. M. Leppert, Köln 2013; *Narodowe i europejskie aspekty polityki historycznej*, ed. B. Korzeniewski, Poznań 2008; *Pamięć zbiorowa i kulturowa. Współczesna perspektywa niemiecka*, ed. M. Saryusz-Wolska, Kraków 2009; W. Pięciak, *Niemiecka pamięć. Współczesne spory w Niemczech o miejsce III Rzeszy w historii, polityce i tożsamości*

the communist power apparatus in Poland were made under the conditions of a state incapacitated by the USSR, by a state that was non-democratic and quasi-totalitarian, and which *de facto* was deprived of democratic control mechanisms. In this sense, it could exercise such policy in an almost absolute manner. In particular, the use and abuse of history in state politics of memory in Poland attained its apogee in the 1960s. It seems that never before and never afterward in the PRL was history used as a tool of political struggle to such a large and significant extent.

The politics of memory of Gomułka's team had a Janus face. It grew out of the necessity of the state's fight against the Church, which, thanks to the changes wrought by October '56, thereafter enjoyed such a stronger position that it openly competed with the power apparatus for the Poles' "hearts and minds" in the scope of the preparations for the jubilee of 1966. History as a science became a victim of the Millennium conflict, because it was mainly instrumentalized by the people of power, and indeed weaponized in the "fratricidal" struggle for memory. Within this framework, the state apparatus wanted to prove that the entire historical process associated with over a 1,000 years of Polish history was teleological, destined for the "crowning" in the form of People's Poland. This was not only an obvious deceit, but also a veritable scientific provocation. The actions of the First Secretary of the Central Committee of the PZPR in the field of history were dictated by current and pragmatic political goals, and in this respect they were negative.

The historicism dominant in the central celebrations of the One-Thousand Years of the Polish State often struck a forced, outright simplistic character. Artificial, and sometimes even folkloric, the character of the celebrations of historical anniversaries made many people feel fed up and adverse (commentators of the period noted this problem).[102] In this regard, the years 1960–1966 created a "millennial world of performances".

The TPP celebrations showed the extent to which state authorities used science to achieve political goals dictated by pragmatism. During the celebrations of the state's jubilee, the past was often treated selectively and even presentistly in order thereby to "justify" a given political thesis. In this respect, the celebrations of the TPP were an opportunity to use the past to sanction the present and show

---

(1989–2001), Kraków 2002; J. Rydel, *Polityka historyczna w Republice Federalnej Niemiec. Zaszłości, Idee, Praktyka*, Kraków 2011; *The politics of memory in postwar Europe*, ed. R. N. Lebow, W. Kansteiner, C. Fogu, Durham 2006.

102 K. Koźniewski, "Czy daliśmy się zmilleniować?", *Kwartalnik Historyczny* 73, 1966, p. 601–604.

that People's Poland was its only heir – the pinnacle of Polish history. This conception ideally fit within the framework of the doctrine of historical materialism, in which communism was the culmination of the historical process.

The process of appropriating history by the communist authorities was an attempt to impose on Poles beliefs about the unique character of the PRL. Such the case, history became a valuating factor. The exaggerated focus on the past also fostered the development of state-fueled nationalism, whose cutting-edge was pointed mainly at West Germany. Playing on anti-German prejudices and phobias was a leitmotif of communist propaganda throughout the TPP celebrations, and it culminated in the wake of the Letter of the Polish Bishops. This phenomenon perfectly suited the wider political context, because in the optics of Gomułka's power apparatus it "justified" before the general public the dependence of the PRL on the USSR, which was held up to be the only guarantor of the inviolability of Poland's western border.

Presentism in the interpretation of the past was, within the framework of the state's TPP celebrations, dictated by political need and by that same token it reflected negatively on the cognitive value of the content presented in this period. Propaganda speeches addressed to mass audiences were usually typified by distorted historical analysis. The works of science and popular-science were less impugnable in this regard. However, a thorough assessment of the cognitive quality and the substantive level of hundreds of various types of publications, exhibitions, brochures, etc. that were related to the TPP is still awaited.

Polish historian Tadeusz Paweł Rutkowski has written that evaluation of the TPP celebrations from the point of view of Polish science is not straightforward. The celebrations released substantial funds for research and engendered numerous publications among them scientific ones. Their effect was also the large-scale popularization of history, in which all Polish historical milieu, with the Polish Historical Society at the apex, took part. Nevertheless, in comparison with the enormous outlay of resources and the efforts of historians, the scientific achievements were not significant, in Rutkowski's opinion, especially since the price for them was the co-opting of the scientific community into the state's political campaign and confrontation with the Church, which had to result in the relative decline of the authority of official historiography.[103]

Polemically it should be noted that during the TPP, history as a science, and especially medievalism, evolved considerably and resulted in many valuable cognitive achievements that were not "contaminated" by the political needs of

---

103 T. P. Rutkowski, *Nauki historyczne...*, p. 434–444.

Poland's communist rulers. Gomułka's historical policy had positive effects for scholar-specialists dealing with the study of the past. The celebration of the TPP, saturated though it was with historicism, had an invigorating impact on the pace and scope of scientific research devoted to the history of Poland. In the period 1960–1966, science gained – and on an unprecedented scale – a powerful patron in the state. It was a golden period for historical science, which hungrily benefited from the possibilities (mainly that of funding) that state authorities unfurled for scholars. The spectrum that was opened for them was very wide indeed. For it involved not only excavation work[104], but also the possibility of publishing their results and editorial initiatives (including source publications, scientific and popular science monographs) and inventorying and protecting monuments of material and spiritual culture. It also gave an opportunity for initiating new scientific ventures and building a broad base for science (e.g., the project to build the National Library in Warsaw). Scientific conferences, numerous lectures, conversations popularizing knowledge about the past, meetings and discussions, several hundred exhibitions related to the subject of the Millennium of Poland, the increased interest in regional history, and the development of tourism on historical routes – this all fostered a deepening of society's historical awareness, as well as the development of education.

The numbers related to this unprecedented mass historical education that Poles then underwent reveal the scale of the phenomenon. According to official data, between 1960 and 1966 some 35,000 lectures and meetings on historical topics took place, ones that attracted 1.7 million people.[105] The number of people who participated in lectures on archaeological topics and visited exhibitions and excavation sites was similarly estimated at 1.5 million.[106]

However, there are indications that in their mass the Poles did not evince deep interest in the past, and their "millennium enthusiasm" was largely superficial and artificially choreographed by the communist state authorities. Of course,

---

104 Excavation works conducted during the TPP celebrations pushed back the beginnings of the formation of Polish cities and refuted the theory of the role of German colonization in their genesis. This kind of searches in: Gdańsk, Szczecin, Wolin, Kamień Pomorski, Kołobrzeg, Gniezno, Poznań, Kruszwica, Kraków, Opole, Wrocław, and Niemcza provided very abundant archaeological material that cast light, e.g., on the condition and level of craft production, the extent of stone construction (sacred and secular buildings), and the penetration of Christian beliefs into the Lesser Poland (Małopolska) region as early as in pre-Mieszko times.
105 "Przemówienie Piotra Gajewskiego", [in:] *Bilans obchodów...*, p. 35.
106 M. Dobrowolski, "Panorama jubileuszu", *Argumenty*, 3 IV 1966, p. 2.

the state's patronage was not largesse. The price that some scholars and scientists paid for the period of prosperity was that of becoming smaller or larger cogs in the state's ideological and propaganda machine that processed the past for the present's legitimacy.

The mass, nationwide celebrations of the One-Thousand Years of the Polish State required considerable organizational skills. In most cases, the celebrations were efficiently carried out. This does not change the fact that participation in them often was not so much a matter of invitation or "advertising", as people were literally compelled, e.g., via blackmail at work, college, and school, being told they would receive no bonus or holiday leave, etc. The other matter, of course, was the costs incurred by state events. At the numerous ceremonies, air shows, and military parade held in 1960–1966/1967, hundreds of millions of zlotys were spent. The exact costs associated with the organization of the TPP may never be known. But their scale was certainly huge. For instance, the spending planned in order to carry out the TPP celebrations in just the years 1958–1960 amounted to 26.5 million zlotys.[107]

The TPP did not meaningfully thwart the Church's preparations for the great jubilee and the celebrations of the Millennium of Poland's Baptism in 1966. It might have overshadowed them with its panache and color, but the spiritual and personal dimension of the Millennium, as well as the efficient and attractive organization of church ceremonies, attracted hosts of people into the orbit of the Church, and not necessarily only the faithful. Nor did society necessarily discern the dispute that was going on around the Millennium, especially before 1966. Believers and non-believers were no doubt none too bothered by participating one day in the state's TPP ceremony – and the next in the Church's Millennium celebrations. All the more as during the communist era, any celebration was an attraction and a break from everyday life. This does not change the fact that in parallel with the TPP celebrations, various behind-the-scenes efforts were being taken to torpedo the Millennium – particularly by the communist Security Service.

The Church and state programs for celebrating the great anniversary were carried out in parallel from 1960, but autonomously so. Both sides also perceived them in a one-dimensional way, which was something largely imposed by the political reality of the time, determined as it was by doctrinal differences – including

---

107 AAN, BP KC PZPR, V/60, Zestawienie postulatów budżetowych nad realizacją programu obchodów Tysiąclecia Państwa Polskiego w latach 1958–1960, Warszawa 1958, without page numbers.

the divergence of goals each party wanted to achieve during the celebrations, the lack of institutional cooperation, and the clash arisen from mutual prejudices. Despite the fact that there were objective premises for cooperation (e.g. the uniqueness of the anniversary, which in itself could become a unifying factor; the deepening of Poland's prestige in the world; the Polonization of the "Recovered Territories"; and the moral rejuvenation of society, something positive from the perspective of both the state and the Church) neither of the parties showed the will to join together within a framework of competitive ceremonies, but rather sought to draw the largest possible portion of society to their own side. Inevitably, the conflict waged by the communist state authorities against the Church negatively affected the course and character of the celebrations of the Millennium. The celebrations of the millennial anniversary of Poland's Baptism, instead of uniting and strengthening society, yielded bitter fruit in the form of deepening the existing divisions between those who were faithful to the Church and those faithful to the party.

Translated by Philip Earl Steele

Vasyl' M. Tkachenko

The inseparable heritage of early medieval Rus'. On the celebration of the 1,150th anniversary of the origin of Russian statehood[1]

Abstract: The chapter discusses the current politics of memory of the Russian Federation in the context of the 1,150th anniversary of the origin of Russian statehood. The main celebrations of the anniversary took place on September 21–23, 2012 in Veliky Novgorod. Despite this, it seems that no consensus as to the date of the original event has ever been reached among the representatives of Russian academia – neither is there any unanimous interpretation of its meaning. Indeed, Russia's jubilee activities were among the matters that influenced the rise of vigilance among Ukrainian scholars concerning the issue of Ukrainian national identity. This attitude is illustrated by numerous publications on the subject of the historic past, published both in scholarly journals and in the commercial press.

Keywords: origins of the Russian statehood, Veliky Novgorod, Kievan Rus', Ukrainian identity, politics of memory

On March 5, 2011, the Presidential Decree No. 267 from March 3, 2011 *On the celebration of the 1,150th anniversary of the origin of Russian statehood* (*O prazdnovanii 1150-letija zarozhdenija rossijskoj gosudarstvennosti*) was published in the Russian Federation. It stipulated that "in order to further consolidate Russian society"[2], the President of the Russian Federation decrees to "take the leadership" of the governmental position "regarding the celebration of the 1,150th anniversary of the origin of Russian statehood" in 2012. The respective steering committee was made responsible for the main activities pertaining to the festivities.[3] The Russian media informed the public that "in 862 AD Rurik

---

1   This chapter is an abbreviated, translated version of the following article: V. M. Tkachenko, "Nepodil'na spadshchina Davn'oï Rusi (pro svjatkuvannja 1150-richja zarodzhennja rosijs'koï derzhavnosti)", *Problemi vsesvitn'oï istoriï: naukovij zhurnal* 1, 2016, p. 24–51.
2   Unless explicitly stated otherwise, all in-text quotations were translated by the translator of the paper.
3   Ukaz Prezidenta Rossijskoj Federacii ot 3 marta 2011. No. 267, [electronic resource] available at: https://rg.ru/2011/03/05/1150-site-dok.html.

took power in Novgorod, and this date is traditionally considered to be 'the starting point' for Russia".[4] The main festivities were to take place on September 21–23, 2012 in Veliky Novgorod. Despite this, it seems that no consensus as to the date of the anniversary[5*] has ever been reached among the representatives of Russian academia – neither is there any unanimous interpretation of the date.[6]

How did the Ukrainian public react to the anniversary initiatives taken in Russia? The famous columnist Ihor Losiev asked in a tone of surprise: "Does this mean that in 862 Anno Domini Russia already existed?", and further: "Who in our country will respond to this 'soft', but rather dangerous challenge? Where is our divided intelligentsia who constantly brawl and entertain themselves with postmodernism?"[7]

A number of Ukrainian scholars publicly addressed the issue of the jubilee of Russian statehood, mostly in the *Den'* newspaper. Practical proposals soon followed. According to the professor of the Ostroh Academy National University, Petro Kraliuk, some Ukrainian scholars suggested that we should celebrate the anniversary of a date 10 years previous to the one announced in Presidential Decree No. 267. This statement was based on the fact that the name *Rus'* was first mentioned in the twelfth-century *Tale of Bygone Years* under the year 852.

---

4   Medvedev velel prazdnovat' 1150-letie rossijskogo gosudarstva, [electronic resource] available at: http://fed.sibnovosti.ru/society/139057-medvedev-velel-prazdnovat-1150-letie-rossiyskogo-gosudarstva.

5   * The footnotes marked with an asterisk were added by the editorial team.
    The only information about Rurik is provided by the *Tale of Bygone Years* (*Povĕstī Vremęninyhŭ Lĕtŭ*) or *Primary Chronicle* originally compiled in Kiev around 1113 and later in the 12th c. updated and edited. This source covers the history of Kievan Rus' from 850 to 1110. It mentions that some tribes, including Eastern Slavs, refused to pay tribute to the Varangians and tried to govern themselves. After they failed and got into fighting each other in order to reestablished political order they invited the Varangians, led by Rurik, who arrived in the Ladoga region in 862 along with his brothers and a large retinue and built the Holmgard settlement near Novgorod. This moment is known as the invitation of the Varagians and since the 19th c., became officially interpreted in Russia as the starting point of Russian history.

6   About present debates see: BBC Russian-Rossija – 1150-letie rossijskogo gosudarstva, [electronic resource] available at: https://www.bbc.com/russian/russia/2011/03/110307_russia_ryurik_anniversary; and Kogda prazdnovat' 1150-letie rossijskogo gosudarstva? Kogda prazdnovat' 1150-letie rossijskogo gosudarstva?, [electronic resource] available at: https://newsland.com/user/4297701455/content/1150-letie-rossiiskogo-gosudarstva-riurikovichi-my/4144590.

7   I. Losev, "Rosija gotuet'sja do '1150-richchja rosijs'koï derzhavi'. Hto v Ukraïni vidpovist' na cej viklik, *Den'* 132/133, 2011.

However, *Rus' land* is not synonymous with Russia.⁸ Until the 19th c. Rus' was the name generally given to Ukrainian lands. This is why the Ostroh Academy initiated a fitting celebration of the 1,160th anniversary of Ukrainian statehood. Thus, we could also speak of the 1,160th anniversary of Ukrainian historiography and Ukrainian literature. Hence it would be a mistake to trace the origins of Ukrainian literature to *Eneïda* (1798) by Ivan Kotliarevsky, who is regarded as the pioneer of modern Ukrainian literature. Alas, understanding of the early medieval period is meager.⁹

Russia's jubilee activities were among the matters that influenced the rise of vigilance among Ukrainian scholars concerning the issue of Ukrainian national identity. This attitude is illustrated by numerous publications on the subject of the historic past, published both in scholarly journals and in the commercial press. A good example of this is the publication under the editorship of Larysa Ivshyna, a monumental collected work called *The power of the soft sign, or the return of the Rus' Law* (*Sila m'jakogo znaka, abo Povernennja Rus'koi pravdi*).¹⁰ In my opinion, the main pathos communicated by this publication lies in its attempt to comprehend the identity of Ukraine through the lens of its historic continuity – Rus'-Ukraine. The second feature is its effort to go beyond political history and to analyze the phenomenon of intensifying system of socio-normative values that manifest our Europeanness in the environment of the Ukrainian *demos* and not *ethnos*.

Since the subject is inexhaustible, we can suggest another, alternative perspective on the origin of Rus'-Ukraine, and do so on the basis of research in the field of the social sciences. This point of view is partly based on Immanuel Wallerstein's world-systems analysis and his concept of world-empires.¹¹

---

8   In the Ukrainian language normally two terms are used: a) *руський* – adjective of (Kievan) Rus' or also of Ruthenia), and b) *російський* – adjective of Russia. In the Russian language two similar terms are used: 1) *русский* and *российский* – both are adjectives of Russia, though the latter is also more commonly used in political contexts, e.g., Russian Federation – *Российская Федерация*, Russian Empire – *Российская Империя*; while the former may refer to both the people of Russia (*русский* – Russian nationality, while *российский* – Russian citizenship), and to Kievan Rus.
  * For the sake of clarity, in this text the spelling of the word Rus' was unified and in all uses and cases an apostrophe was used.
9   "Cja knizhka – strategichnogo znachennja", *Den'* 170/171, 2011, p. 6.
10 *Sila m'jakogo znaka, abo Povernennja Rus'koi pravdi*, ed. L. Ivshina, Kiev 2011.
11 I. Wallerstein, *World system analysis: introduction*, Durham and London 2004. * The author used the Russian edition, published in Moscow in 2006 by the publishing house Territorija Budushchevo, trans. N. Tjukina.

World-systems analysis is a narrative concept. Adhering to the principle of comprehensive history and a single interdisciplinary approach, the supporters of this notion abandon the narrative focused on the history of national states as independent units of study, in favor of destroying the rigid boundaries between economic, political, and sociocultural research methodologies.

It is obvious that each narrative requires its own protagonist. For positivists, everything revolves around the individual and his/her personality. For classical Marxists, the main character was the proletarian, and for the nation-oriented historians – the politician. Yet, for those in favor of world-systems analysis these characters, as well as numerous social structures, are all links in one chain. They are viewed not as elementary particles, but as components of a systemic amalgam, from which they sprang and in accordance with which they act.

An important condition for analysis of the origin of Rus', one applying approaches employed by followers of world-systems analysis, relates to time and space, namely the *chronotope*.[12] This is not an external constant (something that always has been, is, and will be), within which social reality exists. On the contrary, it is constantly changing, while society is a "palpitating organism". It remains unchanged over a long period of time, yet at the same time it is constantly changing. This, obviously, is a paradox – but not a contradiction. That is why the main task of history is to learn how to overcome this paradox.

Antinormanism as a diagnosis for Kievan Rus'

What is the main narrative of Rus', and who takes the central place amongst the main characters in this narration? There is no need to invent a new perspective – in the last centuries, three times there have been debates in Russia's between Normanists and Antinormanists concerning the problem of the Varangians: in the 18th c., the discussion between Gerhard Müller against Mikhail Lomonosov in the Saint Petersburg Academy of Sciences; in the 19th c., the public debate between Mikhail Pogodin and Nikolay Kostomarov at Saint Petersburg University; and since 1965, the debate between Leo Klejn and Igor Shaskolsky. They all focused on the role of the Varangians (Normans) in the formation of Rus'.

---

12 *The concept used in literary theory and philosophy of language, analyzing how configurations of time and space are represented in language and discourse. The term was coined by Russian scholar M. Bakhtin as an element in his theory of meaning in language and literature – see: M. Bakhtin, *Forms of time and of the chronotope in the novel*, [in:] idem, *The Dialogic Imagination*, Austin TX 1981, p. 84–258.

Our role here is reduced to briefly presenting a few bullet points from Omeljan Pritsak's vision of the origin of Rus'.[13] The author, whom I consider to be our mentor in leading the way towards historiosophical research, was the founder and first director (1973–1989) of the Harvard Ukrainian Research Institute. According to Pritsak, "the 200-year long Normanist-Antinormanist confrontation has proven powerless in solving the problem of the origin of Rus'." His opinion resonates with the judgement of the last "troublemaker" on the Norman question, the acclaimed Russian archeologist and dissident persecuted during the Soviet era, Leo Klejn, who believes that no theory of the Norman genesis of Rus' statehood or even scholarly concept exists at all; instead there are only "hypotheses about the ethnic identification of the Varangians, about the extent to which the Scandinavians participated in the history of our country." As for Normanism, it is not represented in any country but Russia, though there were Scandinavian invasions throughout all of Europe and beyond. According to Leo Klejn, in Russia, "this is not an academic movement, but an ideological tendency, which is implanted into science out of patriotic considerations. This is an inferiority complex, so characteristic of our country, whose roots must be sought after in the modern situation." For Ukrainians, commenting on Russian complexes directly leads onto a slippery slope. Let us therefore step aside from the "modern situation" in Russia and just consider Leo Klejn's viewpoint that "not all hypotheses when proven become theories, many of them become not theories, but facts. The debate is about facts".[14]

Omeljan Pritsak states several interesting facts concerning, primarily, the term *Rus'* and its "national" interpretation. In 839, the *Annales Bertiniani* mentioned a ruler of a political organization ("polity") called *Ros* (*Rhos* – Byzant.). The Arabic author, Ibn Khordadbeh, who described trade routes in Eurasia at that time, also noted the existence of two "companies" – Judean Radhanites, who controlled the routes to Khazaria; and non-Judean Rus', who controlled the trade in the north of Eastern Europe. Pritsak asks a rather justified question: how did it happen that the community of Rus' people, who had just come into being, turned out to be such skillful international merchants and took control of such a huge region?

Let us consider the ethnic factor, which seems to be a crucial issue in the formation of Rus' statehood. Omeljan Pritsak comments on this process thus:

---

13 O. Pritsak, *Pohodzhennja Rusi. Starodavni skandinavski dzherela (krim islandskih sag)*, Kiev 1997.
14 L. Klejn, Antinormanizm kak diagnoz, [electronic resource] available at: http://polit.ru/article/2010/12/03/klejn_antinormanism/print/.

Societies of the Baltic region, which were then developing, certainly did not comprise a national culture in its modern sense. The Danes, the Frisians, and the Rus' people were a polyethnic, multilingual community, devoid of territory, comprising marine nomads and inhabitants of partially "eastern" settlements, and sometimes wooded towns and trade settlements of the "western" type. The Rus' people and the Frisians acted as international merchants, which confirms the theory about the formation of the market as an economic organization by merchants, and not by peasants or artisans.[15]

The two latter strata, as representatives of the "lower" culture, had not become familiar with literature or sacred texts, which lay at the foundations of "higher" culture. At that time, the territory of the Rus' people had not yet been clearly defined either.

The ethnic factor goes hand-in-hand with the language factor. The continuity of written tradition is characteristic of a settled empire. Written language acquired the "sacred" character of "national" heredity, i.e., of a settled culture. The change of dynasties did not disrupt linguistic unity. In contrast, a nomadic empire often changed not only the ruling clan (the dynasty), but also its name for itself and its official language. A nomadic empire did not attempt to provide the continuity of "national culture," but strived to wield the unlimited power of an army of young warriors determined to get economic profit. When the nomads overthrew one charismatic ruling clan, they also rejected its language.

International nomadic merchants often cooperated with the local tribal chieftains, helping them to adopt "progressive" governance. For instance, merchants helped to unite different strata of the local population to create a patrimonial state. Throughout medieval times, as Omeljan Pritsak writes, "the towns and states of the Eurasian steppes, and also of the Baltic region, were founded not by the local populations, but by foreign international merchants". At the same time, it makes no sense to try to determine the "nationality" of the Vikings and the Varangians: "They had none. They were just professionals, ready to serve anyone who needed their skills and who could pay for their work".[16]

In urban trade settlements, several languages were spoken. Families or kindred groups used the local language, and two or more *linguae francae* were used for professional purposes. Thus, as Omeljan Pritsak concludes, in the context of Rus':

> it makes no sense to talk about the Swedish national culture of the 9th and 10th c. In the Baltic community, all its components – the Normans, the Veneti (the Slavs), the Balts,

---

15 O. Pritsak, *Pohodzhennja Rusi...*, p. 95.
16 Ibidem, p. 83, 90.

the Finns – were equivalent [...] It was customary (as is known from the Rurikids) to have two or more names, in accordance with professional or marital connections.[17]

Pritsak summarizes a lengthy route leading to the formation of Rus' by distinguishing three stages: the Volga period (c. 839–930), the Dnieper period (c. 930–1036), and the Kievan period (1036–1169). The Kievan stage is essentially different from the two former ones, for during the two first stages, the Rus' people mostly controlled trade routes and tribes, but did not possess territories. When necessary, they defeated their enemies, collected tribute, and controlled trading posts along the two main international routes: the Volga-Don to Bulgaria and Atil, and the Dnieper – from the Varangians through Kiev to Constantinople. In this context only the Kiev period was significantly different, marking the beginning of the cultural consolidation of Rus' and an attempt at its "nationalization."

Real shifts occurred in Rus' during the third stage. Firstly, Novgorod became more significant than Staraya Ladoga, which both linguistically and culturally remained exclusively Scandinavian up to its demise in the middle of the 11th c., while Novgorod had been bilingual from the very beginning. The Novgorod people were mostly descendants of the Veneti, Baltic Slavs who played a key role in the process of adapting the Viking concept of the "barbaric" law to Slavic political culture. Also the oldest surviving copy of the *Rus' Law* (*Russkaja Pravda*), the first legal code of Kievan Rus' and the subsequent Rus' principalities, come from Novgorod, the only place in Rus' where the concept of law was generally recognized, adopted, and self-evident up to the dramatic demise of the Veliky Novgorod Republic in 1479.

Secondly, in 1036, Prince Yaroslav I the Wise (1015–1054), definitively took power in Kiev, crushed the Pechenegs, and consolidated his version of the Roman Empire, the ideological center of which was Saint Sophia's Cathedral in Kiev, and the foundations of which were provided by the system of Novgorod laws. In the next step, Yaroslav introduced a sacral (as a result of the mission of Cyril and Methodius) and legitimate language in his territories, the Church-Slavonic language, whose importance after the demise of Danube Bulgaria decreased significantly on the national level.

Thirdly, Yaroslav started turning Rus' into a territorial community by establishing the princely vagrant army (*druzhina*) in Kiev, Chernihiv, and Pereiaslav lands. As a result of these measures, the names *Rus'* and *Rus' land*, recorded in the second half of the 11th c., started to be used in a new meaning – exclusively relating to southern Rus' (today's Ukraine). Before this, *Rus'* had been

---

17 Ibidem, p. 96.

a foreign ruling leadership with a primitive socio-political organization that rested on seafaring and river nomads who periodically collected tribute for their princes, but did not attach themselves to any specific territory.

Indeed, Yaroslav's "cultural revolution" was the source of a qualitatively new leap from a polyethnic, multilingual community devoid of territory with a "lower" level of culture to a "higher" one, sanctioned through the domination of the Church-Slavonic language. The decline of the independent Bulgarian state left the Church and the Slavonic rite (with its code of spiritual and government-political texts) without a proprietor. This enabled *Rus' land* to appropriate this culture without the fear of losing its own identity. The compilation of the collected chronicles in 1115, created in the first spiritual center of Eastern Europe – Kiev Pechersk Lavra – entailed a unique act that demonstrated "a common historic fate." Omeljan Pritsak's conclusion about the origin of Rus' is unambiguous: "It was then, during the Kiev period, that its own historic self-consciousness appeared and Rus' began to emerge as a legitimate historic entity."[18]

A monopoly on legacy?

The account of the origin of Rus' outlined above is based in an academic perspective dominated by the Hegelian tradition – namely, that when a given social phenomenon, such as the system of state power, is emerging, at that moment it is practically non-existent. The formation of a system, and especially of such a world system as *Rus' land* as an Eastern European counterpart of ancient Rome or Byzantium, is in reality a lengthy historical process. When today we raise the question of marking a specific date for the foundation of Rus'-Ukraine on the national level, the scholars' argument that "on the one hand, it is sort of like that, but on the other hand, it is not" does not suffice. As a rule, certain arbitrary administrative decisions that follow a political rationale are taken on the national level, and they reflect the political background. Such was also the case with the decision concerning the anniversary of the origin of Russia, which was taken in the Russian Federation on the national level.

On a practical level, in Ukraine the debate concerning the origin of Rus' clearly will also continue at the intersection of scholarly thought and political rationale. In 2011–2012, while this topic was relevant for Russia, it was yet to become a burning issue for Ukrainian political elites, thus no decision was made on the national level. Ukrainian society responded to the Russian initiative with

---

18 Ibidem, p. 101.

heated debates, which took place on the airwaves and in the media, while scholarly publications were few and far between. There was a feeling that the political factor in the current situation would be determinative and this affected the nature of the discussion.

In my opinion, a certain level of political correctness and scholarly balance should have been adhered to. Especially during the discussion of such a sacred issue as the one defining who is "the older brother", and thus, presumably, who has a stronger mandate over the historical legacy of Rus'. It is hard to picture an argument between the Italians, the Spanish, the French, the Germans, and the English attempting to determine who of them is the true and only heir to the empire of Ancient Rome. Only one exception must be noted – Mussolini had no doubts here. Yet what can one expect from the leader of Italian fascism? We, however, should learn our lessons from history. Because those who consider the problem from the perspective of whether Rus' was "Ukrainian" or "Russian", emphasizing only the ethnic aspect of this issue and looking for arguments in the context of "land and blood" etc., will ultimately lose the argument.

In consequence, our premises are that early medieval Rus' was a multi-tribal and multi-ethnic territorial-political entity, founded by a trading-military political class, which was generally typical of the early Middle Ages. For instance, the term *Khazars* was also used without any ethnic coloring as a geographical-political concept, and later it started to denote all the subjects of the Khazar king, who constituted the Khazar tribal union. At different times in the existence of the Khazar "federation" it consisted of the Azov and the Volga Bulgarians, the Caucasian and the Don Alans, the Volga Burtas, the trans-Volga Oghuz, the Crimean Goths, the Caucasian highlanders, the Khoresm Iranian Aorsi, the Hungarian Magyars, the Slavs, and the Rus' people. The Khazar language was probably kindred to Old Bulgarian, and is a predecessor of the modern-day Chuvash language. At the same time, the koine of the Jewish-Khazar merchants was the Slavic language.[19] Kievan Rus', in a lot of respects, became an heir to the Khazar Khaganate, when, according to Omeljan Pritsak, "the multilingual trading companies and trading communities, as well as seafaring nomads, adapted the political structure and the charisma of the steppe empires to their needs in order to transform it into the Christian-Slavonic-speaking high culture from which Rus' arose".[20]

---

19 Khazaria, [in:] *Electronic Jewish Library*, [electronic resource] available at: http://www.eleven.co.il/article/14401.
20 O. Pritsak, *Pohodzhennja Rusi...*, p. 101.

Very often in the case of marking anniversaries, political considerations take priority over scholarly concerns. It is no wonder then, that when analyzing the technologies of "jubilee initiatives" in the Russian Federation, the problem of the scholarly justification of a prominent date was far from being a top concern for some initiators of anniversaries. As can be seen from Russian publications, on September 18, 2009, during jubilee ceremonies marking the 1,150th anniversary of Veliky Novgorod, the famous director Nikita Mikhalkov initiated the discussion on the marking of the 1,150th anniversary of the "formation of the state". At the same time, he noted that "the country should be cleaned up, since we live in a terrible mess".[21] The initiative was heard by political leaders, and, as the Russian press agencies reported, the President of Russia, Dmitry Medvedev, concluded that it was necessary "to mark 1,150 years of the origin of the Russian state in 2012".[22]

These jubilee dates did not pan out at once. Veliky Novgorod turned out to be a "stumbling block". First of all, scholars had already voiced a number of questions on the 1,150th anniversary of the foundation of Veliky Novgorod three years earlier. This date, ever so prominent for the city, turned out to be a real mystery. Analysts assumed that since the first mention of the coming of Rurik († 879) is dated at 862, then, for him to "have somewhere to come to", the initiators of the jubilee stepped three years back and waywardly "assigned" the date of the foundation of Novgorod to 859. However, archaeological research conducted in the 20th c. dated the foundation of Novgorod to not earlier than the end of the 9th c., i.e., a few decades after the coming of Rurik. For instance, one of the leading Russian archeologists conducting excavations in this region, Anatoly Kirpichnikov, states that it was Staraya Lagoda (currently a rural village) that became the first capital of the early medieval Rus' state and only later was the capital moved to a settlement next to current Novgorod, one known in the chronicles by its Scandinavian name Holmgard, and now as Rurik's Town (Rurikovo Gorodische). Back then, Novgorod did not yet exist.[23]

---

21 Medvedev prizval otmetit' 1150-letie Rossii, [electronic resource] available at: http://newsland.com/user/4297646261/content/medvedev-prizval-otmetit-1150-letie-rossii/3973597.

22 Medvedev predlozhil otmetit' 1150-letie vozniknovenija rossijskogo gosudarstva, [electronic resource] available at: http://www.newsinfo.ru/news/2009-09-18/medvedev/722293/?mod.

23 V strane novyj superproekt – "1150-letie Rossii", [electronic resource] available at: *http//www.dp.ru/f/2010/07/27/V-strane-novij-superproekt/.

Few people paid any real heed to the considerations of scholars. As can be seen from the media, the governor of Novgorod Oblast, Sergey Mitin, opened hearings with a speech declaring "the Novgorod land as the historical cradle of Russian statehood", while making reference to acclaimed Russian historians (Vasily Tatishchev, Nikolay Karamzin, Mikhail Pogodin, Sergey Solovyov, Vasily Klyuchevsky) who "considered 862 to be the date of the origin of Russian statehood." The governor added that this particular date was deeply respected by the Russian public and authorities in the 19th c.:

> Namely, by the decree of Emperor Nicholas II [(1894–1917) – ed.], the year 862 was given the status of the "primeval event of Russian statehood". The decree was executed by the Ministry of People's Education and several generations of Russians from early childhood adopted the annalistic version of the formation of their state.[24]

The governor built his argument on a historic precedent from 100 years back and appealed to tradition. How could contemporary historians possibly refute this argument?

Consequently, "the process was started". At the beginning of 2011, the leader of the LDPR, Vladimir Zhirinovsky, expressed the will to make Veliky Novgorod the center of the celebration of 1,150 years of Russia. The Russian media reported that the main centers of the 2012 celebrations would be Moscow, Kiev, and Veliky Novgorod. In addition to these three cities, where the main events were to take place, other locations expected to participate were Izborsk (Pskov oblast), Belozersk (Vologodskaja oblast), and Rostov the Great (Yaroslavsk oblast). Three years previously, the Russian government had allocated financing in the amount of 5,000 million Russian rubles for the celebration of 1,150 years of Veliky Novgorod. The media did not draw any attention to the amount of money allocated for the jubilee of the origin of Russian statehood.[25]

Involvement of Kiev

Simultaneously, the problem arose of involving Ukraine in the anniversary celebrations. Naturally, the initiative was supposed to come from the public.

---

24 Forum umnyh ljudej. Novgorodskij gubernator: 1150-letie Rosii: [electronic resource] available at: https://forumnov.com/lofiversion/index.php?t284667.html,%20%D1%81%D0%B2%D0%BE%D0%B1%D0%BE%D0%B4%D0%BD%D1%8B%D0%B9.

25 Novgorodskie vlasti zdut prikaza o prazdnovanii 1150-letija Rossii, [electronic resource] available at: https://forumnov.com/lofiversion/index.php?t278240.html,%20%D1%81%D0%B2%D0%BE%D0%B1%D0%BE%D0%B4%D0%BD%D1%8B%D0%B9.

Consequently, counterparties that apparently specialized in the propaganda of the idea of the "Russian world" were mobilized in Ukraine: the European Institute of Political Culture (Kiev), the news outlets "InfoRos" and "RBK-Ukraine", the Institute for Russians Abroad (Moscow), and the Forum-ua.com portal. On November 12, 2010, the media announced that they were organizing public hearings to which representatives of the Ukrainian authorities were invited, alongside the opposition, scholars, experts, and journalists. There is no conclusive information stating who from those invited actually participated in the hearings. Only two or three speeches given by the participants were made available on the internet, ones including such opinions on the subject as: "Well, I was born in Ukraine (or in Belarus), but now I work in Moscow, and that is why I find it difficult to self-identify what I really am."

The director of the Institute for Russians Abroad Sergey Panteleev voiced the ideology of the above-mentioned assembly. It can be summarized in several statements: traditionally, people born in Ukraine have always been an "empire-building" element in the Russian empire and the Soviet Union; leading Russian geopolitical concepts, namely, "Eurasianism", were created mostly by ethnic Ukrainians (e.g. Petro Savytsky, Petro Suvchynsky or George Vernadsky); at the time, Ukraine could also act as an "adhesive" in Russian-Belarussian relations. Thus, the social demand for Ukraine was formed. The historical, spiritual, and cultural role of Kiev as the traditional center of "the Russian world" was emphasized. Referring to the concept of the Patriarch of Moscow and all Rus', Kirill, Sergey Panteleev expressed his confidence that there was a demand in Russian society for integrational initiatives from Kiev's side, ones which would reflect its status as "the mother of Russian cities" and "the cradle of Russian orthodoxy". In summary, Panteleev initiated the convening of a civil forum in Ukraine, Russia, and Belarus as "an instrument of public diplomacy which would promote the harmonization of relations between our states".[26]

Stressing the fact that Euro-illusions seemed to be dissipating at that time in Ukraine, the participants of these hearings urged the "leaders of Ukraine and the foreign affairs establishment to promptly and pragmatically create a long-term, beneficial and patriotic, strategic, geopolitical Eastern project, rooted in

---

26 S. Panteleev, Rossii, Ukraine i Belorusi nuzhen Grazhdanskij Forum, [electronic resource] available at: *http://www.russkie.org/index.php? module=printnews&id=19893.

the deep-seated interests of Ukrainian society. Primarily, this is for the development of relations with the Russian Federation and Belarus".[27]

These assemblies entered a new stage on April 21, 2011, in the Central House of Journalists in Moscow, where an international round table was held "dedicated to the problems of preparing for the celebrations in 2012 of the 1,150th anniversary of the formation of the Old Rus' state". The contingent making up this assembly was also peculiar – "public activists, scholars, and representatives of official structures of the three countries, who were specialists in working with their compatriots." Sergey Panteleev, who repeated all the statements he had issued in Kiev, again determined the nature and the mood of the reports. Taking into consideration the occasion of the 1,150th anniversary, he somewhat changed the socio-political emphasis of the speech, adding an apparently more scholarly component: "This includes the historical and the social aspect. Moreover, the former one is definitive". The contents of this "scholarly aspect", according to the scientific expert of the assembly from the Institute of Slavonic Studies, Oleg Nemenskiy, lay in the opinion that "historically we are participants of a single state project and a single country. All of us together are Rus'. This is our legendary original beginning, written down in Kiev, which has not lost its importance even now. This date is the font of our self-consciousness".[28]

The resolution of the round table was not very original either: the participants "urged the presidents of Ukraine and Belarus to support the idea of holding jubilee activities in all the countries, heirs to the Old Rus' state". The initiators of this idea also proposed to the heads of Russia, Ukraine, and Belarus that they hold an informal summit dedicated to the jubilee. Plans for developing an international public program of festivities were mentioned, along with the intention to create a respective steering committee. The characteristic feature of the round table lay in the statement that "this event is the first step towards implementing another large-scale idea: the creation of the Public Forum of Russia, Ukraine, and Belarus". The information on who and from what sources would finance all these forums and programs once again was not revealed.[29]

---

27 Konec evroilljuzij: nuzhen li Grazhdanskij Forum Ukrainy, [electronic resource] available at: *http://fraza.ua/analitics/13.11.10/ 103445.html.
28 Sovet po podgotovke prazdnovanija 1150-letija obrazovanija, [electronic resource] available at: *http://russkg.ru/index.php?ohtion=com_content &view+article&id=11.
29 Edinaja Odessa, [electronic resource] at: *http://www.edinaya-odessa.org/publ/print: page,1,28858-obshchestve.

The masterminds of the "Russian world" did not conceal the strategic orientation behind the various jubilee festivities: "Old Rus' can become a new integration center which unites not only Slavonic lands and peoples, but also its neighbors, as was the case many times in the Russian Empire and Soviet times".[30] Tactically, they recommended promoting in the context of Ukraine and Belarus the idea of a common cultural space, which, presumably, already existed *de facto*, and soon could become a common information space. The main aim was to form a successful cooperation with the profile parliamentary committees of the Eastern Slavic countries and to conduct an informal summit of the three heads of state.

The 1,150th jubilee of the origin of Russian statehood was presented by certain circles in Ukraine under the cover of the 1,150th anniversary of the foundation of Kiev's Metropolitanate and the original Baptism of Rus'; during the times of Prince Askold († 882). Under this pretense, a draft resolution (№ 9597) about the celebration on the national level in 2012 was registered in the Verkhovna Rada (parliament) of Ukraine. The Orthodox hierarchs of both the Moscow and Kiev Patriarchates announced the celebrations. Few cared that there was no actual evidence confirming the baptism, while contemporary history dates the foundation of the Kiev Metropolitanate back to the times of the introduction of Christianity in Kievan Rus' by Grand Prince Volodimer the Great (980–1015) in 988. There was a rather vague mention in the reasoning of the clergy that "in the 860s, i.e. around 1,150 years ago, Prince Askold and some Rus' people were baptized, and also a separate Metropolitanate for Rus' was created". This vague "around", or "862 is the most probable date" became the starting point of the jubilee of the Metropolitanate in 2012, i.e., during the celebration of the 1,150th anniversary of the origin of Russian statehood.[31]

---

30 V. Shestakov, 150 let Drevnej Rusi, ili Ocherednaja popytka istoricheski obedinit' Rossiju, Ukrainu i Belarus', [electronic resource] available at: https://fraza.ua/analytics/115162-let-drevney-rusi-ili-ocherednaya-popytka-istoricheski-obedinit-rossiyu-ukrainu-i-belarus.

31 V UPC KP otmetjat 1150-letie uchrezhdenija Kievskoj Mitropolii i Kreshchenija Rusi vo vremena Askol'da, [electronic resource] available at: https://risu.org.ua/ru/index/all_news/orthodox/uoc_kp/45936; K voprosu o nachale russkoj ierarhii. K 1150-letiju osnovanija Kievskoj Mitropolii, [electronic resource] available at: https://www.religion.in.ua/main/history/14789-k-voprosu-o-nachale-russkoj-ierarxii-k-1150-letiyu-osnovaniya-kievskoj-mitropolii.html.

The i's dotted

These public initiatives merely laid the foundations for an event which was truly important for Russian society. On June 22, 2011 in the old Russian city of Vladimir, the President of the Russian Federation Dmitry Medvedev held a general session of the presidium of the Council of Culture and Art and the Council of Science, Technology, and Education. It was dedicated to the preparation for the celebration of the 1,150th anniversary of the origin of the Russian statehood according to Decree No. 267. It should be noted that this meeting confirmed the fact that during 2009–2011, there was an evolution in the assessment of the jubilee date by the Russian authorities: the conversation referred not to the "formation" or the "emergence" but to the "origin" of Russian statehood. This can signify a certain shift in Russian societal awareness, as the term "origin" can be interpreted rather broadly, and, if required, it can even be substantiated rationally.

Dmitry Medvedev also noted that "science has the right to adhere to absolutely different, diametrically opposite opinions about different events". The president noted that teaching history at schools and universities is a different issue, as this is where the problem of searching for consensual views arises, "so that our young citizens would get some general notion of how the formation of our country occurred".[32] Indeed, these reflections voiced by Dmitry Medvedev are justified and generally accepted in the entire civilized world, since the education of future citizens is the task not only of science and education, but also of the political class, as demonstrated by Dmitry Medvedev's speech. Ultimately, science and education are financed by the state, hence, as the Russian president notes,

> we are currently in a unique situation where we are able to celebrate this jubilee duly, and at the same time give an impetus to the development of history, archaeology, and a whole set of other sciences which are connected with the history of our country. *But ultimately, this is done in order to achieve additional opportunities for the development of our country* (italics – V.T.).[33]

Thus, without any prejudice or kowtowing, we should acknowledge that the speech was given by a political leader who defended the interests of his country in the context of the challenges and problems of the time, which Russia was trying to resolve internally, as well as certain global tendencies. It therefore seems that the Ukrainians should have taken the stance of the Russian president

---

32 President of Russia. Official website, [electronic resource] available at: http://state.kremlin.ru/news/12075.
33 Ibidem.

into consideration. For instance, when he signed this decree, he claimed that he was pondering:

> whether or not to sign it, and yet the reasons in favor of celebrating this symbolic jubilee of Russian statehood outweighed the arguments against it, because at this point in time this matters – and not only and indeed not principally scholarly, as it is based in entirely practical reasoning. And the point is obvious: *consolidation of our country, our people, towards the further development of our great and very complicated country* [italics – V.T.].[34]

The interest of Ukraine, which Dmitry Medvedev was not obliged to have at heart, is a different matter, and he diplomatically addressed the issue in his speech:

> Now, in terms of our friends in Ukraine and in Belarus […] Of course it is in our interest that they celebrate all this together with us. But we are rather intelligent and flexible people. The Decree which I have signed, I would like to emphasize this, is a Russian decree, not Ukrainian one. I am the President of the Russian Federation, not of Ukraine. It is called "the celebration of the 1,150th anniversary of the origin of Russian statehood", because it covers the territory of the Russian Federation. Of course, we can view this event as a central link in the emergence of Russian statehood, because we understand what events those were. And in this sense, such an interpretation does not contradict the meaning of this document. Please, if our Ukrainian friends in this respect are ready to cooperate in these processes, I will be very happy. Naturally, at my own level, I will definitely raise this issue in mutual relations with Ukraine and Belarus.[35]

We can see the complexity that the president's statement poses for Ukrainians as to an unambiguous interpretation of the Russian stance. This is based on the fact that modern Russian texts do not have an old spelling of "Russian" (*русский*), as was characteristic of the 11th c., or the spelling of *Rus'* (*руський*), as was common in the 15th c., yet the term "Russian" (*русский*) is widely used, when it is not always clear what it refers to – to "the Russians" as "the Great Russians", or to "Russia's people" as the citizens of Russia, or, ultimately, the population of ancient Rus'.[36] Likewise, in Dmitry Medvedev's speech we hear at the same time both "Russia's statehood" (*российская*), and "Russian statehood" (*русская*).

Some representatives of the Ukrainian side lacked the nerve to overcome the psychology of "a younger brother" and the posture of "little Russianness". They immediately used the 1,150th anniversary as an opportunity to bow to the "older brother". Thus, on September 12, 2012 a conference was held in Kiev, called

---

34 Ibidem.
35 Ibidem.
36 See footnote 8.

"The 1,150th anniversary of the formation of the Old Russian state: history and modern times".[37] Noteworthy is the fact that while the Russian President Dmitry Medvedev mentioned only the "origin", the participants of the Kiev conference started talking about the "formation", not of Old Rus' (from the term "*Rus'*"), but of "Old Russia" (from the term "Russia"). In the speech by Sergey Panteleev, cited above, this view is presented in greater detail: "the tradition of celebrating anniversaries of Russian statehood is reviving".[38] Thus, an event was held in Kiev, where truly laudatory performances were given in honor of the 1,150th anniversary of Russian statehood, during which the indivisible heritage of early medieval Rus' was "appropriated" by Russia. What should we make of this? And how to interpret it, if not from a position of "political responsibility" (Karl Jaspers), then at least from the perspective of "moral responsibility"?[39]

After the "warm-up" in Kiev, jubilee celebrations were held in Veliky Novgorod on September 21–23. The opening day was properly justified: on this day 150 years earlier, Tsar Alexander II opened the monument to the "Millennium of Russia"; on this day in 1380, the Battle of Kulikovo took place, this date is also celebrated as the Day of Russian Unity. As the Russian media reported, the ceremony was attended by the members of the International Committee of the World Day of Russian Unity, the Centre of National Glory, the Foundation of Saint Andrew the First-Called, and by Russian and international scholars and NGO activists.

The day started with a mass and ended with a theatrical performance devoted to the history of the Russian state. Finally, a solemn ceremony of unveiling a monument to the formation of Russian statehood, the "Prince's rock", was held in the Novgorod museum complex "Rurikovo Gorodische". The Russian Institute of Strategic Studies prepared a film "1,150 years of confrontation between Russia and the West" for the jubilee ceremonies. This last event demonstrated Russia's shift towards an intensification of "cold war" psychology.

---

37 The conference "1150-letie obrazovanija Drevnierucckogo gosudarstva: istorija i covremennost'", was held in Kiev 11–12.09.2012, see: *https://guralyuk.livejournal.com/1871600.html.
38 S. Panteleev, Rossii, Ukraine i Belorusi nuzhen Grazhdanskij Forum, [electronic resource] at: *http://www.russkie.org/index.php? module=printnews&id=19893.
39 Uchastniki konferencii "1150-letie obrazovanija Drevnerusskogo gosudarstva" vyskazalis' za edinstvo bratskih vostochnoslavjanskih narodov, [electronic resource] available at: *http://ruskline.ru/news_rl/2012/09/15/uchastniki_konferencii_1150letie_ obrasovaniya_drevnerusskogo_ gosudarstva_vyskazalis_za_edinstvo_bratskih_vost.

The triumph of presentism

The question naturally arises: where does this increased demand for various jubilees and celebrations, which often put historians in such a quandary, come from? The French scholar François Hartog contends that against the background of globalization, the formation of a "global economy", and, at the same time, the increased dangers of losing "world heritage", there has been a real surge in attention to all matters concerning the memory of the past. These recent social upheavals and crises have intensified the desire to renew the disrupted "continuity of time".[40]

Yet the memorial surge of the late 20th and early 21st c. does not signify that society has started to explore its own historical past more scrupulously. On the contrary, according to Hartog, admiration of historical memory has become a true dictate of modernity. Moreover, the adherents of presentism consider that the present is supposed to straightforwardly determine both the past (what me must remember and save, and what we must forget), and the future (what we are building and what fate we are laying for humanity). In summary, the present takes responsibility both for the past and the future. There is a certain rationale here: national consciousness, according to Ernest Renan[41], is not only what is remembered jointly, but also what we must jointly forget.

However, the presentism of the end of the 20th and early 21st c. has some original qualities. At its foundation lies the disappointment in all illusions and ideals. When no faith in a revolutionary idea remains – whether in a socialist society, the nation state, or a better future – then only affluence, comfort, and the tempting changeability of feelings acquire the greatest value. François Hartog lists the most divergent manifestations of such "household" presentism: from the worldview of an unemployed (and untroubled) clochard to the contemplative philosophy of a wealthy tourist; from cosmetic products against obesity and ageing, to the most modern information technologies.

We should note that the present behaves very aggressively in the process of its "self-adoration": it is not enough for the present just to be the present; it strives to secure a place in history, to perpetuate itself in it. Politicians consciously build up their biographies as paths constructed from consecutive steps leading to

---

40 F. Hartog, *Order of time, regimes of historicity*, [electronic resource] available at: *http://magazines.ru/nz/2008/3/ ar3.html; F. Hartog, *Regimes of Historicity: Presentism and Experiences of Time*, New York 2015.
41 E. Renan, "What is a Nation?" [in:] *Becoming National: A Reader*, ed. E. Geoff, R. Grigor, New York and Oxford 1996, p. 41–55.

"historic" acts, while also displaying significant interest in their own family histories (there are active searches through genealogical archives).

Sociologists and political strategists, who construct an image of their patron with references to all possible opinion polls over a period of time, are in great demand. Various anniversaries, whether of commercial companies or educational establishments, become key elements creating an institution's image and brand. The same can be said about various national celebrations, with their fireworks and fancy parades, through which the ruling strata, who profess presentism, try to sanctify their own identity.

In our heyday of presentism, "memory" acquires an ever-growing value, pushing the science of history into second place. Presentism tries to raise the study of the collective memory of a certain region or social stratum to the level of an analogue of the "history of mentalities". Memory, which serves presentism, becomes a way of perceiving and sharing its narrow-minded understanding of the spirit of the present among the wider public. Various realms of memory are constantly constructed and reconstructed according to the current conjuncture, which prompts the most varied, sometimes traumatic reactions from other segments of society. To please the ruling class, national histories are rewritten, different national symbols are created. "National heroes", who are supposed to perpetuate the present fragment in the life of the country and give it the status of a truly historic epoch, are mass-produced with proper grandeur and honors.

In such conditions, historians lose a number of functions that used to be theirs. Historians cease to serve as a "raw nerve", trying to map and think out of the indistinct lines of the future in the past; they cease to be intermediaries between the past and the future. They are replaced by spin-doctors who become liaisons between contemporaries, granting them (at their own permission) a certain place in the modern social hierarchy. Spin-doctors simultaneously select from the past only those things which correspond to the historic memory of statesmen in the present, while at the same time neglecting those things which have lost significance for their noble contemporaries, and which they thus consider irrelevant to the social interest. Ultimately, the disciples of national memory and their comrades talk only about the things that the political leaders want to remember and, by no means, about the ones they wish to forget.

This vernacular and abridged historical memory, damaged as a result of the above-mentioned circumstances, in the short term turns into a free-floating meta-history, because in the battle between memory and history preference is now given to memory. Moreover, the opinion that this "filtered" understanding of history is, in fact, an implementation of the idea of "responsibility to the memory of past generations" has been imposed on public opinion.

What are we celebrating?

According to well-established tradition, the success of celebrating any anniversary whose date has been agreed upon (and this has become standard practice) depends on its meaningfulness. The question of "what super-task we are setting and what ultimate result we are expecting" must always be at the forefront. From the Ukrainian viewpoint, this super-task on the public level was formulated by Larysa Ivshyna in her preface to the book *The power of the soft sign, or the return of the Rus'Law (Sila m'jakogo znaka, abo Povernennja Rus'koi pravdi)*: "to rise to the level of our own history!". At the same time, it would be worthwhile to single out the dominant link that could become paramount in the context of the beginning of the third millennium. We consider, relating to Immanuel Wallerstein's concept, that this could be expressed in the formula: "Rus'-Ukraine as a world system", primarily as a system of power and respective moral and socio-normative culture. Subsequently, we could also analyze the progress of Ukrainian history from this perspective.

The history of Ukraine provides a peculiar illustration of the complexity and ambiguity of the manifestation of a central sociocultural law – namely, the determination of the extent of cultural and social practice involved in unifying the character of a civilization. The main dialectical contradiction which was placed in the genetic pool of the Ukrainian people who formed after the collapse of Rus' lay in the fact that the religious and cultural heritage (primarily Eastern Greek-Byzantine), through the influence of historical circumstances, was able present an appropriate response to the challenge posed by the socio-political system of the West.

The Baptism of Rus' in Kiev over 1,000 years ago had its own peculiar features. Cyril and Methodius, while still in Great Moravia, tried to defend the right of the Slavic community to independence, thus the right to search for their own way between the Roman and Byzantine influences.[42] They tried to solve the Schism, which back then was already looming, by returning to the truths of early Christianity. The evangelism of Kievan Christianity was oriented towards the tradition of the Apostle Paul, which stipulated the unity and equality of all people in Christ. This version of Christianity established the preconditions for the idea of a "free individual", the interest in the inner world of the person, their soul, their search for God, martyrdom, and compassion. The New Testament lay foundations for a free individual in the mentality of the people.[43]

---

42 *Ukrains'kaja cerkva miz Shodom i Zahodom*, ed. P. Yarotsky, Kiev 1966.
43 *Istorija religii v Ukraini u dvoh tomah*, vol. 2: *Ukrains'kje pravoslav'ja*, Kiev 1977.

Ultimately, the mainstream of the socio-normative culture of the Ukrainian people formed in the tradition of early Eastern Christianity, appealing to equality and the Non-possessors Movement. In addition, the interaction of two opposite tendencies – eastern cultural heritage on the one hand, and the innovative rationalist influences of Western social relations on the other hand – pushed Ukrainians towards a synthesis of the East and West, making Ukraine an initiator of unifying traditions. Unfortunately, the outcomes were dramatic. Ukraine, situated between the worlds of Greek-Byzantine and Western Roman cultures, and being a lawful member of both, endeavored throughout its history to unify these two traditions into one living synthetic model. It approached this synthesis in the great epochs of its history, yet, despite numerous opportunities and partial successes, the efforts towards forming an ultimate synthesis fell flat. Ukraine failed to fulfill this mission fully and collapsed under the yoke of extreme external pressure and internal contradictions.

The 20th c. once again presented Ukraine with the task of self-determination. The cofounder of Ukrainian twentieth-century historiography, Mykhailo Hrushevsky[44], saw the solution in a synthesis of the historic experience which the Ukrainian people had gained both during the principality period (prior to the Union of Lublin in 1569) and during the Hetmanate era (from the age of Khmelnitsky until 1764). Yet the liberation movement of 1917–1921 exposed the insufficient statist capacity of the peasantry, who constituted up to 90 percent of the overall Ukrainian population. The solution of the synthesis problem and consequently of the emergence of modern Ukraine once again was postponed until new geopolitical conditions appeared and new driving forces accumulated.

The theorist of Ukrainian statecraft, Vyacheslav Lypynsky, presented the future task in a fundamentally new light: instead of perceiving Ukrainians as an *ethnos*, he urged creating Ukrainianness in the mode of a civil society capable of synthesizing the experiences of East and West. In this context, Lypynsky wrote that "the main difference between Ukraine and Moscow is not language, not tribe, not faith [...], but a political order formed in branches, a different method of organizing the ruling stratum, with differing relations between the top and the bottom, the state and the citizenry – those who govern in respect of those who are governed".[45]

---

44 M. Hruševs'kij, *Istoriia Ukraïny-Rusy*, vol. 1–10, Lviv, Kiev 1991–2000.
45 V. Lypynsky, *Lysty do brativ-hliborobiv. Pro ideju i organizaciju ukraïns'kogo monarhizmu*, Kiev, Philadelphia 1995, p. XXV.

These are distinctive and differing features of the Russians and the Ukrainians that the "ringleaders" of the "triune Russian world" are trying not to notice in close-up, waving the bugaboo of *mazepinstvo*[46] as the manifestation of separatism, radical nationalism, and even racism. This is an extremely sad consequence of our modernity, one which creates a demand for such ideologists who contribute to discord both between Russia and Ukraine and within Ukrainian society itself. As the leading theorist in the field of structural anthropology, Claude Lévi-Strauss, explains: "Any culture develops as a result of the exchange with other cultures. But it is necessary that every culture should offer some resistance, because otherwise it will lose very soon what is inherent to it."[47]

Thus, this "certain resistance" in the sphere of culture is the barrier that some Ukrainians will struggle to overcome. Others will fail to overpower it in the case of the proposed Russian participation in the common jubilee celebrations on account of the 1,150th anniversary of the origin of Russian statehood announced by the leaders of the Russian Federation.

Common ground

In the first edition of this chapter, published in the Russian journal *Politicheskaja konceptologija* just before the celebration of the jubilee in Russia, I warned: "And if, God forbid, during the jubilee celebrations, the pioneers of certain political forces come to issue mutual accusations of racism or radical nationalism, this will be something verging on a crime against humanity".[48]

Unfortunately, the worst happened – after the pompous celebration of the jubilee in 2012, Russia resorted to an act of aggression against Ukraine. In February-March 2014, a military invasion and occupation by Russia of an integral part of Ukraine (the Autonomous Republic of Crimea and city of Sevastopol) occurred. The second stage of the military aggression of the Russian Federation against Ukraine started in April 2014. It was then that military groups supervised, controlled, and financed by Russian special forces proclaimed the

---

46 * Ivan Mazepa, the Hetman of Zaporizhian Host (1687–1708), during the Great Northern War deserted the army of Tsar Peter the Great and sided with King Charles XII of Sweden. Mazepa has been negatively presented in the traditional Russian and Soviet historiography and culture of memory, which derogatorily refers to Ukrainian emancipatory attempts as *mazepinstvo*.
47 See: https://www.scribd.com/document/155012071/Interview-Levi-Strauss-1988-Eribon.
48 *Politicheskaja konceptologija* 2, 2012, p. 160–180.

creation of the Donetsk People's Republic (April 7, 2014) and the Lugansk People's Republic (April 27, 2014). Regular military groups employed by Russia in the war against Ukraine were systematically reinforced by Russian mercenaries from the reserves of the Russian Federation's military forces. At the end of August 2014, Russia's war entered its third stage – the direct military incursion into mainland Ukraine with the use of their regular military forces.

This incursion into Ukraine was accompanied by an unparalleled ideological cover-up claiming that "nationalists" and "fascists" had supposedly come to power in Ukraine. The Kiev establishment, as the separatists claimed, used the army for "punitive actions" against their own people, who had supposedly expressed their will and proclaimed "their" republic in Donbass. Russia, allegedly, had chosen to protect the traditional values established in early medieval Rus' – Orthodoxy, national character, and commonality. In the system of Moscow's traditional values Ukrainians are not a separate nation, but only a component of the "triune Russian world" consisting of the Great Russians, Small Russians, and Belarussians (White Russians), while the territory of Ukraine is merely the "backyard" of Russian statehood. This was ultimately caused by ideological campaigns like the 1,150th anniversary of Russian statehood, which Russia is currently trying to revive within its old imperial boundaries.

In order to avoid the need to analyze Russian biases (this is a matter for a separate paper), we should refer to the famous Russian political commentator, poet, and Russian nationalist, Aleksey Shiropaev (by the way, I treat the notion of nationalism without prejudice, simply as one of the trends present in public opinion). According to Shiropaev, when talking about the "fraternal Ukrainian people", most Russians consider the Ukrainian language and heritage to be a regrettable historical irregularity, a historical anomaly, one which came into being as a result of the harmful Catholic influence of Lithuania and Poland: "And at the same time, the Russians never ask themselves: maybe they themselves are an anomaly?".[49]

However, one positive sign is that a new attitude towards Ukraine is now being formed among the milieu of the Russian democratic intelligentsia, though this process is somewhat ambivalent. This is illustrated by the publications from the Yeltsin era, when such highly esteemed Russian historians as Yury Pivovarov and Andrey Fursov defended the pro-European alternative for Russia's development.

---

49 A. Shiropaev, Ukrainskij i rossijskij puti v istorii: tolchok k razmyshlenijam, [electronic resource] available at: http://www.day.kiev.ua/290619?idsource =298307& mainlang=rus.

Later their paths diverged and currently only Pivovarov, a member of the Russian Academy of Sciences, supports this stance. Nevertheless, at that period, the authors were in agreement:

> It is necessary to look into history more deeply, into the Kiev period, always remembering that the "Kiev model" was not only different from the "'Moscow model', but in many respects was its antipode, and that it was not Moscow, but Lithuania [the Grand Duchy of Lithuania, Ruthenia, and Samogitia – V.T.] that was the "model" successor of Kievan Rus.[50]

Without renouncing the "Kiev legacy" (and they are right, because Rus' was a unique universe of civilization in Eastern Europe, which, in addition to its Kiev "nucleus" also had a huge "external Rus"), the above-mentioned Russian authors admit that

> everything that we call the Russian system started to emerge in the Golden Horde era (we consider this term more adequate than the "appanage epoch"), during the times of the "white-boned" Horde rulers [...]. The historic moment of eternal significance, the birth of the Russian System, was the Great Tsarist Revolution (1517/1565–1649), during which, within the mode of autocracy, the subject of Russian Power was ultimately formed and forged, enabling the creation, construction, carving, imagination, and spatialization of a certain system.[51]

For further perspective on the growth of Ukrainian national identity, when we finally comprehend the fullness of the sense of the term "Rus'-Ukraine" and mark some anniversary, it would make sense to take into consideration Yury Pivovarov and Andrey Fursov's interpretation of those characteristics of the "Russian System" of the Kiev period which have also remained significant for modern Ukraine. Primarily, this refers to the fact that back then Rus' was a European and poly-subjective society. The European type of social development is different from others in that it is founded not only on the fixation of the subjectivity of society, but also on the subject in society itself. The adoption of Christianity became not only a huge spiritual revolution, but also a social one. It created a social model of the individual subject where the physical individual and the social individual were combined.

A Christian society is poly-subjective as a social type: separate individuals, groups, corporations, institutions, and the state become (and are recognized) historical subjects. Either way, in the context of power relations, different

---

50 Y. S. Pivovarov, A. M. Fursov, "Russkaja Sistema: genezis, struktura i funkcionirovanie (tezisy i rabochie gipotezy)", *Russian Historical Journal* 3, 1998, p. 16.
51 Y. S. Pivovarov, A. M. Fursov, "Russkaja Sistema...", p. 16.

principalities of Rus' were "social quadrilaterals" with the vectors constituted by the "prince", "boyardom", "veche", "church", etc. Understandably, different "vectors" were dominant in different lands of Rus'. But even where the dominant "vector" was that of the prince, and even in places, where the prince historically had the best position compared to the other "vectors", where it was not "society" that drove the prince, but rather the prince's power that constructed society (e.g., north-eastern Rus'), this power nevertheless did not have at its disposal a sufficient amount of violence to become absolute and qualitatively alter the correlation of powers or "vectors" in the quadrilateral, let alone break it, or, moreover, deprive the "vectors" of subjectivity.

The arguments of Yury Pivovarov and Andrey Fursov are as follows:

> When [Grand Duke of Vladimir-Suzdal (1157–1174) – ed.] Andrei Yuryevich Bogolyubsky decided to follow the principle that "power is ultimate", "power is everything", and tried to steamroll the boyars and the Church, to become the first absolute monarch in Russian histories (and retrospectively in Russian History) and to turn the "quadrilateral" of power into a singular point of Power from which everything else emerges, he was sent to kingdom come.[52]

At that point, the prince's aspirations had not yet become dominant, and the authorities did not have the force to conduct pervasive violence because the armed people opposed it. A Rus' commoner of pre-Mongol times often was not only armed, but also knew that he could count on the support of the veche.

What happened to the democratic traditions of Rus' later is a separate research topic. The history of a given society is an open system, while its development is not fatally doomed – there are always alternatives, as well as the influence of chance. The historic process could be deemed mystical, were we to exclude the role of chance or accident from it, Karl Marx wrote, and he was right. This statement is especially important today, when we are faced with choices – between the traditions of the democratic system of power and those of autocracy. This is a choice that depends on each of us. It is this choice, above all, that should be brought to public attention by the organizers of festivities, should it ever come to adopting an official decree about the anniversary of Rus'-Ukraine.

However, I believe that Ukraine currently lacks the necessary social consensus on the issue of proclaiming an anniversary of Ukrainian statehood. Moreover, the state itself is not yet in a condition to arouse in the public all the piety necessary for such anniversary festivities. What could definitely unite Ukraine is consolidation in the practice of a high level of social justice and equality of all

---

52 Ibidem, p. 19.

people under the law, which is something that Taras Shevchenko was urging us to do. The 200th anniversary of his birth coincided with the Euromaidan, which was remarkable and serendipitous. We hope that we will be equal to his inescapable longing:

> Will there be judgement? Will there be punishment?
> For the kings and kinglets in this world?
> Will there be truth amongst the people?
> There should be! For the sun will rise
> And scorch the desecrated earth.[53]

Translated by Yuriy Velykoroda

---

53   T. Shevchenko. *Zibrannja tvoriv*, vol. 2: *Poezija 1847–1861*, Kiev 2003, p. 363.

List of affiliations of the authors

Oleksiy Tolochko, Center for Kievan Rus' Studies, Institute of Ukrainian History National Academy of Sciences of Ukraine, Kyiv

Martin Wihoda, Department of History, Masaryk University, Brno

Christian Lübke, Leibniz Institute for the History and Culture of Eastern Europe, University of Leipzig, Leipzig

Matthias Hardt, Leibniz Institute for the History and Culture of Eastern Europe, University of Leipzig, Leipzig

Przemysław Urbańczyk, Institute of Archeology and Ethnology of the Polish Academy of Sciences, Warsaw

Eduard Mühle, Department of History of Eastern Europe, University of Münster, Münster

Marian Rębkowski, Department of Archaeology, University of Szczecin, Szczecin

Teresa Rodzińska-Chorąży, Institute of Art History, Jagiellonian University, Krakow

Igor Kąkolewski, Center for Historical Research of the Polish Academy of Science, Berlin; Institute of Political Science, University of Warmia and Mazury, Olsztyn

Philip Earl Steele, independent scholar, Warsaw

Bartłomiej Noszczak, Institute of National Remembrance, Warsaw

Vasyl' M. Tkachenko, Institute of World History of the National Academy of Sciences of Ukraine, Kyiv

List of figures

Fig. 1: A visualization of the Poznań residential-ecclesial complex from Mieszko I's time (after H. Kóčka-Krenz, Ziemia, człowiek, sztuka. Interdyscyplinarne studia nad ziemią, [in:] Archeologia – historia – kultura – sztuka, ed. U. Mazurczak, Lublin 2015, p. 71–98). The visualition made by Andrzej Gołembnik according to Hanna Kóčka-Krenz 70

Fig. 2: The "tablets" from Podebłocie (after E. Marczak, Wczesnośredniowieczna osada przygrodowa w Podebłociu (stanowisko 3) na tle zespołu osadniczego, Warszawa 2014 [doctoral thesis submitted at the Faculty of History, University of Warsaw; typescript]) 73

Fig. 3: A visualization of the first cathedral church in Poznań (after A. Bukowska and Z. Cozac) 75

Fig. 1: The spread of flat skeletal burial grounds in the 11th c 98

Fig. 2: The spread of the discoveries of Christian religious symbols, end of the 10th and the 11th c 100

Fig. 3: Distribution of the churches founded by Bishop Otto of Bamberg in 1124–1125 (white) and 1128 (black), according to the *Vitae of Saint Otto* 106

Fig. 1: Ostrów Lednicki, a) the plan of the chapel with two semi-cross depressions (drawing M. Rosół), b) the southern depression, view from the east (photo T. Rodzińska-Chorąży) 116

Fig. 2: Early Piast residential compexes and three other examples: a) Ostrów Lednicki I phase, b) Ostrów Lednicki II phase, c) Giecz, d) Przemyśl, e) Poznań, f) Devín (Great Moravia (9th c.), g) Werla (Saxony 10th–11th c.), h) Zürich (after 1000), i) Kraków-Wawel Hill, "Aula of 24 pillars" (by T. Rodzińska-Chorąży) 118

Fig. 3: Kraków-Wawel Hill, tetraconch (St. Mary rotunda): a) the reconstruction of the plan (M. Rosół), b) reconstruction of the form, c) view of the S-E apse (photo T. Rodzińska-Chorąży) 125

Fig. 4: The cathedrals in Poland after 1000: a) Gniezno (by T. Janiak), b) Poznań (by A. Bukowska), c) Kraków (by J. Firlet, Z. Pianowski) 127

Fig. 5: a) Abbey in Tyniec, the southern wall of the church (photo T. Rodzińska-Chorąży), b) Abbey in Mogilno, the western crypt (photo T. Rodzińska-Chorąży) 130

Fig. 6: St. John the Baptist Church in Giecz: a) the plan of the remains with hypothetical form of earlier church (by T. Krysztofiak, T. Rodzińska-Chorąży), b) aerial view of the eastern part of the church with the crypt (photo T. Siuda) 133

Fig. 7: Kraków-Wawel Hill, St. Gereon Church: the plan and reconstruction by J. Firlet, Z. Pianowski (photos of the details T. Rodzińska-Chorąży) 135

Fig. 1: The burial site at Bodzia: the graves, rows of graves, and enclosures. Phase 1 graves are marked darker, those of Phase 2 are marked brighter. (After Buko et al. - A. Buko, T. D. Price, M. Kara, W. Duczko, K. M. Frei, I. Sobkowiak-Tabaka, "A unique medieval cemetery from the 10th/11th c. with chamber-like graves from Bodzia (central Poland). Preliminary result of the multidisciplinary research", *Archäologisches Korrespondenzblatt* 43(3), 2013, p. 423–442) 144

Fig. 2: Grave no. E37, containing a body of a woman deposited in an embryo position (photo: K. Waszczuk) 146

Fig. 3: Grave no. 864/I: details of the bones and sword setup (photo: K. Waszczuk) 147

Fig. 4: Two images of strongholds in eastern and western Wielkopolska (Greater Poland): (a) strongholds built under the early Piast rulers; (b) strongholds of a pre-state chronology, surviving after the early-Piast country was established; (c) strongholds of the pre-state period, destroyed or deserted after the Gniezno state emerged; (d) a line delineating two zones of Wielkopolska, prevalently featuring pre-Piast and early-Piast-strongholds, respectively; (e) tightly laid-out Piast-time strongholds situated east of the "demarcation line" and east of Gniezno; (f) the zone of early-Piast strongholds situated in south-eastern Wielkopolska, in the vicinity of Kalisz (after A. Buko) 152

Editors' remarks

1. The editors chose to include the names of historical rulers in the texts in their most common English form, marking only the names of Slavic rulers appearing for the first time in brackets in the form adopted in the given national language, e.g. Boleslaus (Polish: *Bolesław*, or Czech: *Boleslav*).
2. A transliterated form of the name *Volodimer* was used as it appears in the *Primary Chronicle* or *Tale of Bygone Years*, except for the text: *Searching for the meaning of the Russian way. The ideological setting of the 900th anniversary celebrations of the Baptism of Rus' (1888)* by Mikołaj Banaszkiewicz, where we used the version *Vladimir* as the most common linguistic form used in Russian language.
3. In all texts, the editors use the transcription *Kiev* with the exception of the list of affiliations of the authors where the form *Kyiv* is used.
4. In the case of electronic resources, the dates of access of the websites have been omitted. Some texts in the 2nd part of the volume were written and published in the original languages of the authors and later rewritten and translated for the purpose of the volume, hence, sometimes the electronic resources used for the source texts are not available now. Such resources are marked with an asterisk (*http). The remaining electronic resources have been available until the closing date of the editorial work (31.07.2019).
5. In the texts *Christians and pagans in Kiev during the 10th c.* by Oleksiy Tolochko, *Searching for the meaning of the Russian way. The ideological setting of the 900th anniversary celebrations of the Baptism of Rus' (1888)* by Mikołaj Banaszkiewicz, and *The inseparable heritage of early medieval Rus'. On the celebration of the 1,150th anniversary of the origin of Russian statehood* by Vasyl' M. Tkachenko the authors have included Russian terms and bibliographic addresses in Cyrillic alphabet. To make the volume more accessible for the English-speaking reader the editors chose to transcribe the above mentioned terms and addresses into the Latin alphabet.
6. All quotations from non-English sources were translated into English by the respective translators of the chapters, unless stated otherwise.
7. The footnotes marked with an asterisk (*) were added by the editorial team.
8. In the text *History as a tool in the state's struggle against the Catholic Church during the celebrations of the One-Thousand Years of the Polish State (1956–1966/1967)* by Bartłomiej Noszczak, monthly dates of the quoted Polish daily press have been rendered in Roman numerals because of the footnotes' format.

Polish Studies – Transdisciplinary Perspectives

Edited by Krzysztof Zajas and Jarosław Fazan

- Vol. 1 Artur Płaczkiewicz: Miron Białoszewski: Radical Quest beyond Dualisms. 2012.
- Vol. 2 Kinga Kosmala: Ryszard Kapuściński: Reportage and Ethics or Fading Tyranny of the Narrative. 2012.
- Vol. 3 Michał Nowosielski: Polish Organisations in Germany. Their Present Status and Needs. 2012.
- Vol. 4 Krzysztof Zajas: Absent Culture. The Case of Polish Livonia. 2013.
- Vol. 5 Magdalena Sitarz: Literature as a Medium for Memory. The Universe of Sholem Asch's Novels. 2013.
- Vol. 6 Barbara Przybyszewska-Jarmińska / Lech Sokół (eds.): Poland and Artistic Culture of Western Europe. 14th–20th Century. 2014.
- Vol. 7 Katarzyna Fazan / Anna Róża Burzyńska / Marta Bryś (eds.): Tadeusz Kantor Today. Meta-morphoses of Death, Memory and Presence. Translated by Anda MacBride. 2014.
- Vol. 8 Andrzej Hejmej: Music in Literature. Perspectives of Interdisciplinary Comparative Literature. Translated by Lindsay Davidson. 2014.
- Vol. 9 Grzegorz Niziołek: Warlikowski: Extra Ecclesiam. Translated by Soren Gauger. 2015.
- Vol. 10 Ryszard Koziołek: Sienkiewicz's Bodies. Studies of Gender and Violence. Translated by David Malcolm. 2015.
- Vol. 11 Wojciech Tygielski: Italians in Early Modern Poland. The Lost Opportunity for Modernization? Translated by Katarzyna Popowicz. 2015.
- Vol. 12 Dariusz Jarosz / Maria Pasztor: Polish-French Relations, 1944-1989. Translated by Alex Shannon. 2015.
- Vol. 13 Urszula Augustyniak: History of the Polish –Lithuanian Commonwealth. State – Society – Culture. 2015.
- Vol. 14 Piotr Sobolczyk: Polish Queer Modernism. 2015.
- Vol. 15 Jacek Soszyński / Agnieszka Chamera-Nowak (eds.): Book versus Power. Studies in the Relations between Politics and Culture in Polish History. Editorial assistance by Dan Embree. Translated by Jacek Soszyński 2015.
- Vol. 16 Wojciech Kriegseisen: Between State and Church. Confessional Relations from Reformation to Enlightenment: Poland – Lithuania – Germany – Netherlands. Translated by Bartosz Wójcik and copy-edited by Alex Shannon. 2016.
- Vol. 17 Urszula Sowina: Water, Towns and People. Polish Lands against a European Background until the Mid-16th Century. Translated by Justyna Woldańska. 2016.
- Vol. 18 Grzegorz Krzywiec: Chauvinism, Polish Style. The Case of Roman Dmowski (Beginnings: 1886-1905). Translated by Jarosław Garliński. 2016.
- Vol. 19 Andrzej Sakson: Von Memel bis Allenstein. Die heutigen Bewohner des ehemaligen Ostpreußens: Memelland, Kaliningrader Gebiet, Ermland und Masuren. Übersetzt von Marek Drewnowski. 2016.
- Vol. 20 Antoni Mączak: Unequal Friendship. The Patron-Client Relationship in Historical Perspective. Translated by Alex Shannon. 2017.
- Vol. 21 Olga Szmidt / Katarzyna Trzeciak (eds.): Face in Trouble – From Physiognomics to Facebook. Copy-edited by Soren Gauger. 2017.

Vol. 22　Alina Cała: Jew. The Eternal Enemy? The History of Antisemitism in Poland. 2019.

Vol. 23　Agata Brajerska-Mazur / Edyta Chlebowska (eds.): Jew. On Cyprian Norwid. Studies and Essays. Vol. 1: Syntheses. 2019.

Vol. 24　Beata Nowacka / Zygmunt Ziątek: Ryszard Kapuściński. Biographie d'un écrivain. 2019.

Vol. 25　Stanisław Bylina: Religiousness in the Late Middle Ages. Christianity and Traditional Culture in Central and Eastern Europe in the Fourteenth and Fifteenth Centuries. 2019.

Vol. 26　Igor Kąkolewski / Christian Lübke / Przemysław Urbańczyk (eds.): The Dawning of Christianity in Poland and across Central and Eastern Europe. History and the Politics of Memory. 2020.

www.peterlang.com

www.ingramcontent.com/pod-product-compliance
Lightning Source LLC
LaVergne TN
LVHW092232080526
838199LV00104B/122